AF564456

Couture and Fashion Drafting

Couture and Fashion Drafting

Padmavati B.

Published by

ATLANTIC

PUBLISHERS & DISTRIBUTORS (P) LTD

7/22, Ansari Road, Darya Ganj, New Delhi-110002
Phones : +91-11-40775252, 40775214, 23273880, 23275880
Fax : +91-11-23285873
Web : www.atlanticbooks.com
E-mail : orders@atlanticbooks.com

Branch Office: Chennai
Phones : +91-44-48531784, 28291383
E-mail : chennai@atlanticbooks.com

Printed & bound in India by Atlantic Print Services

PREFACE

Couture and Fashion Drafting is a quintessential book with comprehensive and exceptional illustrations, clear diagrams and step-by-step construction methods, having detailed yet easy to understand explanations. Drafting is based upon the idea that all designs are a combination of two or more of the three major principles of designing:

(i) Silhouetting: Making outline of the desired design,

(ii) Dart manipulation/suppression theory: Adding darts to shape up the garment for preferred appearance, and

(iii) Adding fullness: Adding gathers/pleats/flare to give fullness.

To add to the above principles are the following drafting principles of adding ease:

(i) Wearing ease: Since the vertical measurements are generally straight and do not cover the curves, so small measure of wearing allowance should be added, and

(ii) Designing ease: Designing ease is added to the horizontal measurements and depends on the design, i.e.

  (a) fitting garments do not require designing ease, e.g. corset,

  (b) slight fitting garments require a small measure of ease for moving ease, e.g. shirt, and

(c) considerable measure of ease can be added in loose garments. Generally night wear falls in this category.

This book presents all the information essential to construct drafts and patterns with precision regardless of its intricacy. Various types of women's garments including basic bodice for adults along with corsets, shirts, vests, trousers, skirts, i.e. garments cut on grain line as well as bias cut garments like chudidaar, gored skirt have been covered in 35 chapters. Description of precise measurements of each part of the garment and labelled figures have been given for easy understanding by the readers. This book also provides Glossary of Fabrics which is very precise and informative. Besides, Questions for Practice have been given for the readers to test their theoretical knowledge. The book will ably serve the needs of professional fashion designers and all those concerned with designing and stitching of women's wear. It will also prove useful to the students and teachers of institutes of fashion technology.

Padmavati B.

CONTENTS

1 INTRODUCTION TO FABRICS

ACQUIRING FABRIC KNOWLEDGE

The whole objective of acquiring fabric knowledge is to make the selection and use of fabric more effectual and less haphazard. Fabrics are designed and the process of manufacturing is directed to production of a specific type of material. Fabrics do not just happen, but much care and thought processing goes into their production. Primarily not always the point of view is towards the aesthetic beauty of the end use of the fabric, but mostly towards the efficiency and speed of production as this helps in deciding the value and marketability of the produced fabric.

This does not recommend that to acquire the knowledge of the fabric a fashion designer should stand in awe of the whole modus operandi of fabric manufacturing and treat every fabric as if it were integral and irreplaceable component of the original tapestry.

The user of the fabric should be aware of the elements and process of manufacture of the given fabric and the effect these would have on the properties and behaviour of it. The designer should also have some conception of the central objective of the manufacturer in producing the particular fabric.

The knowledge of the fabric makes the selection procedure more effectual and purposeful.

FABRIC-GARMENT RELATIONSHIP

A fabric is a raw material for the purpose of creation of garments, and rarely serves as a end-product in itself, e.g. Saree, an Indian style of draping the length of fabric by wrapping around the wearer. The purpose of garment manufacturing is to utilize the main properties of the raw material effectively and efficiently not only for its aesthetic value but also for its comfort and purpose. Garment manufacturing is the adaptation of the fabric predominantly, a two-dimensional structure, to suit the subtly variable, three-dimensional human form. The conversion of the exemplified visual ideas into material and the various methods of attaining the visualized result means expense, but this does not prevent designers and production houses from manufacturing elegant, attractive and functional fabrics and garments.

The designers should have a panache and instinct to appreciate the fabric-garment relationship to its optimum. Creative idea is the beginning and the ideas will flow when the designer is fully aware and perceptive to all the aspects of the raw material.

Knowledge of fabric properties and garment construction is an asset to everyone concerned with garments—as a consumer, a designer, or a manufacturer of garment.

FABRIC QUALITIES

Before the garment construction is started, it is important to understand the qualities of the fabric. For a given pattern different fabric would behave differently and give different drape and outlook as a result of which one can be undesired also. It is extremely important to learn about different fabrics available in the market and a few distinctive qualities that would be exhibited by the particular fabric. Here we would discuss about distinctive qualities of the fabrics that should be taken into consideration:

- Shrinkable and Pre-shrunk fabrics.
- Stretch
- Light weight, medium weight and heavy weight fabrics.
- Chemically treated fabrics

Shrinkable and Pre-shrunk Fabrics

Shrinkable Fabrics: The fabrics that shrink on laundering are known as shrinkable fabrics. Thus, pre-shrinking the fabric is very important as laundering the garment would shrink it and cause distortion in the required outlook and size, as garment and its seam would not shrink to the same extent. So it is advised to launder the shrinkable fabrics before the fabric is used for construction of garment.

Pre-shrunk Fabrics: Pre-shrunk fabrics are processed fabrics and are ready to use. Laundering the garments made with these kind of fabrics would not cause any distortion in size and shape.

Stretch

Woven Fabrics: Woven fabrics do not stretch except on bias. Woven fabrics are made up of yarns running at right angles (plain weave) or at 45°-63° (twill weave) to each other. Before a pattern is placed on fabric it is mandatory to understand grain-line of fabric. Grain-line of the fabric decides the way the given garment would drape. For a given woven fabric there are three types of grain-lines:

(i) length-wise grain,

(ii) cross-wise grain and

(iii) bias grain.

(i) Length-wise Grain: Length-wise grain refers to the yarns that run length of the fabric parallel to the selvedge.

(ii) Cross-wise Grain: Cross-wise grain refers to the yarns that run perpendicular to the selvedge or length-wise grain of the fabric.

(iii) Bias Grain: Bias grain refers to the line drawn at 45° to the length-wise grain and cross-wise grain. Bias grain cut fabric would exhibit stretch in woven fabrics.

A garment cut on bias would stretch and drape differently than a garment cut on length-wise grain or cross-wise grain. The length-wise and cross-wise grains do not encompass any stretch, depending on the tautness of the weave the fabric may "provide" but it will not stretch.

Knit Fabrics: Although knit fabric is constructed differently than woven fabrics, the fabric grain is characterized the same way it is for woven fabrics. Though knit fabrics stretch, but the extent of stretch varies on different grain-lines.

Light Weight, Medium Weight and Heavy Weight Fabrics

Light Weight: Light weight fabrics have an airy or loose weave. Generally plain weave. Most suitable as a inner lining fabric of a garment.

Medium Weight: Medium weight fabrics have a tighter weave than light weight fabrics for an amalgamation of warmth and wicking ability.

Heavy Weight: Heavy weight fabrics are generally made of ply yarns with close and compact weave. So, heavy weight fabrics are quite thick and warm, with the wicking quality being slightly poor than medium weight fabrics. Heavy weight fabrics have a brushed finish on the inner side for warmth and wicking and smooth face to resist pilling.

Chemically Treated Fabrics

Chemically treated fabrics are the fabrics that are treated with chemicals or coated with wax, polymers, etc. to protect the fabric from abrasion, oils and environmental changes like humidity, sun exposure, water, etc. Chemically treated fabrics are more durable and strong. Chemically treated fabrics have a smooth finish and luster, as per the treatment.

2 UNDERSTANDING DIFFERENT ASPECTS OF BODY

Fashion designing is all about making a person look more beautiful and creating an illusions when and where essential. Not everyone has a desired body structure for eg. A person has a straight figure but wishes for a hour glass figure. Here we can help by creating a illusion by adding a few curved seams, etc. to the garment. But to decide the persons figure the designer needs a thorough knowledge of figure types.

Before we decide a garment we need to consider structure of: face, neck, shoulders, and overall figure.

DIFFERENT FACE SHAPES

Face shapes should be evaluated carefully to select the very best type of neckline style suitable. This is helpful to curtail countless lines and other facial challenges faced in designing different types of garments. Here we look into necklines that should flatter and act as a gorgeous curtain to create an illusion required to call attention to or conceal the fine lines of a particular face type.

Consider the following rules when selecting necklines for given face type:

Oval Face: This type of face is ideal face type and is characterized by a well-balanced proportion: chin is little narrower than the forehead and softly rounds with high cheek bones. Popularly known as egg-shape face.

Suitable Necklines: All type of necklines suit this face type.

Avoid: None.

Round Face: This type of face is characterized by: a wide forehead, rounded chin and rounded cheek bones. Round faces tend to look short and wide.

Suitable Necklines: Deep and narrow necklines, pointed necklines, e.g. scoop neck, v-neck, glass neck, halter neck, cowl neck, etc.

Avoid: Wide and close necklines, e.g. square neck, round neck, jewel neck, etc.

Oblong Face: Also known as rectangular face. This type of face is characterized by: quite a large forehead, chin is slightly narrower than forehead and softly rounds with wide cheek bones and considerably wide jaw line.

Oblong/rectangular

Suitable Necklines: Necklines that would conceal the long face, e.g. round neck, jewel neck, boat neck, square neck, etc.

Avoid: Deep and narrow necklines that would accentuate the long structure of the face, e.g. scoop neck, halter neck, cowl neck, v-neck, etc.

Square Face: This type of face is characterized by: a broad and deep forehead, wide jaw line and square chin.

Square

Suitable Necklines: Deep and narrow necklines that would give a rounded appearance concealing the square jaw line, e.g. scoop neck, v-neck, glass neck, halter neck, cowl neck, etc.

Avoid: Wide and edged necklines that would accentuate wide jaw line and square chin, e.g. square neck, round neck, crew neck, etc.

Heart Shaped Face: This type of face is characterized by quite a large and wide forehead, wide and high cheek bones, narrow jaw line and a neat sharp chin.

Suitable Necklines: Any smooth curved necklines that would conceal sharp chin, e.g. round neck, jewel neck, scoop neck, boat neck, etc.

Avoid: Sharp pointed necklines which would accentuate sharp chin, e.g. v-neck, halter neck, cowl neck, etc.

Pear Face: This type of face is characterized by quite a narrow and long forehead, high cheek bones, considerably wide jaw line and a sharp chin.

Suitable Necklines: Any smooth curved and deep necklines that would conceal the wide jaw line and sharp chin, e.g. round neck, scoop neck, square neck, glass neck, etc.

Avoid: Sharp pointed necklines that would accentuate long forehead and sharp chin, e.g. v-neck, close halter neck and cowl neck, etc.

Diamond Face: This type of face is characterized by a narrow and long forehead, high cheek bones, narrow jaw line and a sharp chin.

Diamond

Suitable Necklines: Any smooth curved and edged necklines that would give a appearance of oval shape by concealing sharp lines of face, e.g. round neck, square neck, close cowl neck, etc.

Avoid: Sharp pointed and deep-narrow necklines that would emphasize the sharp chin, e.g. v-neck, scoop neck, deep cowl neck, etc.

DIFFERENT NECK TYPES

Like face shapes even neck types should be evaluated carefully to select the very best style suitable for the desired garment. This is helpful to reduce myriad of lines and further challenges faced in designing different types of garments. Here we look into necklines and collars that would cajole and act as an elegant drape to create an illusion required to accentuate or conceal the various lines of a particular neck type.

Ideal Neck Type: This type of neck smoothly starts from face and runs into the shoulder with a elegant curve.

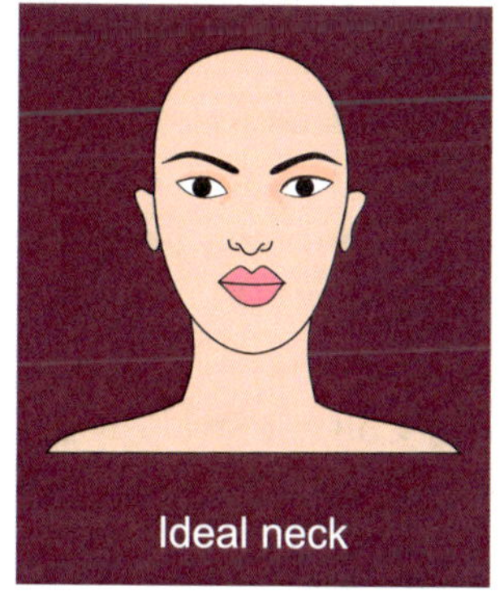

Ideal neck

Suitable Necklines and Collar: People with this type of neck can comfortably carry any necklines and collars.

Avoid: None.

Short Neck Type: This type of neck ends very abruptly into the shoulder, i.e. not much of the neck is discernible.

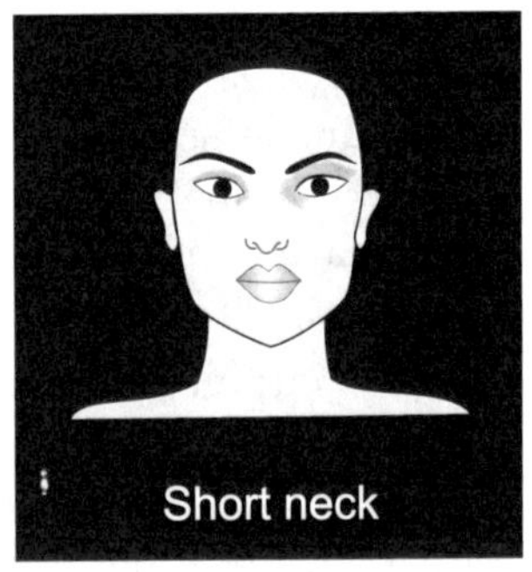
Short neck

Suitable Necklines and Collars: Deep and narrow necklines that would conceal short and stubby neck and create an illusion of long neck e.g.

Necklines: V-neck, scoop neck, halter neck, deep cowl neck.

Collars: Swallow collar, sailor's collar, blouse collar, etc.

Avoid: Close and fitting necklines and collars e.g.

Necklines: Jewel neck, crew neck, close round neck, etc.

Collars: Mandarin collar, shirt collar, cape collar, peter pan collar, polo collar, turtle neck collar, etc.

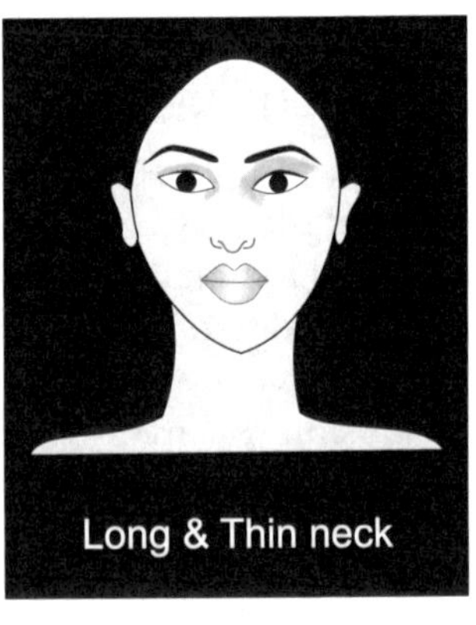
Long & Thin neck

Long and Thin Neck Type: This type of neck is visibly longer and bony without much of flesh around neck and run straight into the shoulder.

Suitable Necklines and Collars: Wide and edged necklines that would emphasize the length elegantly concealing the bony structure e.g.

Necklines: Wide and deep round neck, square neck, boat neck, etc.

Collars: Raised peter pan collar, mandarin collar, turtle neck collar, roll collar, shirt collar, etc.

Avoid: Sharp pointed necklines that would emphasize the bony structure of neck e.g.

Necklines: V-neck, scoop neck, etc.

Collars: Swallow collar, sailor's collar, blouse collar, etc.

Long and Fleshy Neck Type: This type of neck is though long has more of flesh around because of which it looks short and stubby.

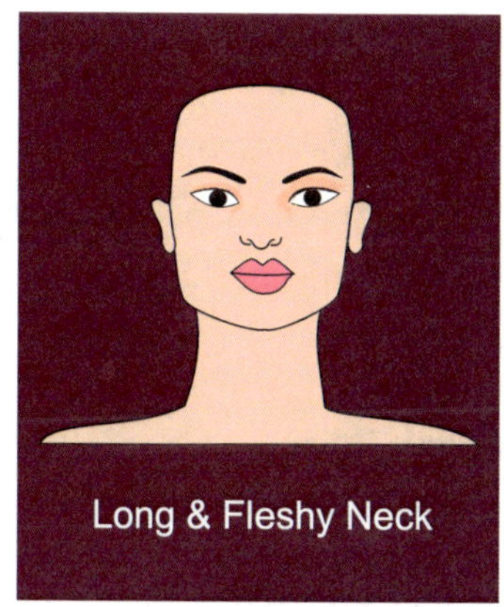

Suitable Necklines and Collars: Narrow and deep necklines, curved as well as edged necklines that would emphasize the length of neck elegantly concealing fleshy structure e.g.

Necklines: Round neck, crew neck, v-neck, scoop neck, heart shaped neckline, etc.

Collars: Polo collar, blouse collar, swallow collar, shirt collar, mandarin collar, etc.

Avoid: Deep and edged necklines that would emphasize on the fleshy structure of the neck e.g.

Necklines: Square neck, glass neck, horse shoe neck, etc.

Collars: Raised peter pan collar, ruffle collar, frilled collar, etc.

FIGURE TYPES

Figure types should be evaluated carefully to select the very best style suitable for the client going hand-in-hand with the trend for the desired garment. This is helpful to curb various challenges faced in designing of different types of garments for a given figure type without emphasizing the section of the body that needs to be passed by. Here we look into proportion of the figure that would cajole and act as a elegant drape to create an illusion required to accentuate a particular figure type while concealing the section not to be noticed.

Pear Shaped Figure: This type of figure is characterized by a slender neck, narrow shoulders, small bust, refined rib cage, shapely feminine waist, munificent lower hips and full thighs.

Suitable Garments: Garments that accentuate the fabulous feminine waistline, e.g.

1. Either short or long blouses, tops and jackets.
2. Pencil skirts.

3. Trousers with exceptional ease around hipline made of flowing fabric.
4. Skirts with softly gathered waistlines.
5. Shoulder pads can be used to broaden the shoulders.
6. Cowl neck, square neck, sweet heart neck give a broader look to shoulders.

Avoid: Garments that accentuate the hipline and narrow shoulder, e.g.

1. Hip length blouses, tops and jackets.
2. Straight cut skirts that would give a square look with inverted cone to top.
3. Straight cut trousers fitting around hipline.
4. Hip belts.

Hour Glass Figure/Eight Shaped Figure: This type of figure is characterized by a small scale bone structure, pronounced bust, narrow waist, shapely curved hips, protruding buttocks and shapely legs. This figure is considered to be a dream figure.

Suitable Garments: Garments that accentuate the great curves, e.g.

1. Short waist length semi-fitted blouses, tops and jackets.
2. Pencil skirts, A-line skirts, gypsy skirts.
3. Trousers with fitted hipline.
4. Waist belts that accentuate the curvy waistline.

Avoid: Garments that disguise the fragile bone structure, e.g.

1. Long blouses, tops and jackets.
2. Straight fit skirts that would conceal the curves.
3. Gathered and bulky waistline garments.

Square Shaped Figure: Also known as straight figure. This type of figure is characterized by an equal width upper and lower torso. An average bust, large rib cage, straight or undefined waist, flat hips and slender legs.

Suitable Garments: Garments that accentuate slender legs and help to elongate upper torso, e.g.

1. Blouse, shirts and jackets should be hip length to mid-thigh length and loose at mid-section.
2. Long tunic tops, blouse and jackets with long bodice and short skirts.
3. Skirts with dropped waistline (e.g. with waist yoke), A-line skirts, straight long skirts.
4. Hip level trousers, jeans, semi-fitted pants, etc.
5. Hip belts.
6. V-neck, glass neck, etc. would help to slenderize the rib cage.

Avoid: Garments that accentuate undefined waistline and large rib cage, e.g.

1. Short waist length blouse, shirts and jackets.
2. Heavily gathered and pleated skirts.
3. Pleated trousers, culottes, etc.
4. Heavy waist belts that accentuate thicker waist.

Diamond Shaped Figure: This type of figure is characterized by narrow shoulders, small bust, broad hips and generous thighs. Narrower on top and toe.

Suitable Garments: Garments that accentuate the elegant and curvy hips and thighs, e.g.

1. Blouse, shirts and jackets should be loose enough at hemlines.
2. Pants that taper slightly to hemline.
3. Hip hugging skirts and trousers.
4. Shoulder pads can be used to broaden shoulders.
5. Puff sleeves, ruffle collars, etc. should be used to create an illusion of curves.

Avoid: Garments that accentuate curve-less waistline and wide hips, e.g.

1. Blouse and jackets with elasticized hemlines.
2. Pants with flared bottoms or hemlines.
3. Gathered and bulky skirts.

4. Hip length tops with v-neck.

Round Shaped Figure: This type of figure is characterized by generous bust, wide rib cage, round back, munificent waist, narrow hips and often shapely willowy legs.

Suitable Garments: Garments that accentuate narrow hips and slender legs, e.g.

1. Less bulky blouse, shirts and jackets.
2. Hip level long tunics and tops.
3. Fitting skirts without gathers at waistline.
4. Tailor fit pants and trousers.
5. Narrow collars, v-necks, etc. should be used to create an illusion of slender neck.
6. Narrow belts blending with the colour of garment.

Avoid: Garments that accentuate munificent middle and round back, e.g.

1. Fitted and short blouses, shirts and tops.
2. Gathered and bulky skirts and pants.
3. Wide round necklines and collars.
4. Wide belts.
5. Puff sleeves, ruffle collars, etc. that would accentuate the fullness of the upper torso.

Inverted Triangular Shaped Figure: This type of figure is characterized by broad shoulders, full bust, average waist, narrow hips and shapely long legs.

Suitable Garments: Garments that accentuate full bust and cleavage, e.g.

1. Blouses, shirts and tops with raglan sleeves.
2. Gathered and bulky skirts to balance broad shoulders.
3. Pants flared at hemline.
4. Deep and low necklines.
5. A low sling hip level belt will draw attention to hips thus balancing the figure.

Avoid: Garments that accentuate broad shoulders and long legs, e.g.

1. Magyar sleeve blouses, shirts and tops.
2. Fitting and tapering skirts and trousers.
3. High round necklines and collars like turtle neck collars, etc.
4. Wide waist belts that would divide and accentuate the longer lower torso.

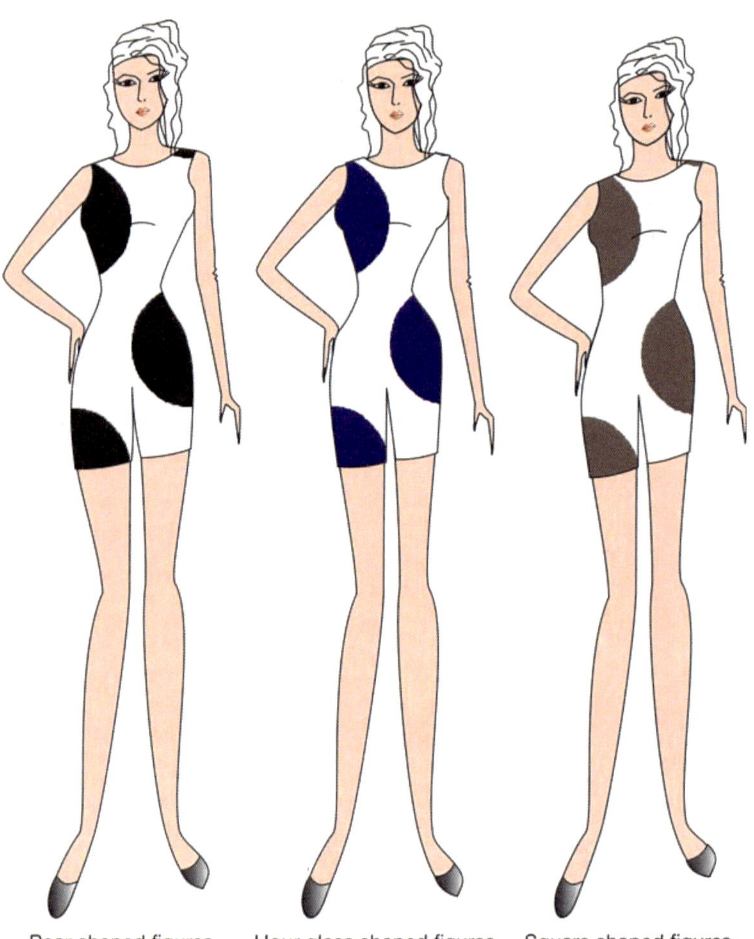

Pear shaped figures   Hour glass shaped figures   Square shaped figures

Figure 1

Diamond shaped figure   Round shaped figure   Inverted triangular shaped figure

Figure 2

3 ADULT BODICE BLOCK AND SLEEVE BLOCK

Bodice Block: A women's upper garment that extends from shoulder to waist.

Suitable Fabric: Light weight to medium weight fabric.

Age Group: 13 years and above.

Size symbol – 10

Scale = cm

Drafting scale = 1/4th cm

Required fabric = 1 m × 90 cm (length × width)

Measurements:

Required length = 42 cm

Round bust = 88 cm

Round waist = 68 cm

Across front = 28 cm

Across back = 35 cm

Highest bust level = 25 cm

Across shoulder = 35 cm

Sleeve length = 20 cm

Top arm/round sleeve = 29 cm

Construction:

1. 0 – 1 = required length + 1 cm [vertically downwards]
   = 43 cm

2. 0 – 2 = ½ round bust + 4 cm (ease) [horizontally]
   = 48 cm

   Complete the rectangle 0 – 1 – 2 – 3.
3. Scye depth/Armhole depth:

   0 – 4 = 1/4th round bust – 4 cm [vertically downwards on line 0 – 1]
   = 18 cm

   Draw a horizontal line from point 4 to line 2 – 3 and mark as 4_1 for bust line.
4. 0 – 5 = highest bust level [vertically downwards on line 0 – 1]
   = 25 cm

   Draw a horizontal line from point 5 to line 2 – 3 and mark as 5_1.

Back:

5. 0 – 6 = 6 – 4 [vertically downwards on line 0 – 4]
   = 9 cm

   i.e. point 6 is the mid-point of line 0 – 4.
6. Across Back:

   6 – 6_1 = ½ across back [horizontally]
   = 17.5 cm

   Draw a vertical line upwards and downwards from point 6 to line 0 – 2 and 4 – 4_1 and mark as v and v_1, respectively.
7. 0 – 7 = 7 – 6 [vertically downwards on line 0 – 1]
   = 4.5 cm

   i.e. point 7 is the mid-point of line 0 – 6.
8. 7 – 7_1 = ½ across back [horizontally]

   Draw a horizontal line from point 7 to line v – v_1 and mark as 7_1.
9. Neckline:

   0 – 8 = 1/12th round bust [horizontally on line 0 – 2]
   = 7.3 cm

$8 - 8_1$ = 1.5 cm [vertically upwards]

Join $8_1 - 0$ in a smooth curve for neckline.

10. Shoulder Line:

    v – 9 = 2.5 cm (shoulder drop) [vertically downwards on line $v - v_1$]

    $9 - 9_1$ = 3 cm [perpendicular to line $v - v_1$ outwards]

    Join $8_1 - 9_1$ in a straight line for shoulder line.

11. Armhole:

    $4 - 10 = 10 - 4_1$ [horizontally on line $4 - 4_1$]

    = 24 cm

    i.e. point 10 is the mid-point of line $4 - 4_1$.

    Join $9_1 - 6_1 - 10$ in a smooth curve for armhole.

12. Waistline:

    1 – 11 = 1/4th round waist + 3 cm (dart width) + 2 cm (ease) [horizontally on line 1 – 3]

    = 22 cm

13. Side Seams:

    Join 11 – 10 in a straight line for side seams.

14. Dart:

    (a) Waistline dart

    (i) Dart position:

    1 – N = 1/12th round bust [horizontally on line 1 – 11]

    = 7.3 cm

    (ii) Dart length: Draw a vertical line upwards from point N to line $5 - 5_1$ and mark as N_1.

    $N - N_1$ is the required dart length for waistline dart.

    (iii) Dart width:

    $N - S = N - S_1$ = 1.5 cm (on either side of point N) [horizontally]

Join $S - N_1$ and $S_1 - N_1$ in straight lines for the required waistline dart.

(b) Shoulder dart:

(i) Dart position:

$8_1 - R = R - 9_1$ [on line $8_1 - 9_1$]

= 7.4 cm

i.e. R is the mid-point of line $8_1 - 9_1$.

(ii) Dart length:

$R - R_1$ = 1/12th round bust + 1 cm [perpendicular to line $8_1 - 9_1$ downwards]

= 8.3 cm

$R - R_1$ is the required dart length for the shoulder dart.

(iii) Dart width:

$R - Q = R - Q_1$ = 1 cm (on either side of point R) [on line $8_1 - 9_1$]

Join $Q - R_1$ and $Q_1 - R_1$ in straight lines for the required shoulder dart.

15. Back Opening:

0 – 7 is back opening (or as required to pull over the top)

Finish the opening with a fly or dress hooks or as desired.

16. Back bodice block is along the points:

$0 - 1 - N - 11 - 10 - 6_1 - 9_1 - R - 8_1 - 0$,

where;

0 – 1 is on fold.

$0 - 8_1$ is neckline.

$8_1 - R - 9_1$ is shoulder line.

$9_1 - 6_1 - 10$ is armhole.

0 – 7 is back opening.

10 – 11 is side seam.

1 – N – 11 is waistline.

Front:

1. Neckline:

   2 – 12 = 1/12th round bust [horizontally on line 2 – 0]
   = 7.3 cm

   2 – 12_1 = 1/12th round bust (for depth) [vertically downwards on line 2 – 3]
   = 7.3 cm

   Join 12 – 12_1 in a smooth curve for round neck.

2. Shoulder:

   Join 12 – 7_1 in a straight line.

   (i) 12 – T = 8_1 – Q of back bodice block [on line 12 – 7_1]

   (ii) T – T_1 = 3 cm (for shoulder dart) [on line 12 – 7_1]

   (iii) T_1 – 13 = Q_1 – 9_1 of back bodice block [on line 12_1 – 7_1]

   12 –13 is the required shoulder line with dart.

3. Armhole:

   (i) 12_1 – 14 = 14 – 4_1 [vertically downwards on line 2 – 3]
   = 5.4 cm

   i.e. 14 is the mid-point of line 12_1 – 4_1.

   (ii) 14 – 14_1 = ½ across front + 2 cm (dart width) + 1 cm (ease) [horizontally]
   = 17 cm

   Join 13 – 14_1 – 10 in a smooth curve for armhole.

4. Waistline:

   3 – 15 = 1/4th round waist + 4 cm (dart width) + 2 cm (ease) [horizontally on line 3 – 1]
   = 23 cm

5. Side Seams:

   Join 15 – 10 in a straight line for side seams.

6. Darts:

   (a) Waistline dart:

   (i) Dart position:

   3 – M = 1/12th round bust [horizontally on line 3 – 1]
   = 7.3 cm

   (ii) Dart length:

   $5_1 - 5_2$ = 1/12th round bust [horizontally on line $5_1 - 5$]
   = 7.3 cm

   $5_2 - M_1$ = 1.5 cm [vertically downwards]

   Join $M_1 - M$ in a straight line for waist line dart.

   $M - M_1$ is the required dart length for the waistline dart.

   (iii) Dart width:

   $M - P = M - P_1$ = 2 cm (on either side of point M) [horizontally on line 3 – 15]

   Join $P - M_1$ and $P_1 - M_1$ in straight lines for waistline dart.

   (b) Shoulder dart:

   (i) Dart position: $T - B = B - Q_1$ [on line 12 – 13]
   = 1.5 cm

   i.e. B is the mid-point of line $T - T_1$.

   Point B is the dart position for shoulder line dart.

   (ii) Dart length:

   $4_1 - B_1$ = 1/12th round bust + 2 cm [on line 4 – 10] [horizontally]
   = 9.3 cm

   $B - B_1$ is the required dart length.

(iii) Dart width: B – T = B – T_1 = 1.5 cm

Join T – B_1 and T_1 – B_1 in straight lines for the required shoulder dart.

22. Front bodice block is along the points:

12_1 – 3 – M – 15 – 10 – 14_1 – 13 – B – 12 – 12_1,

where:

12_1 – 3 is on fold.

12 – 12_1 is neckline.

12 – B – 13 is shoulder line.

13 – 14_1 – 10 is armhole.

10 – 15 is side seam.

3 – M – 15 is waistline.

Add seam allowance of 1.5 cm (or as required) and hem allowance of 3 cm (or as required) and mark corresponding balance points and grain-line on each draft and pattern piece.

Bodice Block

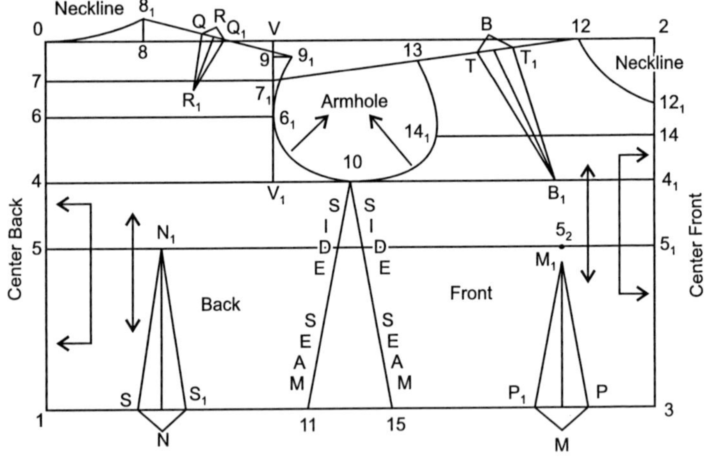

Plain Sleeve Block

Measurements:

Sleeve length = 26 cm

Top arm = 24 cm

Round bust = 88 cm

Construction:

1. 0 – 1 = sleeve length [vertically downwards]
   = 26 cm
2. 0 – 2 = 1/12th round bust + 2 cm [vertically downwards on line 0 – 1]
   = 88/12 + 2
   = 9 cm
3. 2 – 3 = 1/4th round bust – 2 cm [horizontally]
   = 20 cm
4. 1 – 4 = ½ top arm + 1 cm (ease) [horizontally]
   = 24/2 + 1 cm
   = 13 cm

   Join 4 – 3 in a straight line for side seam.
5. 0 – 5 = 2 cm [horizontally]

   Join 3 – 5 in a straight line.
6. Divide 3 – 5 into four equal parts and mark as 6, 7 and 8, respectively.
   (i) 6 – 6_1 = 1 cm [perpendicular downwards to line 3 – 5]
   (ii) 7 – 7_1 = 2.5 cm [perpendicular upwards to line 3 – 5]
   (iii) 8 – 8_1 = 1 cm [perpendicular upwards to line 3 – 5]
7. For Back Sleeve Crown:

   Join 5 – 7_1 – 6 – 3 in a curve as shown in the figure.
8. For Front Sleeve Crown:

   Join 5 – 8_1 – 7 – 6_1 – 3 in a curve as shown in the figure.

Add seam allowance of 1.5 cm (or as required) and hem allowance of 3 cm (or as required) and mark corresponding balance points and grain-line on each draft and pattern piece.

Sleeve Block

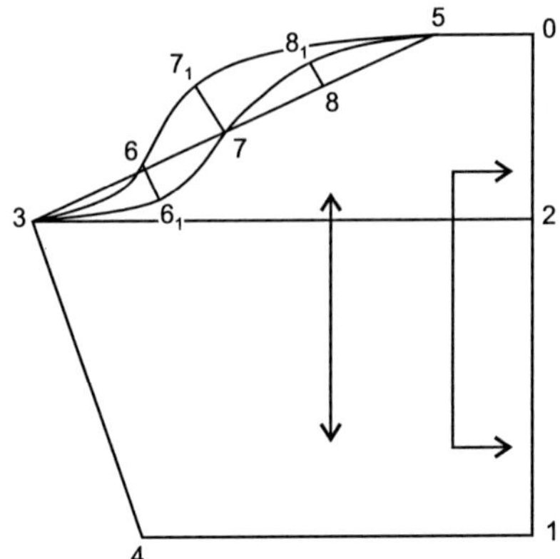

Full View of Sleeve Block

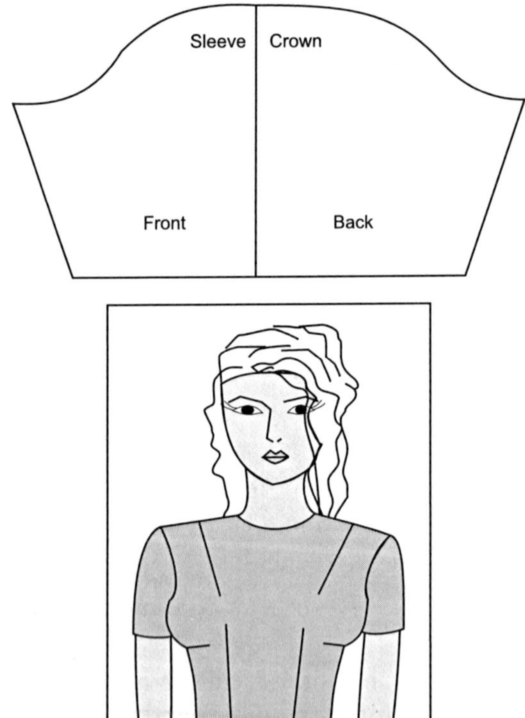

4 DART MANIPULATION THEORY

SLASH AND SPREAD METHOD

1. Construct a bodice block (front) without shoulder dart.
2. Mark different possible positions for darts and mark each point as 1, 2, 3,....., 10 on the bodice block as shown in the diagram.
3. Draw straight lines from these points to the dart head of waistline dart.
4. These lines thus drawn are slash lines to obtain new dart by suppressing waistline dart.
5. Make 10 bodice blocks each with a single slash line.
6. Cutout waistline dart in every bodice block.
7. Cut through the slash line in each case and suppress waistline dart. This would open the slashed line giving the new dart.

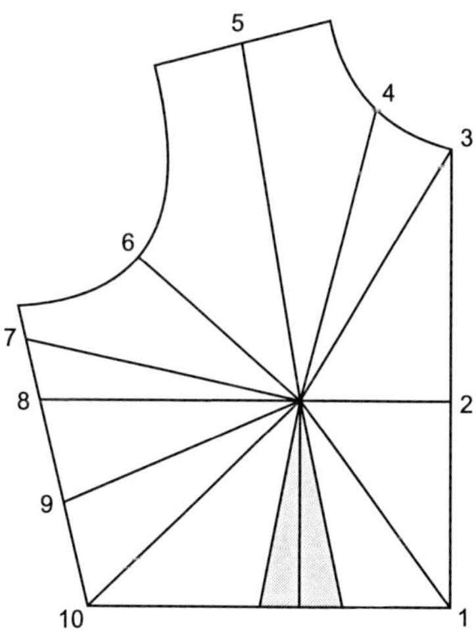

Darts are used to give shape and enhance the bust and show the slenderness of waistline without causing distortion in the garment. Dart width is predominantly based on the figure types and cup size of the bust.

Dart manipulation theory gives the options of different dart positions which can be used selectively for a desired style and silhouette.

1. Lower Center Front Dart (waistline point on center front)

(i) Cut through the slash line without separating.

(ii) Repress the waistline dart while spreading the slashed line.

(iii) Trace out the obtained bodice block with lower center front dart.

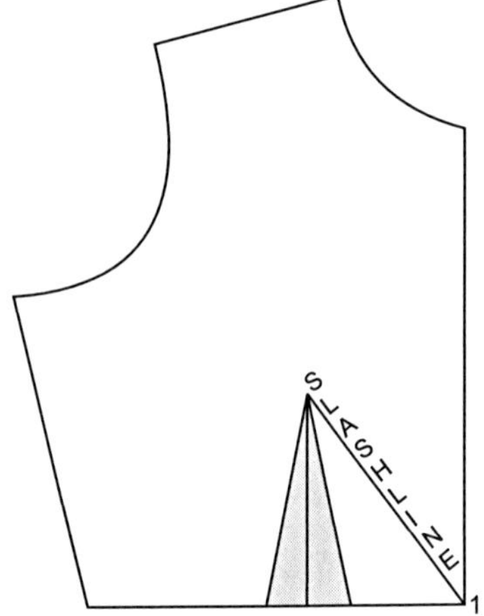

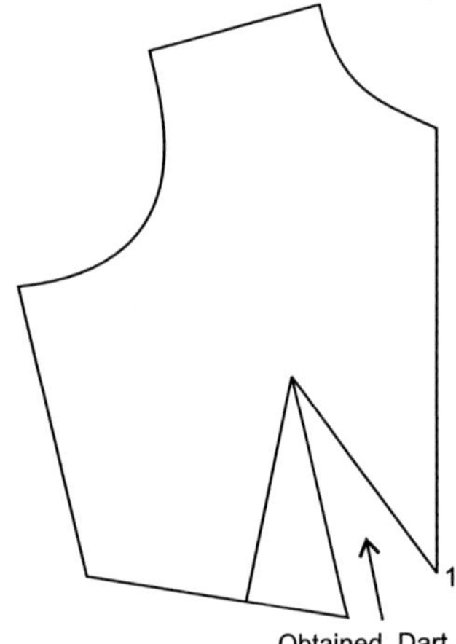

2. Straight Center Front Dart (line drawn perpendicular from center front to dart head)

(i) Cut through the slash line without separating.

(ii) Repress the waistline dart while spreading the slashed line.

(iii) Trace out the obtained bodice block with straight center front dart.

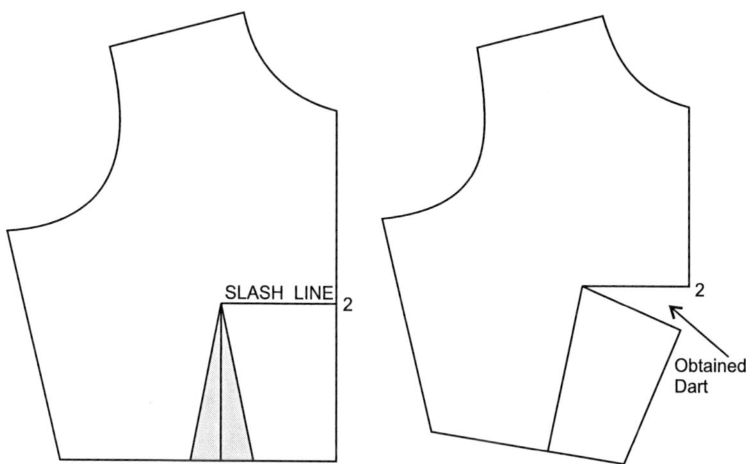

3. Central Neckline Dart (neckline point on center front)

(i) Cut through the slash line without separating.

(ii) Repress the waistline dart while spreading the slashed line.

(iii) Trace out the obtained bodice block with central neckline dart.

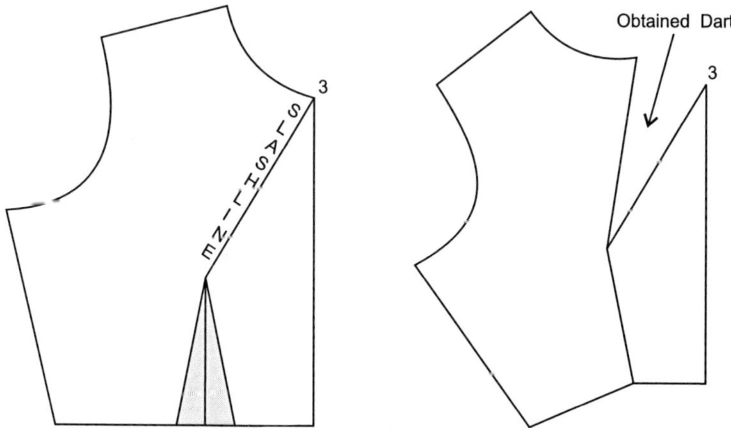

4. Neckline Dart (mid point of neckline)

(i) Cut through the slash line without separating.

(ii) Repress the waistline dart while spreading the slashed line.

(iii) Trace out the obtained bodice block with neckline dart.

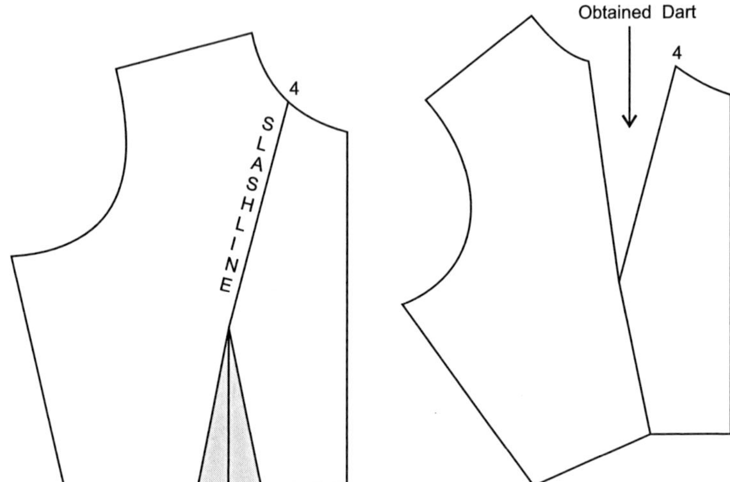

5. Shoulder Dart (mid point of shoulder line)

(i) Cut through the slash line without separating.

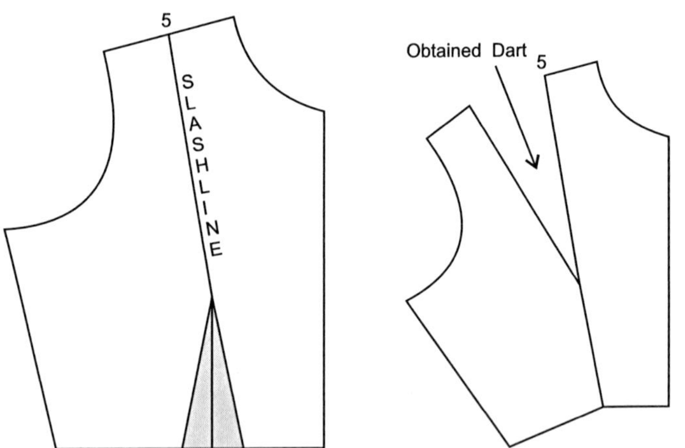

(ii) Repress the waistline dart while spreading the slashed line.

(iii) Trace out the obtained bodice block with shoulder dart.

6. Armhole Dart (point 14_1 of the front bodice block)

(i) Cut through the slash line without separating.

(ii) Repress the waistline dart while spreading the slashed line.

(iii) Trace out the obtained bodice block with armhole dart.

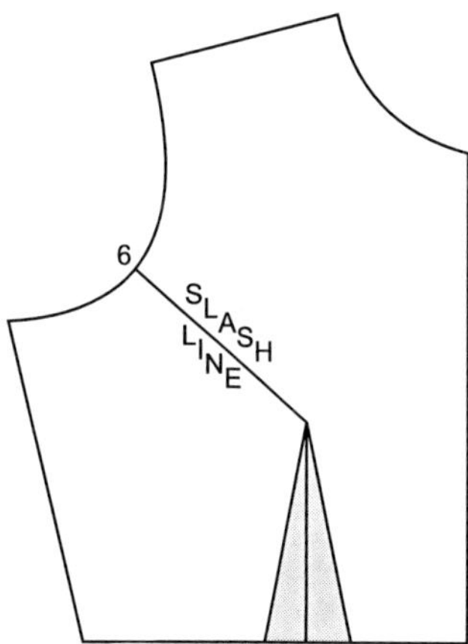

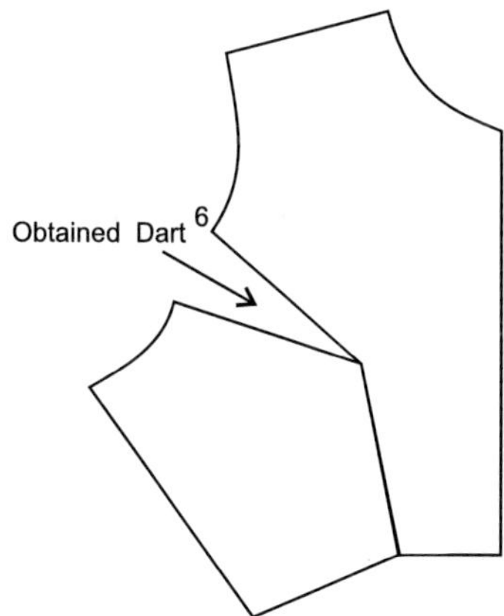

7. Upper Side Seam Dart (2 cm – 3 cm below point 10 of front bodice block)

(i) Cut through the slash line without separating.

(ii) Repress the waistline dart while spreading the slashed line.

(iii) Trace out the obtained bodice block with upper side seam dart.

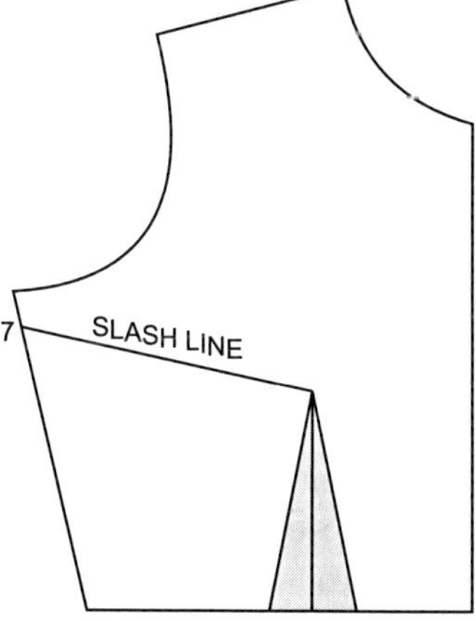

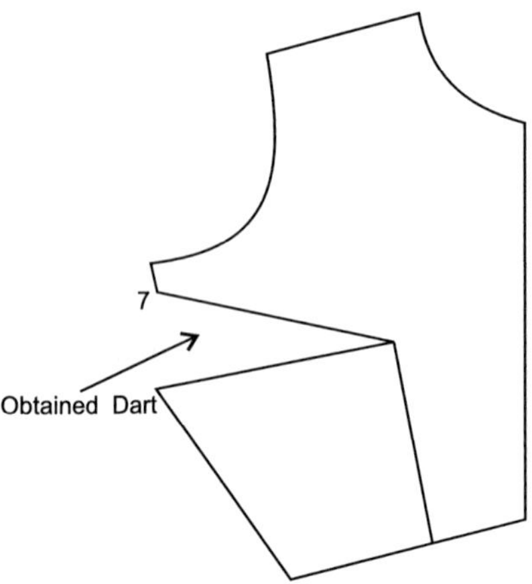

8. Straight Side Seam Dart (parallel to waistline)

(i) Cut through the slash line without separating.

(ii) Repress the waistline dart while spreading the slashed line.

(iii) Trace out the obtained bodice block with straight side seam dart.

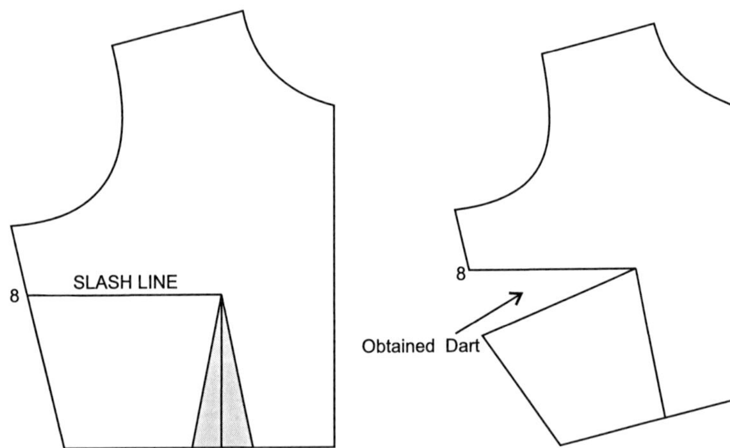

9. Lower Side Seam Dart (point anywhere between straight side seam dart and pt. 15 of front bodice block)

(i) Cut through the slash line without separating.

(ii) Repress the waistline dart while spreading the slashed line.

(iii) Trace out the obtained bodice block with lower side seam dart.

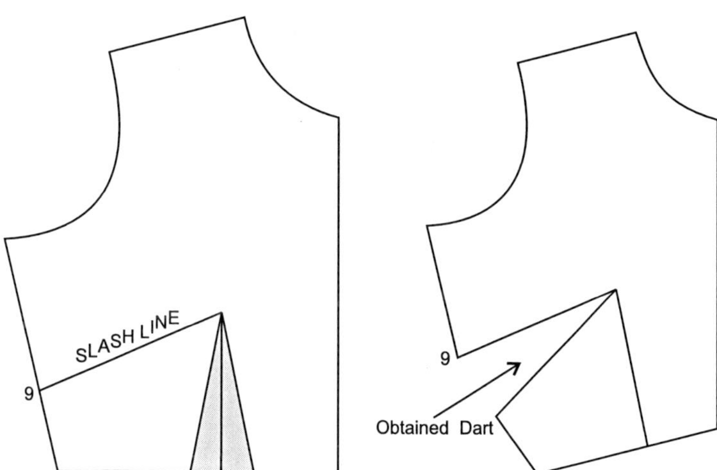

10. French Dart

(i) Cut through the slash line without separating.

(ii) Repress the waistline dart while spreading the slashed line.

(iii) Trace out the obtained bodice block with French dart.

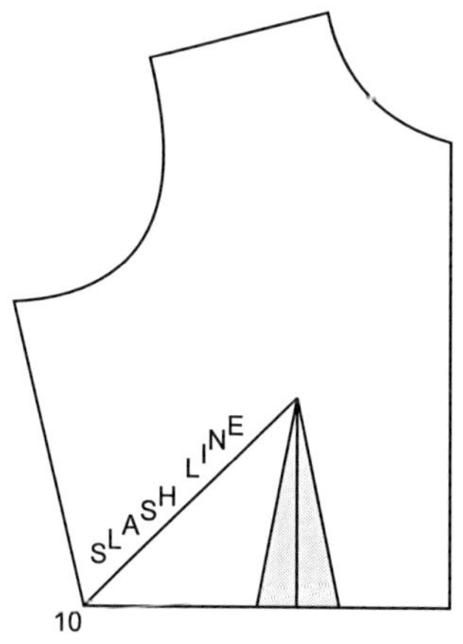

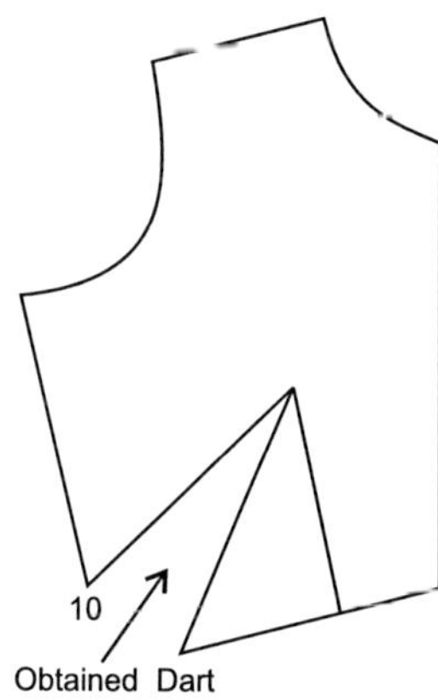

11. Double Waistline Dart

Waistline dart is replaced by double waistline darts. Single waistline dart of 4 cm is replaced by two waistline darts of 2 cm each.

(i) Draw a straight line upwards from point P and P_1 to line A – B and mark as R and R_1, respectively.

(ii) (a) First Dart:

Dart position: Point P is the position for the first dart.

Dart length: P – R is the required dart length.

Dart width: P – E = P – E_1 = 1 cm (on either side of point P).

Join E – R and E_1 – R in straight lines for the first dart.

(b) Second Dart:

Dart position: Point P_1 is the position for the second dart.

Dart length: P_1 – R_1 is the required dart length.

Dart width: P_1 – G = P_1– G_1 = 1 cm (on either side of point P_1).

Join G – R_1 and G_1 – R_1 in straight lines for the second dart.

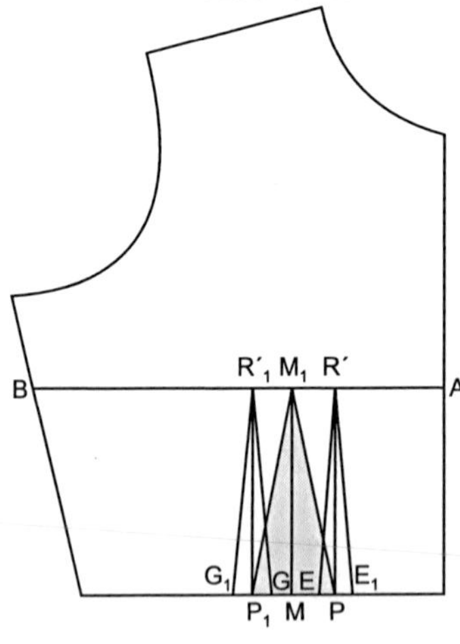

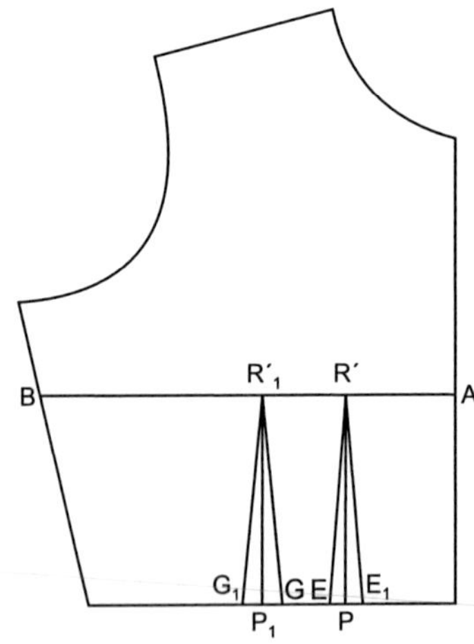

5 SKIRTS

SKIRTS

A skirt is a tube shaped or cone shaped lower garment generally worn by women which hangs from the waist to knees, calf or ankles.

[Adding 1 cm to back section facilitates side seam pockets]

Basic Skirt for Adults

A tube shaped knee length lower garment generally worn by women that hangs from waist to knee.

Suitable Fabric: Light weight to medium weight fabric.

Age Group: 13 yrs. and above

Size symbol – 10

Scale – cm

Drafting scale – 1/4th cm or 1/6th cm

Required fabric – 70 cm × 100 cm (length × width)

Measurements:

Required length = 60 cm

Round waist = 68 cm

Round hips = 94 cm

Hip level = 20.3 cm

Belt width = 2 cm

Construction:

1. 0 – 1 = required length + 1 cm – belt width [vertically downwards]

   = 59 cm

2. 0 – 2 = ½ round hips + 4 cm (ease) [horizontally]
   = 51 cm

   Complete the rectangle 0 – 1 – 2 – 3.

3. 0 – 4 = hip level – belt width [vertically downwards on line 0 – 1]
   = 18.3 cm

   Draw a horizontal line from point 4 to line 2 – 3 and mark as 4_1.

4. 0 – 5 = ½ (0 – 2) + 1 cm [horizontally]
   = 26.5 cm

   Draw a line vertically downwards from point 5 to line 1 – 3 through line 4 – 4_1 and mark as:

   5_1 on line 1 – 3, and 4_2 on line 4 – 4_1.

5. 4_2 – 6 = 2 cm [vertically upwards on line 4_2 – 4].

Back:

6. 0 – 7 = 1/4th round waist + 4 cm (dart width) + 1 cm [horizontally on line 0 – 5]
   = 22 cm

7. 7 – 8 = 2.5 cm [vertically upwards]

   Join 8 – 6 in a smooth outward curve for seam line.

   Join 8 – 0 in a smooth inward curve for waistline.

8. Darts: Divide 0 – 8 into three equal parts and mark as N and T, respectively.

   (a) First Dart:

      (i) Dart position: Point N is the dart position for the first dart.

      (ii) Dart length: N – N_1 = 1/12th round hips – 1 cm [vertically downwards]
      = 6.8 cm

      (iii) Dart width: N – S = N – S_1 = 1 cm (on either side of point N) [on line 0 – 8]

Join $S - N_1$ and $S_1 - N_1$ in straight lines for the required dart.

(b) Second Dart:

(i) Dart position: Point T is the dart position for the second dart.

(ii) Dart length:

$T - T_1$ = 1/12th round hips – 1.5 cm [perpendicular downwards to line 0 – 8]

= 6.3 cm

(iii) Dart width: $T - R = T - R_1 = 1$ cm (on either side of point T) [on line 0 – 8]

Join $R - T_1$ and $R_1 - T_1$ in straight lines for the required dart.

9. For Opening: 6 – A = 3 cm (upwards on line 6 – 8 or as required)

Opening should be finished with a zip or as desired.

10. Back basic skirt block is along the points:

$0 - 1 - 5_1 - 4_2 - 6 - 8 - T - N - 0$

where:

0 – 1 is on fold.

8 – A is side opening on one side.

$8 - 6 - 4_2 - 5_1$ is side seams.

$1 - 5_1$ is hemline, and 0 – N – T – 8 is waistline.

Front:

1. $2 - 7_f$ = 1/4th round waist + 4 cm (dart width) – 1 cm [horizontally on line 2 – 5]

= 20 cm

2. $7_f - 8_f$ = 2.5 cm [vertically upwards]

Join $8_f - 6$ in a smooth outward curve for seam line.

Join $8_f - 2$ in a smooth inward curve for waistline.

3. Darts: Divide $0 - 8_f$ into three equal parts and mark as M and J, respectively.

(a) First dart:

(i) Dart position: Point M is the dart position for the first dart.

(ii) Dart length: $M - M_1$ = 1/12th round hips [vertically downwards]

= 7.8 cm

(iii) Dart width: $M - P = M - P_1$ = 1 cm (on either side of point M) [on line $2 - 8_f$]

Join $P - M_1$ and $P_1 - M_1$ in straight lines for the required dart.

(b) Second dart:

(i) Dart position: Point J is the dart position for the second dart.

(ii) Dart length: $J - J_1$ = 1/12th round hips – 1.5 cm [perpendicular downwards to line $2 - 8_f$]

= 6.3 cm

(iii) Dart width: $J - K = J - K_1$ = 1 cm (on either side of point J) [on line $2 - 8_f$]

Join $K - J_1$ and $K_1 - J_1$ in straight lines for the required dart.

4. For Opening: $6 - A_1$ = 3 cm (upwards on line $6 - 8_f$ or as required)

   Opening should be finished with a zip or as desired.

5. Front basic skirt block is along the points:

   $2 - 3 - 5_1 - 4_2 - 6 - 8_f - J - M - 2$,

   where:

   $2 - 3$ is on fold.

   $8_f - A_1$ is side opening on one side.

   $8_f - 6 - 4_2 - 5_1$ is side seams.

   $2 - 5_1$ is hemline.

   $8_f - J - M - 2$ is waistline.

Add seam allowance of 1.5 cm (or as required) and hem allowance of 3 cm (or as required) and mark corresponding balance points and grain line on each draft and pattern piece.

Belt:

1. A – B = round waist [horizontally]
   = 68 cm
2. A – C = 4 cm (with intake) [vertically downwards]
   Complete the rectangle A – B – C – D.
3. For overlap:
   B – E = D – F = 2.5 cm [horizontally outwards]
   Join E – F in a straight line or in a smooth outward curve for overlap.
   (Use interfacing equal to ½ of belt width to give firmness to the belt.)

Add seam allowance of 1.5 cm (or as required) and put up corresponding balance points and grain line on each pattern piece.

Basic Skirt:

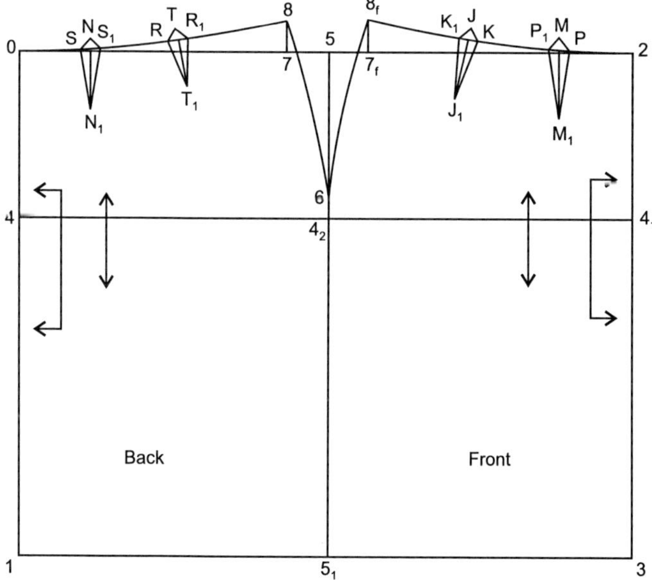

Belt:

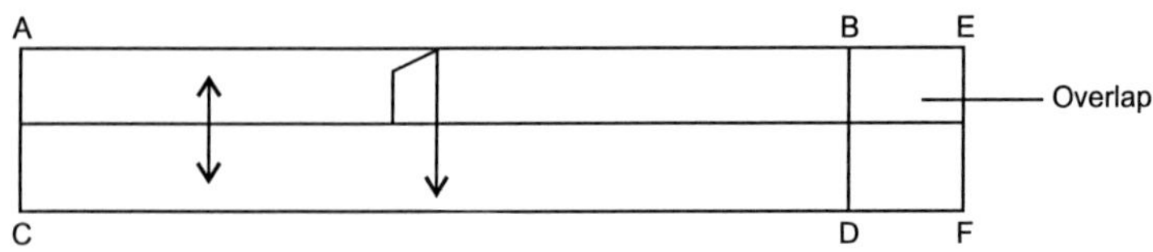

Basic Skirt for Adults (Single Dart)

Basic Skirt for Adults: A tube shaped knee length lower garment generally worn by women that hangs from waist to knee.

Suitable Fabric: Light weight to medium weight fabric.

Age group: 13 yrs. and above

Size symbol – 10

Scale – cm

Drafting scale – 1/4th cm or 1/6th cm

Required fabric – 70 cm × 100 cm (length × width)

Measurements:

Required length = 60 cm

Round waist = 68 cm

Round hips = 94 cm

Hip level = 20.3 cm

Belt width = 1 cm

Construction:

1. 0 – 1 = required length + 1 cm – belt width [vertically downwards]
   = 60 cm
2. 0 – 2 = ½ round hips + 4 cm (ease) [horizontally]
   = 51 cm

   Complete the rectangle 0 – 1 – 2 – 3.
3. 0 – 4 = hip level – belt width [vertically downwards on line 0 – 1]
   = 19.3 cm

BASIC SKIRT (DOUBLE DARTS) AND VARIATION

Basic skirt

Basic skirt with frills

Draw a horizontal line from point 4 to line 2 – 3 and mark as 4_1.

4. 0 – 5 = ½ (0 – 2) +1 cm [horizontally]

   = 26.5 cm

   Draw a line vertically downwards from point 5 to line 1 – 3 through line 4 – 4_1 and mark as:

   5_1 on line 1 – 3, and

   4_2 on line 4 – 4_1

5. 4_2 – 6 = 2 cm [vertically upwards on line 4_2 – 4]

Back:

6. 0 – 7 = 1/4th round waist + 2 cm (dart width) + 1 cm [horizontally on line 0 – 5]

   = 20 cm

7. 7 – 8 = 2.5 cm [vertically upwards]

   Join 8 – 6 in a smooth outward curve for seam line.

   Join 8 – 0 in a smooth inward curve for waistline.

8. Darts: Divide 0 – 8 into 2 equal parts and mark as T.

   (i) Dart position: Point T is the dart position.

   (ii) Dart length:

   T – T_1 = 1/12th round hips – 1.5 cm [perpendicular downwards to line 0 – 8]

   = 6.3 cm

   (iii) Dart width: T – R = T – R_1 = 1 cm (on either side of point T) [on line 0 – 8]

   Join R – T_1 and R_1 – T_1 in straight lines for the required dart.

9. For Opening: 6 – A = 3 cm (upwards on line 6 – 8 or as required)

   Opening should be finished with a zip or as desired.

10. Back basic back skirt block is along the points:

    0 – 1 – 5_1 – 4_2 – 6 – 8 – T – 0,

where:

0 – 1 is on fold.

8 – A is side opening on one side or a back opening can be given on center back 0 – 4.

8 – 6 – 4_2 – 5_1 is side seams.

1 – 5_1 is hem line.

0 – T – 8 is waistline.

Front:

1. 2 – 7_f = 1/4th round waist + 2 cm (dart width) – 1 cm [horizontally on line 2 – 5]
   = 18 cm
2. 7_f – 8_f = 2.5 cm [vertically upwards]
   Join 8_f – 6 in a smooth outward curve for seam line.
   Join 8_f – 2 in a smooth inward curve for waistline.
3. Darts: Divide 0 – 8_f into 2 equal parts and mark as M.
   (i) Dart position: Point M is the dart position.
   (ii) Dart length: M – M_1 = 1/12th round hips [vertically downwards]
   = 7.8 cm
   (iii) Dart width: M – P = M – P_1 = 1 cm (on either side of point M) [on line 2 – 8_f]
   Join P – M_1 and P_1 – M_1 in straight lines for the required dart.
4. For Opening: 6 – A_1 = 3 cm (upwards on line 6 – 8_f or as required)
   Opening should be finished with a zip or as desired.
5. Front basic skirt block is along the points:
   2 – 3 – 5_1 – 4_2 6 – 8_f – M – 2,
   where:
   2 – 3 is on fold.
   8_f – A_1 is side opening on one side or as required.

$8_f - 6 - 4_2 - 5_1$ is side seams.

$2 - 5_1$ is hem line.

$2 - M - 8_f$ is waistline.

Add seam allowance of 1.5 cm (or as required) and hem allowance of 3 cm (or as required) and mark corresponding balance points and grain line on each draft and pattern piece.

Belt:

1. A – B = round waist [horizontally]
   = 68 cm
2. A – C = 2 cm (with intake) [vertically downwards]
   Complete the rectangle A – B – C – D.
3. For Overlap:
   B – E = D – F = 2.5 cm [horizontally outwards]
   Join E – F in a straight line or in a smooth outward curve for overlap.
   (Use interfacing equal to ½ of belt width to give firmness to the belt.)

Add seam allowance of 1.5 cm (or as required) and put up corresponding balance points and grain line on each pattern piece.

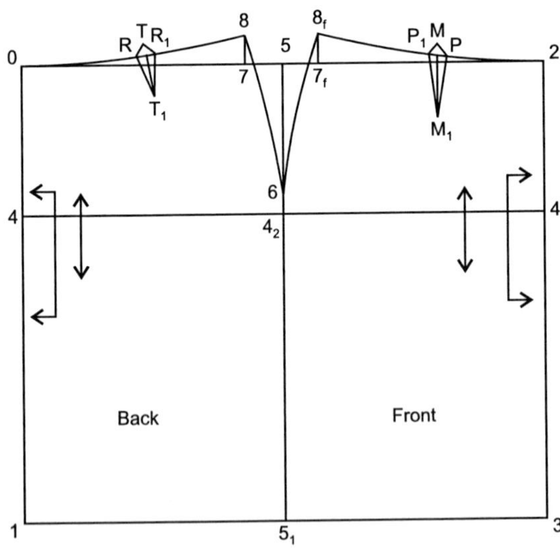

Belt:

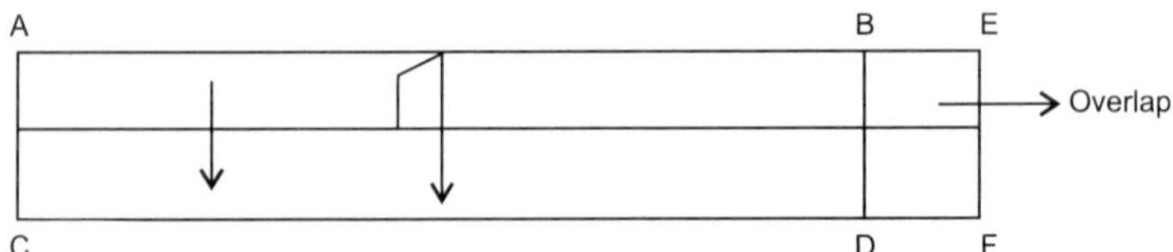

Fish Cut Skirt

Fish Cut Skirt: An ankle length lower garment worn from waist till ankle, generally by women, it is fitting till knee length and is flared at hem. It should be teamed with a halter neck top to enhance the look of the wearer or as desired.

Suitable Fabric: Light weight to medium weight fabric.

Age Group: 13 yrs. and above.

Size symbol – 10

Scale – cm

Drafting scale – 1/4th cm or 1/6th cm

Required fabric – 2.10 m × 90 cm (length × width)

Measurements:

Required length (waist to ankle) = 104 cm

Round waist = 68 cm

Round hips = 94 cm

Hip level = 21 cm

Waist to knee = 58 cm

Round knees = 64 cm (measurement should be taken around both knees together with slight ease)

Belt width = 2 cm

Construction:

1. 0 – 1 = required length + 1 cm – belt width [vertically downwards]
   = 103 cm
2. 0 – 2 = ½ round hips + 4 cm (ease) [horizontally]
   = 51 cm

Complete the rectangle 0 – 1 – 2 – 3.

BASIC SKIRT (SINGLE DART) AND VARIATION

Basic skirt

Basic skirt with frills

3. 0 – 4 = ½ of (0 – 2) – 1 cm [horizontally]
   = 24.5 cm

   Draw a vertical line downwards from point 4 to line 1 – 3 and mark as 4_1.

   Line 4 – 4_1 divides front and back block. Front skirt block is 1 cm lesser in width than back skirt block to facilitate inserted side seam pockets.

4. Hip Level

   0 – 5 = hip level – belt width [vertically downwards]
   = 19 cm

   Draw a horizontal line from point 5 to line 2 – 3 through line 4 – 4_1 and mark as:

   5_1 on line 4 – 4_1, and

   5_2 on line 2 – 3.

5. Knee Length

   0 – 6 = waist to knee – belt width [vertically downwards]
   = 56 cm

   Draw a horizontal line from point 6 to line 2 – 3 through line 4 – 4_1 and mark as:

   6_1 on line 4 – 4_1, and

   6_2 on line 2 – 3.

6. 5_1 – 7 = 2.5 cm [vertically upwards]

Back:

7. Waistline:

   (i) 2 – 8 = 1/4th round waist + 3 cm (dart) + 1 cm [horizontally]
   = 21 cm

   (ii) 8 – 9 = 2.5 cm [vertically upwards]

   Join 9 – 2 in a smooth curve for waistline.

8. Join 9 – 7 in a smooth curve for side seam.

9. Knee Line:

$6_2 - 10$ = 1/4th round knees + 2 cm (ease) + 1 cm [horizontally]
= 19 cm

Draw a vertical line downwards from point 10 to line 3 – 1 and mark as 10_1.

10. For Dart:

(i) Dart position: 2 – N = 1/12th round hips [on line 2 – 9]
= 7.8 cm

(ii) Dart length: $N - N_1$ = 1/8th round hips – 1 cm [vertically downwards]
= 10.75 cm

(iii) Dart width: N – R = $N - R_1$ = 1.5 cm [on either side of point N on line 2 – 9]

Join $R - N_1$ and $R_1 - N_1$ in straight lines for the required dart.

11. Fish Cut Shape:

(i) Drop a vertical line downwards from point N_1 to line $3 - 10_1$ through lines

$5_2 - 5_1$ and $6_2 - 10$ and mark as:

A on line $5_2 - 5_1$,

A_1 on line $6_2 - 10$, and

A_2 on line $3 - 10_1$.

(ii) For Back Central Panel:

(a) Cut through line: $R - N_1 - A - A_1 - A_2$.

Central panel is along the points:

$2 - 6_2 - 3 - A_2 - A_1 - N_1 - R - 2$.

(b) Pivot line $3 - 6_2$ at point 6_2 by 8 cm (or as required) and mark as C.

(c) Pivot line $A_2 - A_1$ at point A_1 by 8 cm (or as required) and mark as C_1.

(d) Trace out the obtained pattern for central panel of fish cut skirt.

(e) Fish cut skirt back central panel is along the points:

$2 - 6_2 - C - C_1 - A_1 - A - N_1 - R - 2$.

Cut 2 – pieces of the above block for fish cut skirt.

(iii) For Side Panel:

(a) Cut through line: $R_1 - N_1 - A - A_1 - A_2$.

Side panel is along the points:

$R_1 - N_1 - A_1 - A_2 - 10_1 - 10 - 5_1 - 7 - 9$.

(b) Pivot line $A_2 - A_1$ at point A_1 by 8 cm (or as required) and mark as D.

(c) Pivot line $10_1 - 10$ at point 10 by 8 cm (or as required) and mark as D_1.

(d) Trace out the obtained pattern for side panel of fish cut skirt.

(e) Fish cut skirt back side panel is along the points:

$R_1 - N_1 - A_1 - D - D_1 - 10 - 5_1 - 7 - 9 - R_1$.

Cut two pieces of the above block for fish cut skirt.

(iv) Total of four panels, i.e. two pieces of central and two pieces of side panel are to be cut to complete the back section of fish cut skirt.

Front:

1. Waistline:

(i) 0 – 11 = 1/4th round waist + 3 cm (dart) – 1 cm [horizontally]

= 19 cm

(ii) 11 – 12 = 2.5 cm [vertically upwards]

Join 12 – 0 in a smooth curve for waist line.

2. Join 12 – 7 in a smooth curve for side seam.
3. Knee Line: 6 – 13 = 1/4th round knees + 2 cm (ease) – 1 cm [horizontally]
   = 17 cm

   Draw a vertical line downwards from point 13 to line 1 – 3 and mark as 13_1.
4. Dart:
   (i) Dart position: 0 – M = 1/12th round hips [on line 0 – 12]
   = 7.8 cm
   (ii) Dart length: M – M_1 = 1/8th round hips [vertically downwards]
   = 11.75 cm
   (iii) Dart width: M – S = M – S_1 = 1.5 cm [on either side of point M on line 0 – 12]

   Join S – M_1 and S_1 – M_1 in straight lines for the required dart.
5. Fish Cut Shape:
   (i) Drop a vertical line downwards from point M_1 to line 1 – 13_1 through lines 5 – 5_1 and 6 – 13 and mark as:

   B on line 5 – 5_1,

   B_1 on line 6 – 13, and

   B_2 on line 1 – 13_1.
   (ii) For front central panel:
   (a) Cut through line: S – M_1 – B – B_1 – B_2.

   Front central panel is along the points:

   0 – 6 – 1 – B_2 – B_1 – B – M_1 – S – 0.
   (b) Pivot line 1 – 6 at point 6 by 8 cm (or as required) and mark as E.
   (c) Pivot line B_2 – B_1 at point B_1 by 8 cm (or as required) and mark as E_1.

(d) Trace out the obtained pattern for central panel of fish cut skirt.

(e) Fish cut skirt front central panel is along the points:

$0 - 6 - E_1 - E - B_1 - M_1 - S - 0$.

Cut two pieces of the above block for fish cut skirt.

(iii) For Side Panel:

(a) Cut through line: $S_1 - M_1 - B - B_1 - B_2$.

Side panel is along the points:

$S_1 - M_1 - B - B_1 - B_2 - 13_1 - 13 - 5_1 - 7 - 12 - S_1$.

(b) Pivot line $B_2 - B_1$ at point B_1 by 8 cm (or as required) and mark as F.

(c) Pivot line $13_1 - 13$ at point 13 by 8 cm (or as required) and mark as F_1.

(d) Trace out the obtained pattern for side panel of fish cut skirt.

(e) Fish cut skirt back side panel is along the points:

$S_1 - M_1 - B_1 - F_1 - F - 13 - 5_1 - 7 - 12 - S_1$.

Cut two pieces of the above block for fish cut skirt.

(iv) Total of four panels, i.e. two pieces of central and two pieces of side panel are to be cut to complete the front section of fish cut skirt.

6. Give a side or center back opening of 15 cm (or as required) and finish with a fly (zip).

Add seam allowance of 1.5 cm (or as required) and hem allowance of 3 cm (or as required) and mark corresponding balance points and grain line on each draft and pattern piece.

Belt:

1. A – B = round waist [horizontally]
   = 68 cm
2. A – C = 4 cm (with intake) [vertically downwards]
   Complete the rectangle A – B – C – D.
3. For Overlap:
   B – E = D – F = 2.5 cm [horizontally outwards]
   Join E – F in a straight line or in a smooth outward curve for overlap.
   (Use interfacing equal to ½ of belt width to give firmness to the belt.)

Add seam allowance of 1.5 cm (or as required) and put up corresponding balance points and grain line on each draft and pattern piece.

Fish Cut Skirt Block

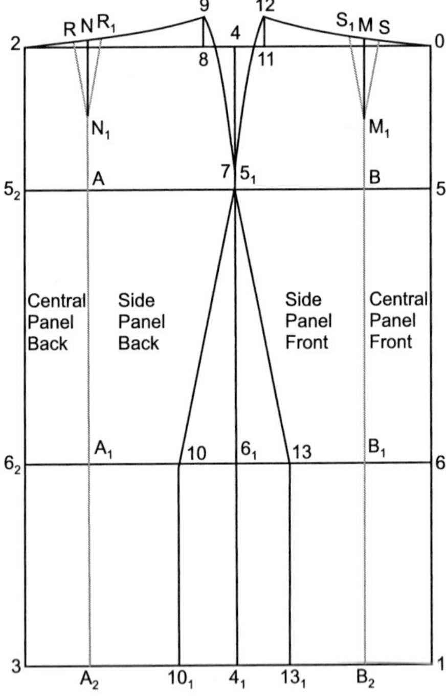

Back Fish Skirt Block

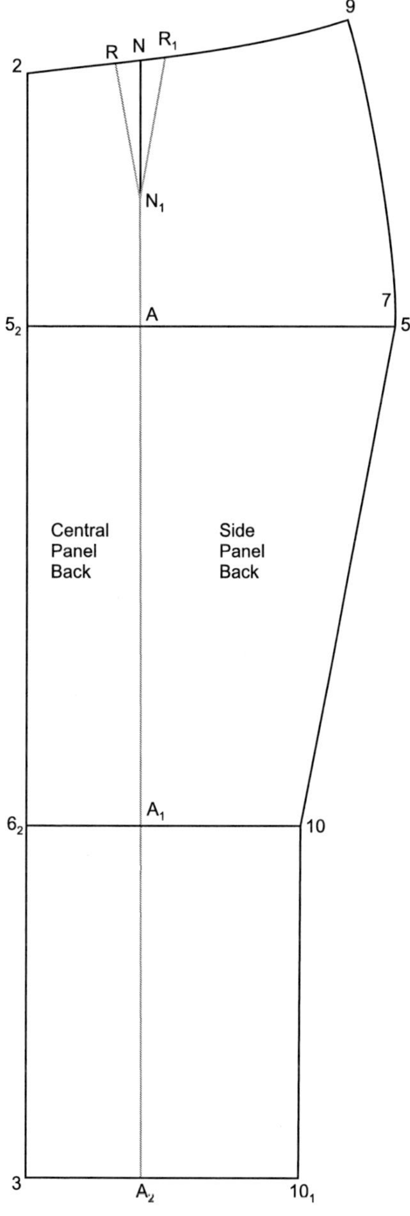

Back Central Panel

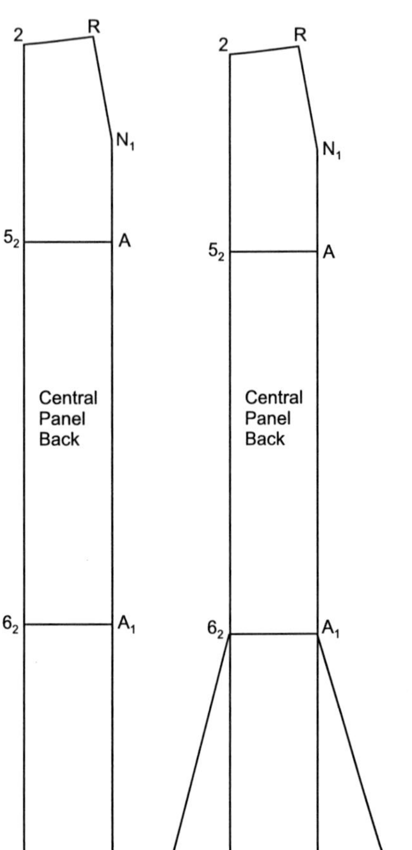

Final Central Panel

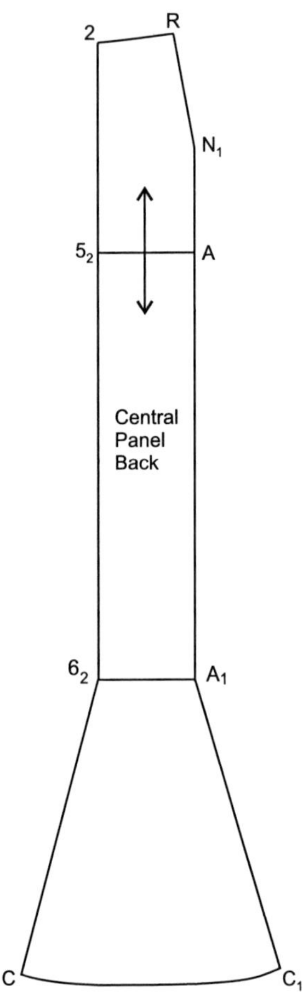

Back Side Panel

Final Side Panel

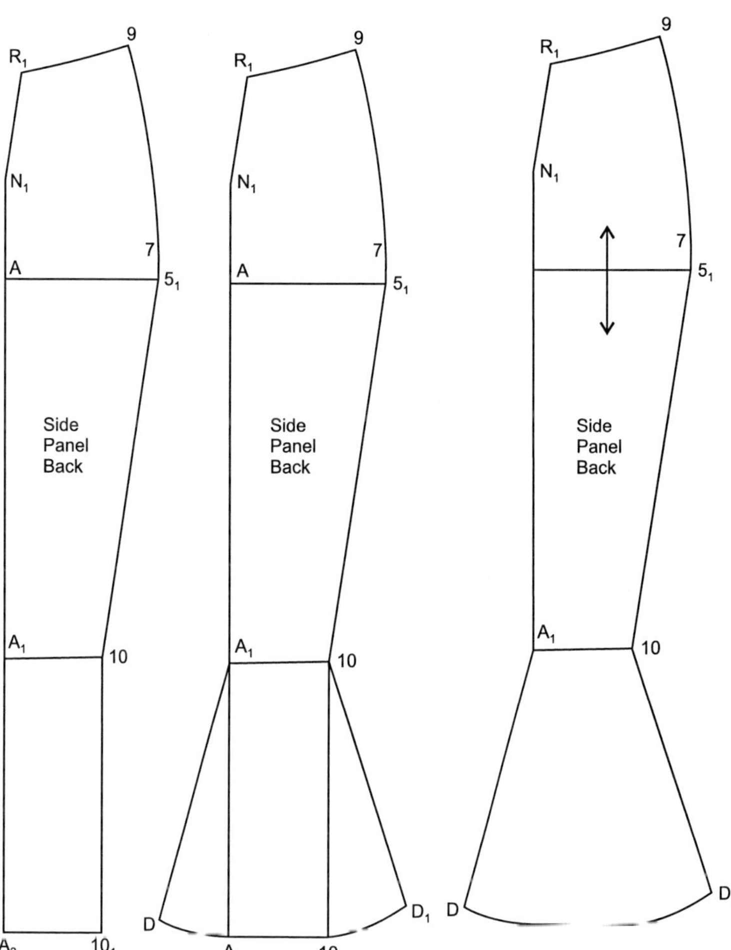

Front Fish Skirt Block

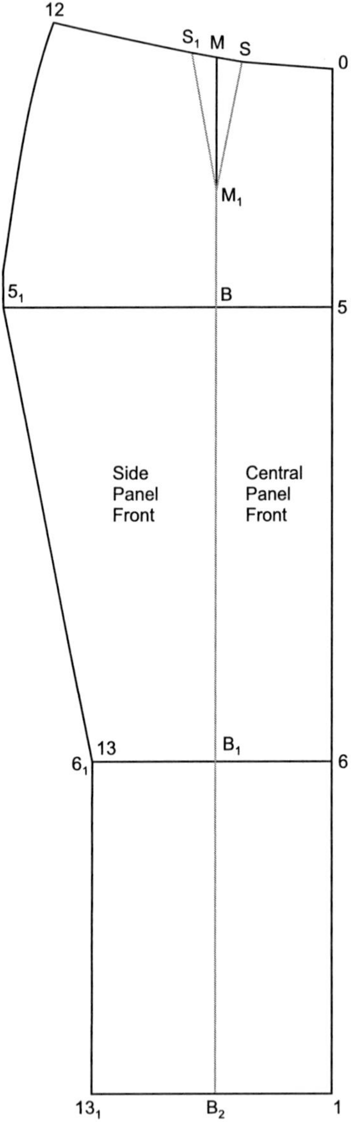

Front Central Panel

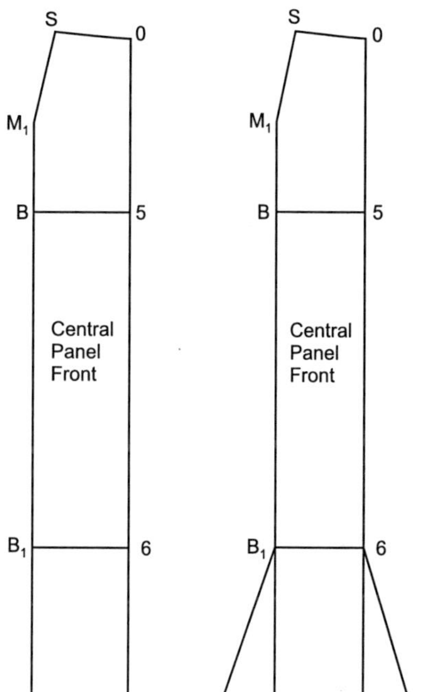

Final Central Panel

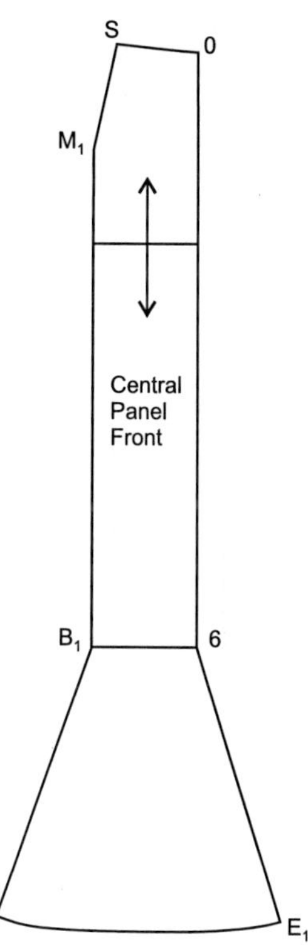

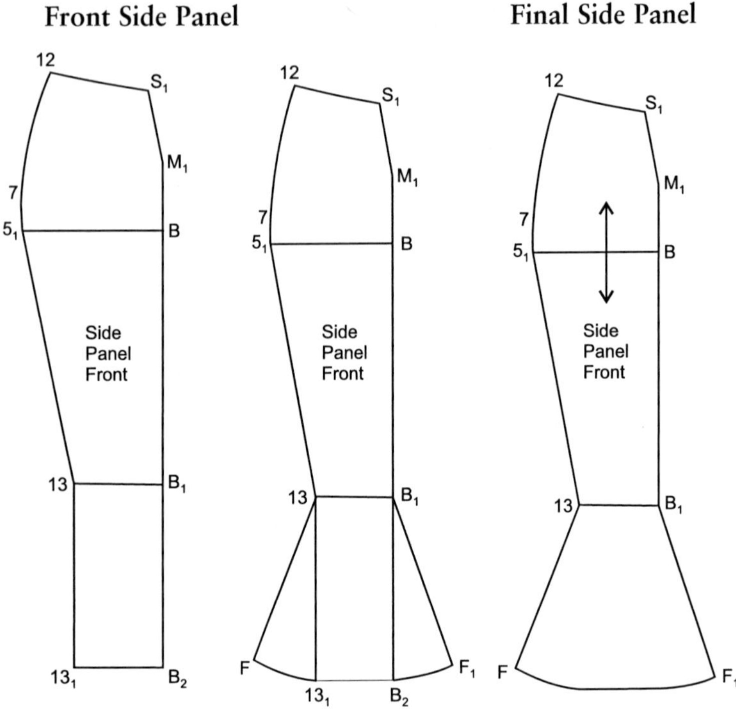

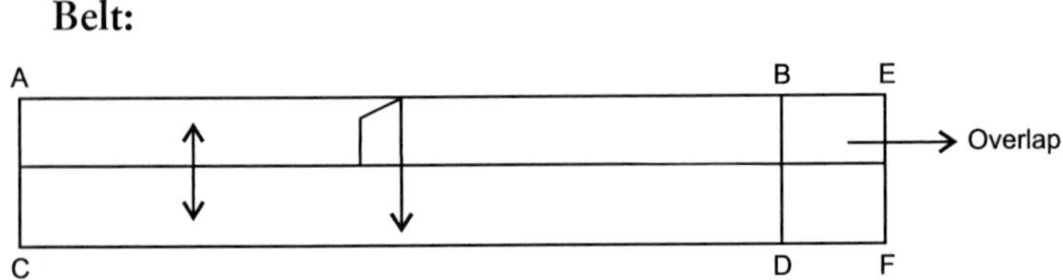

Pencil Skirt

An ankle length lower garment worn from waist till ankle, generally by women, it is fitting at waist and hips and tapers down to ankle. A slit has to be given to this skirt to facilitate walking.

Suitable Fabric: Medium weight to heavy weight fabric.

FISH CUT SKIRT AND VARIATION

Fish cut skirt

Fish cut skirt with yoke and triangular panels

Age Group: 13 yrs. and above

Size symbol – 10

Scale – cm

Drafting scale – 1/4th cm or 1/6th cm

Required fabric – 2.10 m × 54 cm (length × width)

Measurements:

Required length (waist to ankle) = 104 cm

Round waist = 68 cm

Round hips = 94 cm

Hip level = 21 cm

Waist to knee = 58 cm

Round bottom/round ankles = 66 cm (this measurement should be taken by keeping feet slightly apart)

Belt width = 2 cm

Construction:

1. 0 – 1 = required length + 1 cm – belt width [vertically downwards]
   = 103 cm
2. 0 – 2 = ½ round hips + 3 cm (ease or as required) [horizontally]
   = 50 cm

   Complete the rectangle 0 – 1 – 2 – 3.
3. 0 – 4 = ½ (0 to 2) – 1 cm [horizontally]
   = 25 cm

   Draw a vertical line downwards from point 4 to line 1 – 3 and mark as 4_1.
4. Hip level

   0 – 5 = hip level – belt width [vertically downwards]
   = 19 cm

   Draw a horizontal line from point 5 to line 2 – 3 through line 4 – 4_1 and mark as:

5_1 on line 4 – 4_1, and
5_2 on line 2 – 3.

5. 5_1 – 6 = 2 cm [vertically upwards]

Back:

6. Waistline:

   0 – 7 = 1/4th round waist + 3 cm (dart) + 1 cm [horizontally]
   = 21 cm

   7 – 8 = 2.5 cm [vertically upwards]

   Join 0 – 8 in a smooth inward curve for waistline.

7. Join 8 – 6 in a smooth outward curve for side seam.
8. Hem Line:

   1 – 9 = 1/4th round bottom [horizontally]
   = 17.5 cm

   Join 9 – 5_1 in a straight line for side seam.

9. Dart:

   (i) Dart position: 0 – N = 1/12th round hips [horizontally]
   = 7.8 cm

   (ii) Dart length: N – N_1 = 1/8th round hips – 1 cm [vertically downwards]
   = 10.75 cm

   (iii) Dart width: N – S = N – S_1 = 1.5 cm (on either side of point N) [horizontally]

   Join S – N_1 and S_1 – N_1 in straight lines for the required dart.

10. Back Slit:

    0 – 10 = waist to knee [vertically downwards]
    = 58 cm

    10 – 1 is the required center back slit.

11. Back pencil skirt block is along the points:

    0 – N – 8 – 6 – 5_1 – 9 – 3 – 10 – 0

    0 – 1 is on fold.

$8 - 6 - 5_1 - 9$ is side seam.

$10 - 1$ is center back slit.

Front:

1. Waistline:

   $2 - 7_f$ = 1/4th round waist + 3 cm (dart) – 1 cm [horizontally]

   = 19 cm

   $7_f - 8_f$ = 2.5 cm [vertically upwards]

   Join $2 - 8_f$ in a smooth inward curve for waistline.

2. Join $8_f - 6$ in a smooth outward curve for side seam at hip level.

3. Hem Line:

   $3 - 9_f$ = 1/4th round bottom – 1 cm [horizontally on line 3 – 1]

   = 15.5 cm

   Join $9_f - 5_f$ in a straight line for side seam.

4. Dart:

   (i) Dart position:

   2 – M = 1/12th round hips [horizontally]

   = 7.8 cm

   (ii) Dart length: $M - M_1$ = 1/8th round hips [vertically downwards]

   = 11.75 cm

   (iii) Dart width: $M - P = M - P_1$ = 1 cm (on either side of point M) [horizontally]

   Join $P - M_1$ and $P_1 - M_1$ in straight lines for the required dart.

5. Front pencil skirt block is along the points:

   $2 - M - 8_f - 6 - 5_1 - 9_f - 3 - 2$

   2 – 3 is on fold.

   $8_f - 6 - 5_1 - 9_f$ is side seam.

Add seam allowance of 1.5 cm (or as required) and hem allowance of 3 cm (or as required) and mark corresponding balance points and grain line on each draft and pattern piece.

Belt:

1. A – B = round waist
   = 68 cm
2. A – C = 4 cm (with intake)
   Complete the rectangle A – B – C – D.
3. For Overlap:
   B – E = D – F = 2.5 cm [horizontally outwards]
   Join E – F in a straight line or in a smooth outward curve for overlap.
   (Use interfacing equal to ½ of belt width to give firmness to the belt.)

Add seam allowance of 1.5 cm (or as required) and put up corresponding balance points and grain line on each draft and pattern piece.

Pencil Skirt:

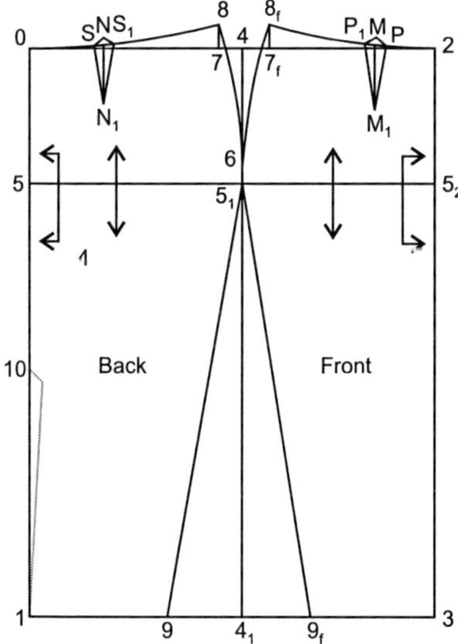

Belt:

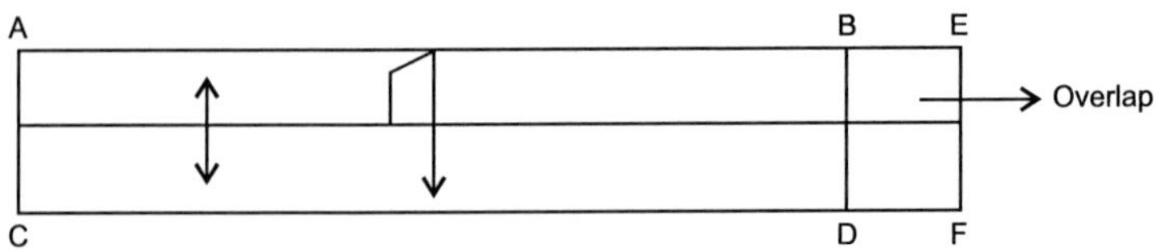

A-line Skirt

A-line Skirt: A-line skirt is a knee to ankle length bias cut skirt that is fitting at waist and flared at hemline.

Suitable Fabric: Light weight to medium weight fabric.

Age Group: Any age.

Size symbol – 10

Scale – cm

Drafting scale – 1/4th cm or 1/6th cm

Required fabric – 1.10 m × 90 cm (length × width)

Measurements:

Required length (waist to knee) = 54 cm

Round waist = 68 cm

Round hips = 94 cm

Hip level = 21 cm

Belt width = 2 cm

Construction:

1. 0 – 1 = required length + 1 cm – belt width [vertically downwards]
   = 52 cm
2. Hip Level:
   0 – 2 = hip level – belt width [vertically downwards on line 0 – 1]
   = 19 cm
3. Hip Line:
   2 – 3 = 1/4th round hips + 4 cm (ease and shape) [horizontally]
   = 27.5 cm

PENCIL SKIRT AND VARIATION

Back view

Pencil skirt

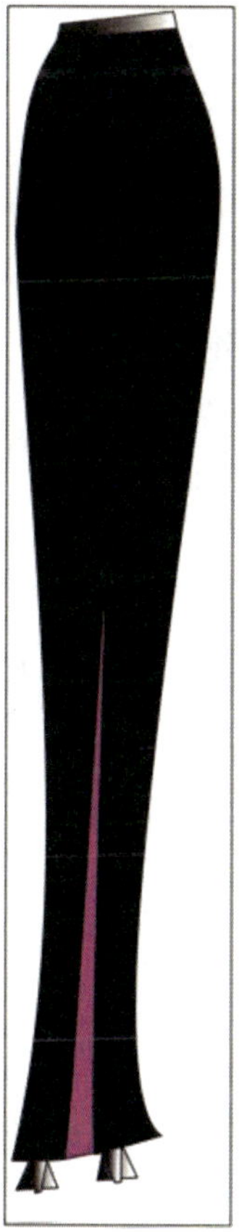

Pencil skirt with yoke

4. Waistline:

   0 – 4 = 1/4th round waist + 2 cm (dart width) [horizontally]

   = 19 cm

5. To Shape Waistline:

   4 – 5 = 2.5 cm [vertically upwards]

   Join 5 – 0 in a smooth curve for waistline.

6. Side Seams:

   Join 5 – 3 in a straight line and extend downwards and mark as 6, where:

   5 – 6 = (0 – 1) + 2.5 cm

   = 52 cm + 2.5 cm

   = 54.5 cm

7. Hem Line:

   Join 6 – 1 in a smooth curve for hem line.

8. For Dart: waistline dart.

   (i) Dart position: 0 – N = 1/12th round hips [on line 0 – 5]

   = 7.8 cm

   (ii) Dart length: N – N_1 = 1/10th round hips [perpendicular to line 0 – 5]

   = 9.4 cm

   (iii) Dart width:

   N – S = N – S_1 = 1 cm (on either side of point N) [on line 0 – 5]

   Join S – N_1 and S_1 – N_1 in straight lines for the required waistline dart.

9. For Side Opening:

   5 – A = 1/8th round hips [downwards on line 5 – 6]

   = 11.75 cm

This opening is given in skirt to slip into the skirt comfortably and can be finished with a fly (zip) or as required.

10. For A-line skirt block cut along the points:

    0 – 1 – 6 – A – 5 – N – 0,

    where:

    0 – 1 is on fold.

    5 – 6 is side seams.

    6 – 1 is hem line.

    Cut two pieces of the above block, one piece for front and one piece for back.

Add seam allowance of 1.5 cm (or as required) and hem allowance of 3 cm (or as required) and mark corresponding balance points and grain line on each draft and pattern piece.

Belt:

1. A – B = round waist

   = 68 cm

2. A – C = 4 cm (with intake)

   Complete the rectangle A – B – C – D.

3. For Overlap:

   B – E = D – F = 2.5 cm [horizontally outwards]

   Join E – F in a straight line or in a smooth outward curve for overlap.

   (Use interfacing equal to 1/2 of belt width to give firmness to the belt.)

Add seam allowance of 1.5 cm (or as required) and put up corresponding balance points and grain line on each draft and pattern piece.

A-line Skirt:

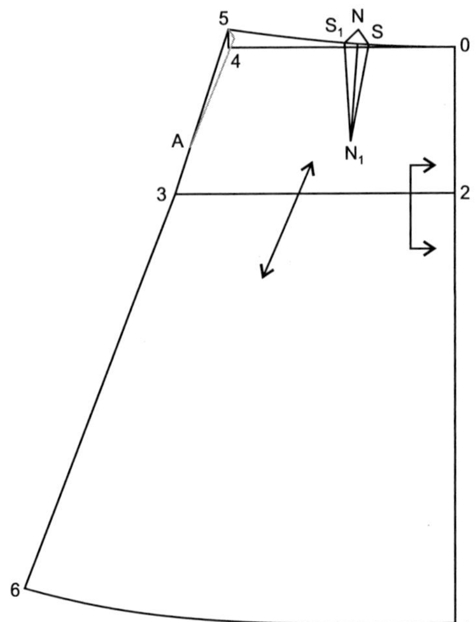

Belt:

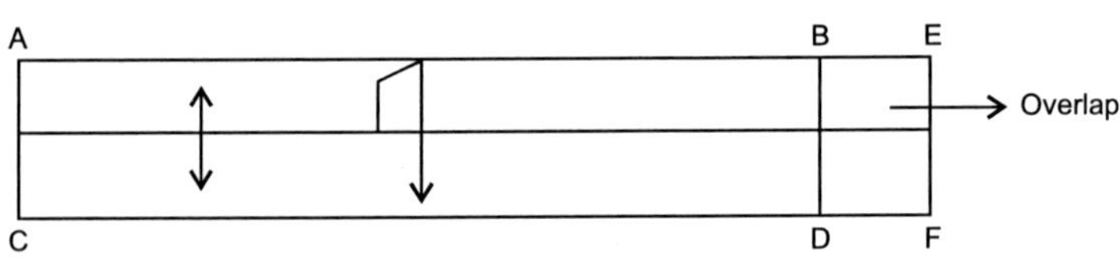

A-LINE SKIRT & VARIATION

A-line skirt (knee length)

A-line skirt (full length) shaped with yoke

6 MINI SKIRT

A-LINE MINI SKIRT

A short mid-thigh length lower garment fitting at waist and slightly flared at hem line.

Suitable Fabric: Medium to heavy weight fabric.

Group: 13 years and above.

Size symbol – 10

Scale – cm

Drafting scale – 1/4th cm or 1/6th cm

Required fabric – 64 cm × 62 cm (length × width)

Measurements:

Knee length = 56 cm

Required length = ½ knee length

= 28 cm

Round waist = 72 cm (low waist)

Round hips = 94 cm

Hip level = 20.3 cm

Belt width = 2 cm

Construction:

1. 0 – 1 = required length + 1 cm – belt width [vertically downwards]

   = 27 cm

2. Hip Level:

   0 – 2 = hip level – belt width [vertically downwards on line 0 – 1]

   = 18.3 cm

3. Hip Line:

   2 – 3 = 1/4th round hips + 2 cm (ease) [horizontally]

   = 25.5 cm

4. 0 – 4 = 2 – 3 [horizontally]

   Join 3 – 4 in a straight line.

5. Waistline:

   0 – 5 = 1/4th round waist + 3 cm (dart width) [horizontally on line 0 – 4]

   = 21 cm

6. To Shape Waistline:

   5 – 6 = 2.5 cm [vertically upwards]

   Join 0 – 6 in a smooth curve for shaping the waistline.

7. To Shape Side Seam at Hip Level:

   3 – 7 = 2 cm [vertically upwards on line 3 – 4]

   Join 7 – 6 in a smooth curve to shape side seam at hip level.

8. Hem Line:

   1 – 8 = 1/4th round hips + 6 cm [horizontally]

   = 29.5 cm

   Join 3 – 8 in a straight line.

9. To Shape Hem Line:

   8 – 9 = 1 cm [upwards on line 8 – 3]

   Join 9 – 1 in a smooth curve for hem line.

10. For Dart:

    (i) Dart position: 0 – N = 1/12th round hips [on line 0 – 6]

    = 7.8 cm

(ii) Dart length: $N - N_1$ = 1/12th round hips – 1 cm [perpendicular downwards to line 0 – 6]

= 6.8 cm

(iii) Dart width: $N - S = N - S_1$ = 1.5 cm (on either side of point N) [on line 0 – 6]

Join $S - N_1$ and $S_1 - N_1$ in straight lines for the required dart.

11. For mini skirt block cut along the points:

    0 – 1 – 9 – 3 – 7 – 6 – N – 0,

    where:

    0 – 1 is on fold.

    6 – 7 – 3 – 9 is side seams.

    Cut two pieces of the above mini skirt block; one piece for front and one piece for back to complete the mini skirt.

Add seam allowance of 1.5 cm (or as required) and hem allowance of 3 cm (or as required) and mark corresponding balance points and grain line on each draft and pattern piece.

Belt:

1. A – B = round waist [horizontally]

   = 72 cm

2. A – C = 4 cm (with intake) [vertically downwards]

   Complete the rectangle A – B – C – D.

3. For Overlap:

   B – E = D – F = 2.5 cm [horizontally outwards]

   Join E – F in a straight line or in a smooth outward curve for overlap.

   (Use interfacing equal to ½ of belt width to give firmness to the belt.)

Add seam allowance of 1.5 cm (or as required) and put up corresponding balance points and grain line on each draft and pattern piece.

A-line Mini Skirt:

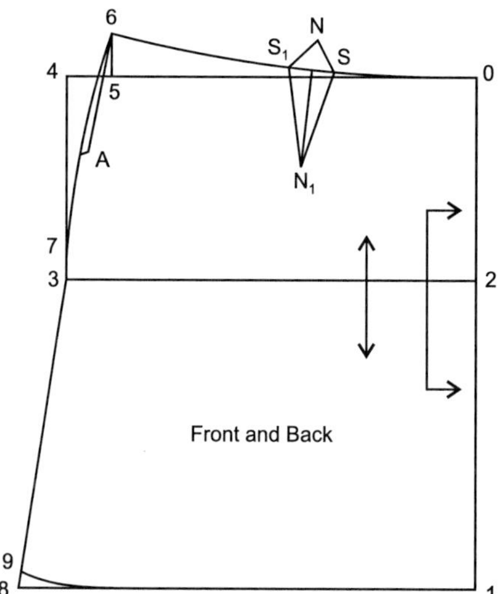

Belt:

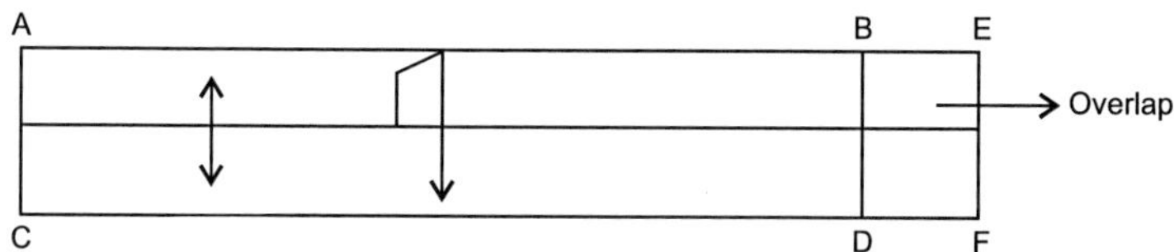

MINI SKIRT WITH INVERTED BOX PLEATS

A short mid-thigh length lower garment with immediate pleats facing each other. For inverted box pleats the immediate pleats are stitched to some length downwards.

Suitable Fabric: Light weight to medium weight fabric.

Age Group: 13 years and above.

Size symbol – 10

Scale – cm

Drafting scale – 1/4th cm or 1/6th cm

Required fabric – 66 cm × 82 cm (length × width)

Measurements:

Knee length = 56 cm

Required length = ½ knee length

= 28 cm

Round waist = 72 cm (low waist)

Round hips = 94 cm

Hip level = 17.3 cm

Belt width = 1 cm

Number of pleats = 16

Pleat intake = 4 cm

Construction:

1. 0 – 1 = required length + 1 cm – belt width [vertically downwards]

   = 28 cm

2. Hip Level:

   0 – 2 = hip level + 0.5 cm – belt width [vertically downwards on line 0 – 1]

   = 16.8 cm

3. Waist Line

   0 – 3 = 1/4th round waist + (1/4th number of pleats × pleat intake) [horizontally]

   = 18 cm + 16 cm

   = 34 cm

4. Hip Line:

   2 – 4 = 1/4th round hips + (1/4th number of pleats × pleat intake) + 1.5 cm (ease) [horizontally]

   = 41 cm

5. Hem Line:

   1 – 5 = 2 – 4 [horizontally]

   = 41 cm

   Join 5 – 4 in a straight line for side seams.

6. To Shape Waist Line:

   3 – 6 = 2 cm [vertically upwards]

Join 0 – 6 in a smooth curve for waistline.

Join 6 – 4 in a smooth curve for side seam.

7. For Pleats: Divide 0 – 3 into three equal parts and mark as A and B, respectively.
8. Inverted pleats face each other.
   (a) First pleat:
      (i) Pleat position: $A - A_1 = A - A_2 = 4$ cm (on either side of point A) [on line 0 – 3]
      (ii) Pleat length: $A_1 - A_3 = A_2 - A_4$ = hip level – 3 cm [vertically downwards]

         = 14.3 cm
      (iii) For box pleat: Extend the pleat length upwards to meet the line 0 – 6.

         Bring together points A_1 and A_2 and stitch till points A_3 and A_4.
   (b) Second pleat:
      (i) Pleat position: $B - B_1 = B - B_2 = 4$ cm (on either side of point B) [on line 0 – 3]
      (ii) Pleat length: $B_1 - B_3 = B_2 - B_4$ = hip level – 4 cm [vertically downwards]

         = 13.3 cm
      (iii) For box pleat: Extend the pleat length upwards to meet the line 0 – 6.

         Bring together points B_1 and B_2 and stitch till points B_3 and B_4.
9. For Opening:

   6 – G = hip level – 4 cm [downwards on line 6 – 4]

   = 13.3 cm
10. Inverted box pleats mini skirt block is along the points:

    $0 - 1 - 5 - 4 - G - 6 - B_2 - B - B_1 - A_2 - A - A_1 - 0$,

    where:

    0 – 1 is on fold.

$0 - A_1 - A - A_2 - B_1 - B - B_2 - 6$ is waistline.

6 – G is opening on one side which can be finished with a zip or as desired.

6 – 4 – 5 is side seams.

1 – 5 is hem line.

Add seam allowance of 1.5 cm (or as required) and hem allowance of 3 cm (or as required) and mark corresponding balance points and grain line on each draft and pattern piece.

Belt:

1. A – B = round waist [horizontally]

   = 72 cm
2. A – C = 2 cm (with intake) [vertically downwards]

   Complete the rectangle A – B – C – D.
3. For Overlap:

   B – E = D – F = 2.5 cm [horizontally outwards]

   Join E – F in a straight line or in a smooth outward curve for overlap.

   (Use interfacing equal to ½ of belt width to give firmness to the belt.)

Add seam allowance of 1.5 cm (or as required) and put up corresponding balance points and grain line on each draft and pattern piece.

Inverted Box Pleats Mini Skirt:

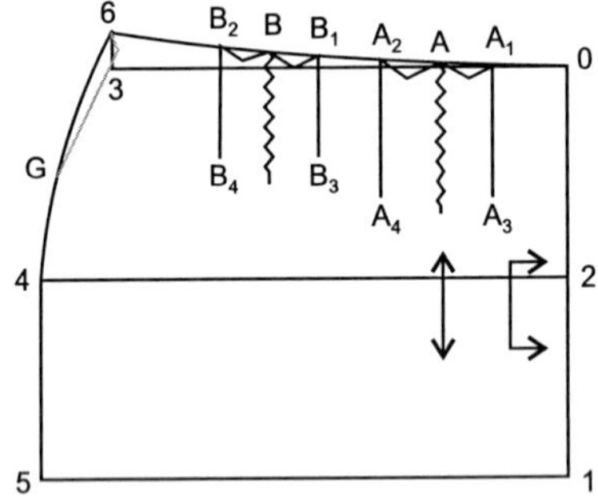

Belt:

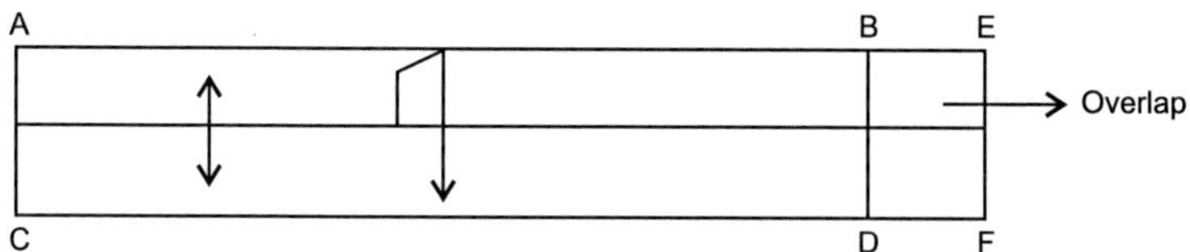

MINI SKIRT STRAIGHT FIT

A mid thigh-length slightly fitting lower garment with a small slit to facilitate walking.

Suitable Fabric: Medium to heavy weight fabric.

Age Group: 13 years and above.

Size symbol – 10

Scale – cm

Drafting scale – 1/4th cm or 1/6th cm

Required fabric – 34 cm × 104 cm or 70 cm × 53 cm (length × width)

Measurements:

Knee length = 56 cm

Required length = ½ knee length

= 28 cm

Round waist = 72 cm (low waist)

Round hips = 94 cm

Hip level = 17.3 cm

Belt width = 2 cm

Construction:

1. 0 – 1 = required length + 1 cm – belt width [vertically downwards]

   = 27 cm

2. Hip Level:

   0 – 2 = hip level + 0.5 cm – belt width [vertically downwards on line 0 – 1]

   = 15.8 cm

3. Waistline:

   0 – 3 = 1/4th round waist + 2 cm (dart width) [horizontally]

   = 20 cm

4. To Shape Waistline:

   3 – 4 = 2.5 cm [vertically upwards]

   Join 4 – 0 in a smooth curve for waistline.

5. Hip Line:

   2 – 5 = 1/4th round hips + 1.5 cm (ease) [horizontally]

   = 25 cm

   Join 5 – 4 in a smooth curve for side seam.

6. Hem Line:

   1 – 6 = 2 – 5 [horizontally]

   = 25 cm

   Join 6 – 5 in a straight line for side seam.

7. Dart:

   (a) Dart position: 0 – M = 1/12th round hips [horizontally on line 0 – 3]

   = 7.8 cm

   (b) Dart length: M – M_1 = 1/12th round hips – 1.5 cm [vertically downwards]

   = 6.3 cm

   (c) Dart width: M – P = M – P_1 = 1 cm (on either side of point M) [horizontally]

   Join P – M_1 and P_1 – M_1 in straight lines for the required dart and extend upwards to meet the line 0 – 4.

8. For Opening:

   4 – 5 is the opening on one side of the skirt that should be finished with a zip or as desired.

9. For Side Slits: Side slits or center back slit should be provided in straight fit mini skirt for walking ease.

6 – A = 5 cm (or as required) [vertically upwards on line 6 – 5]

10. Straight fit mini skirt block is along the points:

 0 – 1 – 6 – A – 5 – 4 – M – O.

 where:

 0 – 1 is on fold.

 4 – G is side opening on one side which should be finished with zip or as desired.

 0 – M – 4 is waistline.

 4 – 5 – A is side seams.

 A – 6 is side slits.

 1 – 6 is hem line.

 Front and back block for straight fit mini skirt are similar, so cut two pieces each for front and back.

Add seam allowance of 1.5 cm (or as required) and hem allowance of 3 cm (or as required) and mark corresponding balance points and grain line on each draft and pattern piece.

Belt:

1. A – B = round waist [horizontally]

 = 72 cm

2. A – C = 4 cm (with intake) [vertically downwards]

 Complete the rectangle A – B – C – D.

3. For Overlap:

 B E – D – F = 2 cm [horizontally outwards]

 Join E – F in a straight line or in a smooth outward curve for overlap.

 (Use interfacing equal to ½ of belt width to give firmness to the belt.)

Add seam allowance of 1.5 cm (or as required) and put up corresponding balance points and grain line on each draft and pattern piece.

Straight Fit Mini Skirt:

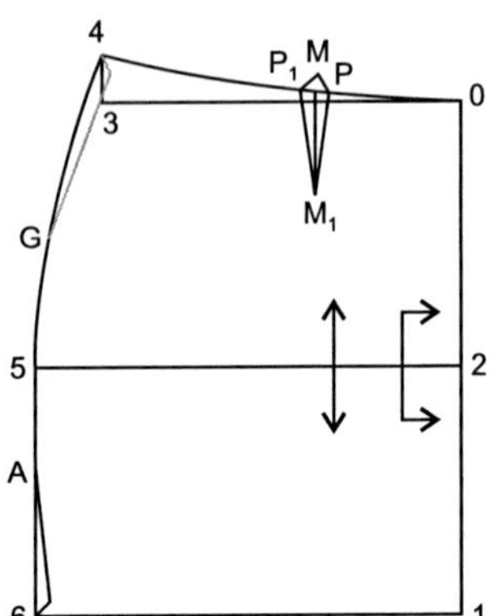

Belt:

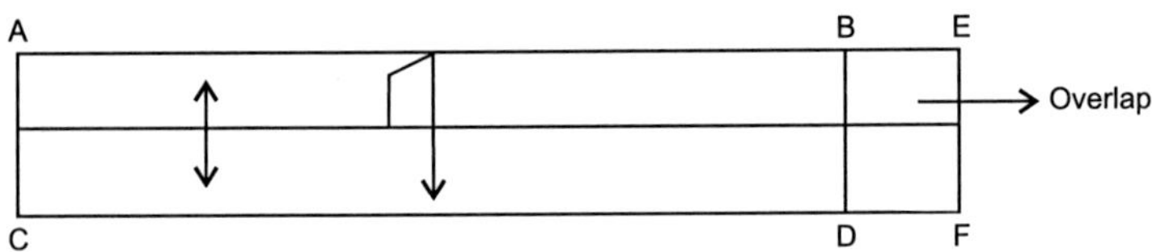

MINI SKIRTS

Straight fit

Inverted box pleats

A-line

7 GORED SKIRT

GORED SKIRTS

A gored skirt is a vertical paneled lower garment worn generally by women, which is fitting at waist and flared at hem.

4-gored Skirt

4-gored skirt is a 4-vertical paneled conical shaped lower garment generally worn by women, which is fitting at waist and flared at hem.

Suitable Fabric: Light weight to medium weight fabric.

Age Group: 13 yrs. and above.

Size symbol – 10

Scale – cm

Drafting scale – 1/4th cm or 1/6th cm

Required fabric – 2.10 m × 90 cm (length × width)

Measurements:

Required length (waist to ankle) = 104 cm

Round waist = 68 cm

Round hips = 94 cm

Hip level = 21 cm

Belt width = 2 cm

Construction:

1. 0 – 1 = required length + 1 cm – belt width [vertically downwards]
   = 103 cm
2. Hip Level:
   0 – 2 = hip level – belt width [vertically downwards on line 0 – 1]
   = 19 cm
3. Hip Line:
   2 – 3 = 1/4th round hips + 8 cm (to give shape) [horizontally]
   = 31.5 cm
4. Waistline:
   0 – 4 = 1/4th round waist + 3 cm (dart) [horizontally]
   = 20 cm
5. Side Seams:
   4 – 5 = 2.5 cm [vertically upwards]
   Join 5 – 3 in a straight line and extend and mark as 6, where:
   5 – 6 = (0 – 1) + 2.5 cm
   = 105.5 cm
6. Hem Line:
   Join 6 – 1 in a smooth curve for hem line.
7. To Shape Waistline:
   Join 5 – 0 in a smooth curve for waistline.
8. Dart:
   (i) Dart position: 0 – N = 1/12th round hips [on line 0 – 5]
   = 7.8 cm
   (ii) Dart length: N – N_1 = 1/8th round hips [perpendicular to line 0 – 5]
   = 11.75 cm

(iii) Dart width: N – S = N – S_1 = 1.5 cm (on either side of point N) [on line 0 – 5]

Join S – N_1 and S_1 – N_1 in straight lines for the required dart.

9. 4-gored skirt block is along the points:

0 – 1 – 6 – 3 – 5 – N – 0.

where:

5 – 3 – 6 is side seam.

0 – 1 is the center front and center back seam.

1 – 6 is hem line.

Cut four pieces of the obtained pattern to complete the skirt.

Add seam allowance of 1.5 cm (or as required) and hem allowance of 3 cm (or as required) and mark corresponding balance points and grain line on each draft and pattern piece.

Belt:

1. A – C = belt width [vertically downwards]
   = 4 cm (with intake)
2. A – B = round waist [horizontally]
   = 68 cm

   Complete the rectangle A – B – C – D.
3. For Overlap:

   B – E = D – F = 2.5 cm [horizontally outwards]

   Join E – F in a straight line or in a smooth outward curve for overlap.

   (Use interfacing equal to ½ of belt width to give firmness to the belt.)

Add seam allowance of 1.5 cm (or as required) and put up corresponding balance points and grain line on each draft and pattern piece.

4-gored Skirt:

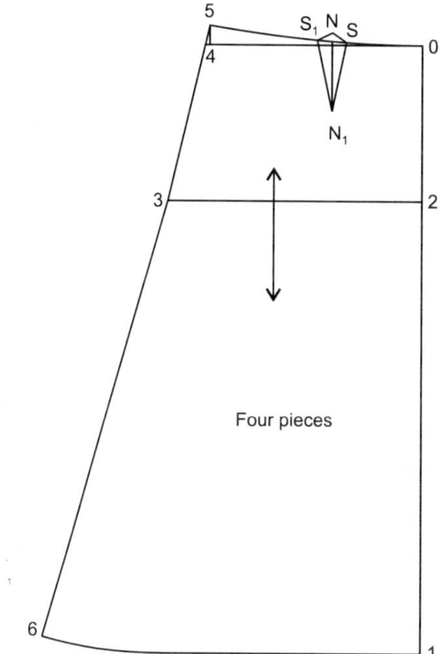

Belt:

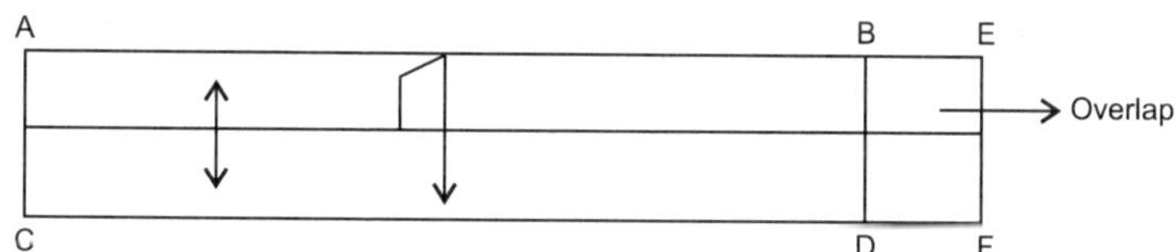

6-gored Skirt

6-gored skirt is a 6-vertical paneled conical shaped lower garment generally worn by women, which is fitting at waist and flared at hem. 6-gored skirt has more flare at hem than 4-gored skirt.

Suitable Fabric: Light weight to medium weight fabric.

Age Group: 13 yrs. and above

Size symbol – 10

Scale – cm

4-GORED SKIRT & VARIATIONS

4-Gored skirt

4-Gored skirt with front opening and slit

4-Gored skirt (knee length)

Drafting scale – 1/4th cm or 1/6th cm

Required fabric – 2.10 m × 1 m (length × width)

Measurements:

Required length (waist to ankle) = 104 cm

Round waist = 68 cm

Round hips = 94 cm

Hip level = 21 cm

Belt width = 2 cm

Construction:

1. 0 – 1 = required length + 1 cm – belt width [vertically downwards]

   = 103 cm

2. Hip Level:

   0 – 2 = hip level – belt width [vertically downwards on line 0 – 1]

   = 19 cm

3. Hip Line:

   2 – 3 = 1/4th round hips + 8 cm (to give shape) [horizontally]

   = 31.5 cm

4. Waistline:

   0 – 4 = 1/4th round waist + 3 cm (dart) [horizontally]

   = 20 cm

5. To Shape Waistline:

   4 – 5 = 2.5 cm [vertically upwards]

   Join 5 – 0 in a smooth curve for waistline.

6. Side Seams:

   Join 5 – 3 in a straight line and extend and mark as 6, where:

   5 – 6 = (0 – 1) + 2.5 cm = 105.5 cm

7. Hem Line:

   Join 6 – 1 in a smooth curve for hem line.

8. Central Gore:
   (i) 0 – 7 = 1/3rd (0 – 5) [on line 0 – 5]
   = 7 cm
   (ii) 2 – 8 = 1/3rd (2 – 3) [on line 2 – 3]
   = 10.5 cm

   Join 7 – 8 in a straight line and extend the line downwards to meet line 1 – 6 and mark as 9.
   (iii) 7 – N = 1.5 cm [on line 7 – 0]

   Join N – 8 in a straight line.
   (iv) Central Gore (central panel) is along the points: 0 – 1 – 9 – 8 – N – 0.

   where:

   0 – 1 is on fold.

   N – 8 – 9 is central-side seam.

   Cut two pieces of central panel for: One front and one back.
9. Side Panels:
   (i) 7 – N_1 = 1.5 cm [on line 7 – 5]

   Join N_1 – 8 in a straight line.
   (ii) Side panel is along the points:

   N_1 – 8 – 9 – 6 – 3 – 5 – N_1.

   where:

   5 – 3 – 6 is side seam.

   N_1 – 8 – 9 is side-central seam.

   Cut four pieces of side panels to complete the 6-paneled skirt.

Add seam allowance of 1.5 cm (or as required) and hem allowance of 3 cm (or as required) and mark corresponding balance points and grain line on each draft and pattern piece.

Belt:

1. A – B = round waist [horizontally]
   = 68 cm

2. A – C = 4 cm (with intake) [vertically downwards]
   Complete the rectangle A – B – C – D.
3. For Overlap:
   B – E = D – F = 2.5 cm [horizontally outwards]
   Join E – F in a straight line or in a smooth outward curve for overlap.
   (Use interfacing equal to ½ of belt width to give firmness to the belt.)

Add seam allowance of 1.5 cm (or as required) and put up corresponding balance points and grain line on each draft and pattern piece.

6-gored Skirt:

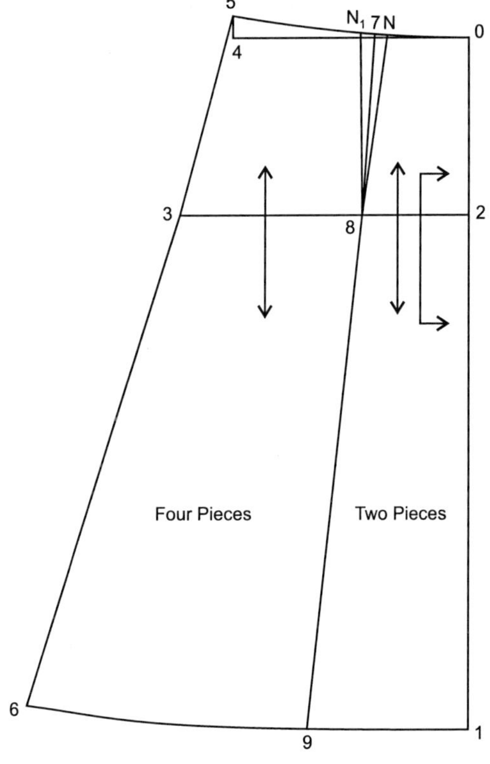

Belt:

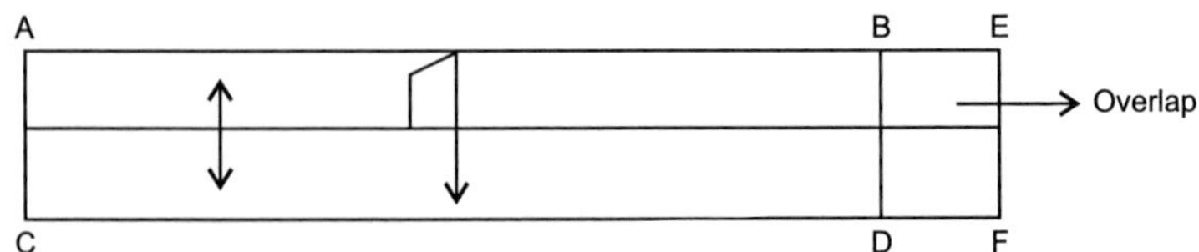

12-gored Skirt

12-gored skirt is a 12-vertical paneled conical shaped lower garment, generally worn by women, which is fitting at waist and flared at hem. 12-gored skirt has more flare at hem than 6-gored skirt.

Suitable Fabric: Light weight to medium weight fabric.

Age Group: 13 yrs. and above.

Size symbol – 10

Scale – cm

Drafting scale – 1/4th cm or 1/6th cm

Required fabric – 4.20 m × 1 m (length × width)

Measurements:

Required length (waist to ankle) = 104 cm

Round waist = 68 cm

Round hips = 94 cm

Hip level = 21 cm

Belt width = 2 cm

Construction:

1. 0 – 1 = required length + 1 cm – belt width [vertically downwards]
   = 103 cm
2. 0 – 2 = hip level – belt width [vertically downwards on line 0 – 1]
   = 19 cm
3. 2 – 3 = 1/4th round hips + 9 cm (to give shape) [horizontally]
   = 32.5 cm

6-GORED SKIRT AND VARIATION

6-Gored skirt

6-Gored skirt with double slits

6-Gored skirt with yoke

4. 0 – 4 = 1/4th round waist + 4 cm [horizontally]
   = 21 cm
5. 4 – 5 = 2.5 cm [vertically upwards]

   Join 5 – 3 in a straight line and extend and mark as 6, where:

   5 – 6 = (0 – 1) + 2.5 cm
   = 105.5 cm
6. Join 6 – 1 in a smooth curve for hem line.
7. First Gore:
   (i) 0 – 7 = 1/3rd (0 – 5) [on line 0 – 5]
   = 7 cm
   (ii) 2 – 8 = 1/3rd (2 – 3) [horizontally on line 2 – 3]
   = 10.8 cm
   (iii) Join 7 – 8 in a straight line and extend the line downwards to meet the line 1 – 6 and mark as 9.
   (iv) 7 – N = 1 cm [on line 7 – 0]

   Join N – 8 in a straight line to shape.
   (v) First gore is along the points:

   0 – 1 – 9 – 8 – N – 0.

   Cut four pieces of first gore for the required 12-gored skirt.
8. Second Gore:
   (i) 7 – 10 = 1/3rd (0 – 5) [on line 7 – 5]
   = 7 cm
   (ii) 8 – 11 = 1/3rd (2 – 3) [horizontally on line 8 – 3]
   = 10.8 cm
   (iii) Join 10 – 11 in a straight line and extend the line downwards to meet the line 1 – 6 and mark as 12.
   (iv) 7 – N_1 = 1 cm [on line 7 – 5]

   Join N_1 – 8 in a straight line to shape.

(v) 10 – M = 1 cm [on line 10 – 5]

Join M – 11 in a straight line to shape.

(vi) Second gore is along the points:

N_1 – 8 – 9 – 12 – 11 – M – N_1.

Cut four pieces of second gore for the required 12-gored skirt.

9. Third Gore:

(i) 10 – M_1 = 1 cm [on line 10 – 5]

Join M_1 – 11 in a straight line to shape.

(ii) Third gore is along the points:

M_1 – 11 – 12 – 6 – 5 – M_1.

Cut four pieces of third gore for the required 12-gored skirt.

10. Finish the skirt with a side opening of 1/8th round hips or as desired.

Add seam allowance of 1.5 cm (or as required) and hem allowance of 3 cm (or as required) and mark corresponding balance points and grain line on each draft and pattern piece.

Belt:

1. A – B = round waist [horizontally]

   = 68 cm

2. A – C = 4 cm (with intake) [vertically downwards]

   Complete the rectangle A – B – C – D.

3. For Overlap:

   B – E = D – F = 2.5 cm [horizontally outwards]

   Join E – F in a straight line or in a smooth outward curve for overlap.

   (Use interfacing equal to ½ of belt width to give firmness to the belt.)

Add seam allowance of 1.5 cm (or as required) and put up corresponding balance points and grain line on each draft and pattern piece.

12-gored Skirt:

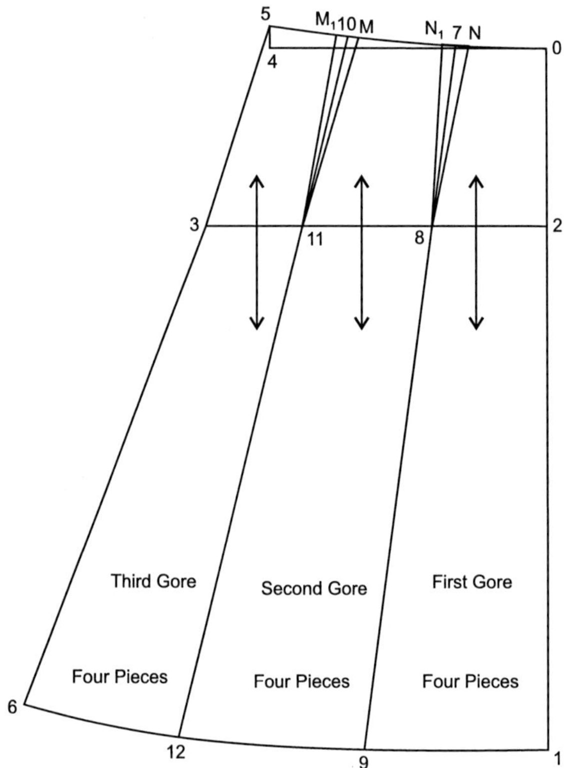

Belt:

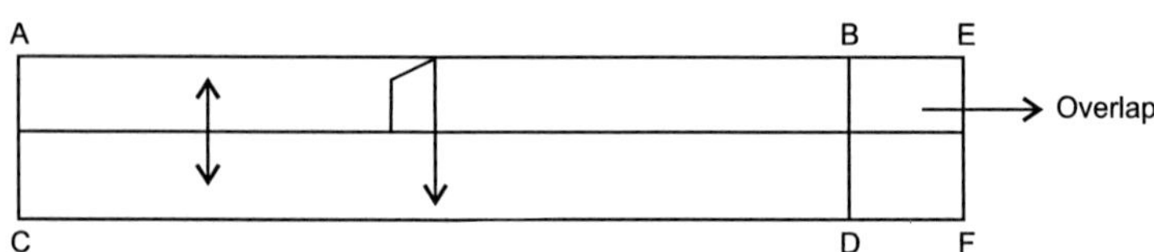

12-GORED SKIRT & VARIATION

12-Gored skirt

12-Gored skirt with front slit

12-gored skirt with yoke

8 WRAPAROUND SKIRT

WRAPAROUND SKIRT 1

Wraparound Skirt: A tube shaped seamless knee to ankle length lower garment that is straight fit and wraps or overlaps on front and is buttoned or tied into a knot by the extended waistline belt on one side of the waist.

Suitable Fabric: Light weight to heavy fabric.

Age Group: 13 yrs. and above.

Size symbol – 10

Scale – cm

Drafting scale – 1/4th cm or 1/6th cm

Required fabric – 55 cm × 1.25 m (length × width)

Measurements:

Required length = 52 cm

Round waist = 68 cm

Round hips = 94 cm

Hip level = 21 cm

Belt width = 2 cm

Construction:

1. 0 – 1 = required length + 1 cm – belt width [vertically downwards]
   = 51 cm
2. 0 – 2 = ½ round hips + 1/8th round waist (for wrap) + 6 cm (ease) [horizontally]

= 47 cm + 8.5 cm + 6 cm

= 61.5 cm

Complete the rectangle 0 – 1 – 2 – 3.

Back:

3. 0 – 4 = 1/4th round hips + 2 cm (ease) [horizontally on line 0 – 2]

   = 25.5 cm

   Draw a vertical line downwards from point 4 to line 1 – 3 and mark as 4_1.

   For dart width:

   = (0 – 4) – 1/4th round waist

   = 8.5 cm

   Divide 8.5 cm into 3 parts – 2 parts for 2 darts and 1 part for side seam.

4. Darts:

   (i) 4 – P = 2 cm [horizontally on line 4 – 0]

   4 – 4_2 = hip level – 2.5 cm (for shaping sides) [vertically downwards on line 4 – 4_1]

   = 18.5 cm

   Join P – 4_2 in a straight line for side dart.

   (ii) Divide 0 – P into three equal parts and mark as 5 and 6 for dart positions.

   (a) Dart at point 5:

   - Dart length: 5 – 5_1 = 1/10th round hips – 1 cm [vertically downwards]

     = 8.4 cm

   - Dart width: 5 – N = 5 – N_1 = 1. 5 cm (on either side of point 5) [horizontally]

     Join N – 5_1 and N_1 – 5_1 in straight lines for the required dart.

(b) Dart at point 6:

- Dart length: $6 - 6_1$ = 1/10th round hips – 1 cm [vertically downwards]
  = 8.4 cm
- Dart width: $6 - M = 6 - M_1$ = 1. 5 cm (on either side of point 6) [horizontally]

  Join $M - 6_1$ and $M_1 - 6_1$ in straight lines for the required dart.

5. 0 – 1 is center back on fold.

Front:

1. 4 – 7 = 1/4th round hips + 2 cm (ease) [horizontally on line 4 – 2]
   = 25.5 cm

   Draw a vertical line downwards from point 7 to line 1 – 3 and mark as 7_1.
2. Darts:

   (i) $4 - P_1$ = 2 cm [horizontally on line 4 – 2]

   Join $P_1 - 4_2$ in straight line for side dart.

   (ii) Divide $P_1 - 7$ into three equal parts and mark as 8 and 9 for dart positions.

   (a) Dart at point 8:

   - Dart length: $8 - 8_1$ = 1/10th round hips [vertically downwards]
     = 9.4 cm
   - Dart width: $8 - R = 8 - R_1$ = 1.5 cm (on either side of point 8) [horizontally]

     Join $R - 8_1$ and $R_1 - 8_1$ in straight lines for the required dart.

   (b) Dart at point 9:

   - Dart length: $9 - 9_1$ = 1/10th round hips [vertically downwards]
     = 9.4 cm

- Dart width: $9 - T = 9 - T_1 = 1.5$ cm (on either side of point 9) [horizontally]

  Join $T - 9_1$ and $T_1 - 9_1$ in straight lines for the required dart.

3. $7 - 7_1$ is the center front line.
4. To complete the wraparound skirt:

   (i) 4 – A = 2.5 cm [vertically upwards]

   (a) Join A – 0 in a smooth curve and increase the dart lengths upwards to meet the line A – 0.

   (b) Join A – 7 in a smooth curve and increase the dart length upwards to meet the line A – 7.

   (ii) 2 – B = 1.5 cm [vertically upwards]

   Join B – 7 in a smooth curve.
5. Wraparound skirt block is along the points:

   $0 - 1 - 4_1 - 7_1 - 3 - B - 7 - 9 - 8 - A - 6 - 5 - 0$.

   where:

   0 – 1 is on fold.

   B – 3 are free ends to wraparound or overlap on front.

Add seam allowance of 1.5 cm (or as required) and hem allowance of 3 cm (or as required) and mark corresponding balance points and grain line on each draft and pattern piece.

Belt:

1. A – B = round waist [horizontally] (0 – 2 after deduction of darts)

   = 95 cm
2. A – C = 4 cm (with intake) [vertically downwards]

   Complete the rectangle A – B – C – D.

   (Use interfacing equal to ½ of belt width to give firmness to the belt.)

Add seam allowance of 1.5 cm (or as required) and put up corresponding balance points and grain line on each draft and pattern piece.

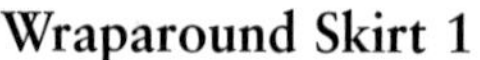

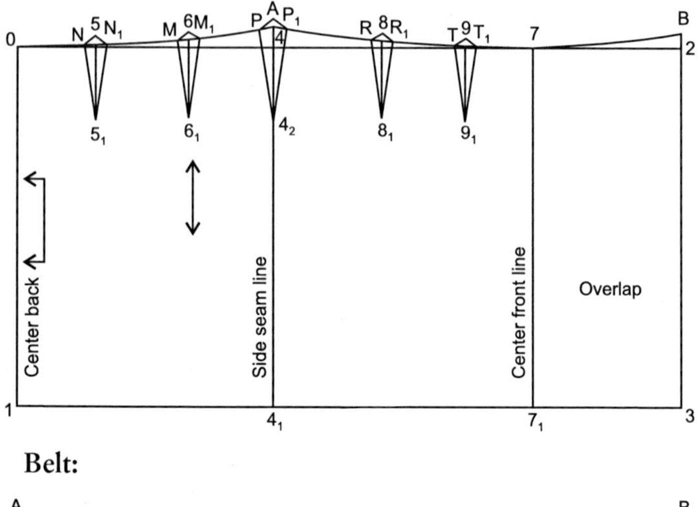

WRAPAROUND SKIRT 2

Flared Wraparound Skirt: A half circular seamless knee to ankle length lower garment that wraps or overlaps at front and is buttoned or tied into a knot by the extended waistline belt on one side of the waist. This skirt is fitting at waist and flared at hem. A bias cut skirt.

Suitable Fabric: Light weight to medium weight fabric.

Age Group: 13 yrs. and above

Size symbol – 10

Scale – cm

Drafting scale – 1/4th cm or 1/6th cm

Required fabric – 1.60 m × 80 cm (length × width)

Measurements:

Required length = 52 cm

Round waist = 68 cm

WRAPAROUND SKIRT & VARIATION

Wraparound skirt (full length)

Wraparound skirt (knee length) without belt

Round hips = 94 cm

Hip level = 21 cm

Belt width = 2 cm

Construction:

1. To wrap on front: Circumference = round waist + 1/4th round waist (for overlap) = 85 cm
2. For ½ circular skirt: Circumference = πr

   $85 \text{ cm} = r \times 22/7$

   $\therefore\ r = 85 \times 7/22$

   $= 27.04$ cm
3. 0 – 1 = radius + required length + 1 cm – belt width [vertically downwards]

   = 77.04 cm
4. 0 – 2 = 0 – 1 [horizontally]

   Complete the square 0 – 1 – 2 – 3.
5. 0 – 4 = radius [horizontally on line 0 – 2]

   = 27.04 cm
6. Taking 0 – 4 as radius draw an arc with point 0 as center to line 0 – 1 and mark as 5 for waistline.

   4 – 5 is waistline.
7. Taking 0 – 1 as radius draw an arc with point 0 as center to point 2 for hem line.
8. ½ circular wrap around skirt block is along the points: 4 – 2 – 1 – 5 – 4,

   where:

   5 – 1 is on fold.

   4 – 2 are free ends to wrap around front.
9. Finish the hem line with a facing or beading or as desired.

Add seam allowance of 1.5 cm (or as required) and hem allowance of 3 cm (or as required) and mark corresponding balance points and grain line on each draft and pattern piece.

Belt:

1. A – B = round waist [horizontally]
   = 85 cm
2. A – C = 4 cm (with intake) [vertically downwards]
   Complete the rectangle A – B – C – D.
   (Use interfacing equal to ½ of belt width to give firmness to the belt.)

Add seam allowance of 1.5 cm (or as required) and put up corresponding balance points and grain line on each draft and pattern piece.

Wraparound Skirt 2:

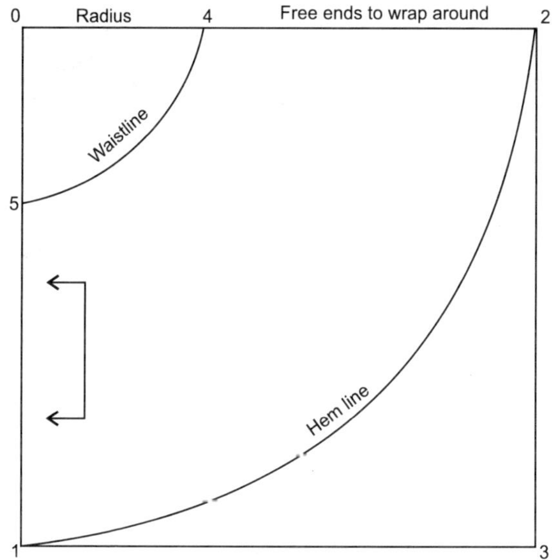

Belt:

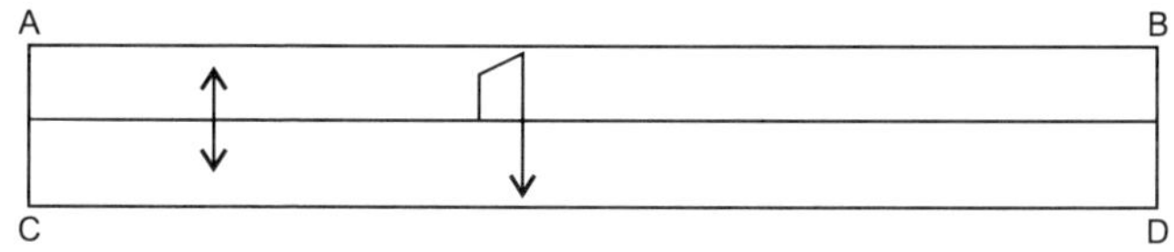

WRAPAROUND SKIRT & VARIATION (HALF CIRCULAR)

Wraparound skirt (full length)

Wraparound skirt (knee length) without belt

9 PANELED SKIRT

PANELED SKIRT/GYPSY SKIRT

Paneled Skirt: Also known as gypsy skirt is a knee to ankle length lower garment, generally worn by women, which has got horizontal panel and each panel is gathered to the hem of its upper panel. Has a great feminine look.

Suitable Fabric: Light weight fabric.

Age Group: Any

Size symbol – 10

Scale – cm

Drafting scale – 1/4th cm or 1/6th cm

Required fabric – 2 m × 90 cm (length × width)

Measurements:

Required length (waist to ankle) = 104 cm

Round waist = 68 cm

Round hips = 94 cm

Hip level = 21 cm

Belt width = 2 cm

Construction:

1. 0 – 1 = required length + 1 cm – belt width [vertically downwards]

   = 103 cm

First Panel:

2. 0 – 2 = hip level – belt width + 2.5 cm [vertically downwards on line 0 – 1]
   = 22.5 cm
3. 2 – 3 = 1/4th round hips + 10 cm [horizontally]
   = 33.5 cm
4. 0 – 4 = 1/4th round waist + 10 cm [horizontally]
   = 27 cm
5. 4 – 5 = 2.5 cm [vertically upwards]
   Join 5 – 0 in a straight line to shape the waistline.
6. Join 3 – 5 in a straight line for side seam of first panel.
7. First panel is along the points:
   0 – 2 – 3 – 5 – 0.
   Where:
   0 – 2 is on fold.
   5 – 3 is side seam.

Second Panel:

8. 2 – 6 = 1/3rd required length [vertically downwards]
   = 34.6 cm
9. 2 – 7 = 2 × 1/4th round hips + 5 cm (or as required for gathers) [horizontally]
   = 52 cm
   Extend from point 3 horizontally for point 7.
10. 6 – 8 = 2 – 7 [horizontally]
    Join 7 – 8 in a straight line for side seam.
11. Second panel is along the points:
    2 – 6 – 8 – 7 – 2.
    where:
    2 – 6 is on fold.
    7 – 8 is side seam.

Third Panel:

12. 6 – 9 = 3 × 1/4th round hips + 5 cm (or as required for gathers) [horizontally]
    = 75.5 cm

    Extend from point 8 horizontally for point 9.
13. 1 – 10 = 6 – 9 [horizontally]

    Join 9 – 10 in a straight line for side seam.
14. Third panel is along the points:

    6 – 1 – 10 – 9.

    where:

    6 – 1 is on fold.

    9 – 10 is side seam.

    1 – 10 is the hem line for paneled skirt.

First Panel:

1. Cut along 0 – 2 – 3 – 5 – 0 for first panel where 0 – 2 is on fold.
2. Finish 0 – 5 waistline with a facing and elastic approximately 2.5 cm wide and 55 cm in length or as required.

Second Panel:

1. Cut along 2 – 6 – 8 – 7 – 2 for second panel where 2 – 6 is on fold.
2. Gather 2 – 7 of second panel to 2 – 3 of first panel and finish with a lace or a tasseled lace or a linear embroidery or as desired.

Third Panel:

1. Cut along 6 – 1 – 10 – 9 – 6 for third panel where 6 – 1 is on fold.
2. Gather 6 – 9 of third panel to 6 – 8 of second panel and finish with a lace or a tasseled lace or a linear embroidery or as desired.
3. Finish 1 – 10, hem line with a linear lace or linear tasseled lace or linear embroidery or as desired.

Add seam allowance of 1.5 cm (or as required) and hem allowance of 3 cm (or as required) and mark corresponding balance points and grain line on each draft and pattern piece.

Paneled Skirt:

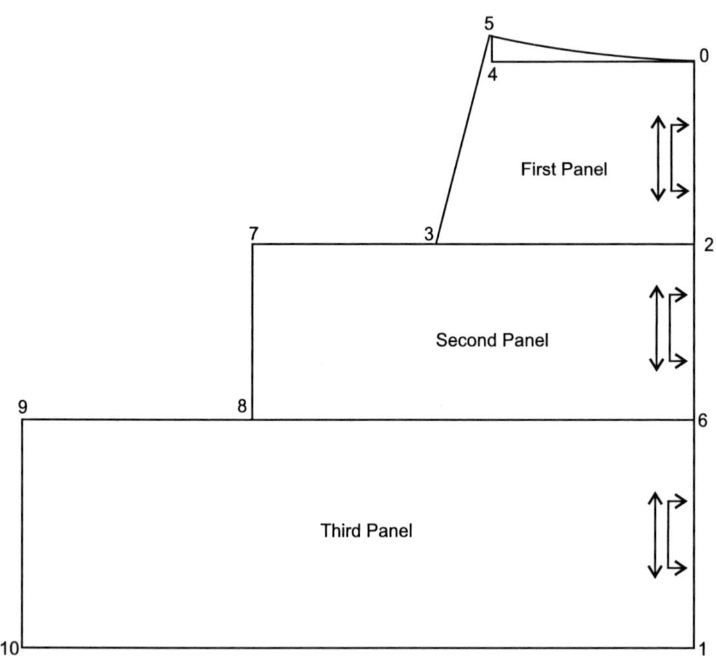

Pixie Skirt 1

Pixie Skirt: A seamless knee length to calf length lower garment worn, generally by women, teamed with a fitting top or as desired. A circular skirt without trimming the edges at hem is called a pixie skirt.

Suitable Fabric: Light weight fabric.

Age Group: Any

Size symbol – 10

Scale – cm

Drafting scale – 1/4th cm or 1/6th cm

Required fabric – 1.3m × 1.3 m (length × width)

PANELED SKIRT/GYPSY SKIRT

Paneled skirt

Paneled skirt without belt

Measurements:

Required length = 52 cm

Round waist = 68 cm

Belt width = 2 cm

Construction:

1. Circumference = round waist + 10 cm (for gathers)
   = 78 cm
2. Circumference = $2\pi r$ (r = radius)
   78 cm = $2 \times 22/7 \times r$
   $\therefore$ r = 12.4 cm
3. 0 – 1 = radius + required length + 1 cm – belt width [vertically downwards]
   = 63.4 cm
4. 0 – 2 = 0 – 1 [horizontally]
   = 63.4 cm

   Complete the square 0 – 1 – 2 – 3.
5. 0 – 4 = radius [horizontally on line 0 – 2]
   = 12.4 cm

   Draw an arc with 0 – 4 as radius from point 4 with 0 as center to line 0 – 1 and mark as 5.
6. Pixie skirt block is along the points:

   4 – 2 – 3 – 1 – 5 – 4.

   where:

   4 – 2 and 5 – 1 is on fold.

   4 – 5 is waistline.

   1 – 3 – 2 is hem line.
7. Give a small opening on one side of the skirt to slip in if the belt is not finished with a elastic.

Add seam allowance of 1.5 cm (or as required) and hem allowance of 3 cm (or as required) and mark corresponding balance points and grain line on each draft and pattern piece.

Belt:

1. A – C = 2 × required belt width (with intake) [vertically downwards]
   = 4 cm
2. A – B = round waist + 2 cm (overlap) [horizontally]
   = 72 cm

   Complete the rectangle A – B – C – D.

Add seam allowance of 1.5 cm (or as required) and mark corresponding balance points and grain line on each draft and pattern piece.

Pixie Skirt 1

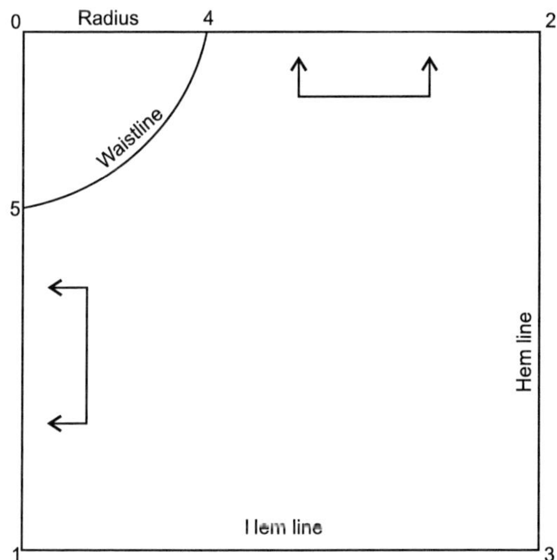

Belt:

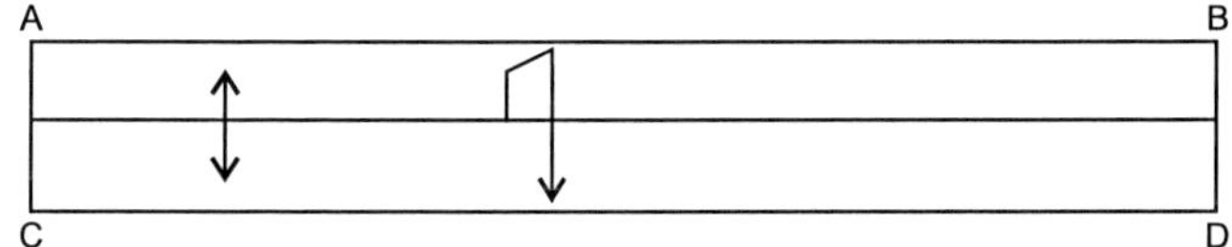

Pixie Skirt 2

Pixie Skirt: A knee length to calf length lower garment worn, generally by women, teamed with a fitting top. A circular skirt without trimming the edges at hem is stitched to a yoke at hip level to enhance the waist and hip curve.

Suitable Fabric: For yoke: Medium weight fabric.
For skirt: Light weight fabric.

Age Group: Any

Size symbol – 10

Scale – cm

Drafting scale – 1/4th cm or 1/6th cm

Required Fabric: Yoke = 20 cm × 1 m (length × width)

Skirt = 56 cm × 56 cm (length × width)

Measurements:

Required length = 52 cm

Round waist = 68 cm

Round hips = 94 cm

Hip level = 17 cm

Belt width = 2 cm

Construction:

Yoke:

1. 0 – 1 = hip level + 1 cm – belt width [vertically downwards]
   = 18 cm
2. 0 – 2 = 1/4th round waist + 3 cm (dart width) [horizontally]
   = 20 cm
3. 2 – 3 = 2.5 cm [vertically upwards]
   Join 3 – 0 in a smooth curve for waistline.
4. 1 – 4 = 1/4th round hips + 2 cm [horizontally]
   = 25.5 cm
   Join 3 – 4 in a smooth curve for side seams of the yoke.
5. 1 – 5 = 1 cm [vertically downwards]
   Join 4 – 5 in a smooth curve to shape the yoke.

6. For Dart:
   (i) Dart position: 0 – N = 1/12th round hips [on line 0 – 3]
   = 7.8 cm
   (ii) Dart length: $N - N_1$ = 1/10th round hips [vertically downwards]
   = 9.4 cm
   (iii) Dart width: $N - S = N - S_1$ = 1.5 cm (on either side of point N) [on line 0 – 3]
   Join $S - N_1$ and $S_1 - N_1$ in straight lines for the required dart.
7. For yoke block cut along the points:
   0 – 5 – 4 – 3 – N – 0.
   where:
   0 – 5 is on fold.
   3 – 4 is side seams.
   4 – 5 is the hem line of yoke.
   Cut two pieces of the above block, one piece for front and one piece for back to complete the required yoke.
8. Give a small opening to slip into the skirt which should be finished with a fly (zip), skirt hooks or as required.

Skirt:

9. Circumference = 4 × {hem line of yoke + 8 cm (gathers)}
   = 4 × {25.5 cm + 8 cm}
   = 134 cm
10. Circumference = $2\pi r$ (where r = radius)
   134 cm = $2\pi r$
   ∴ r = 21.3 cm
11. 6 – 7 = radius + required length + 1 cm – (yoke + belt width) [vertically downwards]
   = 53.3 cm

12. 6 – 8 = 6 – 7 [horizontally on line 6 – 8]
    = 53.3 cm

    Complete the square 6 – 7 – 8 – 9.

13. 6 – 10 = radius [horizontally on line 6 – 8]
    = 21.3 cm

    Draw an arc with 6 – 10 as radius from point 10 with 6 as the center to line 6 – 7 and mark as 11.

14. For skirt block cut along the points:

    10 – 8 – 9 – 7 – 11 – 10,

    where:

    10 – 8 and 11 – 7 is on fold.

    10 – 11 is the required hip line to be stitched to yoke to complete pixie skirt.

    7 – 9 – 8 is the hem line.

15. 10 – 11 of skirt block should be stitched to 5 – 4 of yoke.

Add seam allowance of 1.5 cm (or as required) and hem allowance of 3 cm (or as required) and mark corresponding balance points and grain line on each draft and pattern piece.

Belt:

1. A – C = belt width [vertically downwards]
   = 4 cm (with intake)

2. A – B = round waist [horizontally]
   = 68 cm

   Complete the rectangle A – B – C – D.

Add seam allowance of 1.5 cm (or as required) and mark corresponding balance points and grain line on each pattern piece.

Pixie Skirt 2

Yoke:

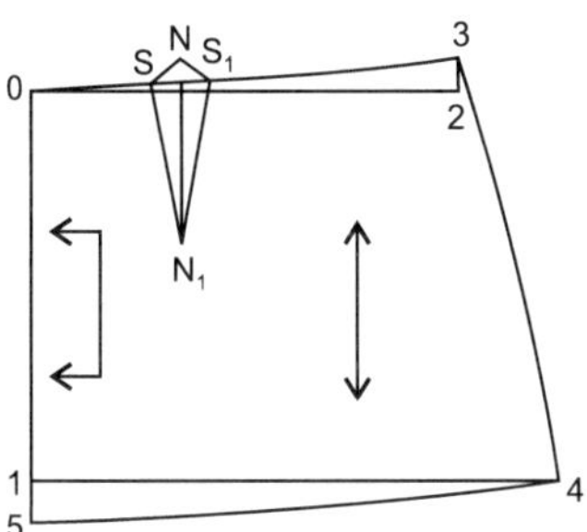

Skirt:

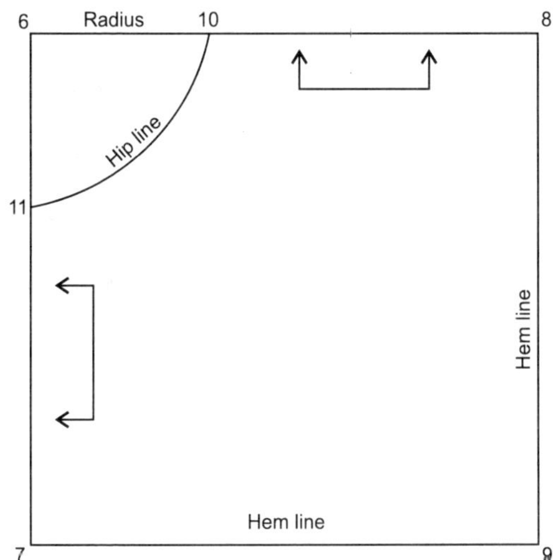

Belt:

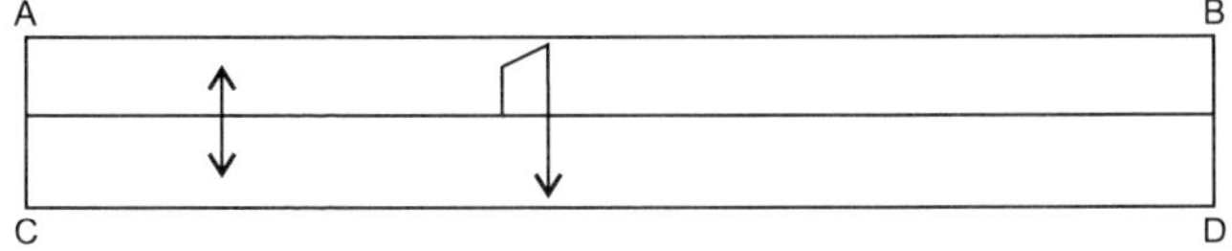

PIXIE SKIRT & PIXIE SKIRT WITH YOKE

Pixie skirt

Pixie skirt with yoke

10 WOMEN'S VEST

VEST

A sleeveless jacket or waistcoat worn as a second garment on shirt or blouse for some purpose or as a uniform.

Suitable Fabric: Medium to heavy weight fabric. Interlining of light weight smooth fabric like satin should be used to give body to the vest.

Age Group: Any

Size symbol – 10

Scale – cm

Drafting scale – 1/4th cm

Fabric required – 90 cm × 60 cm (length × width)

Measurements:

Required length = 42 cm

Round bust = 88 cm

Round waist = 68 cm

Across shoulder = 35 cm

Highest bust level = 25 cm

Across back = 35 cm

Across front = 28 cm

Construction:

Back:

1. 0 – 1 = required length + 1 cm [vertically downwards]
   = 43 cm

2. Armhole Depth:

   0 – 2 = 1/4th round bust – 3 cm [vertically downwards on line 0 – 1]

   = 19 cm

3. Bust Line:

   2 – 3 = 1/4th round bust + 3 cm (ease for 2nd garment or as required) [horizontally]

   = 25 cm

4. Waistline:

   1 – 4 = 1/4th round waist + 3 cm (dart width) + 1 cm [horizontally]

   = 21 cm

   Join 3 – 4 in a straight line for side seams.

5. Shoulder:

   0 – 5 = ½ across shoulder [horizontally]

   = 17.5 cm

6. Neckline:

   0 – 6 = 1/12th round bust + 1 cm [horizontally on line 0 – 5]

   = 8.3 cm

   6 – 7 = 1.5 cm [vertically upwards]

   Join 7 – 0 in a smooth curve for neckline.

7. Shoulder Line:

   5 – 8 = 0.5 cm [vertically downwards]

   Join 7 – 8 in a straight line for shoulder line.

8. Armhole:

   0 – 9 = ½ armhole depth [vertically downwards on line 0 – 1]

   = 8.5 cm

   9 – 10 = ½ across back [horizontally/perpendicular to center back]

   = 17.5 cm

   Join 8 – 10 – 3 in a smooth curve for armhole.

9. Dart:

   (i) Dart position: 1 – N = 1/12th round bust + 0.5 cm [horizontally on line 1 – 4]

   = 7.8 cm

   (ii) Dart length: N – N_1 = 1/8th round bust [vertically upwards]

   = 11 cm

   (iii) Dart width: N – S = N – S_1 = 1.5 cm (on either side of point N) [on line 1 – 4]

   Join S – N_1 and S_1 – N_1 in straight lines for the required dart.

10. For back vest block cut along the points:

    0 – 1 – N – 4 – 3 – 10 – 8 – 7 – 0.

    where:

    0 – 1 is on fold.

    7 – 0 is neckline.

    7 – 8 is shoulder line.

    8 – 10 – 3 is armhole.

    3 – 4 is side seams.

Front:

1. $0_f - 1_f$ = required length + 2.5 cm [vertically downwards]

   = 44.5 cm

2. Armhole Depth:

   $0_f - 2_f$ = 1/4th round bust – 2 cm [vertically downwards on line $0_f - 1_f$]

   = 20 cm

3. Bust Line:

   $2_f - 3_f$ = 1/4th round bust + 3 cm (ease) + 0.5 cm (dart width) [horizontally]

   = 25.5 cm

4. Waistline:

   $1_f - 4_f$ = 1/4th round waist + 4 cm (dart width) + 1 cm [horizontally]

   = 22 cm

   Join $3_f - 4_f$ in a straight lines for side seams.

5. Shoulder:

   $0_f - 5_f$ = ½ across shoulder [horizontally]

   = 17.5 cm

6. Neckline:

   $0_f - 6_f$ = 1/12th round bust + 1 cm [horizontally on line $0_f - 5_f$]

   = 8.3 cm

   $0_f - 7_f$ = 1/12th round bust + 3 cm [vertically downwards on line $0_f - 1_f$]

   Join $6_f - 7_f$ in a smooth curve for neckline.

7. Shoulder Line:

   $5_f - 8_f$ = 2 cm [vertically downwards]

   Join $7_f - 8_f$ in a straight line for shoulder line.

8. Armhole:

   $2_f - 9_f$ = 1/4th armhole depth [vertically upwards on line $9_f - 0_f$]

   = 4.25 cm

   $9_f - 10_f$ = ½ across front + 0.5 cm (dart width) [horizontally/perpendicular to center front]

   = 14.5 cm

   Join $8_f - 10_f - 3_f$ in a smooth curve for armhole.

9. Dart:

   0_f – A = highest bust level [vertically downwards on line $0_f - 1_f$]

   = 25 cm

   Draw a horizontal line from point A to line $3_f - 4_f$ and mark as B.

A – C = 1/12th round bust [horizontally on line A – B]
= 7.3 cm

(a) Waistline Dart: Double Darts

I. First Dart:

(i) Dart position: 1_f – M = 1/12th round bust – 2 cm [horizontally on line 1_f – 4_f]
= 5.3 cm

(ii) Dart length: M – M_1 = 15 cm (2 cm below line A – B) [vertically upwards]

(iii) Dart width: M – P = M – P_1 = 1 cm (on either side of point M) [on line 1_f – 4_f]

Join P – M_1 and P_1 – M_1 in straight lines for the first dart.

II. Second Dart:

(i) Dart position: M – L = 4 cm [horizontally on line 1_f – 4_f]

(ii) Dart length: L – L_1 = 15 cm (2 cm below line A – B) [vertically upwards]

(iii) Dart width: L – K = L – K_1 = 1 cm (on either side of point L) [on line 1_f – 4_f]

Join K – L_1 and K_1 – L_1 in straight lines for the second dart.

(b) Armhole Dart:

(i) Dart position: Point 10_f is the position for armhole dart.

(ii) Dart length: C – J = 3 cm [upwards on line C – 10_f]

10_f – J is the required dart length for armhole dart.

(iii) Dart width: 10_f – R = 10_f – R_1 = 0.75 cm (¾ cm) (on either side of point 10_f) [on line 8_f – 10_f – 3_f]

Join R – J and R_1 – J in straight lines for the required armhole dart.

10. For front vest block cut along the points:

    $7_f - 1_f - M - L - 4_f - 3_f - 10_f - 8_f - 6_f - 7_f$.

    where:

    $7_f - 1_f$ is front open.

    $6_f - 7_f$ is neckline.

    $6_f - 8_f$ is shoulder line.

    $8_f - 10_f - 3_f$ is armhole.

    $3_f - 4_f$ is side seams.

Add seam allowance of 1.5 cm (or as required) and hem allowance of 3 cm (or as required) and mark corresponding balance points and grain line on each draft and pattern piece.

Vest:

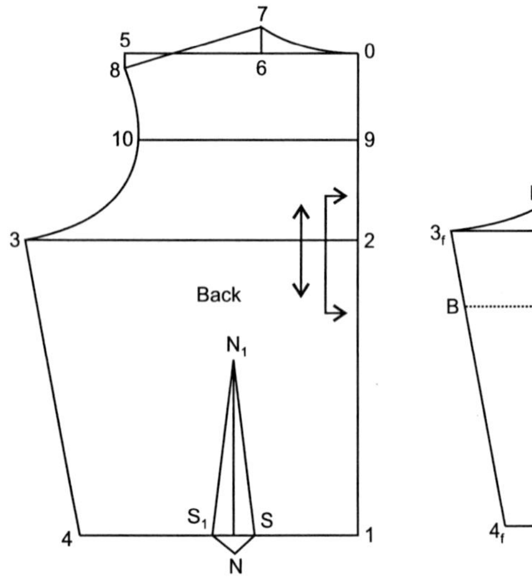

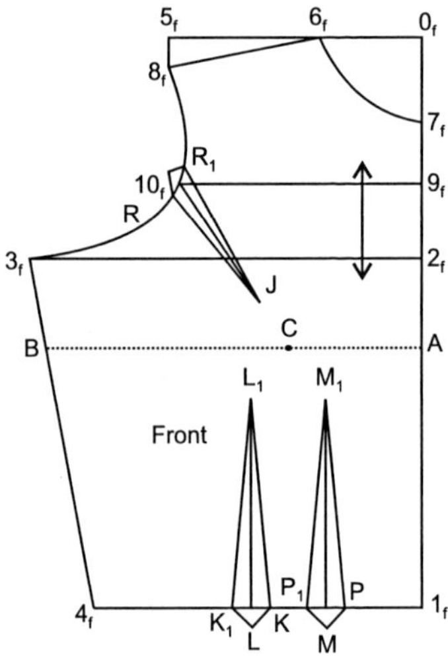

VEST & VARIATION

Vest

Double breasted vest

11 SHIRTS: PLAIN SHIRT WITH FULL SLEEVES

SHIRT

A loose or slightly fitting upper garment with collar and sleeves and is buttoned down in front. Can be teamed with a trousers, skirt etc.

Suitable Fabric: Light or medium weight fabric.

Age Group: Any

Size symbol – 10

Scale – cm

Drafting scale – 1/4th cm

Fabric required – 1.5 m × 90 cm (length × width)

Measurements:

Required length = 59 cm

Round bust = 88 cm

Round waist = 68 cm

Waist length = 40 cm

Round hem = 90 cm (12 cm above hips)

Round hips = 94 cm

Across shoulder = 35 cm

Highest bust level = 25 cm

Construction:

Back:

1. 0 – 1 = required length + 1 cm [vertically downwards]
   = 60 cm

2. Armhole Depth:

   0 – 2 = 1/4th round bust – 3 cm [vertically downwards on line 0 – 1]

   = 19 cm

3. Bust Line:

   2 – 3 = 1/4th round bust + 2 cm (ease) [horizontally]

   = 24 cm

4. Waist Length:

   0 – 4 = waist length [vertically downwards on line 0 – 1]

   = 40 cm

5. Waistline:

   4 – 5 = 1/4th round waist + 3 cm (dart width) + 1 cm (ease) [horizontally]

   = 21 cm

   Join 5 – 3 in a straight line.

6. Hip Line:

   1 – 6 = 1/4th round hem + 2 cm [horizontally]

   = 24.5 cm

   Join 6 – 5 in a straight line.

7. Shoulder:

   0 – 7 = ½ across shoulder + 1 cm [horizontally]

   = 18.5 cm

   Draw a vertical line downwards from point 7 to line 2 – 3 and mark as 8.

8. Neckline:

   0 – 9 = 1/12th round bust [horizontally on line 0 – 7]

   = 7.3 cm

   9 – 10 = 1.5 cm [vertically upwards]

   Join 10 – 0 in a smooth curve for neckline.

9. Shoulder Line:

   7 – 11 = 0.5 cm [vertically downwards on line 7 – 8]

   Join 11 – 10 in a straight line for shoulder line.

10. Armhole:

    11 – 12 = 12 – 8 [vertically on line 11 – 8]

    = 9.25 cm

    Join 11 – 12 – 3 in a smooth curve for armhole.

11. Dart: Waistline dart (double headed dart)

    (i) Dart position: 4 – N = 1/12th round bust [horizontally]

    = 7.3 cm

    (ii) Dart length: Upward dart length:

    $N - N_1$ = 1/10th round bust [vertically upwards]

    = 8.8 cm

    Downward dart length:

    $N - N_2$ = 1/10th round hips [vertically downwards]

    = 9.4 cm

    $N_1 - N_2$ is the required dart length for double-headed dart.

    (iii) Dart width: $N - S = N - S_1$ = 1.5 cm (on either side of point N) [on line 4 – 5]

    Join $S - N_1$ and $S - N_2$ in straight lines and join $S_1 - N_1$ and $S_1 - N_2$ in straight lines for the required double-headed dart.

12. Yoke Section:

    0 – K = 1/12th round bust – 1 cm (or as required) [vertically downwards]

    = 6.3 cm

    Draw a horizontal line from point K to armhole line 11 – 12 – 3 and mark as K_1.

13. For back shirt block cut along the points:

    $K - 1 - 6 - 5 - 3 - 12 - K_1 - K$,

    where:

    K – 1 is on fold.

$K_1 - 12 - 3$ is armhole.

$3 - 5 - 6$ is side seams.

14. For yoke cut along the points:

    $0 - K - K_1 - 11 - 10 - 0$,

    where:

    $0 - K$ is on fold.

    $10 - 0$ is neckline.

    $10 - 11$ is shoulder line.

    $11 - K_1$ is armhole section.

Front:

1. $0_f - 1_f$ = required length + 2 cm [vertically downwards]

   = 61 cm

2. Armhole Depth:

   $0_f - 2_f$ = 1/4th round bust – 3 cm [vertically downwards on line $0_f - 1_f$]

   = 19 cm

3. Bust Line:

   $2_f - 3_f$ = 1/4th round bust + 2 cm (ease) [horizontally]

   = 24 cm

4. Waist Length:

   $0_f - 4_f$ = waist length + 1 cm [vertically downwards on line $0_f - 1_f$]

   = 41 cm

5. Waistline:

   $4_f - 5_f$ = 1/4th round waist + 3 cm (dart width) + 1 cm (ease) [horizontally]

   = 21 cm

   Join $5_f - 3_f$ in a straight line.

6. Hip Line:

   $1_f - 6_f$ = 1/4th round hem + 2 cm [horizontally]

   = 24.5 cm

   Join $6_f - 5_f$ in a straight line.

7. Shoulder:

   $0_f - 7_f$ = ½ across shoulder + 1 cm [horizontally]
   = 18.5 cm

   Draw a vertical line downwards from point 7_f to line $2_f - 3_f$ and mark as 8_f.

8. Neckline:

   $0_f - 9_f$ = 1/12th round bust [horizontally on line $0_f - 7_f$]
   = 7.3 cm

   $0_f - 10_f$ = 1/8th round bust [vertically downwards]
   = 11 cm

   Join $9_f - 10_f$ in a straight line for neckline.

9. Shoulder Line:

   $7_f - 11_f$ = 2 cm [vertically downwards on line $7_f - 8_f$]

   Join $11_f - 9_f$ in a straight line for shoulder line.

10. Armhole:

    $8_f - 12_f$ = 3 cm [vertically upwards on line $8_f - 11_f$]

    Join $11_f - 12_f - 3_f$ in a smooth curve for armhole.

11. Dart:

    0_f – A = highest bust level [vertically downwards on line $0_f - 1_f$]
    = 25 cm

    A – B = 1/12th round bust [horizontally]
    = 7.3 cm

    (a) Waistline dart: double-headed dart

    (i) Dart position: 4_f – M = 1/12th round bust [horizontally on line $4_f - 5_f$]
    = 7.3 cm

    (ii) Dart length: upward dart length: B – M_1 = 1.5 cm [vertically downwards on line B – M]

    M – M_1 is the upward dart length.

Downward dart length:

$M - M_2$ = 1/10th round hips [vertically downwards]

= 9.4 cm

$M_1 - M_2$ is the required dart length for double-headed dart.

(iii) Dart width: $M - P = M - P_1$ = 1.5 cm (on either side of point M) [on line $4_f - 5_f$]

Join $P - M_1$ and $P - M_2$ in straight lines and join $P_1 - M_1$ and $P_1 - M_2$ in straight lines for the required double-headed dart.

(b) Side seam dart:

(i) Dart position: $3_f - T$ = 1/10th round bust [downwards on line $3_f - 5_f$]

= 8.8 cm

(ii) Dart length: $B - T_1$ = 5 cm [on line B – T]

$T - T_1$ is the required dart length.

(iii) Dart width: $T - R = T - R_1$ = 0.6 cm (on either side of point T) [on line $3_f - 5_f$]

Join $R - T_1$ and $R_1 - T_1$ in straight lines for the required side seam dart.

12. Yoke Section:

$11_f - L$ = 3 cm (or as required) [downwards on line $11_f - 12_f - 3_f$]

Draw a line from point L parallel to shoulder line ($11_f - 9_f$) to meet neckline ($9_f - 10_f$) and mark as L_1.

13. For front shirt block cut along the points:

$10_f - 1_f - 6_f - 5_f - T_1 - 3_f - 12_f - L - L_1 - 10_f$,

where:

$10_f - 1_f$ is front open that should be finished with shirt placket.

$L_1 - 10_f$ is neckline.

$L - 12_f - 3_f$ is armhole.

$3_f - T - 5_f - 6_f$ is side seams.

14. For front yoke section cut along the points:

 $9_f - L_1 - L - 11_f - 9_f$,

 where:

 $9_f - L_1$ is neckline section.

 $11_f - L$ is armhole section.

Add seam allowance of 1.5 cm (or as required) and hem allowance of 3 cm (or as required) and mark corresponding balance points and grain line on each draft and pattern piece.

Yoke:

1. Place front and back yoke sections together at shoulder line, i.e. line 10 – 11 of back to $10_f - 11_f$ of front (as shown in the diagram) and mark as Q on neckline and Q_1 on armhole.
2. Trace out the obtained block for yoke and mark front and back sections.
3. For yoke block cut along the points:

 $L_1 - Q - 0 - K - K_1 - Q_1 - L - L_1$,

 where:

 0 – K is on fold.

 $L - Q_1 - K_1$ is armhole section.

 $L_1 - Q - 0$ is neckline section.

Add seam allowance of 1.5 cm (or as required) and mark corresponding balance points and grain line on each draft and pattern piece.

Blouse Collar: Half roll collar.

1. Trace out the neckline $9_f - 10_f$ of front shirt block.
2. Extend line $10_f - 9_f$ upwards and mark as E, where:

 $9_f - E$ = ½ back neckline

 = 7.6 cm
3. Pivot line $E - 9_f$ at point 9_f by 2 cm downwards and mark as E_1.

4. $E_1 - E_2$ = 3 cm (or as required) {not to exceed 4 cm} [perpendicular to line $9_f - E$]
5. $10_f - F$ = 3 cm (or as required) [perpendicular to line $10_f - 9_f$]
6. $10_f - G$ = 4 cm [upwards on line $10_f - 9_f$]

   $G - G_1$ = 6 cm (or as required) [perpendicular upwards to line $10_f - 9_f$]

   Join $G_1 - E_2$ in a smooth curve as shown in the diagram.
7. $G - F_1$ = 3 cm (or as required) [upwards on line $G - G_1$]

   Join $F_1 - F$ in a straight line.
8. For blouse collar cut along the points:

   $10_f - G - 9_f - E_1 - E_2 - G_1 - F_1 - F - 10_f$.

   where:

   $E_1 - E_2$ is on fold.

   $E_1 - 9_f - G - 10_f$ should be stitched to neckline of shirt.

Add seam allowance of 1.5 cm (or as required) and mark corresponding balance points and grain line on each draft and pattern piece.

Shirt Sleeve

Measurements:

Sleeve length = 58.6 cm

Round wrist = 16 cm

Cuff width = 4 cm

Construction:

1. 0 – 1 = sleeve length + 1 cm – cuff width [vertically downwards]

   = 55.6 cm
2. Sleeve Crown:

   0 – 2 = 1/4th round bust – 4 cm [vertically downwards on line 0 – 1]

   = 18 cm

3. Crown Width:

   2 – 3 = 1/4th round bust – 4 cm [horizontally]

   = 18 cm

   Join 3 – 0 in a straight line.

4. Round Wrist:

   1 – 4 = ½ round wrist + 2 cm (ease) [horizontally]

   = 10 cm

   Join 4 – 3 in a straight line for side seams.

5. To Shape Sleeve Crown:

   (i) Divide line 3 – 0 into four equal parts and mark as R, S and T, respectively.

   (ii) R – R_1 = 1.25 cm [perpendicular downwards to line 3 – 0]

   (iii) S – S_1 = 2.5 cm [perpendicular upwards to line 3 – 0]

   (iv) T – T_1 = 1.25 cm [perpendicular upwards to line 3 – 0]

6. For front sleeve crown join 0 – T_1 – S – R_1 – 3 in a smooth 'S' shape.

7. For back sleeve crown join 0 – S_1 – R – 3 in a smooth 'S' shape.

8. For shirt sleeve block cut along the points:

   0 – 1 – 4 – 3 – R – S_1 – 0,

   where:

   0 – 1 is on fold.

   Open the sleeve block and shape front sleeve crown.

   Front sleeve is along the points: 0 – 1 – 4 – 3 – R_1 – S – T_1 – 0.

   Back sleeve is along the points: 0 – 1 – 4 – 3 – R – S_1 – 0.

Open Cuff:

1. 0_c – 1_c = 4 cm [vertically downwards]

2. 0_c – 2_c = round wrist + 4 cm [horizontally]

   = 20 cm

   Complete the rectangle 0_c – 1_c – 2_c – 3_c.

3. Shape at points 1_c and 3_c in a smooth curve (or as required) for open cuffs.
4. For cuff block cut along the points:

   $0_c - 1_c - 3_c - 2_c - 0_c$,

   where:

   $3_c - 1_c$ is on fold.

   $0_c - 2_c$ of cuff block should be stitched to 1 – 4 of sleeve block with a 1 cm pleat on 1 – 4 of sleeve block.

   (Inter facing should be used to provide firmness to cuffs.)

Add seam allowance of 1.5 cm (or as required) and mark corresponding balance points and grain line on each draft and pattern piece.

Back Shirt Block: Back Shirt Block (Yoke Cut and Separated)

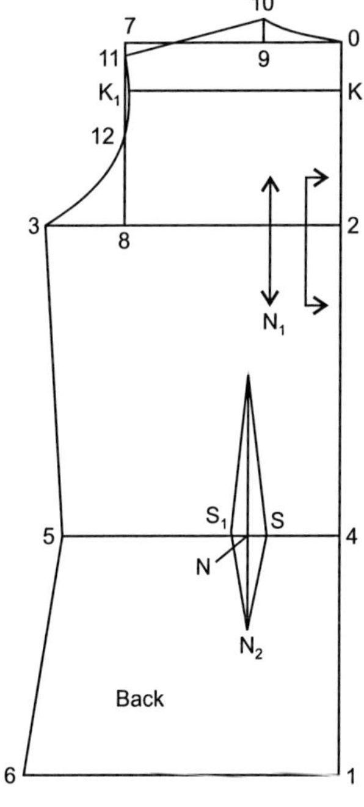

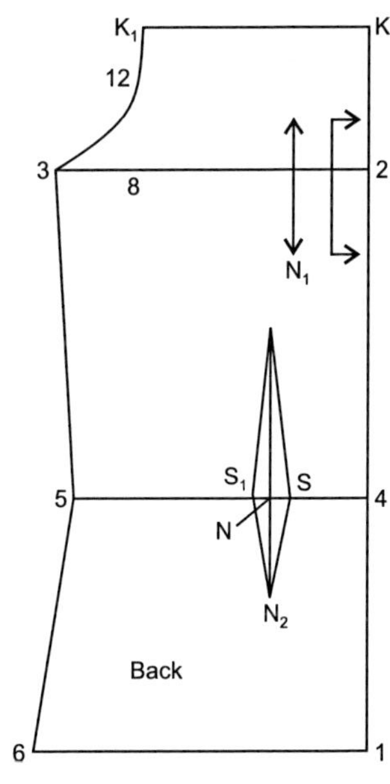

Front Shirt Block: Front Shirt Block (Yoke Cut and Separated)

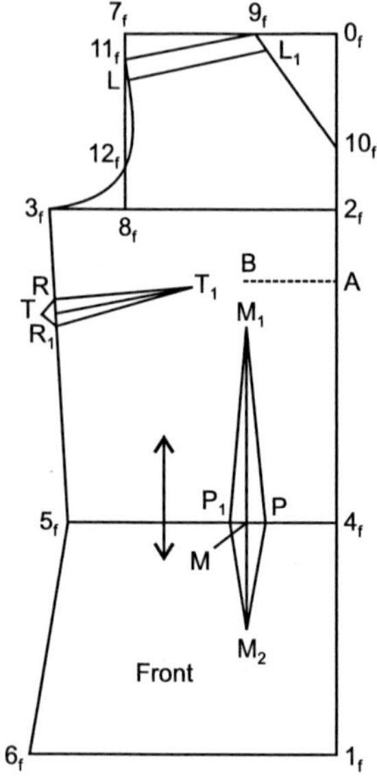

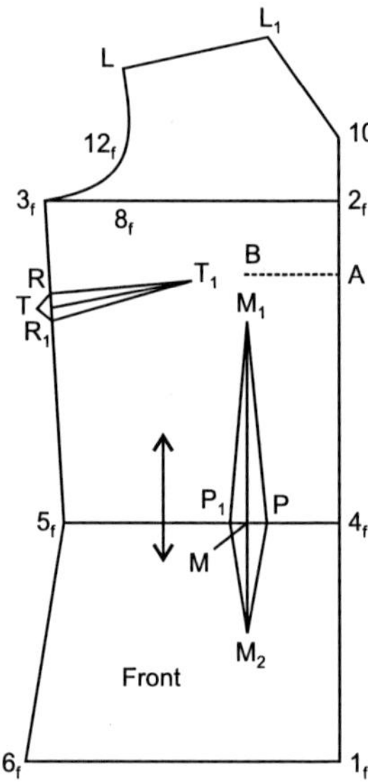

Blouse Collar:

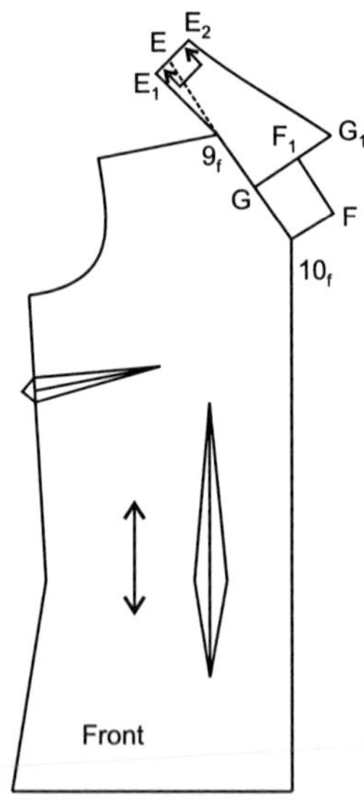

Blouse Collar:

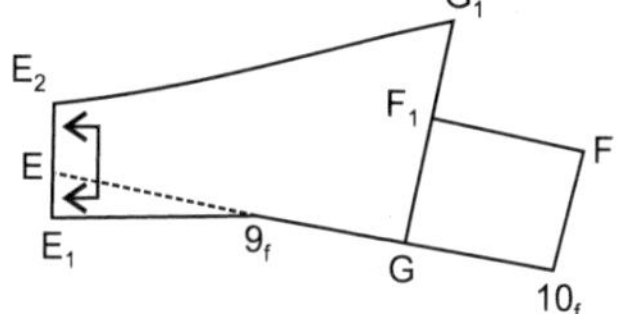

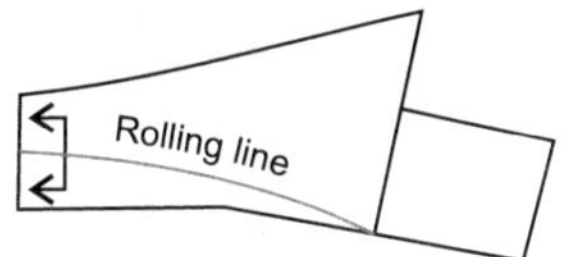

Yoke:

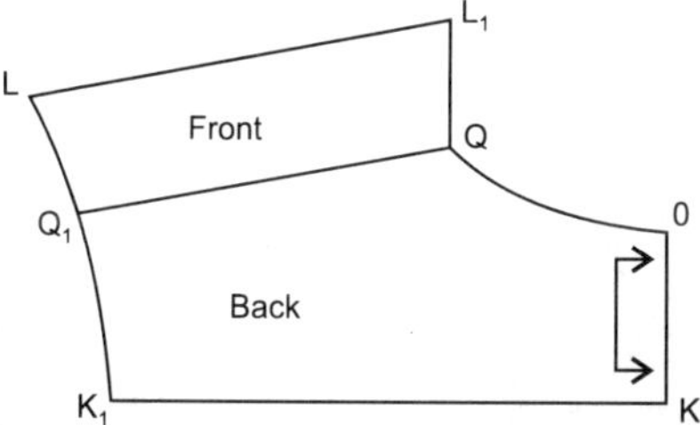

Shirt Sleeve:

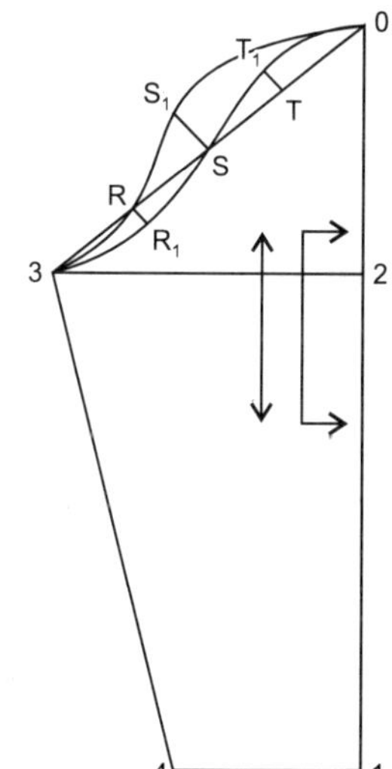

Cuffs:

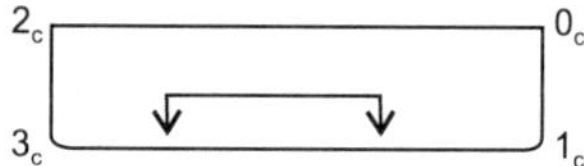

SHIRT & VARIATION

Plain shirt

Plain shirt with open cuffs & Pleated front

12 CORSET

EDWARDIAN CORSET

Edwardian Corset: A tight fitting women's garment worn during Edwardian era, extends from bust line to lower waist. Generally worn to conceal waistline and accentuate bust line. Corsets have to be finished with continuous longitudinal ribs or canvas.

Suitable Fabric: Medium weight fabric as inner lining and outer fabric as desired.

Age Group: 13 years and above.

Size symbol – 10

Scale – cm

Drafting scale – 1/4th cm

Required fabric – 33 cm × 88 cm (length × width)

Measurements:

Waist length = 42 cm

Round bust = 88 cm

Round waist = 68 cm

Across front = 28 cm

Construction:

1. 0 – 1 = waist length + 1 cm [vertically downwards]
   = 43 cm
2. 0 – 2 = ½ round bust – 4 cm [horizontally]
   = 40 cm

   Complete the rectangle 0 – 1 – 2 – 3.

3. Armhole Depth:

   0 – 4 = 1/4th round bust – 4 cm [vertically downwards on line 0 – 1]

   = 18 cm

4. Bust Line:

   Draw a horizontal line from point 4 to line 2 – 3 and mark as 4_1.

5. $4 - 4_2$ = 1/4th round bust [horizontally on line $4 - 4_1$]

   = 22 cm

   Draw a vertical line downwards from point 4_2 to line 1 – 3 and mark as 5.

   [4_2 – 5 is the dividing line of front and back corset block]

6. 4 – 6 = 2.5 cm [vertically upwards on line 4 – 0]

7. $6 - 6_1$ = ½ across front [horizontally]

   = 16 cm

8. Armhole:

   Join $6_1 - 4_2$ in a smooth curve for armhole.

9. Waistline:

   1 – 7 = 1/4th round waist [horizontally on line 1 – 3]

   = 17 cm

10. Side Seam (front):

    Join $7 - 4_2$ in a straight line for side seam (front).

11. $5 - 7_1$ = 5 – 7 (on other side of point 5) [horizontally on line 1 – 3]

    = 5 cm

12. Side Seam (back):

    Join $7_1 - 4_2$ in a straight line for side seam (back).

13. Front Shape:

    1 – 8 = 5 cm (or as required) [vertically downwards]

    Join 8 – 7 in a smooth inward curve or as required for shape.

For one piece corset block:

(i) Cut through the points:

$6 - 8 - 7 - 7_1 - 3 - 4_1 - 4_2 - 6_1 - 6$.

Cut out through the points: $7 - 4_2 - 7_1 - 7$.

(ii) Bring together points $7 - 7_1$ and mark as P.

(iii) Trace out the obtained block for one piece corset block.

For 3-paneled corset block:

(a) Central Panel:

(i) 1 – M = 1/12th round bust [on line 1 – 3]

= 7.3 cm

Join 6_1 – M in a smooth curve and extend downwards to meet the line 8 – 7 and mark as M_1.

(ii) Central corset panel is along the points:

$6 - 8 - M_1 - M - 6_1 - 6$.

where:

6 – 8 is on fold.

$6_1 - M - M_1$ is central side seam.

(b) Back Panel:

(i) 3 – N = 1/12th round bust [horizontally on line 3 – 1]

= 7.3 cm

(ii) $4_2 - N_1$ = 1/12th round bust [horizontally on line $4_2 - 4_1$]

= 7.3 cm

Join N_1 – N in a smooth curve.

(iii) Back corset panel is along the points:

$N_1 - N - 3 - 4_1 - N_1$.

where:

4_1 – 3 is back opening, which should be finished with a draw string passed through eyelets made on line 4_1 – 3 for a traditional corset.

$N_1 - N$ is the back side seam.

Cut two pieces of the above block.

(c) Side Corset Panel:

(i) Cut out section $7 - 4_2 - 7_1 - 7$.

(ii) Bring together points $7 - 7_1$ and mark as P and trace out the obtained block.

(iii) Side corset panel is along the points:

$6_1 - M - M_1 - P - N - N_1 - 4_2 - 6_1$.

where:

$6_1 - M - M_1$ is side central seam.

$N_1 - N$ is side back seam.

Add seam allowance of 1.5 cm (or as required) and hem allowance of 3 cm (or as required) and mark corresponding balance points and grain line on each draft and pattern piece.

Edwardian Corset:

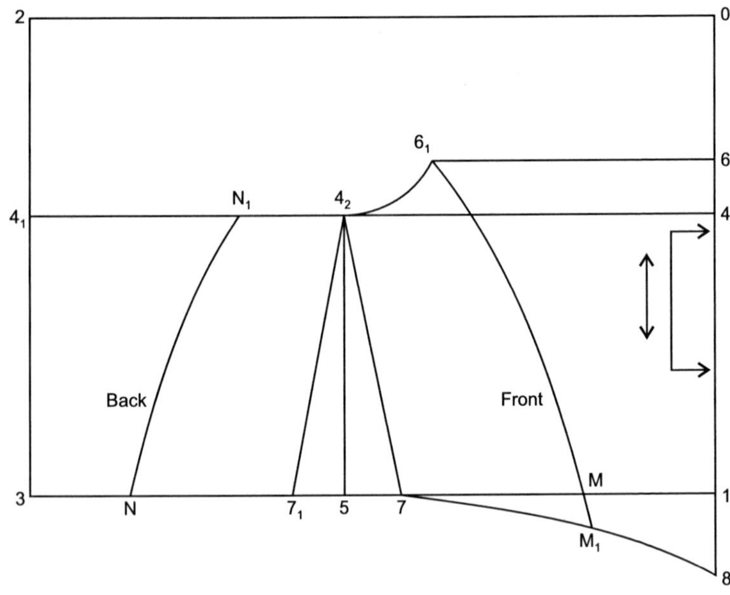

One Piece Corset Block:

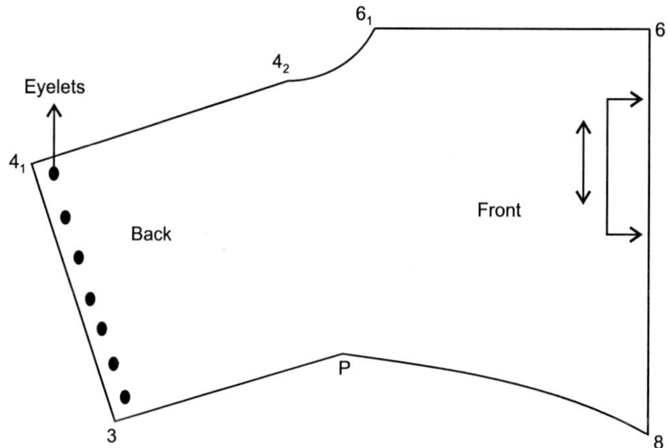

Front, Side and Back Corset Panels (separated):

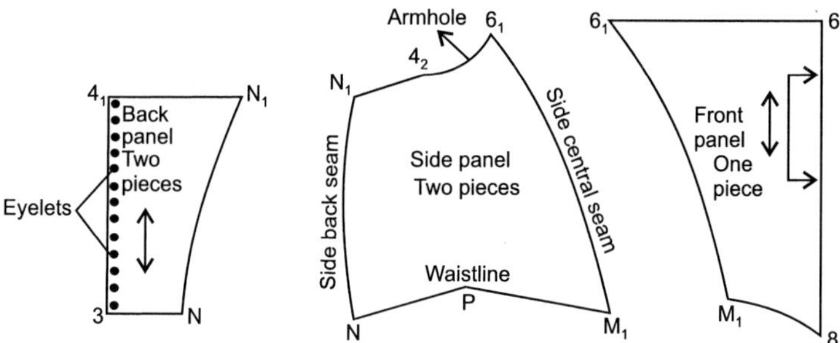

Front, Side and Back Corset Panels (stitched):

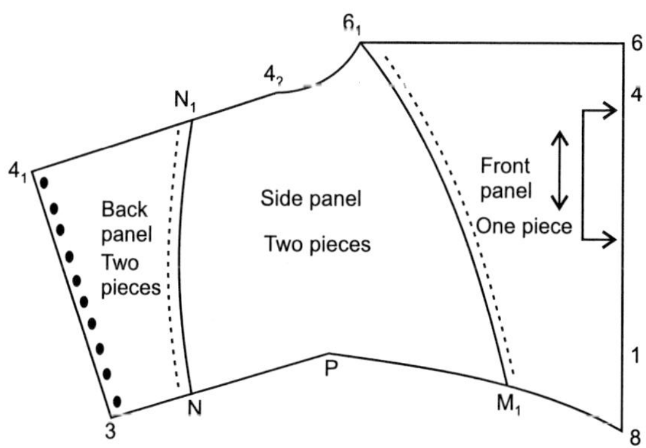

CORSET

A tight fitting women's upper garment that extends from bust line to lower waist. Generally worn to conceal waistline and accentuate bust line. Corsets have to be finished with continuous longitudinal ribs or canvas.

Suitable Fabric: Medium weight fabric.

Age Group: 13 years and above.

Size symbol – 10

Scale – cm

Drafting scale – 1/4th cm

Required fabric – 46 cm × 90 cm (length × width)

Measurements:

Required length = 42 cm

Round bust = 88 cm

Round waist = 68 cm

Across front = 28 cm

Across shoulder = 35 cm

Construction:

Back:

1. 0 – 1 = required length + 1 cm [vertically downwards]
   = 43 cm
2. Armhole Depth:
   0 – 2 = 1/4th round bust – 4 cm [vertically downwards on line 0 – 1]
   = 18 cm
3. Bust Line:
   2 – 3 = 1/4th round bust [horizontally]
   = 22 cm
4. Waistline:
   1 – 4 = 1/4th round waist + 3 cm (dart width) [horizontally]
   = 20 cm

5. Side Seam:

   Join 4 – 3 in a straight line for side seams.

6. Shoulder:

   0 – 5 = ½ across shoulder – 1 cm [horizontally]

   = 16.5 cm

   Draw a vertical line downwards from point 5 to line 2 – 3 and mark as 6.

7. Neckline:

   5 – 7 = 2.5 cm (or as required for shoulder width) [horizontally on line 5 – 0]

   Join 7 – 2 in a deep curve for neckline.

8. Shoulder Line:

   5 – 8 = 1 cm (shoulder drop) [vertically downwards on line 5 – 6]

   Join 8 – 7 in a straight line for shoulder line.

9. Armhole:

   8 – 9 = 9 – 6 [vertically downwards on line 8 – 6]

   = 8.5 cm

   that means point 9 is the mid-point of line 8 – 6.

   Join 8 – 9 – 3 in a smooth curve for armhole.

10. Dart:

    Waistline dart:

    (i) Dart position: 1 – N = 1/12th round bust [horizontally on line 1 – 4]

    = 7.3 cm

    (ii) Dart length: N – N_1 = 1/8th round bust [vertically upwards]

    = 11 cm

    (iii) Dart width: N – S = N – S_1 = 1.5 cm (on either side of point N) [horizontally on line 1 – 4]

    Join S – N_1 and S_1 – N_1 in straight lines for the required waistline dart.

11. To separate central back panel and side back panel:
    (a) Central back panel:
        (i) Join $9 - N_1$ in a smooth curve.
        (ii) For central back panel cut along the points:
            $2 - 1 - S - N_1 - 9 - 8 - 5 - 7 - 2$,
            where:
            2 – 1 is on fold.
            7 – 2 is neckline.
            8 – 7 is shoulder line.
            1 – S is waistline.
            $9 - N_1 - S$ is central side seam.
    (b) For side back panel cut along the points:
        $9 - N_1 - S_1 - 4 - 3 - 9$,
        where:
        $9 - N_1 - S_1$ is side central seam.
        9 – 3 is remaining armhole.
        3 – 4 is side seams.
        $4 - S_1$ is remaining waistline.
        Cut two pieces of side back panels for corset block.

Front:

1. $0_f - 1_f$ = required length + 1 cm [vertically downwards]
   = 43 cm
2. Armhole Depth:
   $0_f - 2_f$ = 1/4th round bust – 3 cm [vertically downwards on line $0_f - 1_f$]
   = 19 cm
3. Bust Line:
   $2_f - 3_f$ = 1/4th round bust [horizontally]
   = 22 cm

4. Waistline:

   $1_f - 4_f$ = 1/4th round waist + 3 cm (dart width) [horizontally]

   = 20 cm

5. Side Seam:

   Join $4_f - 3_f$ in a straight line for side seams.

6. Shoulder:

   $0_f - 5_f$ = ½ across shoulder – 1 cm [horizontally]

   = 16.5 cm

   Draw a vertical line downwards from point 5_f to line $2_f - 3_f$ and mark as 6_f.

7. Neckline:

   $5_f - 7_f$ = 2.5 cm (or as required for shoulder width) [horizontally on line $5_f - 0_f$]

   $2_f - 8_f$ = 2.5 cm (or as required) [vertically upwards]

   Join $7_f - 8_f$ in a deep curve for neckline.

8. Shoulder Line:

   $5_f - 9_f$ = 1 cm (shoulder drop) [vertically downwards on line $5_f - 6_f$]

   Join $9_f - 7_f$ in a straight line for shoulder line.

9. Armhole:

   $6_f - 10_f$ = 3 cm [vertically upwards on line $6_f - 9_f$]

   Join $9_f - 10_f - 3_f$ in a smooth curve for armhole.

10. Darts:

    0_f – A = highest bust level [vertically downwards on line $0_f - 1_f$]

    = 25 cm

    A – B = 1/12th round bust [horizontally]

    = 7.3 cm

    (a) Waistline dart:

    (i) Dart position: 1_f – M = 1/12th round bust [horizontally on line $1_f - 4_f$]

    = 7.3 cm

(ii) Dart length: $B - M_1 = 2$ cm [vertically downwards on line $B - M$]

Join $M - M_1$ in straight line.

$M - M_1$ is the required waistline dart length.

(iii) Dart width: $M - P = M - P_1 = 1.5$ cm (on either side of point M) [horizontally]

Join $P - M_1$ and $P_1 - M_1$ in straight lines for the required dart.

(b) Armhole dart:

(i) Dart position: Point 10_f is the required dart position for armhole dart.

(ii) Dart length: $B - J = 2.5$ cm [upwards on line $B - 10_f$]

Join $10_f - J$ in a straight line.

$10_f - J$ is the required dart length for armhole dart.

(iii) Dart width: $10_f - R = 10_f - R_1 = 0.5$ cm (on either side of point 10_f) [on line $3_f - 10_f - 9_f$]

Join $R - J$ and $R_1 - J$ in straight lines for the required armhole dart.

11. To separate center front panel and front side panel:

(a) For center front panel:

(i) Join $M_1 - J$ in a smooth curve.

(ii) For center front corset panel cut along the points:

$8_f - 1_f - P - M_1 - J - R_1 - 9_f - 7_f - 8_f$.

where:

$8_f - 1_f$ is center front open which can be finished with buttons, frogs or as required.

$P - M_1 - J - R_1$ is central side seam.

$7_f - 8_f$ is neckline.

$9_f - 7_f$ is shoulder line.

$9_f - R_1$ is armhole section.

Cut 2-pieces of center front panel for corset block.

(b) For front side panel cut along the points:

$R - J - M_1 - P_1 - 4_f - 3_f - R$,

where:

$R - J - M_1 - P_1$ is side central seam.

$R - 3_f$ is remaining armhole.

$3_f - 4_f$ is side seams.

$4_f - P_1$ is remaining waistline.

Cut two pieces of side front panels for corset block.

Add seam allowance of 1.5 cm (or as required) and hem allowance of 3 cm (or as required) and mark corresponding balance points and grain line on each draft and pattern piece.

Corset:

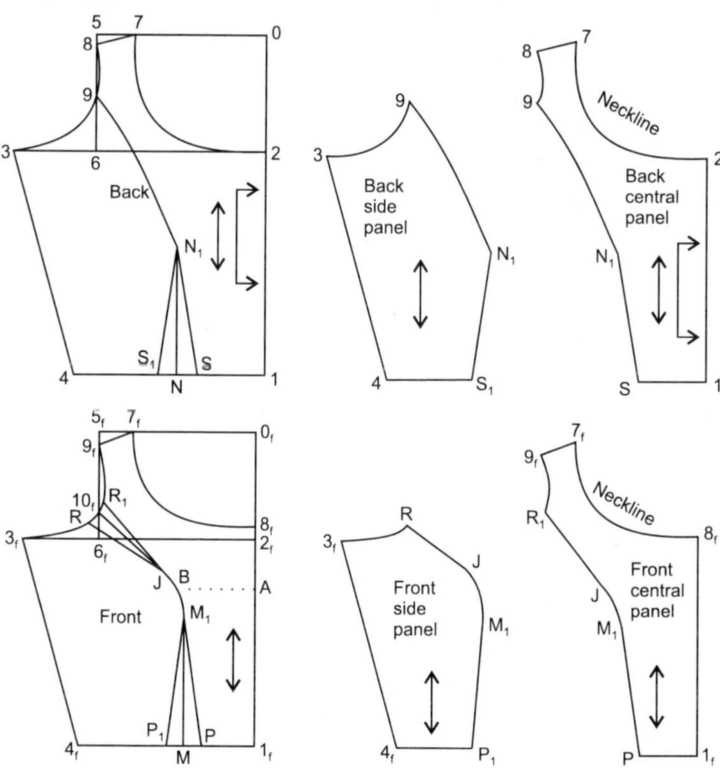

CORSETS

Edwardian corset

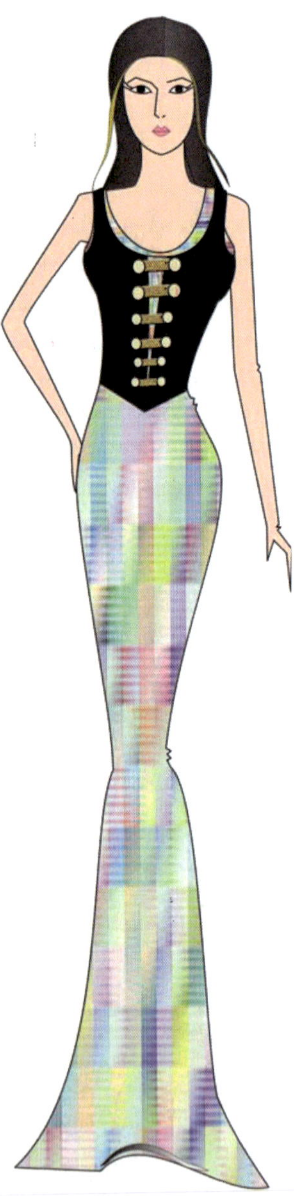

Bodice corset

13 TUNICS (SLEEVELESS)

STRAIGHT FIT TUNIC

Straight Fit Tunic: It is a slightly fitting midthigh to knee length upper garment generally worn by women and girls sometimes teamed with jeans, trousers, etc.

Suitable Fabric: Satin, viscose, soft and smooth fabric.

Age Group: Any.

Size symbol – 10

Scale – cm

Drafting scale – 1/4th cm or 1/6th cm

Required fabric – 1.5 m × 90 cm (length × width)

Measurements:

Required length = 70 cm

Round bust = 88 cm

Round waist = 68 cm

Round hips = 94 cm

Waist length = 40.3 cm

Hip level = 21 cm

Across shoulder = 35 cm

Construction:

Back:

1. 0 – 1 = required length + 1 cm [vertically downwards]
   = 71 cm

2. Armhole Depth:

   0 – 2 = 1/4th round bust – 4 cm [vertically downwards on line 0 – 1]

   = 18 cm

3. Bust Line:

   2 – 3 = 1/4th round bust + 2 cm (ease) [horizontally]

   = 24 cm

4. Waist Length:

   0 – 4 = waist length [vertically downwards on line 0 – 1]

   = 40.3 cm

5. Waistline:

   4 – 5 = 1/4th round waist + 3 cm (dart width) + 1 cm (ease) [horizontally]

   = 22 cm

   Join 5 – 3 in a straight line.

6. Hip Level:

   4 – 6 = hip level [vertically downwards on line 4 – 1]

   = 21 cm

7. Hip Line:

   6 – 7 = 1/4th round hips + 2 cm (ease) [horizontally]

   = 25.5 cm

   Join 7 – 5 in a straight line.

8. Hem Line:

   1 – 8 = 6 – 7 [horizontally for straight fit tunic]

   = 25.5 cm

   Join 8 – 7 in a straight line.

9. Shoulder:

   0 – 9 = ½ across shoulder [horizontally]

   = 17.5 cm

   Draw a vertical line downwards from point 9 to line 2 – 3 and mark as 10.

10. Neckline:

    0 – 11 = 1/12th round bust [horizontally on line 0 – 9]

    11 – 12 = 1.5 cm [vertically upwards on line 0 – 1]

    Join 0 – 12 in a smooth inward curve for back neckline.

11. Shoulder Line:

    9 – 13 = 0.5 cm [vertically downwards on line 9 – 10]

    Join 13 – 12 in a straight line for shoulder.

12. Armhole:

    13 – 14 = 10 – 14 [vertically]

    = 8.75 cm

    that means point 14 is the mid-point of line 13 – 10.

    Join 13 – 14 – 3 in a smooth curve for armhole.

13. For Dart: waistline double-headed dart.

    (i) Dart position:

    4 – N = 1/12th round bust [horizontally on line 4 – 5]

    = 7.3 cm

    (ii) Dart length: double headed dart.

    Upward dart length:

    $N - N_1$ = 1/10th round bust [vertically upwards]

    = 8.8 cm

    Downward dart length:

    $N - N_2$ = 1/10th round hips [vertically downwards]

    = 9.4 cm

    $N_1 - N_2$ is the required dart length for the double-headed dart.

    (iii) Dart width: $N - S = N - S_1$ = 1.5 cm (on either side of point N) [horizontally]

    Join $S - N_1$ and $S - N_2$ in straight lines and join $S_1 - N_1$ and $S_1 - N_2$ in straight lines for the required double-headed dart.

14. For back straight fit tunic block cut along the points:
 12 – 0 – 1 – 8 – 7 – 5 – 3 – 14 – 13 – 11 – 12,
 where:
 0 – 1 center back is on fold.
 3 – 5 – 7 – 8 is side seams.
 1 – 8 is hem line.

Front:

1. $0_f - 1_f$ = required length + 2.5 cm [vertically downwards]
 = 72.5 cm
2. Armhole Depth:
 $0_f - 2_f$ = 1/4th round bust – 4 cm [vertically downwards on line $0_f - 1_f$]
 = 18 cm
3. Bust Line:
 $2_f - 3_f$ = 1/4th round bust + 2 cm (ease) [horizontally]
 = 24 cm
4. Waist Length:
 $0_f - 4_f$ = waist length + 1.5 cm (for dart) [vertically downwards on line $0_f - 1_f$]
 = 43.5 cm
5. Waistline:
 $4_f - 5_f$ = 1/4th round waist + 3 cm (dart width) + 1 cm (ease) [horizontally]
 = 22 cm
 Join $3_f - 5_f$ in a straight line.
6. Hip Level:
 $4_f - 6_f$ = hip level [vertically downwards on line $4_f - 1_f$]
 = 21 cm
7. Hip Line:
 $6_f - 7_f$ = 1/4th round hips + 2 cm (ease) [horizontally]
 = 25.5 cm
 Join $5_f - 7_f$ in a straight line.

8. Hem Line:

   $1_f - 8_f = 6_f - 7_f$ [horizontally]

   = 25.5 cm

   Join $7_f - 8_f$ in a straight line.

9. Shoulder:

   $0_f - 9_f$ = ½ across shoulder [horizontally]

   = 17.5 cm

   Draw a vertical line downwards from point 9_f to line $2_f - 3_f$ and mark as 10_f.

10. Neckline:

    $0_f - 11_f$ = 1/12th round bust [horizontally on line $0_f - 9_f$]

    = 7.3 cm

    $0_f - 12_f$ = 1/12th round bust + 1 cm [vertically downwards on line $0_f - 1_f$]

    = 8.3 cm

    Join $11_f - 12_f$ in a smooth curve for neckline.

11. Shoulder Line:

    $9_f - 13_f$ = 2 cm [vertically downwards on line $9_f - 10_f$]

    Join $13_f - 11_f$ in a straight line for shoulder.

12. Armhole:

    $10_f - 14_f$ = 2.5 cm [vertically upwards on line $10_f - 13_f$]

    Join $13_f - 14_f - 3_f$ in a smooth curve for armhole.

13. For Dart:

    0_f – A = highest bust level [vertically downwards on line $0_f - 1_f$]

    = 25 cm

    A – B = 1/12th round bust [horizontally]

    = 7.3 cm

(a) Waistline dart: Double-headed dart.

(i) Dart position: $4_f - M$ = 1/12th round bust [horizontally on line $4_f - 5_f$]
= 7.3 cm

(ii) Dart length: Double-headed dart.

Upward dart length: $B - M_1$ = 2 cm [vertically downwards on line B – M]

$M - M_1$ is the required upward dart length.

Downward dart length:

$M - M_2$ = 1/10th round hips [vertically downwards]
= 9.4 cm

$M_1 - M_2$ is the required dart length for double-headed dart.

(iii) Dart width: $M - P = M - P_1$ = 1.5 cm (on either side of point M) [horizontally]

Join $P - M_1$ and $P - M_2$ in straight lines and join $P_1 - M_1$ and $P_1 - M_2$ in straight lines for the required double-headed dart.

(b) Side seam dart:

(i) Dart position: $5_f - T$ = 1/8th round bust [upwards on line $5_f - 3_f$]
= 11 cm

(ii) Dart length: $B - T_1$ = 5 cm [on line B – T]

$T - T_1$ is the required dart length.

(iii) Dart width: $T - R = T - R_1$ = 0.8 cm (on either side of point T) [on line $5_f - 3_f$]

Join $R - T_1$ and $R_1 - T_1$ in straight lines for the required side seam dart.

14. For Opening: 12_f – A [vertically downwards on line $12_f - 1_f$] is the front opening and should be finished with kurta placket or as required.

15. For front straight fit tunic block cut along the points:

    $12_f - 1_f - 8_f - 7_f - 5_f - T - 3_f - 14_f - 13_f - 11_f - 12_f$,

    where:

    $12_f - 1_f$ is on fold.

    $3_f - T - 5_f - 7_f - 8_f$ is side seams.

    $1_f - 8_f$ is hem line.

Add seam allowance of 1.5 cm (or as required) and hem allowance of 3 cm (or as required) and mark corresponding balance points and grain line on each draft and pattern piece.

Straight Fit Tunic:

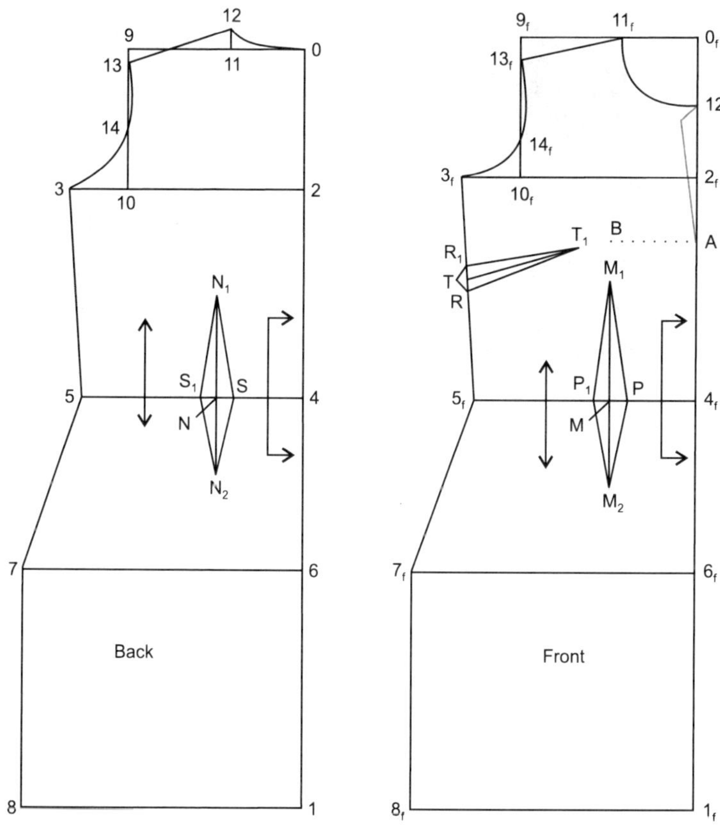

STRAIGHT FIT TUNIC & VARIATION

Straight fit tunic

Straight fit tunic (variation)

A-LINE TUNIC

A-line Tunic [First Garment]

A-line Tunic: It is a slightly fitting mid-thigh to knee length upper garment that is slightly flared at hem and generally worn by women and girls sometimes teamed with jeans, trousers, etc.

Suitable Fabric: Light weight to medium weight smooth fabric.

Age Group: Any.

Size symbol – 10

Scale – cm

Drafting scale – 1/4th cm or 1/6th cm

Required fabric – 1.5 m × 1 m (length × width)

Measurements:

Required length = 82 cm

Round bust = 88 cm

Round hips = 94 cm

Waist length = 40.3 cm

Hip level = 21 cm

Across shoulder = 35 cm

Construction:

Back:

1. 0 – 1 = required length + 1 cm [vertically downwards]
   = 83 cm
2. Armhole Depth:
   0 – 2 = 1/4th round bust – 4 cm [vertically downwards on line 0 – 1]
   = 18 cm
3. Bust Line:
   2 – 3 = 1/4th round bust + 2 cm [horizontally]
   = 24 cm

4. Waist Length:

   0 – 4 = waist length [vertically downwards on line 0 – 1]

   = 40.3 cm

5. Hip Level:

   4 – 5 = hip level [vertically downwards on line 4 – 1]

   = 21 cm

6. Hip Line:

   5 – 6 = 1/4th round hips + 2 cm (ease) [horizontally]

   = 25.5 cm

   Join 3 – 6 in a straight line and extend downwards and mark as 7,

   where:

   3 – 7 = 2 – 1

   = 65 cm

7. Hem Line:

   Join 7 – 1 in a smooth curve for hem Line.

8. Draw a horizontal line from point 4 to line 3 – 7 and mark as 8.

9. Shoulder:

   0 – 9 = ½ across shoulder [horizontally]

   = 17.5 cm

   Draw a vertical line downwards from point 9 to line 2 – 3 and mark as 10.

10. Neckline:

    0 – 11 = 1/12th round bust [horizontally on line 0 – 9]

    = 7.3 cm

    0 – 12 = 1.5 cm [vertically downwards on line 0 – 1]

    Join 11 – 12 in a smooth curve for neckline.

11. Shoulder Line:

    9 – 13 = 2 cm (shoulder drop according to shoulder type) [vertically downwards]

    Join 13 – 11 in a straight line for shoulder.

12. Armhole:

    13 – 14 = 14 – 10 [vertically on line 13 – 10]

    that means point 14 is the mid-point of line 13 – 10 = 8 cm.

    Join 13 – 14 – 3 in a smooth curve for armhole.

13. For Dart:

    Waistline dart: double headed dart.

    (i) Dart position: 4 – N = 1/12th round bust [horizontally on line 4 – 8]
    = 7.3 cm

    (ii) Dart length: double headed dart: upward dart: $N - N_1$ = 1/8th round bust [vertically upwards] = 11 cm

    Downward dart: $N - N_2$ = 1/10th round hips [vertically downwards]
    = 9.4 cm

    $N_1 - N_2$ is the required dart length for the double-headed dart.

    (iii) Dart width: $N - S = N - S_1$ = 1.5 cm (on either side of point N) [horizontally]

    Join $S - N_1$ and $S - N_2$ in straight lines and join $S_1 - N_1$ and $S_1 - N_2$ in straight lines for the required waistline dart.

14. For back tunic block cut along the points:

    12 – 1 – 7 – 6 – 8 – 3 – 14 – 13 – 11 – 12,

    where:

    3 – 8 – 6 – 7 is side seams.

    12 – 1 is on fold.

Front:

1. $0_f - 1_f$ = required length + 2.5 cm [vertically downwards]
   = 84.5 cm
2. Armhole Depth:
   $0_f - 2_f$ = 1/4th round bust – 2.5 cm [vertically downwards on line $0_f - 1_f$]
   = 19.5 cm
3. Bust Line:
   $2_f - 3_f$ = 1/4th round bust + 1 cm (dart width) + 2 cm (ease) [horizontally]
   = 25 cm
4. Waist Length:
   $0_f - 4_f$ = waist length + 1.5 cm [vertically downwards]
   = 41.8 cm
5. Hip Level:
   $4_f - 5_f$ = hip level [vertically downwards on line $4_f - 1_f$]
   = 21 cm
6. Hip Line:
   $5_f - 6_f$ = 1/4th round hips + 2 cm [horizontally]
   = 25.5 cm

   Join $3_f - 6_f$ in a straight line and extend downwards and mark as 7_f, where:

   $3_f - 7_f$ = $2_f - 1_f$
   = 65 cm
7. Hem Line:
   Join $7_f - 1_f$ in a smooth outward curve for hem line.
8. Waistline:
   Draw a horizontal line from point 4_f to line $3_f - 7_f$ and mark as 8_f.

9. Shoulder:

   $0_f - 9_f$ = ½ across shoulder [horizontally]
   = 17.5 cm

   Draw a vertical line downwards from point 9_f to line $2_f - 3_f$ and mark as 10_f.

10. Neckline:

    $0_f - 11_f$ = 1/12th round bust [horizontally on line $0_f - 9_f$]
    = 7.3 cm

    $0_f - 12_f$ = 1/12th round bust + 2 cm (for neckline depth) [vertically downwards]
    = 9.3 cm

    Join $11_f - 12_f$ in a smooth curve for scoop neck.

11. Shoulder Line:

    $9_f - 13_f$ = 2 cm (shoulder drop) [vertically downwards]

    Join $13_f - 11_f$ in a straight line for shoulder.

12. Armhole:

    $10_f - 14_f$ = 3.5 cm [vertically upwards on line $10_f - 13_f$]

    Join $13_f - 14_f - 3_f$ in a smooth curve for armhole.

13. For Dart:

    0_f – A = highest bust level [vertically downwards on line $0_f - 1_f$]
    = 2.5 cm

    A – B = 1/12th round bust [horizontally]
    = 7.3 cm

    (a) Waistline dart: double-headed dart.

    (i) Dart position: 4_f – M = 1/12th round bust [horizontally on line $4_f - 8_f$]
    = 7.3 cm

(ii) Dart length: double-headed dart.

Upward dart length: $B - M_1$ = 1.5 cm [vertically downwards on line $B - M$]

$M - M_1$ is the required upward dart length.

Downward dart length:

$M - M_2$ = 1/10th round hips [vertically downwards]

= 9.4 cm

$M_1 - M_2$ is the required dart length for the double-headed dart.

(iii) Dart width: $M - P = M - P_1$ = 1.5 cm (on either side of point M) [horizontally]

Join $P - M_1$ and $P - M_2$ in straight lines and join $P_1 - M_1$ and $P_1 - M_2$ in straight lines for the required waistline dart.

(b) Armhole Dart:

(i) Dart position: Point 14_f is the position for armhole dart.

(ii) Dart length: $B - J$ = 3 cm [upwards on line $B - 14_f$]

$J - 14_f$ is the required dart length for armhole dart.

(iii) Dart width: $14_f - R = 14_f - R_1$ = 1 cm (on either side of point 14_f) [on line $3_f - 13_f$]

Join $R - J$ and $R_1 - J$ in straight lines for the required armhole dart.

14. For front tunic block cut along the points:

$12_f - 1_f - 7_f - 8_f - 3_f - 14_f - 13_f - 11_f - 12_f$,

where:

$3_f - 8_f - 6_f - 7_f$ is side seams.

$12_f - 1_f$ is on fold.

Add seam allowance of 1.5 cm (or as required) and hem allowance of 2 cm (or as required) and mark corresponding balance points and grain line on each draft and pattern piece.

A-line Tunic [First Garment]:

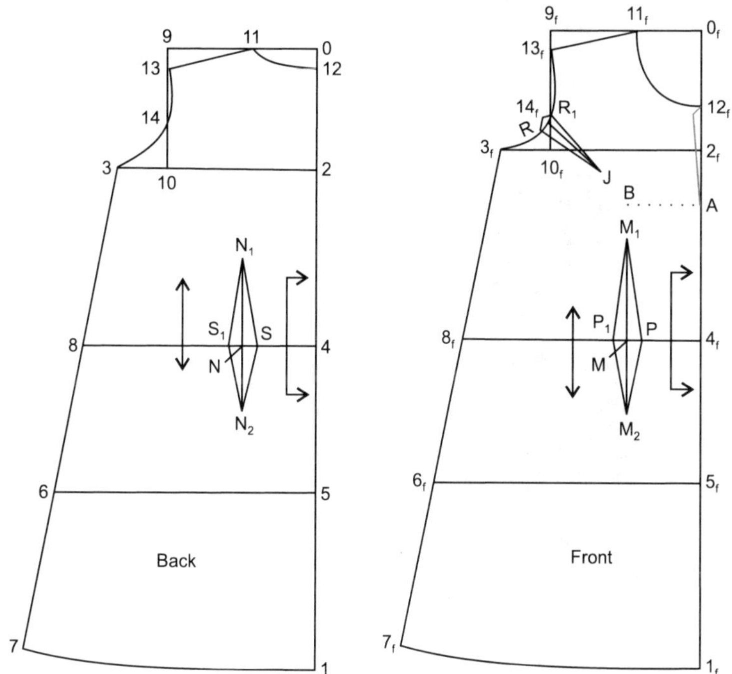

A-line Tunic (Second Garment)

A-line Tunic: This tunic is a mid-thigh to knee length sleeve less upper garment worn on a T-shirt, shirt or a tank top.

Suitable Fabric: Terry cot, cotton, denim, etc.

Age Group: 13 yrs. and above.

Size symbol – 10

Scale – cm

Drafting scale – 1/4th cm or 1/6th cm

Required fabric – 1.5 m × 1 m (length × width)

Measurements:

Required length = 82 cm

Round bust = 88 cm

Round hips = 94 cm

A-LINE TUNIC AND VARIATION (1ST GARMENT)

A-line tunic

A-line tunic with sleeves

Waist length = 40.3 cm

Hip level (waist to hips) = 21 cm

Across shoulder = 35 cm

Construction:

Back:

1. 0 – 1 = required length + 1.5 cm [vertically downwards]

   = 83.5 cm

2. Armhole Depth:

   0 – 2 = 1/4th round bust – 2 cm [vertically downwards on line 0 – 1]

   = 20 cm

3. Bust Line:

   2 – 3 = 1/4th round bust + 3 cm [horizontally]

   = 25 cm

4. Waist Length:

   0 – 4 = waist length [vertically downwards on line 0 – 1]

   = 40.3 cm

5. Hip Level:

   4 – 5 = hip level [vertically downwards on line 4 – 1]

   = 21 cm

6. Hip Line:

   5 – 6 = 1/4th round hips + 5 cm (or as required for shape) [horizontally]

   = 28.5 cm

   Join 3 – 6 in a straight line and extend downwards and mark as 7, where:

   3 – 7 = 2 – 1 [downwards]

   = 62 cm

7. Hem Line:

   Join 7 – 1 in a smooth curve for hem line.

8. Waistline:

   Draw a horizontal line from point 4 to line 3 – 7 and mark as 8.

9. Shoulder:

   0 – 9 = ½ across shoulder [horizontally]

   = 17.5 cm

   Draw a vertical line downwards from point 9 to line 2 – 3 and mark as 10.

10. Neckline:

    0 – 11 = 1/12th round bust + 1 cm [horizontally]

    = 7.3 cm

    11 – 12 = 1.5 cm [vertically upwards]

    Join 12 – 0 in a smooth curve for neckline.

11. Shoulder Line:

    9 – 13 = 0.5 cm [vertically downwards on line 9 – 10]

    Join 13 – 12 in a straight line for shoulder.

12. Armhole:

    13 – 14 = 10 – 14 [vertically]

    that means point 14 is the mid-point of line 13 – 10 = 9.75 cm

    Join 13 – 14 – 3 in a smooth curve for armhole.

13. For Dart: waistline dart (double-headed dart)

    (i) Dart position: 4 – N = 1/12th round bust + 0.5 cm [horizontally on line 4 – 8]

    = 7.8 cm

    (ii) Dart length: double headed dart.

    Upward dart length: $N - N_1$ = 1/10th round bust [vertically upwards]

    = 8.8 cm

    Downward dart length:

    $N - N_2$ = 1/10th round hips [vertically downwards]

    = 9.4 cm

$N_1 - N_2$ is the required dart length for the double-headed dart.

(iii) Dart width: $N - S = N - S_1 = 1.5$ cm (on either side of point N) [horizontally]

Join $S - N_1$ and $S - N_2$ in straight lines and join $S_1 - N_1$ and $S_1 - N_2$ in straight lines for the required double-headed dart.

14. For back tunic block cut along the points:

    0 – 1 – 7 – 6 – 8 – 3 – 14 – 13 – 12 – 0,

    where:

    0 – 1 is on fold.

    3 – 8 – 6 – 7 is side seams.

Front:

1. $0_f - 1_f$ = required length + 3 cm [vertically downwards]
   = 85 cm
2. Armhole Depth:

   $0_f - 2_f$ = 1/4th round bust – 2 cm [vertically downwards]
   = 20 cm
3. Bust Line:

   $2_f - 3_f$ = 1/4th round bust + 3 cm [horizontally]
   = 25 cm
4. Waist Length:

   $0_f - 4_f$ = waist length + 1.5 cm [vertically downwards on line $0_f - 1_f$]
   = 41.8 cm
5. Hip Level:

   $4_f - 5_f$ = hip level [vertically downwards on line $4_f - 1_f$]
   = 20.3 cm

6. Hip Line:

   $5_f - 6_f$ = 1/4th round hips + 5 cm (or as required for shape) [horizontally]

   = 28.5 cm

   Join $3_f - 6_f$ in a straight line and extend downwards and mark as 7_f, where:

   $3_f - 7_f = 2_f - 1_f$ [downwards]

   = 63.5 cm

7. Hem Line:

   Join $7_f - 1_f$ in a smooth curve for hem line.

8. Waistline:

   Draw a horizontal line from point 4_f to line $3_f - 7_f$ and mark as 8_f.

9. Shoulder:

   $0_f - 9_f$ = ½ across shoulder [horizontally]

   = 17.5 cm

   Draw a vertical line downwards from point 9_f to line $2_f - 3_f$ and mark as 10_f.

10. Neckline:

    $0_f - 11_f$ = 1/12th round bust + 1 cm [horizontally on line $0_f - 9_f$]

    = 8.3 cm

    $0_f - 12_f$ = 1/12th round bust + 3 cm [vertically downwards on line $0_f - 1_f$]

    = 10.3 cm

    Join $11_f - 12_f$ in a smooth curve for U shape neckline.

11. Shoulder Line:

    $9_f - 13_f$ = 2 cm (shoulder drop according to shoulder type) [vertically downwards]

    Join $13_f - 11_f$ in a straight line for shoulder.

12. Armhole:

    $10_f - 14_f$ = 3 cm [vertically upwards on line $10_f - 13_f$]

    Join $13_f - 14_f - 3_f$ in a smooth curve for armhole.

13. For Darts:

$0_f - A$ = highest bust level [vertically downwards]
= 25 cm

$A - B$ = 1/12th round bust + 0.5 cm [horizontally]
= 7.8 cm

(a) Waistline dart: double-headed dart.

(i) Dart position: $4_f - M$ = 1/12th round bust + 0.5 cm [horizontally on line $4_f - 8_f$]
= 7.8 cm

(ii) Dart length: double-headed dart.

Upward dart length: $B - M_1$ = 2 cm [vertically downwards on line B – M]

$M - M_1$ is the upward dart length.

Downward dart length:

$M - M_2$ = 1/10th round hips [vertically downwards]
= 9.4 cm

$M_1 - M_2$ is the required dart length for the double-headed dart.

(iii) Dart width: $M - P = M - P_1$ = 1.5 cm [horizontally on line $4_f - 8_f$]

Join $P - M_1$ and $P - M_2$ in straight lines and join $P_1 - M_1$ and $P_1 - M_2$ in straight lines for the required double-headed dart.

(b) Side Seam Dart:

(i) Dart position: $5_f - T$ = 1/8th round bust + 1 cm [upwards on line $8_f - 3_f$]
= 12 cm

(ii) Dart length: $B - T_1$ = 4 cm [on line B – T]

$T - T_1$ is the required dart length for the side seams dart.

(iii) Dart width:

$T - R = T - R_1 = 1$ cm [on line $8_f - 3_f$]

Join $R - T_1$ and $R_1 - T_1$ in straight lines for the required side seams dart.

14. For front A-line tunic block cut along the points:

$12_f - 1_f - 7_f - 6_f - 8_f - T - 3_f - 14_f - 13_f - 11_f - 12_f$, where:

$12_f - 1_f$ is on fold.

$3_f - T - 8_f - 6_f - 7_f$ is side seams.

12_f – A is opening if required which can be finished with continuous placket and buttons or dress hooks or as required.

Add seam allowance of 1.5 cm (or as required) and hem allowance of 3 cm (or as required) and mark corresponding balance points and grain line on each draft and pattern piece.

A-line Tunic (Second Garment):

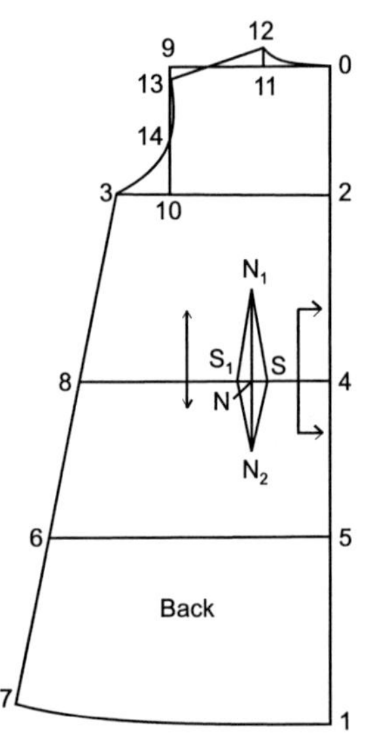

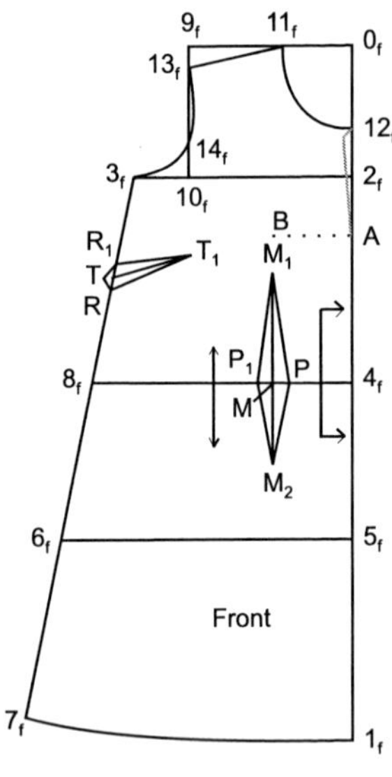

14 FROCKS

MINI FROCK

Low waist mini frock with half circular skirt.

Suitable Fabric: Medium weight to heavy weight fabric.

Age Group: 13 yrs. and above (this construction is suitable for age of 13 years and above).

Size symbol – 10

Scale – cm

Drafting scale – 1/4th cm or 1/6th cm

Required fabric – 1.5 m × 1 m (length × width)

Measurements:

Required length = 70 cm

Round bust = 88 cm

Round waist = 68 cm

Round hips = 94 cm

Waist length = 42 cm

Hip level (waist to hips) = 20.3 cm

Across shoulder = 35 cm

Highest bust level = 25 cm

Bodice length = waist length + 1/10th round hips + 2 cm [low waist length]

= 42 cm + 11.4 cm

= 53.4 cm

A-LINE TUNIC AND VARIATION (2ND GARMENT)

A-line tunic

A-line tunic with side slits and front opening

Skirt length = required length – bodice length
= 70 cm – 53.4 cm
= 16.6 cm

Construction:

Back:

1. 0 – 1 = bodice length + 1 cm [vertically downwards]
   = 54.4 cm
2. Armhole Depth:
   0 – 2 = 1/4th round bust – 4 cm [vertically downwards on line 0 – 1]
   = 18 cm
3. Bust Line:
   2 – 3 = 1/4th round bust + 2 cm (ease) [horizontally]
   = 24 cm
4. Waist Length:
   0 – 4 = waist length [vertically downwards on line 0 – 1]
   = 42 cm
5. Waistline:
   4 – 5 = 1/4th round waist + 2.5 cm (dart width) + 1 cm (ease) [horizontally]
   = 20.5 cm
   Join 3 – 5 in a straight line.
6. Lower Waistline:
   1 – 6 = 1/4th round hips [horizontally]
   = 23.5 cm
   Join 6 – 5 in a straight line.
7. Shoulder:
   0 – 7 = ½ across shoulder [horizontally]
   = 17.5 cm
   Draw a vertical line downwards from point 7 to line 2 – 3 and mark as 8.

8. Neckline:

   0 – 9 = 1/12th round bust (or as required) [horizontally on line 0 – 7]

   = 7.33 cm

   0 – 10 = 1.5 cm [vertically downwards on line 0 – 1]

   Join 9 – 10 in a smooth curve for neckline.

9. Shoulder Line:

   7 – 11 = 2 cm (shoulder drop) [vertically downwards on line 7 – 8]

   Join 11 – 9 in a straight line for shoulder.

10. Armhole:

    11 – 12 = 12 – 8 [vertically downwards on line 11 – 8]

    = 8 cm

    that means point 12 is the mid-point of line 11 – 8.

    Join 11 – 12 – 3 in a smooth curve for armhole.

11. Darts: waistline dart [double headed dart]

    (i) Dart position:

    4 – N = 1/12th round bust [horizontally on line 4 – 5]

    = 7.33 cm

    (ii) Dart length: double-headed dart.

    Upward dart length:

    $N - N_1$ = 1/10th round bust [vertically upwards]

    = 8.8 cm

    [**Note:** Point N_1 should be at least 3 cm below the bust line 2 – 3]

    Downward dart length:

    $N - N_2$ = 1/10th round hips [vertically downwards]

    = 9.4 cm

    [**Note:** Point N_2 should be at least 2 cm above the hip line 1 – 6]

$N_1 - N_2$ is the required dart length for double-headed dart.

(iii) Dart width:

$N - S = N - S_1 = 1.25$ cm (on either side of point N) [horizontally on line 4 – 5]

Join $S - N_1$ and $S - N_2$ in straight lines and join $S_1 - N_1$ and $S_1 - N_2$ in straight lines for the required double-headed dart.

12. Back bodice block of mini frock is along the points:

10 – 1 – 6 – 5 – 3 – 12 – 11 – 9 – 10,

where:

10 – 1 is on fold.

9 – 10 is neckline.

9 – 11 is shoulder.

11 – 12 – 3 is armhole.

3 – 5 – 6 is side seams.

Front:

1. $0_f - 1_f$ = bodice length + 1.5 cm (dart width) + 1 cm [vertically downwards]

   = 56.4 cm

2. Armhole Depth:

   $0_f - 2_f$ = 1/4th round bust – 4 cm [vertically downwards on line $0_f - 1_f$]

   = 18 cm

3. Bust Line:

   $2_f - 3_f$ = 1/14th round bust + 2 cm (ease) [horizontally]

   = 24 cm

4. Waist Length:

   $0_f - 4_f$ = waist length + 1.5 cm (dart width) [vertically downwards on line $0_f - 1_f$]

   = 43.5 cm

5. Waistline:

   $4_f - 5_f$ = 1/4th round waist + 2.5 cm (dart width) + 1 cm (ease) [horizontally]

   = 20.5 cm

   Join $5_f - 3_f$ in a straight line.

6. Lower Waistline:

   $1_f - 6_f$ = 1/4th round hips [horizontally]

   = 23.5 cm

   Join $6_f - 5_f$ in a straight line.

7. Shoulder:

   $0_f - 7_f$ = ½ across shoulder [horizontally]

   = 17.5 cm

   Draw a vertical line downwards from point 7_f to line $2_f - 3_f$ and mark as 8_f.

8. Neck Line:

   $0_f - 9_f$ = 1/12th round bust (equal to 0 – 9 of back bodice) [horizontally on line $0_f - 7_f$]

   = 7.33 cm

   $0_f - 10_f$ = 1/12th round bust (or as required for depth) [vertically downwards on line $0_f - 1_f$]

   = 7.33 cm

   Join $9_f - 10_f$ in a smooth curve for round neck.

9. Shoulder Line:

   $7_f - 11_f$ = 2 cm (shoulder drop) [vertically downwards on line $7_f - 8_f$]

   Join $11_f - 9_f$ in a straight line for shoulder.

10. Armhole:

    $8_f - 12_f$ = 2.5 cm [vertically upwards on line $8_f - 11_f$]

    Join $11_f - 12_f - 3_f$ in a smooth curve for armhole.

11. Darts:

    0_f – A = highest bust level [vertically downwards on line $0_f - 1_f$]

    = 25 cm

A – B = 1/12th round bust [horizontally]
= 7.33 cm

(a) Waistline dart: double-headed dart.

(i) Dart position: 4_f – M = 1/12th round bust [horizontally on line 4_f – 5_f]
= 7.33 cm

(ii) Dart length: double headed dart.

Upwards dart length: B – M_1 = 1.5 cm [vertically downwards on line B – M]

Join M – M_1 in a straight line. M – M_1 is the required upward dart length.

Downward dart length:

M – M_2 = 1/10th round hips [vertically downwards]
= 9.4 cm

M_1 – M_2 is the required dart length for double-headed dart.

(iii) Dart width:

M – P = M – P_1 = 1.25 cm (on either side of point M) [horizontally on line 4_f – 5_f]

Join P – M_1 and P – M_2 in straight lines and join P_1 – M_1 and P_1 – M_2 in straight lines for the required double-headed dart.

(b) Straight side seam dart:

(i) Dart position: Extend line A – B to meet the line 3_f – 5_f and mark as T (draw a cropped/dotted line)

(ii) Dart length: B – T_1 = 4 cm [on line B – T]

T – T_1 is the required dart length for side seam dart.

(iii) Dart width: T – R = T – R_1 = 1 cm (on either side of point T) [on line 5_f – 3_f]

Join $R - T_1$ and $R_1 - T_1$ in straight lines for the required side seam dart.

12. Front bodice block for mini frock is along the points:

    $10_f - 1_f - 6_f - 5_f - T - 3_f - 12_f - 11_f - 9_f - 10_f$,

    where:

    $10_f - 1_f$ is on fold.

    $9_f - 10_f$ is neckline.

    $9_f - 11_f$ is shoulder line.

    $11_f - 12_f - 3_f$ is armhole.

    $3_f - T - 5_f - 6_f$ is side seams.

    $10_f - A$ is front opening to slip into the frock which can be finished with continuous placket and dress hooks or zip or as required.

Skirt: Half Circular Skirt

Circumference = 4 × (6 – 1)

= 94 cm

Now

Circumference = ½ (2πr)

i.e. 94 cm = πr (since π = 22/7)

∴ r = 29.9 cm

1. 13 – 14 = r + required length for skirt + 1 cm [vertically downwards]

   = 29.9 cm + 16.6 cm + 1 cm

   = 47.5 cm

2. 13 – 15 = 13 – 14 [horizontally]

   = 47.5 cm

   Complete the square 13 – 14 – 15 – 16.

3. 13 – 17 = radius [horizontally on line 13 – 15]

   = 29.9 cm

4. 13 – 18 = 13 – 17 [vertically downwards on line 13 – 14]

   = 29.9 cm

Join points 17 – 18 in an arc using a compass for waistline.

5. Join points 14 – 15 in an arc for hem line.
6. Skirt block for mini frock is along the points:

   17 – 15 – 14 – 18 – 17,

   where:

   18 – 14 is on fold (line 18 – 14 should be slashed for side seams to give a better effect).

   17 – 18 is waistline.

   14 – 15 is hem line.

Add seam allowance of 1.5 cm (or as required) and hem allowance of 3 cm (or as required) and mark corresponding balance points and grain line on each draft and pattern piece.

Mini frock:

Bodice:

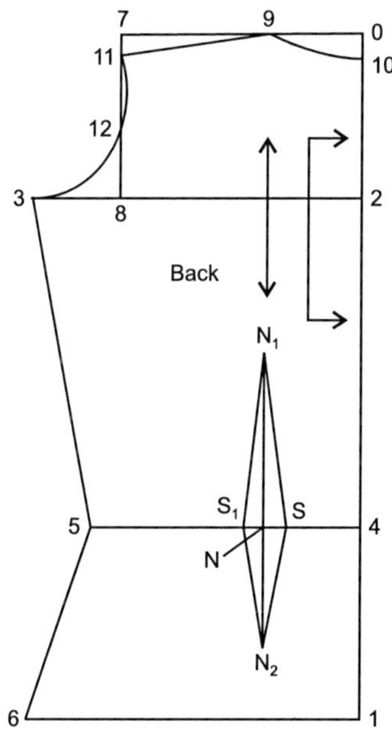

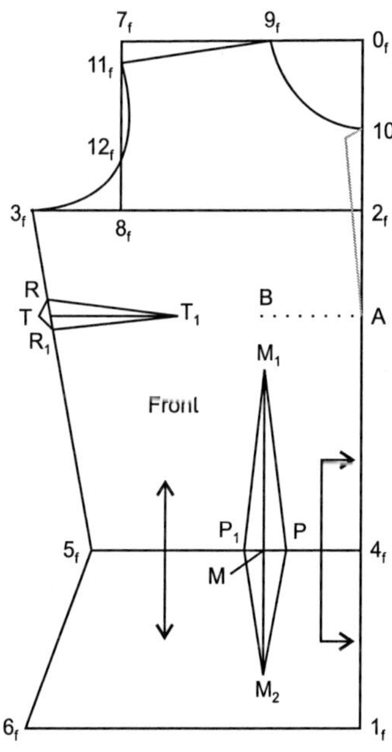

Skirt:

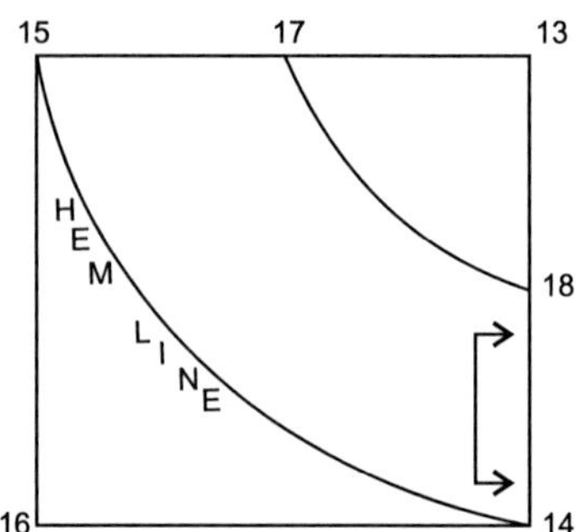

MIDDY

Mid-calf length women's upper garment.

Suitable Fabric: Medium weight to heavy weight fabric.

Age Group: 13 yrs. and above.

Size symbol – 10

Scale – cm

Drafting scale – 1/4th cm or 1/6th cm

Required fabric – 2 m × 1 m (length × width)

Measurements:

Required length = 90 cm

Round bust = 88 cm

Round waist = 68 cm

Round hips = 94 cm

Waist length = 42 cm

Hip level (waist to hips) = 21 cm

Across shoulder = 35 cm

Sleeve length = 18 cm

Top arm = 24 cm

Construction:

Back:

1. 0 – 1 = required length + 1 cm [vertically downwards]
 = 91 cm

2. Armhole Depth:

   0 – 2 = 1/4th round bust – 3 cm [vertically downwards on line 0 – 1]

   = 19 cm

3. Bust Line:

   2 – 3 = 1/4th round bust + 2 cm (ease) [horizontally]

   = 24 cm

4. Waist Length:

   0 – 4 = waist length [vertically downwards on line 0 – 1]

   = 42 cm

5. Hip Level:

   4 – 5 = hip level [vertically downwards on line 4 – 1]

   = 21 cm

6. Hip Line:

   5 – 6 = 1/4th round hips + 2 cm (ease and shape) [horizontally]

   = 25.5 cm

   Join 3 – 6 in a straight line and extend downwards and mark as 7, where:

   3 – 7 = 2 – 1

   = 72 cm

7. Hem Line:

   Join 7 – 1 in a smooth curve for hem line.

8. Waistline:

   Draw a horizontal line from point 4 to line 3 – 7 and mark as 8.

9. Shoulder:

   0 – 9 = ½ across shoulder + 1 cm [horizontally]

   = 18.5 cm

   Draw a vertical line downwards from point 9 to line 2 – 3 and mark as 10.

10. Neckline:

    0 – 11 = 1/12th round bust [horizontally on line 0 – 9]
    = 7.33 cm

    11 – 12 = 1.5 cm [vertically upwards]

    Join 12 – 0 in a smooth curve for neckline.

11. Shoulder Line:

    9 – 13 = 0.5 cm (shoulder drop) [vertically downwards on line 9 – 10]

    Join 13 – 12 in a straight line for shoulder line.

12. Armhole:

    13 – 14 = 14 – 10 [vertically downwards on line 13 – 10]
    = 9.25 cm

    that means point 14 is the mid-point of line 13 – 10.

    Join 13 – 14 – 3 in a smooth curve for armhole.

13. Darts: Waistline dart (double-headed dart)

    (i) Dart position: 4 – N = 1/12th round bust [horizontally]
    = 7.33 cm

    (ii) Dart length:

    Upward dart length: $N - N_1$ = 1/10th round bust [vertically upwards]
    = 8.8 cm

    Downward length: $N - N_2$ = 1/10th round hips [vertically downwards]
    = 9.4 cm

    $N_1 - N_2$ is the required dart length for the double-headed dart.

    (iii) Dart width: N – S = $N - S_1$ = 1 cm (on either side of point N) [horizontally on line 4 – 8]

    Join $S - N_1$ and $S - N_2$ in straight lines and join $S_1 - N_1$ and $S_1 - N_2$ in straight lines for the required double-headed dart at waistline.

14. Back A-line tunic is along the points:

    0 – 1 – 7 – 3 – 14 – 13 – 12 – 0,

    where:

    0 – 1 is on fold.

    12 – 0 is neckline.

    12 – 13 is shoulder.

    13 – 14 – 3 is armhole.

    3 – 7 is side seams.

    7 – 1 is hem line.

Front:

1. $0_f - 1_f$ = required length + 1.5 cm [vertically downwards]

   = 91.5 cm

2. Armhole Depth:

   $0_f - 2_f$ = 1/4th round bust – 1.5 cm [vertically downwards on line $0_f - 1_f$]

   = 20.5 cm

3. Bust Line:

   $2_f - 3_f$ = 1/4th round bust + 1 cm (dart width) + 2 cm (ease) [horizontally]

   = 25 cm

4. Waist Level:

   $0_f - 4_f$ = waist length [vertically downwards on line $0_f - 1_f$]

   = 42 cm

5. Hip Level:

   $4_f - 5_f$ = hip level [vertically downwards on line $4_f - 1_f$]

   = 21 cm

6. Hip Line:

   $5_f - 6_f$ = 1/4th round hips + 3 cm (ease and shape) [horizontally]

   = 26.5 cm

Join $3_f - 6_f$ in a straight line and extend downwards and mark as 7_f, where:

$3_f - 7_f$ = 3 – 7 (of back block)
= 72 cm

7. Hem Line:

Join $7_f - 1_f$ in a smooth curve for hem line.

8. Waistline:

Draw a horizontal line from point 4_f to line $3_f - 7_f$ and mark as 8_f.

9. Shoulder:

$0_f - 9_f$ = ½ across shoulder + 1 cm [horizontally]
= 18.5 cm

Draw a vertical line downwards from point 9_f to line $2_f - 3_f$ and mark as 10_f.

10. Neckline:

$0_f - 11_f$ = 1/12th round bust [horizontally on line $0_f - 9_f$]
= 7.33 cm

$0_f - 12_f$ = 1/10th round bust (or as required) [vertically downwards on line $0_f - 1_f$]
= 8.8 cm

Join $11_f - 12_f$ in a smooth curve for neckline.

11. Shoulder Line:

$9_f - 13_f$ = 2 cm (shoulder drop) [vertically downwards on line $9_f - 10_f$]

Join $13_f - 11_f$ in a straight line for shoulder line.

12. Armhole:

$10_f - 14_f$ = 3.5 cm [vertically upwards on line $9_f - 13_f$]

Join $13_f - 14_f - 3_f$ in a smooth curve for armhole.

13. Darts:

0_f – A = highest bust level [vertically downwards on line $0_f - 1_f$]
= 25 cm

A – B = 1/12th round bust [horizontally]
= 7.33 cm

(a) Waistline dart: double headed dart

(i) Dart position: 4_f – M = 1/12th round bust [horizontally on line 4_f – 8_f]
= 7.33 cm

(ii) Dart length: Upward dart length: B – M_1 = 2 cm [vertically downwards on line B – M]

M – M_1 is the required upward dart length.

Downward dart length:

M – M_2 = 1/10th round hips [vertically downwards]
= 9.4 cm

M_1 – M_2 is the required dart length for double-headed dart.

(iii) Dart width: M – P = M – P_1 = 1 cm (on either side of point M) [horizontally on line 4_f – 8_f]

Join P – M_1 and P – M_2 in straight lines and join P_1 – M_1 and P_1 – M_2 in straight lines for the required double-headed dart.

(b) Armhole dart:

(i) Dart position: Point 14_f is the dart position for armhole dart.

(ii) Dart length: B – J = 3 cm [upwards on line B – 14_f]

J – 14_f is the required dart length for armhole dart.

(iii) Dart width: 14_f – R = 14_f – R_1 = 1 cm (on either side of point 14_f) [on line 3_f – 13_f]

Join R – J and R_1 – J in straight lines for the required armhole dart.

14. For Opening: To slip on the tunic slash 12_f – A and finish with a continues placket and dress hooks or as desired.

15. Front A-line tunic block is along the points:

    $12_f - 1_f - 7_f - 3_f - 14_f - 13_f - 11_f - 12_f$,

    where:

    $12_f - 1_f$ is on fold.

    $11_f - 12_f$ is neckline.

    $11_f - 13_f$ is shoulder.

    $13_f - 14_f - 3_f$ is armhole.

    $3_f - 7_f$ is side seams.

    $7_f - 1_f$ is hem line.

    12_f – A is front opening.

Add seam allowance of 1.5 cm (or as required) and hem allowance of 3 cm (or as required) and mark corresponding balance points and grain line on each draft and pattern piece.

Sleeves: Short Plain Sleeves

Measurements:

Sleeve length = 18 cm

Top arm = 24 cm

Round bust = 88 cm

Construction:

1. 0 – 1 = sleeve length [vertically downwards]
   = 18 cm
2. Sleeve Crown:
   0 – 2 = 1/12th round bust + 2 cm [vertically downwards on line 0 – 1]
   = 88/12 + 2
   = 7.33 + 2 cm
   = 9.33 cm
3. 2 – 3 = 1/4th round bust – 2 cm [horizontally]
   = 20 cm
4. 1 – 4 = ½ top arm + 1 cm (ease) [horizontally]
   = 24/2 + 1 cm
   = 13 cm

   Join 4 – 3 in a straight line for side seam.

5. 0 – 5 = 2 cm [horizontally]

   Join 3 – 5 in a straight line.

6. Divide 3 – 5 into four equal parts and mark as 6, 7 and 8, respectively.

   (i) $6 - 6_1$ = 1 cm [perpendicular downwards to line 3 – 5]

   (ii) $7 - 7_1$ = 2.5 cm [perpendicular upwards to line 3 – 5]

   (iii) $8 - 8_1$ = 1 cm [perpendicular upwards to line 3 – 5]

7. For Back Sleeve Crown:

   Join $5 - 7_1 - 6 - 3$ in a curve as shown in the figure.

8. For Front Sleeve Crown:

   Join $5 - 8_1 - 7 - 6_1 - 3$ in a curve as shown in the figure.

Add seam allowance of 1.5 cm (or as required) and hem allowance of 3 cm (or as required) and mark corresponding balance points and grain line on each draft and pattern piece.

Middy:

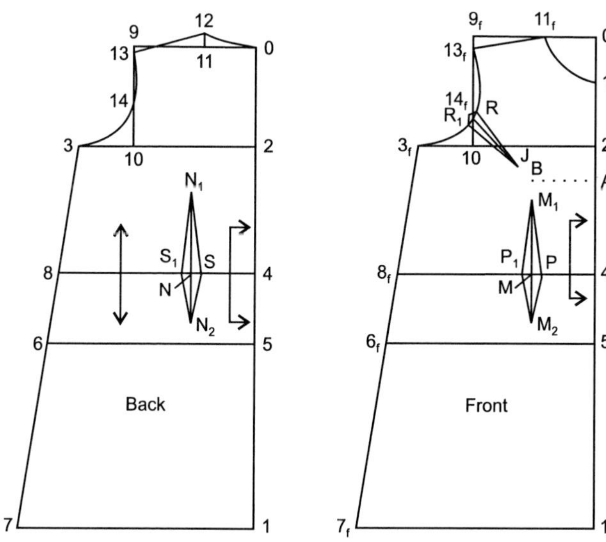

Sleeve:

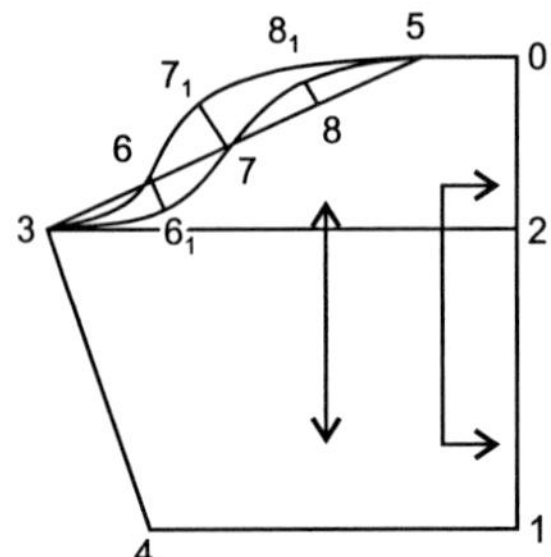

PUFFED AND GATHERED FROCK

In puffed and gathered frock the waistline darts are replaced with lots of gather to give a puffed look to the bodice of the frock.

Suitable Fabric: Any light weight to medium weight fabric.

Age Group: 13 yrs. and above.

Size symbol – 10

Scale – cm

Drafting scale – 1/4th cm or 1/6th cm

Required fabric – 3 m × 1 m (length × width)

Measurements:

Required length = 90 cm

Round bust = 88 cm

Round waist = 68 cm

Round hips = 94 cm

Waist length = 40.3 cm

Hip level (waist to hips) = 21 cm

Across shoulder = 35 cm

Construction:

Bodice Block

Back:

1. 0 – 1 = waist length + 3 cm (for puffed look) [vertically downwards]

   = 45 cm

2. Armhole Depth:

0 – 2 = 1/4th round bust – 3 cm [vertically downwards on line 0 – 1]

= 19 cm

3. Bust Line:

2 – 3 = 1/4th round bust + 2 cm (ease) [horizontally]

= 24 cm

4. Waistline:

1 – 4 = 1/4th round waist + 7 cm (or as required for puff) [horizontally]

= 24 cm

Join 3 – 4 in a straight line for side seams.

5. Shoulder:

0 – 5 = ½ across shoulder (for sleeveless) [horizontally]

= 17.5 cm

Draw a vertical line downwards from point 5 to line 2 – 3 and mark as 6.

6. Neckline (boat neck):

0 – 7 = 1/12th round bust + 4 cm [horizontally on line 0 – 5]

= 11.3 cm

0 – 8 = 1.5 cm [vertically downwards on line 0 – 1]

Join 7 – 8 in a smooth curve for boat neck.

7. Shoulder Line:

5 – 9 = 1.5 cm (shoulder drop) [vertically downwards on line 5 – 6]

Join 9 – 7 in a straight line for shoulder.

8. Armhole:

9 – 10 = 10 – 6 [vertically on line 9 – 6]

= 8.5 cm

that means point 10 is the mid-point of line 9 – 6.

Join 9 – 10 – 3 in a smooth curve for armhole.

9. To Shape Waistline

   1 – 11 = 1.5 cm [vertically downwards]

   Join 11 – 4 in a smooth curve for shaping waistline.

10. Back bodice block for puffed frock is along the points:

   8 – 11 – 4 – 3 – 10 – 9 – 7 – 8,

   where:

   8 – 11 is on fold.

   7 – 8 is neckline.

   7 – 9 is shoulder line.

   9 – 10 – 3 is armhole.

   3 – 4 is side seams.

   4 – 11 is waistline.

Front:

1. $0_f - 1_f$ = waist length + 3 cm (for puffed look) [vertically downwards]

   = 45 cm

2. Armhole:

   $0_f - 2_f$ = 1/4th round bust – 3 cm [vertically downwards on line $0_f - 1_f$]

   = 19 cm

3. Bust Line:

   $2_f - 3_f$ = 1/4th round bust + 2 cm (ease) [horizontally]

   = 24 cm

4. Waistline:

   $1_f - 4_f$ = 1/4th round waist + 8 cm (or as required for puff) [horizontally]

   = 25 cm

   Join $3_f - 4_f$ in a straight line for side seams.

5. Shoulder:

   $0_f - 5_f$ = ½ across shoulder [horizontally]

   = 17.5 cm

Draw a vertical line downwards from point 5_f to line $2_f - 3_f$ and mark as 6_f.

6. Neckline (boat neck):

   $0_f - 7_f$ = 1/12th round bust + 4 cm [horizontally on line $0_f - 5_f$]

   = 11.3 cm

   $0_f - 8_f$ = 1/12th round bust [vertically downwards on line $0_f - 1_f$]

   = 7.3 cm

   Join $7_f - 8_f$ in a smooth curve for boat neck.

7. Shoulder Line:

   $5_f - 9_f$ = 1.5 cm (shoulder drop) [vertically downwards on line $5_f - 6_f$]

   Join $9_f - 7_f$ in a straight line for shoulder.

8. Armhole:

   $6_f - 10_f$ = 2.5 cm [vertically upwards on line $6_f - 9_f$]

   Join $9_f - 10_f - 3_f$ in a smooth curve for armhole.

9. To Shape Waistline:

   $1_f - 11_f$ = 2 cm [vertically downwards]

   Join $11_f - 4_f$ in a smooth curve.

10. Front bodice block for puffed frock is along the points:

    $8_f - 11_f - 4_f - 3_f - 10_f - 9_f - 7_f - 8_f$,

    where:

    $8_f - 11_f$ is on fold.

    $7_f - 8_f$ is neckline.

    $7_f - 9_f$ is shoulder.

    $9_f - 10_f - 3_f$ is armhole.

    $3_f - 4_f$ is side seams.

    $4_f - 11_f$ is waistline.

Skirt

Gathers = 2 × round waist [horizontally]

= 136 cm

1. 12 – 13 = required length – waist length [vertically downwards]

   = 48 cm

2. Waist Line:

   12 – 14 = 1/4th gathers [horizontally]

   = 34 cm

3. Hem Line:

   13 – 15 = waist line + 10 cm (flare) [horizontally]

   = 44 cm

   Join 14 – 15 in a straight line for side seams.

4. To Shape Hem Line:

   14 – 16 = 12 – 13 [downwards on line 14 – 15]

   Shape 16 – 13 in a smooth curve for hem line.

5. Skirt block for puffed frock is along the points:

   12 – 13 – 16 – 14 – 12,

   where:

   12 – 13 is on fold.

   12 – 14 is waistline.

   14 – 16 is side seams.

   13 – 16 is hem line.

   Cut two pieces of the skirt block each for front and back.

   - 12 – 14 of skirt block should be gathered to 11 – 4 of back and 11_f – 4_f of front bodice block.
   - Waistline seam should be finished with draw string/pull string for puffed frock.

Add seam allowance of 1.5 cm (or as required) and hem allowance of 3 cm (or as required) and mark corresponding balance points and grain line on each draft and pattern piece.

Puffed and Gathered Frock

Bodice:

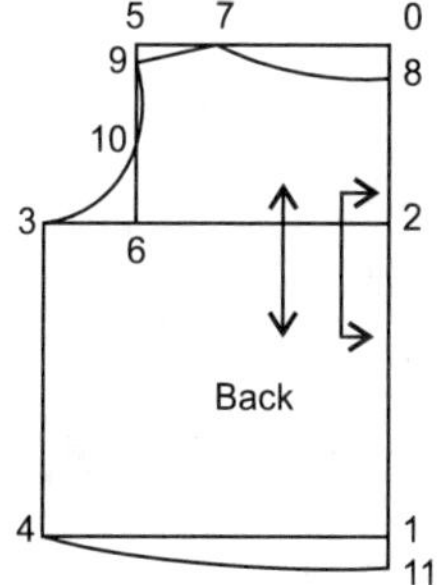

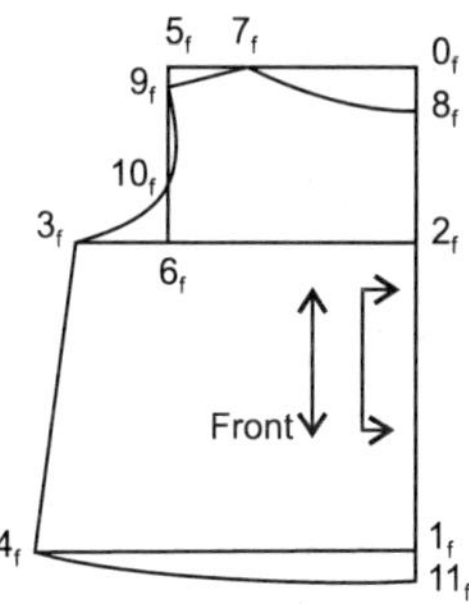

Skirt:

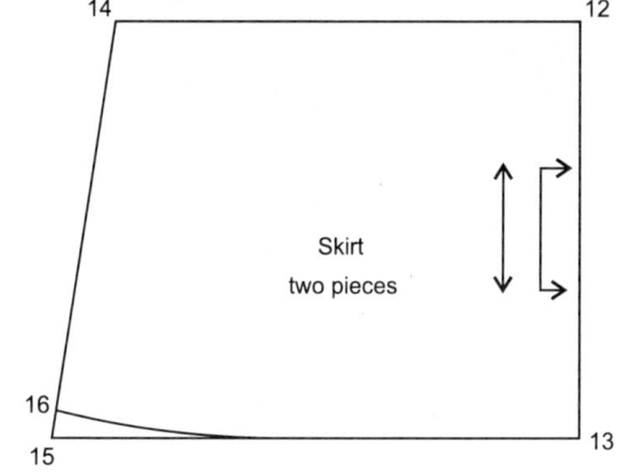

FROCKS

Mini frock Middy Puffed & gathered frock

15 EVENING GOWN

EVENING GOWN

A full length upper garment worn by women's in evening for party or occasions as such.

Suitable Fabric: *For gown:* Light weight to medium weight fabric.

For fish panels: Light weight sheer fabric or light weight fabric.

Suitable Age: 13 years and above.

Size symbol – 10

Scale – cm

Drafting scale – 1/4th cm or 1/6th cm

Required fabric – 3 m × 1 m (length × width)

Measurements:

Required length = 146 cm

Round bust = 88 cm

Round waist = 68 cm

Round hips = 94 cm

Waist length = 41 cm

Hip level (waist to hips) = 21 cm

Knee length (waist to knee) = 58 cm

Round knees (both knees together) = 58 cm

Across shoulder = 35 cm

Construction:

Back:

1. 0 – 1 = required length + 1.5 cm [vertically downwards]
   = 147.5 cm
2. Armhole Depth:
   0 – 2 = 1/4th round bust – 5 cm [vertically downwards on line 0 – 1]
   = 17 cm
3. Bust Line:
   2 – 3 = 1/4th round bust + 1 cm (ease) (or as required) [horizontally]
   = 23 cm
4. Waist Level:
   0 – 4 = waist length [vertically downwards on line 0 – 1]
   = 41 cm
5. Waistline:
   4 – 5 = 1/4th round waist + 3 cm (dart width) [horizontally]
   = 20 cm
   Join 5 – 3 in a straight line.
6. Hip Level:
   4 – 6 = hip level [vertically downwards on line 4 – 1]
   = 21 cm
7. Hip Line:
   6 – 7 = 1/4th round hips + 1 cm (ease) (or as required) [horizontally]
   = 24.5 cm
   Join 7 – 5 in a straight line.
8. Knee Length:
   4 – 8 = knee length [vertically downwards on line 4 – 1]
   = 58 cm

9. Knee Line:

   8 – 9 = ½ round knees + 2 cm (ease) (or as required for walking) [horizontally]

   = 29 cm

   Join 9 – 7 in a straight line.

10. Hem Line:

    1 – 10 = 1/4th round hips + 8 cm (for flare) (or as required) [horizontally]

    = 31.5 cm

    Join 10 – 9 in a straight line.

11. To Shape Hem Line:

    9 – 11 = 8 – 1 [downwards on line 9 – 10]

    = 48.5 cm

    Join 11 – 1 in a smooth curve.

12. Shoulder:

    0 – 12 = ½ across shoulder – 1 cm [horizontally]

    = 16.5 cm

    Draw a vertical line downwards from point 12 to line 2 – 3 and mark as 13.

13. Neckline:

    12 – 14 = 3 cm (or as required) [horizontally on line 12 – 0]

    2 – 15 = 3 cm (or as required) [vertically upwards on line 2 – 0]

    Join 14 15 in a smooth curve for deep wide scoop neck.

14. Shoulder Line:

    12 – 16 = 0.5 cm [vertically downwards on line 12 – 13]

    Join 16 – 14 in a straight line for shoulder line.

15. Armhole:

    16 – 17 = 13 – 17 [vertically]

    = 8.25 cm

that means point 17 is the mid-point of line 16 – 13.

Join 16 – 17 – 3 in a smooth curve for armhole.

16. Dart: waistline dart (double-headed dart)

    (i) Dart position: 4 – N = 1/12th round bust [horizontally on line 4 – 5]
    = 7.3 cm

    (ii) Dart length:

    Upward dart length: N – N_1 = 1/8th round bust [vertically upwards]
    = 11 cm

    Downward dart length:

    N – N_2 = 1/10th round hips [vertically downwards]
    = 9.4 cm

    N_1 – N_2 is the required dart length for double-headed dart.

    (iii) Dart width: N – S = N – S_1 = 1.5 cm (on either side of point N) [on line 4 – 5]

    Join S – N_1 and S – N_2 in straight lines and join S_1 – N_1 and S_1 – N_2 in straight lines for the required double-headed dart.

17. Evening gown block is along the points:

    15 – 1 – 11 – 9 – 7 – 5 – 3 – 17 – 16 – 14 – 15,

    where:

    15 – 1 is on fold.

    15 – C is back opening and should be finished with a zip [where; 4 – C = 4 cm (or as required)]

    3 – 5 – 7 – 9 – 11 is side seams.

    14 – 15 is neckline

    16 – 17 – 3 is armhole.

    16 – 14 is shoulder line.

    1 – 11 is hem line.

18. For Fish Cut Shape:
    (i) Divide line 8 – 9 into three equal parts and mark as v and x, respectively.
    (ii) Divide line 1 – 11 into three equal parts and mark as v_1 and x_1, respectively.
    (iii) Join v – v_1 and x – x_1 in straight lines.
    (iv) Slash lines: 8 – 1, v – v_1 and x – x_1.
19. Panels to stitch into the slashed lines:
    (i) 18 – 19 = v – v_1 [vertically downwards]

    19 – 20 = 15 cm (or as required for flare) [horizontally]

    Join 18 – 20 in straight line.
    (ii) 18 – 21 = 18 – 19 [downward on line 18 – 20]

    Join 21 – 19 in a smooth curve.
20. Fish panel is along the points: Five pieces of fish panels should be cut for the five slashed lines in the evening gown block back block.

    18 – 19 – 21 – 18,

    where:

    18 – 19 is on fold.

    18 – 21 is seam line that should be stitched to slashed lines 8 – 1, v – v_1 and x – x_1.

    19 – 21 is hem line.

Front:

1. $0_f - 1_f$ = required length + 3 cm [vertically downwards]

   = 149 cm
2. Armhole Depth:

   $0_f - 2_f$ = 1/4th round bust – 5 cm [vertically downwards on line $0_f - 1_f$]

   = 17 cm

3. Bust Line:

   $2_f - 3_f$ = 1/4th round bust + 1 cm (ease) (or as required) [horizontally]

   = 23 cm

4. Waist Level:

   $0_f - 4_f$ = waist length + 1.5 cm (dart width) [vertically downwards on line $0_f - 1_f$]

   = 42.5 cm

5. Waistline:

   $4_f - 5_f$ = 1/4th round waist + 3 cm (dart width) [horizontally]

   = 20 cm

   Join $5_f - 3_f$ in a straight line.

6. Hip Level:

   $4_f - 6_f$ = hip level [vertically downwards on line $4_f - 1_f$]

   = 21 cm

7. Hip Line:

   $6_f - 7_f$ = 1/4th round hips + 1 cm (ease) (or as required) [horizontally]

   = 24.5 cm

   Join $7_f - 5_f$ in a straight line.

8. Knee Length:

   $4_f - 8_f$ = knee length [vertically downwards on line $4_f - 1_f$]

   = 58 cm

9. Knee Line:

   $8_f - 9_f$ = ½ round knees + 2 cm (ease) (or as required for walking) [horizontally]

   = 29 cm

   Join $9_f - 7_f$ in a straight line.

10. Hem Line:

$1_f - 10_f$ = 1/4th round hips + 8 cm (for flare) (or as required) [horizontally]

= 31.5 cm

Join $10_f - 9_f$ in a straight line.

11. To Shape Hem Line:

$9_f - 11_f = 8_f - 1_f$ [downwards on line $9_f - 10_f$]

= 48.5 cm

Join $11_f - 1_f$ in a smooth curve.

12. Shoulder:

$0_f - 12_f$ = ½ across shoulder – 1 cm [horizontally]

= 16.5 cm

Draw a vertical line downwards from point 12_f to line $2_f - 3_f$ and mark as 13_f.

13. Neckline:

$12_f - 14_f$ = 3 cm (or as required) [horizontally on line $12_f - 0_f$]

$2_f - 15_f$ = 2 cm (or as required) [vertically upwards on line $2_f - 0_f$]

Join $14_f - 15_f$ in a smooth curve for deep wide scoop neck.

14. Shoulder Line:

$12_f - 16_f$ = 0.5 cm [vertically downwards on line $12_f - 13_f$]

Join $16_f - 14_f$ in a straight line for shoulder line.

15. Armhole:

$13_f - 17_f$ = 2.5 cm [vertically upwards]

Join $16_f - 17_f - 3_f$ in a smooth curve for armhole.

16. Dart:

0_f – A = highest bust level [vertically downwards on line $0_f - 1_f$]

= 25 cm

A – B = 1/12th round bust [horizontally]
= 7.3 cm

(a) Waistline dart: (double-headed dart)

(i) Dart position: 4_f – M = 1/12th round bust [horizontally on line 4_f – 5_f]
= 7.3 cm

(ii) Dart length: Upward dart length: B – M_1 = 2 cm [vertically downwards]

M – M_1 is the required upward dart length.

Downward dart length:

M – M_2 = 1/10th round hips [vertically downwards]
= 9.4 cm

M_1 – M_2 is the required dart length for double-headed dart.

(iii) Dart width: M – P = M – P_1 = 1.5 cm (on either side of point M) [on line 4_f – 5_f]

Join P – M_1 and P – M_2 in straight lines and join P_1 – M_1 and P_1 – M_2 in straight lines for the required double-headed waistline dart.

(b) Side seam dart:

(i) Dart position: 3_f – T = 1/12th round bust [downwards on line 3_f – 5_f]
= 7.3 cm

(ii) Dart length: B – T_1 = 3 cm [on line B – T]

T – T_1 is the required dart length.

(iii) Dart width: T – R = T – R_1 = 0.8 cm (on either side of point T) [on line 3_f – 5_f]

Join R – T_1 and R_1 – T_1 in straight lines for the required side seam dart.

17. Evening gown front block is along the points:

15_f – 1_f – 11_f – 9_f – 7_f – 5_f – T – 3_f – 17_f – 16_f – 14_f – 15_f,

where:

$15_f - 1_f$ is on fold.

$3_f - T - 5_f - 7_f - 9_f - 11_f$ is side seams.

$14_f - 15_f$ is neckline

$16_f - 17_f - 3_f$ is armhole.

$16_f - 14_f$ is shoulder line.

$1_f - 11_f$ is hem line.

18. For Fish Cut Shape:
    (i) Divide line $8_f - 9_f$ into three equal parts and mark as y and z, respectively.
    (ii) Divide line $1_f - 11_f$ into three equal parts and mark as y_1 and z_1, respectively.
    (iii) Join $y - y_1$ and $z - z_1$ in straight lines.
    (iv) Slash lines: $8_f - 1_f$, $y - y_1$ and $z - z_1$.
19. Panels to stitch into the slashed lines:
    (i) $18_f - 19_f = y - y_1$ [vertically downwards]

    $19_f - 20_f = 15$ cm (or as required for flare) [horizontally]

    Join $18_f - 20_f$ in straight line.
    (ii) $18_f - 21_f = 18_f - 19_f$ [downward on line 18 – 20]

    Join $21_f - 19_f$ in a smooth curve.
20. Fish panel is along the points: Five pieces of fish panels should be cut for the five slashed lines in the evening gown block back block.

    $18_f - 19_f - 21_f - 18_f$,

    where:

    $18_f - 19_f$ is on fold.

    $18_f - 21_f$ is seam line that should be stitched to slashed lines $8_f - 1$, $y - y_1$ and $z - z_1$.

    $19_f - 21_f$ is hem line.

Add seam allowance of 1.5 cm (or as required) and hem allowance of 3 cm (or as required) and mark corresponding balance points and grain line on each draft and pattern piece.

Evening Gown:

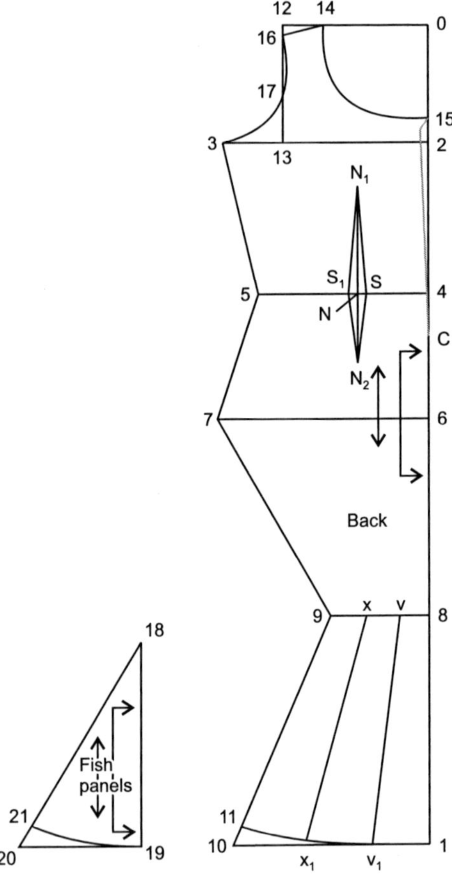

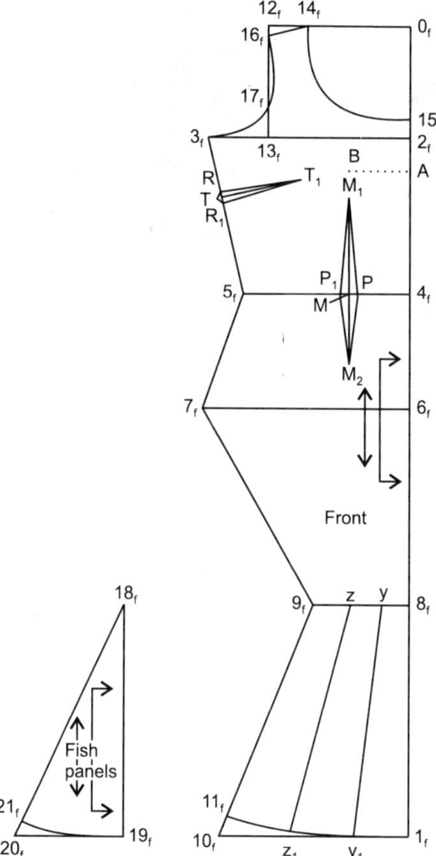
12_f
14_f
0_f
16_f
17_f
15_f
3_f
13_f
2_f
B
A
R
T_1
T
M_1
R_1
P_1
P
5_f
M
4_f
M_2
7_f
6_f
Front
18_f
9_f
z
y
8_f
Fish panels
21_f
11_f
20_f
19_f
10_f
z_1
y_1
1_f

EVENING GOWN & VARIATIONS

Evening gown & variations

Evening gown (empire waist)

Evening Gown (shoulder-less)

16 NIGH-TIE

NIGH-TIE

A knee to ankle length loose upper garment worn as night wear for sleeping.

Suitable Fabric: Light weight soft fabric.

Age Group: Any

Size symbol – 10

Scale – cm

Drafting scale – 1/4th cm or 1/6th cm

Fabric required – 2.10 m × 54 cm (length × width)

Measurements:

Required length = 120 cm

Round bust = 88 cm

Across shoulder = 35 cm

Yoke length = 1/4th round bust – 5.5 cm = 16.5 cm

Construction:

Back:

1. 0 – 1 = required length + 1 cm [vertically downwards]
   = 121 cm
2. Armhole Depth:
   0 – 2 = 1/4th round bust – 3 cm [vertically downwards on line 0 – 1]
   = 19 cm

3. Bust Line:

   2 – 3 = 1/4th round bust + 3 cm [horizontally]
   = 25 cm

4. Shoulder:

   0 – 4 = ½ across shoulder + 1 cm [horizontally]
   = 18.5 cm

   Draw a perpendicular downwards from point 4 to line 2 – 3 and mark as 5.

5. Hem Line:

   1 – 6 = 1/4th round bust + 8.5 cm (for flare or as required) [horizontally]
   = 30.5 cm

   Join 3 – 6 in a straight line for side seam.

6. Neckline:

   0 – 7 = 1/12th round bust [horizontally on line 0 – 9]
   = 7.3 cm

   0 – 8 = 1.5 cm (or as required for depth of neckline) [vertically downwards]

   Join 7 – 8 in a smooth curve for neckline.

7. Shoulder Line:

   4 – 9 = 2 cm (shoulder drop according to shoulder type) [vertically downwards]

   Join 9 – 7 in a straight line for shoulder.

8. Armhole:

   9 – 10 = 10 – 5 [vertically]
   = 8.5 cm

   that means point 10 is the mid-point of 9 – 5.

   Join 9 – 10 – 3 in a smooth curve for armhole.

9. To Shape Hem Line:

   3 – 11 = 2 – 1 [downwards on line 3 – 6]
   = 102 cm

   Join 11 – 1 in a smooth curve to shape the hem line.

10. For back nigh-tie block cut along the points:

    8 – 1 – 11 – 3 – 10 – 9 – 7 – 8,

    where:

    8 – 1 is on fold.

    3 – 11 is side seams.

    1 – 11 is hem line

    7 – 8 is neckline.

    7 – 9 is shoulder line.

    9 – 10 – 3 is armhole.

Front:

Yoke:

1. $0_f - 1_f$ = yoke length + 1 cm [vertically downwards]

   = 17.5 cm

2. $0_f - 2_f$ = ½ across shoulder + 1 cm [horizontally]

   = 18.5 cm

   Complete the rectangle $0_f - 1_f - 2_f - 3_f$.

3. $1_f - 4_f$ = 1.5 cm [vertically downwards]

   Join $3_f - 4_f$ in a smooth curve.

4. Neckline:

   $0_f - 5_f$ = 1/12th round bust [horizontally on line $0_f - 2_f$]

   = 7.3 cm

   $0_f - 6_f$ = 1/12th round bust + 1 cm (or as required for depth of neckline) [vertically downwards]

   = 8.3 cm

   Join $5_f - 6_f$ in a smooth curve for neckline.

5. Shoulder Line:

   $2_f - 7_f$ = 2 cm [vertically downwards]

   Join $7_f - 5_f$ in a straight line for shoulder.

6. Armhole:

   Join $7_f - 3_f$ in a smooth curve for armhole.

7. For giving a front opening cut two pieces of the yoke and finish the opening with plackets and hooks or as desired.

Skirt:

Skirt length = full length – yoke length = 103 cm

8. $8_f - 9_f$ = skirt length + 1 cm [vertically downwards]
   = 104 cm
9. $8_f - 10_f$ = 20 cm (or as required for gathers) [horizontally]

   $9_f - 11_f = 8_f - 10_f$ [horizontally]

   Complete the rectangle $8_f - 9_f - 10_f - 11_f$.
10. Bust Line:

    $10_f - 12_f$ = 1/4th round bust + 3 cm [horizontally]
    = 25 cm
11. Hem Line:

    $11_f - 13_f$ = 1/4th round bust + 8.5 cm (or as requires for flare) [horizontally]
    = 30.5 cm

    Join $12_f - 13_f$ in a straight line for side seams.
12. For Armhole:

    $12_f - 14_f$ = 3 cm [downwards on line $12_f - 13_f$]

    $10_f - 15_f = 1_f - 3_f$ of yoke.

    Join $15_f - 14_f$ in a smooth curve for armhole.
13. $12_f - 16_f = (8_f - 9_f)$ [downwards on line $12_f - 13_f$]
    = 104 cm

    Join $16_f - 11_f$ in a smooth curve for hem line.
14. Front skirt block of nigh-tie is along the points:

    $8_f - 9_f - 11_f - 16_f - 14_f - 15_f - 8_f$,

    where:

    $8_f - 9_f$ is on fold.

    $15_f - 14_f$ is armhole section.

    $9_f - 11_f - 16_f$ is hem line.

Add seam allowance of 1.5 cm (or as required) and hem allowance of 3 cm (or as required) and mark corresponding balance points and grain line on each draft and pattern piece.

Nigh-tie:

Back Block:

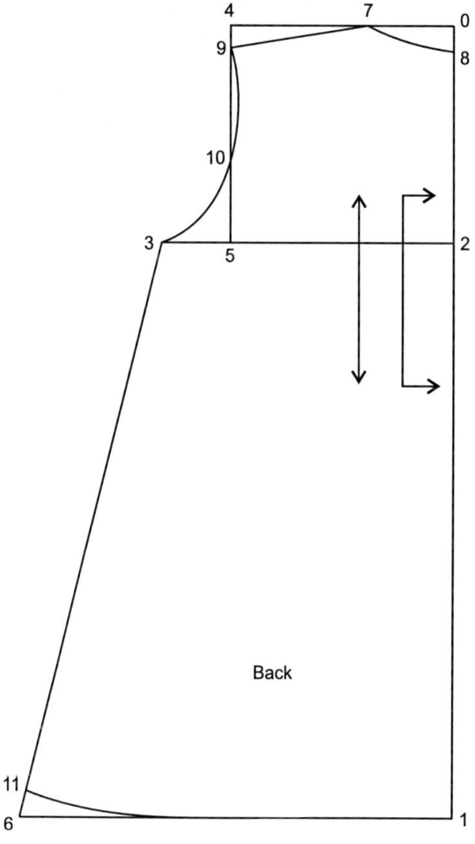

Front Block: Yoke and Skirt

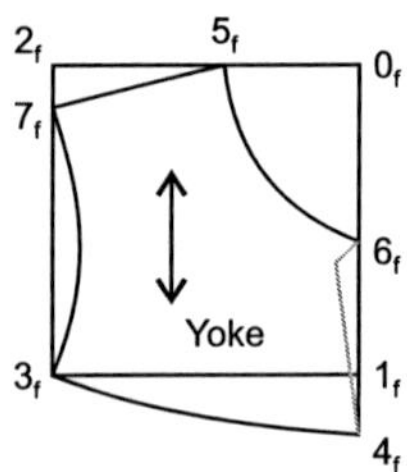

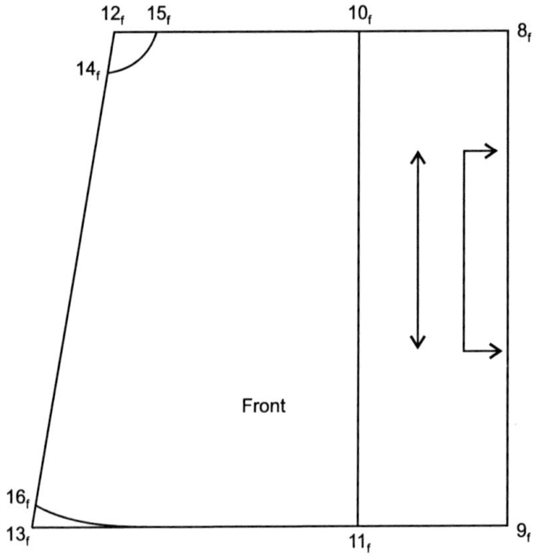

NIGH-TIE & VARIATION

Nigh-tie (full length)

Nigh-tie (knee length)

17 OVER COAT

OVER COAT

Over coat or a night gown is a second garment of knee to ankle length worn on a nigh-tie or a night suit, it can also be used as a bathing robe.

Suitable Fabric: Light weight soft fabric or medium weight soft fabric.

Age group: Any

Size symbol – 10

Scale – cm

Drafting scale – 1/4th cm or 1/6th cm

Fabric required – 3.80 m × 90 cm (length × width)

Measurements:

Required length = 120 cm

Round bust = 88 cm

Round hips = 94 cm

Waist length = 42 cm

Across shoulder = 35 cm

Construction:

Back:

1. 0 – 1 = required length + 2 cm [vertically downwards]
   = 122 cm

2. Armhole Depth:

   0 – 2 = 1/4th round bust – 3 cm [vertically downwards on line 0 – 1]

   = 19 cm

3. Bust Line:

   2 – 3 = 1/4th round bust + 3 cm [horizontally]

   = 25 cm

4. Shoulder:

   0 – 4 = ½ across shoulder + 2 cm [horizontally]

   = 19.5 cm

   Draw a perpendicular downwards from point 4 to line 2 – 3 and mark as 5.

5. Waist Length:

   0 – 6 = waist length [vertically downwards on line 0 – 1]

   = 42 cm

6. Waistline:

   6 – 7 = 1/4th round waist + 2 cm (dart width) + 2 cm (ease) [horizontally]

   = 21 cm

   Join 7 – 3 in a straight line.

7. Hem Line:

   1 – 8 = 1/4th round hips + 8 cm (or as required for flare) [horizontally]

   = 31.5 cm

8. Side Seam:

   Join 7 – 8 in a straight line.

9. Neckline:

   0 – 9 = 1/12th round bust [horizontally on line 0 – 4]

   = 7.3 cm

   9 – 10 = 1.5 cm [vertically upwards]

   Join 10 – 0 in a smooth curve for neckline.

10. Shoulder Line:

    4 – 11 = 0.5 cm [vertically downwards on line 4 – 5]

    Join 11 – 10 in a straight line for shoulder line.

11. Armhole:

    11 – 12 = 12 – 5 [vertically]

    = 9.25 cm

    Join 11 – 12 – 3 in a smooth curve for armhole.

12. Dart: Waistline dart (double-headed dart)

    (i) Dart position: 4 – N = 1/12th round bust [horizontally]

    = 7.3 cm

    (ii) Dart length: Upward dart length:

    $N - N_1$ = 1/10th round bust [vertically upwards]

    = 8.8 cm

    Downward dart length:

    $N - N_2$ = 1/10th round hips [vertically downwards]

    = 9.4 cm

    $N_1 - N_2$ is the required dart length for double-headed dart.

    (iii) Dart width: $N - S = N - S_1$ = 1 cm (on either side of point N) [horizontally on line 6 – 7]

    Join $S - N_1$ and $S - N_2$ in straight lines and join $S_1 - N_1$ and $S_1 - N_2$ in straight lines for the required double-headed waistline dart.

13. For back night gown block cut along the points:

    0 – 1 – 8 – 7 – 3 – 12 – 11 – 10 – 0,

    where:

    0 – 1 is on fold.

    3 – 7 – 8 is side seams.

    1 – 8 is hem line.

Front:

1. $0_f - 1_f$ = required length + 3 cm [vertically downwards]

   = 123 cm

2. Armhole Depth:

   $0_f - 2_f$ = 1/4th round bust – 3 cm [vertically downwards on line $0_f - 1_f$]

   = 19 cm

3. Bust Line:

   $2_f - 3_f$ = 1/4th round bust + 3 cm (ease) [horizontally]

   = 25 cm

4. Shoulder:

   $0_f - 4_f$ = ½ across shoulder + 2 cm [horizontally]

   = 19.5 cm

   Draw a vertical line downwards from point 4_f to line $2_f - 3_f$ and mark as 5_f.

5. Waist Length:

   $0_f - 6_f$ = waist length + 1 cm (dart width) [vertically downwards]

   = 43 cm

6. Waistline:

   $6_f - 7_f$ = 1/4th round waist + 2 cm (dart width) + 2 cm (ease) [horizontally]

   = 21 cm

   Join $7_f - 3_f$ in a straight linc.

7. Hem Line:

   $1_f - 8_f$ = 1/4th round hips + 8 cm (or as required for flare) [horizontally]

   = 31.5 cm

8. Side Seams:

   Join $8_f - 7_f$ for side seams.

9. For Overlap:
   (i) $6_f - 9_f$ = 1/12th round bust [horizontally outwards]
   = 7.3 cm
   (ii) $9_f - 10_f = 6_f - 1_f$ [vertically downwards]
   = 80 cm
   Join $10_f - 1_f$ in a straight line.
10. Neckline:
   $0_f - 11_f$ = 1/12th round bust [horizontally on line $0_f - 4_f$]
   = 7.3 cm
   Join $11_f - 9_f$ in a smooth curve for neckline.
11. Shoulder Line:
   $4_f - 12_f$ = 2 cm [vertically downwards on line $4_f - 5_f$]
   Join $12_f - 11_f$ in a straight line for shoulder line.
12. Armhole:
   $5_f - 13_f$ = 2.5 cm [vertically upwards]
   Join $12_f - 13_f - 3_f$ in a smooth curve for armhole.
13. Darts:
   $0_f - A$ = highest bust level [vertically downwards on line $0_f - 1_f$]
   = 25 cm
   A – B = 1/12th round bust [horizontally]
   = 7.3 cm
   (a) Waistline dart: double-headed dart.
   (i) Dart position: $6_f - M$ = 1/12th round bust [horizontally on line $6_f - 7_f$]
   = 7.3 cm
   (ii) Dart length: Upward dart length: $B - M_1$ = 2 cm [vertically downwards on line B – M]
   $M - M_1$ is the required upward dart length.

Downward dart length:

$M - M_2$ = 1/10th round hips [vertically downwards]
= 9.4 cm

$M_1 - M_2$ is the required dart length for double-headed dart.

(iii) Dart width: $M - P = M - P_1$ = 1 cm (on either side of point M) [horizontally on line $6_f - 7_f$]

Join $P - M_1$ and $P - M_2$ in straight lines and join $P_1 - M_1$ and $P_1 - M_2$ in straight lines for the required double-headed dart.

(b) Side seam dart:

(i) Dart position: $3_f - T$ = 1/10th round bust [downwards on line $3_f - 7_f$]
= 8.8 cm

(ii) Dart length: $B - T_1$ = 4 cm [downwards on line B – T]

$T - T_1$ is the required dart length.

(iii) Dart width: $T - R = T - R_1$ = 0.6 cm (on either side of point T) [on line $3_f - 7_f$]

Join $R - T_1$ and $R_1 - T_1$ in straight lines for the required side seam dart.

14. For front gown block cut along the points:

$9_f - 10_f - 8_f - 7_f - T - 3_f - 13_f - 12_f - 11_f - 9_f$, where:

$10_f - 8_f$ is hem line.

$3_f - T_f - 7_f - 8_f$ is side seam.

$9_f - 10_f$ is for overlap.

Cut two pieces of front block each for right and left side.

Lapels:

1. Trace out the shoulder and neckline of front night gown block.

2. Trace out line $9_f - 11_f$.
3. Extend line $9_f - 11_f$ upwards and mark as E, where:
   $11_f - E$ = ½ back neckline
   = 7.5 cm
4. Width of lapel
   $E - E_1$ = 6 cm (or as required) [perpendicular to line $9_f - E$]
   Join $E_1 - 9_f$ in a smooth curve as shown in the diagram or as required.
5. For lapel block cut along the points:
   $9_f - 11_f - E - E_1 - 9_f$,
   where:
   $E - E_1$ is on fold.
   $9_f - E$ should be stitched to neckline of night gown.
   Lapels should be finished with a interfacing.

Waistline Belt:

1. 0 – 1 = 4 cm [vertically downwards]
2. 0 – 2 = round waist + 20 cm (or as required) [horizontally]
   = 88 cm
   (to wrap around waist and tie into a knot)
   Complete the rectangle 0 – 1 – 2 – 3.
3. For waistline belt cut along the points:
   0 –1 – 2 – 3.

Add seam allowance of 1.5 cm (or as required) and hem allowance of 3 cm (or as required) and mark corresponding balance points and grain line on each draft and pattern piece.

18 TROUSERS

CONSTRUCTION OF BASIC TROUSERS

Basic Trousers: Lower garment worn by women and girls length from waist to ankle (full length), with separate legs joined at crotch, and waistline darts. Generally teamed with shirt, tunic, etc.

Suitable Fabric: Medium to heavy fabric.

Age Group: Any

Size symbol – 10

Scale – cm

Drafting scale – 1/4th cm or 1/6th cm

Fabric required – 2.25 m × 57 cm

Measurements:

Full length = 104 cm

Round waist = 68 cm

Round hips = 94 cm

Hip level = 19 cm

Body rise = 28 cm

Knee length = 58 cm

Round bottom = 40 cm

Belt width = 2 cm

Night Gown:

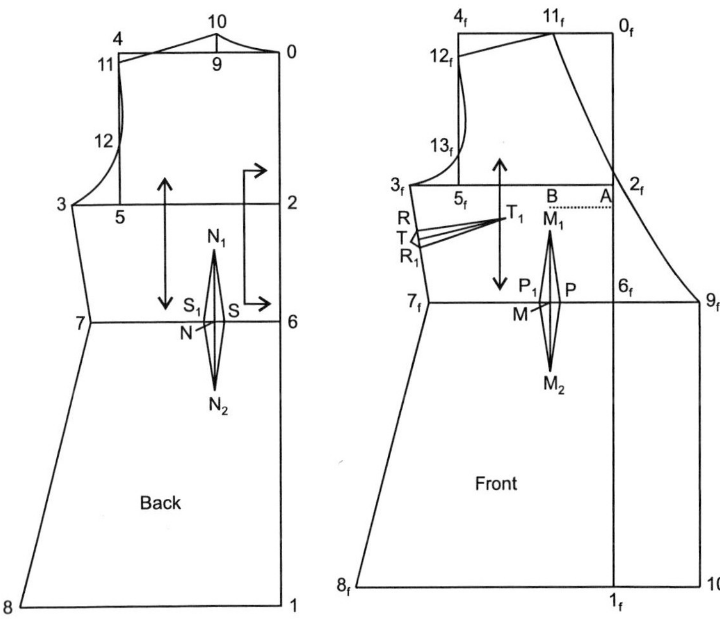
10
4
11
9
0
12
3
5
2
N_1
S_1
S
7
N
6
N_2
Back
4_f
11_f
0_f
12_f
13_f
3_f
5_f
B
A
2_f
R
T_1
M_1
T
R_1
P_1
P
6_f
7_f
M
9_f
M_2
Front
8_f
1_f
10_f
8
1

Lapels:

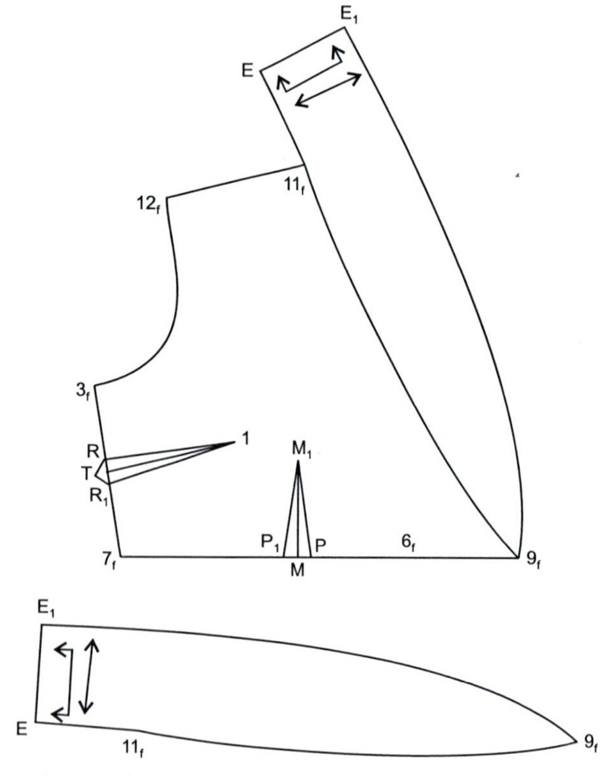

Waistline Belt:

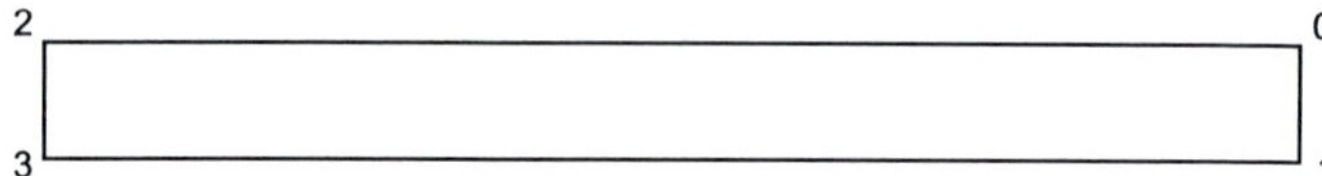

OVER COAT & VARIATION

Night gown (full length)

Night gown (knee length)

Construction:

1. 0 – 1 = required length + 1 cm – belt width [vertically downwards]
   = 103 cm
2. 0 – 2 = ½ round hips + 4 cm (ease) [horizontal]
   = 51 cm

   Complete the rectangle 0 – 1 – 2 – 3.
3. 0 – 4 = hip level – belt width [vertically downwards on line 0 – 1]
   = 17 cm

   Draw a horizontal line from point 4 to line 2 – 3 and mark as 4_1.
4. 0 – 5 = body rise – belt width [vertically downwards]
   = 26 cm

   Draw a horizontal line from point 5 to line 2 – 3 and mark as 5_1.
5. 0 – 6 = knee length – belt width [vertically downwards]
   = 56 cm

   Draw a horizontal line from point 6 to line 2 – 3 and mark as 6_1.

Back:

6. 2 – 7 = ½ (0 to 2) + 1 cm [horizontally on line 2 – 0]
   = 26.5 cm

   Draw a vertical line downwards from point 7 to line 1 – 3 through lines 4 – 4_1, 5 – 5_1 and 6 – 6_1 and mark as:

   4_2 on line 4 – 4_1.

   5_2 on line 5 – 5_1.

   6_2 on line 6 – 6_1.

   7_1 on line 1 – 3.
7. 7 – 8 = 2 cm [horizontally on line 7 – 2]

   Join 8 – 4_2 in a smooth curve to shape side seam hip level.

8. For Waist:

   $8 - 8_1$ = 1/4th round waist + 3 cm (dart width) + 1 cm [horizontally on line 8 – 2]

   = 21 cm

9. Waistline:

   $8_1 - 9$ = 2.5 cm [vertically upwards]

   Join 9 – 8 in a smooth curve for waistline.

10. Crotch Depth:

    $5_1 - 10$ = 1/10th round hips [extend horizontally outwards]

    = 9.4 cm

    Join $9 - 4_1 - 10$ in a smooth curve using tailors curve for back crotch depth.

11. Hem/bottom:

    $7_1 - 11$ = ½ round bottom + 1 cm [horizontally on line $7_1 - 3$]

    = 21 cm

    Join $10 - 6_1 - 11$ in a smooth curve for inside leg length.

12. For Crease Line:

    (i) $11 - J = 7_1 - J$ [horizontally on line $7_1 - 3$]
    i.e. J is the mid-point of line $11 - 7_1$
    = 10.5 cm

    (ii) $6_1 - J_1 = 6_2 - J_1$ [horizontally on line $6_1 - 6_2$]
    i.e. J_1 is the mid-point of line $6_1 - 6_2$
    = 13.25 cm

    (iii) Join $J - J_1$ in a straight line and extend upwards to meet the line 9 – 8 and mark as J_2.

13. For Dart:

    (i) Dart position: 9 – N = 8 – N [on line 9 – 8]
    i.e. N is the mid point of line 9 – 8
    = 10.5 cm

(ii) Dart length: $N - N_1$ = 1/12th round hips – 1 cm [perpendicular downwards to line 9 – 8]
= 6.8 cm

(iii) Dart width: $N - S = N - S_1$ = 1.5 cm (on either side of point N) [on line 9 – 8]

Join $S - N_1$ and $S_1 - N_1$ in straight lines for the required dart.

14. For back trousers block cut along the points:

$8 - 4_2 - 5_2 - 6_2 - 7_1 - J - 11 - 6_1 - 10 - 4_1 - 9 - J_2 - N - 8$,

where:

$8 - 4_2 - 5_2 - 6_2 - 7_1$ is side seams and outside leg length.

$10 - 6_1 - 11$ is inside leg length.

$9 - 4_1 - 10$ is back crotch depth.

$J_2 - J_1 - J$ is trousers crease line.

Cut two pieces of back trousers block to complete the trousers.

Front:

1. 7 – 12 = 2 cm [horizontally on line 7 – 0]

Join $12 - 4_2$ in a smooth curve to shape side seam hip level.

2. For Waist:

$12 - 12_1$ = 1/4th round waist + 4 cm (dart width) – 1 cm [horizontally on line 7 – 0]
= 20.5 cm

3. Waistline:

$12_1 - 13$ = 1 cm [vertically downwards]

Join 12 – 13 in a smooth curve for front waistline.

4. Front Fork:

5 – 14 = 1/12th round hips – 1 cm [extend horizontally outwards]
= 6.8 cm

Join 13 – 4 – 14 in a smooth curve for front fork.

5. Hem/bottom:

   $7_1 - 15$ = ½ round bottom – 1 cm [horizontally on line $7_1 - 1$]
   = 19 cm

   Join 14 – 6 – 15 in a smooth curve for inside leg length.

6. Crease Line:

   (i) $7_1 - L = 15 - L$ [horizontally on line $7_1 - 15$]
   i.e. L is the mid-point of line $7_1 - 15$
   = 9.75 cm

   (ii) $6_2 - L_1 = 6 - L_1$ [horizontally on line $6_2 - 6$]
   i.e. L_1 is the mid-point of line $6_2 - 6$
   = 12.75 cm

   (iii) Join $L - L_1$ in a straight line and extend upwards to meet the line 12 – 13 and mark as M.

7. For Darts: Two darts.

   (a) First dart:

   (i) Dart position: M is the position for first dart.

   (ii) Dart length: $M - M_1$ = 1/12th round hips [vertically downwards]
   = 7.8 cm

   (iii) Dart width: $M - P = M - P_1$ = 1 cm (on either side of point M) [on line 12 – 13]

   Join $P - M_1$ and $P_1 - M_1$ in straight lines for the required first dart.

   (b) Second dart:

   (i) Dart position: $P_1 - R$ = 4 cm [on line $P_1 - 12$]

   (ii) Dart length: $R - R_1$ = 1/12th round hips [vertically downwards]
   = 7.8 cm

(iii) Dart width: $R - Q = R - Q_1 = 1$cm (on either side of point R) [on line 12 – 13]

Join $Q - R_1$ and $Q_1 - R_1$ in straight lines for the required second dart.

8. For front trousers block cut along the points:

   $12 - 4_2 - 5_2 - 6_2 - 7_1 - L - 15 - 6 - 14 - 4 - 13 - M - R - 12$,

   where:

   $12 - 4_2 - 5_2 - 6_2 - 7_1$ is side seams and outside leg length.

   14 – 6 – 15 is inside leg length.

   13 – 4 – 14 is the front fork.

   $M_1 - L_1 - L$ is the crease line for front trousers.

   Cut two pieces of front trousers block to complete the trousers.

Add seam allowance of 1.5 cm (or as required) and hem allowance of 3 cm (or as required) and mark corresponding balance points and grain line on each draft and pattern piece.

Belt:

1. A – B = round waist = 72 cm [horizontally]
2. A – C = 4 cm (with intake) [vertically downwards]

   Complete the rectangle A – B – C – D.
3. For Overlap:

   B – E = D – F = 2.5 cm [horizontally outwards]

   Join E – F in a straight line or in a smooth outward curve for overlap.

   (Use interfacing equal to ½ of belt width to give firmness to the belt.)

Add seam allowance of 1.5 cm (or as required) and put up corresponding balance points and grain line on each draft and pattern piece.

Basic Trousers:

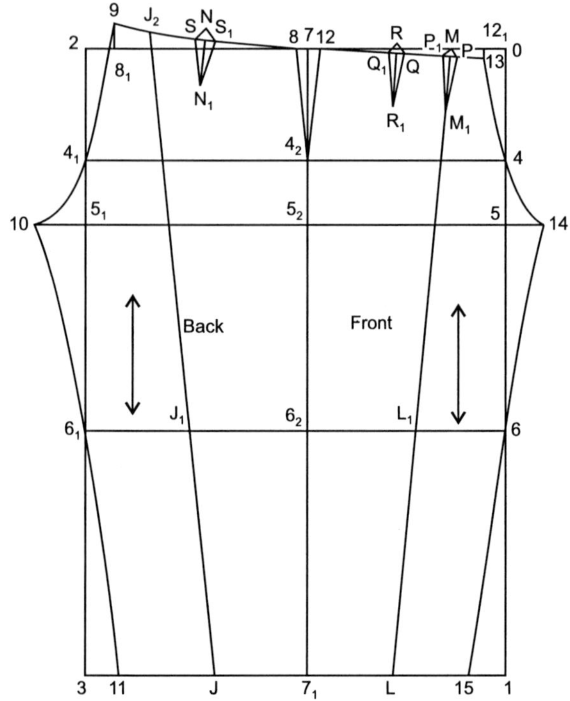

Belt:

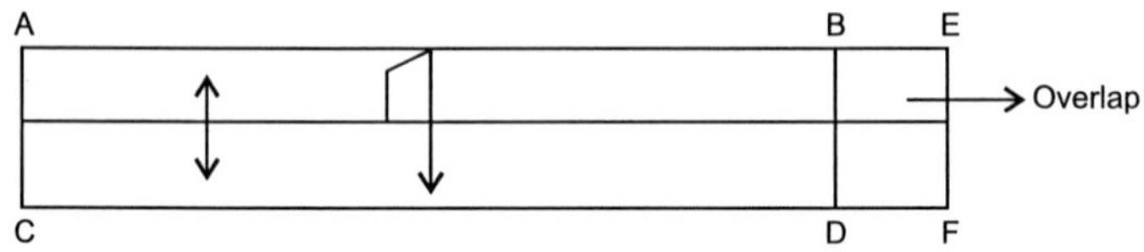

FLAT FRONTS

Lower garment worn by women and girls length from waist to ankle (full length), with separate legs joined at crotch, without waistline darts at front. Generally teamed with shirt, tunic, etc.

Suitable Fabric: Light to heavy fabric.

Age Group: Any

Measurements:

Size symbol – 10

Scale – cm

Drafting scale – 1/4th cm or 1/6th cm

Fabric required – 2.25 m × 57 cm

Measurements:

Full length = 104 cm

Round waist = 68 cm

Round hips = 94 cm

Hip level = 19 cm

Body rise = 28 cm

Knee length = 58 cm

Belt width = 2 cm

Construction:

1. 0 – 1 = required length + 1 cm – belt width [vertically downwards]
   = 103 cm
2. 0 – 2 = ½ round hips + 4 cm (ease) [horizontally]
   = 51 cm

   Complete the rectangle 0 – 1 – 2 – 3.
3. 0 – 4 = hip level – belt width [vertically downwards on line 0 – 1]
   = 17 cm

   Draw a horizontal line from point 4 to line 2 – 3 and mark as 4_1.
4. 0 – 5 = body rise – belt width [vertically downwards on line 0 – 1]
   = 26 cm

   Draw a horizontal line from point 5 to line 2 – 3 and mark as 5_1.
5. 0 – 6 = knee length – belt width [vertically downwards on line 0 – 1]
   = 56 cm

Draw a horizontal line from point 6 to line 2 – 3 and mark as 6_1.

Back:

6. 2 – 7 = ½ (0 to 2) + 1 cm [horizontally on line 2 – 0]
   = 26.5 cm

   Draw a vertical line downwards from point 7 to line 1 – 3 through lines 4 – 4_1, 5 – 5_1, 6 – 6_1 and mark as:

   4_2 on line 4 – 4_1,

   5_2 on line 5 – 5_1,

   6_2 on line 6 – 6_1, and

   7_1 on line 1 – 3.

   Line 7 – 7_1 divides front and back block to construct trousers.

7. 7 – 8 = 3 cm [horizontally on line 7 – 2]

   Join 8 – 4_2 in a smooth curve to shape side seam at hip level.

8. For Waist:

   8 – 8_1 = 1/4th round waist + 3 cm (dart width) + 1 cm [horizontally on line 8 – 2]
   = 21 cm

9. Waistline:

   8_1 – 9 = 2.5 cm [vertically upwards]

   Join 9 – 8 in a smooth curve for waistline.

10. Crotch Depth:

    5_1 – 10 = 1/10th round hips [horizontally outwards]
    = 9.4 cm

    Join 9 – 4_1 – 10 in a smooth curve using tailors curve for back crotch depth.

11. Hem/bottom:

    7_1 – 11 = ½ round bottom + 1 cm [horizontally on line 7_1 – 3]
    = 21 cm

    Join 10 – 6_1 – 11 in a smooth curve for inside leg length.

12. For Dart:
    (i) Dart position: 9 – N = 8 – N [on line 9 – 8]
    i.e. N is the mid-point of line 9 – 8
    = 10.5 cm
    (ii) Dart length: N – N_1 = 1/12th round hips – 1 cm [vertically downwards]
    = 6.8 cm
    (iii) Dart width: N – S = N – S_1 = 1.5 cm (on either side of point N) [on line 8 – 9]
    Join S – N_1 and S_1 – N_1 in straight lines for the required dart.
13. For Crease Line:
    (i) 7_1 – J = 11 – J [horizontally on line 7_1 – 11]
    i.e. J is the mid-point of line 7_1 – 11
    = 10.5 cm
    (ii) 6_1 – J_1 = 6_2 – J_1 [horizontally on line 6_1 – 6_2]
    i.e. J_1 is the mid-point of line 6_1 – 6_2
    = 13.25 cm
    (iii) Join J – J_1 in a straight line and extend upwards to meet the line 8 – 9 and mark as J_2.
14. For back trousers block cut along the points:
    8 – 4_2 – 5_2 – 6_2 – 7_1 – J – 11 – 6_1 – 10 – 4_1 – 9 – J_2 – N – 8.
    8 – 4_2 – 5_2 – 6_2 – 7_1 is side seams and outside leg length.
    10 – 6_1 – 11 is inside leg length.
    9 – 4_1 – 10 is back crotch depth.
    J_2 – J_1 – J is crease line.
    Cut two pieces of back trousers block to complete the trousers.

Front:

1. 7 – 12 = 3 cm [horizontally on line 7 – 0]
   Join 12 – 4_2 in a smooth curve to shape side seam at hip level.

2. For Waist:

   $12 - 12_1$ = 1/4th round waist – 1 cm [horizontally on line 12 – 0]
   = 16 cm

3. Waistline:

   $12_1 - 13$ = 1 cm [vertically downwards]

   Join 12 – 13 in a smooth curve for waistline.

4. Front Fork:

   5 – 14 = 1/12th round hips – 1 cm [horizontally outwards]
   = 6.8 cm

   Join 13 – 4 – 14 in a smooth curve using tailors curve for front fork.

5. Hem/bottom:

   $7_1 - 15$ = ½ round bottom – 1 cm [horizontally on line $7_1 - 1$]
   = 19 cm

   Join 14 – 6 – 15 in a smooth curve for inside leg length.

6. For Crease Line:

   (i) $7_1 - L = 15 - L$ [horizontally on line $7_1 - 15$]
   i.e. L_1 is the mid-point of line $7_1 - 15$ = 9.5 cm

   (ii) $6_2 - L_1 = 6 - L_1$ [horizontally on line $6_2 - 6$]
   i.e. L_1 is the mid-point of line $6_2 - 6$ = 12.75 cm

   (iii) Join $L - L_1$ in a straight line and extend upwards to meet the line 12 – 13 and mark as L_2.

7. For flat front trousers block cut along the points:

   $12 - 4_2 - 5_2 - 6_2 - 7_1 - L - 15 - 6 - 14 - 4 - 13 - L_2 - 12$.

   $12 - 4_2 - 5_2 - 6_2 - 7_1$ is side seams and outside leg length.

   14 – 6 – 15 is inside leg length.

   13 – 4 – 14 is front fork.

   $L_2 - L_1 - L$ is the crease line.

Cut two pieces of front trousers block to complete the trousers.

Add seam allowance of 1.5 cm (or as required) and hem allowance of 3 cm (or as required) and mark corresponding balance points and grain line on each draft and pattern piece.

Belt:

1. A – B = round waist = 68 cm [horizontally]
2. A – C = 4 cm (with intake) [vertically downwards]

   Complete the rectangle A – B – C – D.
3. For Overlap:

   B – E = D – F = 2.5 cm [horizontally outwards]

   Join E – F in a straight line or in a smooth outward curve for overlap.

   (Use interfacing equal to ½ of belt width to give firmness to the belt.)

Add seam allowance of 1.5 cm (or as required) and put up corresponding balance points and grain line on each draft and pattern piece.

Flat Fronts:

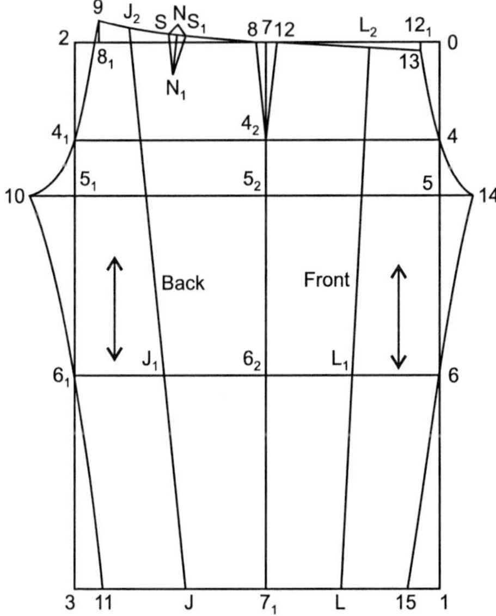

Belt:

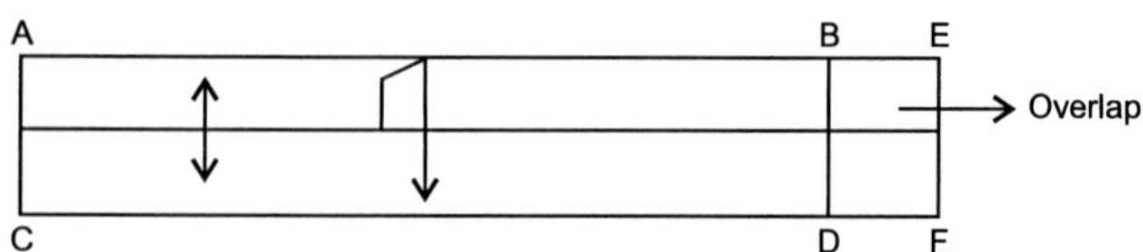

TROUSERS

Basic trousers

Flat fronts

19 PANTS

HAREM PANTS

Full length (waist to ankle) lower garment gathered or pleated at waist and ankle, worn by women and girls. Generally teamed with short waist length tops.

Suitable Fabric: Light weight fabric.

Age Group: Any

Measurements:

Size symbol – 10

Scale – cm

Drafting scale – 1/4th cm or 1/6th cm

Fabric required – 2 m × 1 cm (length × width)

Measurements:

Required length = 104 cm

Round waist = 68 cm

Round hips = 94 cm

Round ankle = 24 cm

Hip level = 20 cm

Round ankle belt width = 2 cm (without intake)

Round Hips:

Number of pleats = 48

Pleat intake = 4 cm

Round Ankle:

Number of pleats = 12

Pleat intake = 2 cm

Yoke:

Required yoke length = hip level – 2 cm [vertically downwards] = 18 cm

Construction:

Yoke:

1. 0 – 1 = 18 cm + 1 cm [vertically downwards] = 19 cm
2. 0 – 2 = 1/4th round hips + 2 cm (ease) [horizontally]
   = 25.5 cm

   Complete the rectangle 0 – 1 – 2 – 3.
3. 0 – 4 = 1/4th round waist + 3 cm [horizontally on line 0 – 2] = 20 cm

Front:

4. Join 3 – 4 in a straight line for front yoke shape.

Back:

5. 4 – 5 = 2.5 cm [vertically upwards]

   Join 3 – 5 in a straight line for back yoke shape.

   Join 5 – 0 in a smooth curve to shape waistline.
6. 0 – 1 is on fold.

   Cut two pieces one for each side.

Pants:

1. 6 – 7 = required length – yoke length + 2 cm (for puffed look) [vertically downwards]
   = 88 cm
2. 6 – 8 = 1/4th round hips + 2 cm (ease) + 1/4th number of pleats × pleat intake [horizontally]
   = 25.5 cm + 48 cm = 73.5 cm
3. 8 – 9 = 1/3rd round hips – yoke length [vertically downwards]
   = 13.3 cm

4. 7 – 10 = ½ round ankle + 1 cm (ease) + ½ number of pleats × pleat intake [horizontally]
 = 13 cm + 12 cm = 25 cm

   Join 9 – 10 in a smooth curve for inside leg length.

5. Harem pants block is along the points:

   6 – 7 – 10 – 9 – 8 – 6,

   where:

   6 – 7 is on fold.

   6 – 8 is round hips with pleats (mark the pleats).

   7 – 10 is round ankle (mark the pleats).

   9 – 10 is inside leg length.

Ankle Belt:

1. 11 – 12 = 2 × 2 cm [vertically downwards]
 = 4 cm
2. 11 – 13 = ½ round ankle + 1 cm (ease) [horizontally]
 = 7 cm

   Complete the rectangle 11 – 12 – 13 – 14.

3. Ankle belt is along the points:

   11 – 12 – 13 – 14.

   11 – 12 is on fold.

   To finish harem pants:

   - Pleat 8 – 6 of pants to 3 – 1 of yoke.
   - Pleat 10 – 7 of pants to 13 – 11 of ankle belt.

Add seam allowance of 1.5 cm (or as required) and nefa allowance of 3 cm (or as required) put up corresponding balance points and grain line on each draft and pattern piece.

Harem Pants:

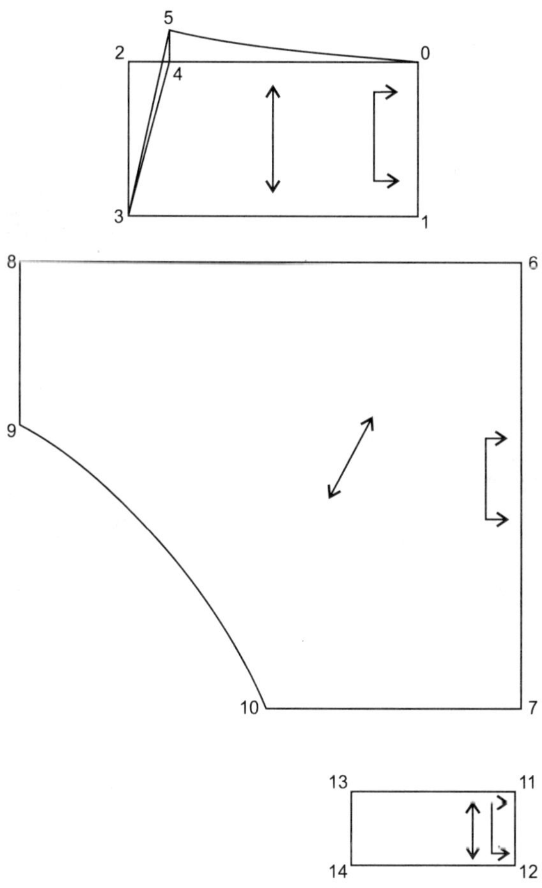

HAREM PANTS & VARIATION

Harem pants

Harem pants with key holes

20 BELL BOTTOMS

BELL BOTTOMS

Lower garment worn by women and girls length from waist to ankle (full length), with separate legs joined at crotch, and waistline darts. Flared at bottom or hem from knee line of the trousers to give a bell like appearance. Generally teamed with short shirt, etc.

Suitable Fabric: Light to heavy fabric.

Age Group: Any

Measurements:

Size symbol – 10

Scale – cm

Drafting scale – 1/4th cm or 1/6th cm

Fabric required – 1.50 m × 90 cm

Measurements:

Required length = 104 cm

Round waist = 68 cm

Round hips = 94 cm

Round knee = 38 cm

Hip level = 20 cm

Body rise = 25 cm

Knee length = 56 cm

Belt width = 2 cm

Construction:

1. 0 – 1 = required length + 1 cm – belt width [vertically downwards]
   = 103 cm
2. 0 – 2 = ½ round hips + 4 cm (ease) [horizontally]
   = 51 cm

   Complete the rectangle 0 – 1 – 2 – 3.
3. Hip Level:

   0 – 4 = hip level – belt width [vertically downwards on line 0 – 1]
   = 18 cm

   Draw a horizontal line from point 4 to line 2 – 3 and mark as 4_1.
4. Body Rise:

   0 – 5 = body rise – belt width [vertically downwards on line 0 – 1]
   = 23 cm

   Draw a horizontal line from point 5 to line 2 – 3 and mark as 5_1.
5. Knee Level:

   0 – 6 = knee length – belt width [vertically downwards on line 0 – 1]
   = 54 cm

   Draw a horizontal line from point 6 to line 2 – 3 and mark as 6_1.

Back:

6. 2 – 7 = ½ (0 – 2) + 1 cm [horizontally on line 2 – 0]
   = 26.5 cm

   Draw a vertical line downwards from point 7 to line 1 – 3 through lines 4 – 4_1, 5 – 5_1, 6 – 6_1 and mark as:

   4_2 on line 4 – 4_1

   5_2 on line 5 – 5_1

   6_2 on line 6 – 6_1, and

   7_1 on line 1 – 3.

7. $7 - 8 = 2$ cm [horizontally on line $7 - 2$]

   Join $8 - 4_2$ in a smooth curve for shaping side seams at hip level.

8. Waistline:

   $8 - 8_1 =$ 1/4th round waist + 3 cm (dart width) + 1 cm [horizontally]
   = 21 cm

9. Shaping Waistline:

   $8_1 - 9 = 2.5$ cm [vertically upwards]

   Join $9 - 8$ in a smooth curve for shaping the waistline.

10. Crotch:

    $5_1 - 10 =$ 1/10th round hips (extend outwards) [horizontally]
    = 9.4 cm

    $10 - 10_1 = 1.5$ cm [vertically downwards]

    Join $9 - 4_1 - 10_1$ in a smooth curve for shaping crotch depth.

11. Knee Level:

    $6_2 - 11 = 2.5$ cm [horizontally on line $6_2 - 6_1$]

    Join $5_2 - 11$ in a straight line.

    Join $11 - 7_1$ in a straight line for bell bottom shape.

12. Round Knee:

    $11 - 11_1 =$ ½ round knee + 1 cm (ease) + 1 cm [horizontally on line $11 - 6_1$]
    = 21 cm

13. Inside Leg Length:

    Join $10_1 - 11_1$ in a smooth curve.

    Join $11_1 - 3$ in a straight line.

14. Dart:

    (i) Dart position: $8 - N = 9 - N$ [on line $8 - 9$] = 10.5 cm

    (ii) Dart length: $N - N_1$ = 1/12th round hips – 1 cm [perpendicular downwards to line $8 - 9$] = 6.8 cm

(iii) Dart width: $N - S = N - S_1$ = 1.5 cm (on either side of point N) [on line 8 – 9]

Join $S - N_1$ and $S_1 - N_1$ in straight lines for the required dart.

15. For back bell bottoms block cut along the points:

    $8 - 4_2 - 5_2 - 11 - 7_1 - 3 - 11_1 - 10_1 - 4_1 - 9 - N - 8$, where:

    $8 - 4_2 - 5_2 - 11 - 7_1$ is outside leg length/outside leg seams.

    $10_1 - 11_1 - 3$ is inside leg length/inside leg seams.

    $9 - 4_1 - 10_1$ is back crotch depth.

    $7_1 - 3$ is hem line for bell bottom.

    Cut two pieces of back block.

Front:

1. 7 – 12 = 2 cm [horizontally on line 7 – 0]

   Join $12 - 4_2$ in a smooth curve to shape side seams at hip level.

2. Waistline:

   $12 - 12_1$ = 1/4th round waist + 3 cm (dart width) – 1 cm [horizontally on line 12 – 0]

   = 19 cm

3. $12_1 - 13$ = 1 cm [vertically downwards]

   Join 12 – 13 in a smooth curve to shape front waistline.

4. Crotch:

   5 – 14 = 1/12th round hips – 1 cm (extend outwards) [horizontally]

   = 6.8 cm

   Join 13 – 4 – 14 in a smooth curve to shape front fork.

5. Knee Level:

   $6_2 - 15$ = 2.5 cm [horizontally on line $6_2 - 6$]

6. Outside Leg Length

   Join $5_2 - 15$ in a straight line.

   Join $15 - 7_1$ in a straight line.

7. Round Knee:

   $15 - 15_1$ = ½ round knee + 1cm (ease) – 1 cm [horizontally on line 15 – 6]

   = 19 cm

8. Inside Leg Length:

   Join $14 - 15_1$ in a smooth curve.

   Join $15_1 - 1$ in a straight line for bell bottom shape.

9. Dart:

   (i) Dart position: 12 – M = 1/12th round hips [on line 12 – 13]

   = 7.8 cm

   (ii) Dart length: $M - M_1$ = 1/12th round hips – 1 cm [perpendicular downwards to line 12 – 13] = 6.8 cm

   (iii) Dart width: $M - P = M - P_1$ = 1.5 cm (on either side of point M) [on line 12 – 13]

   Join $P - M_1$ and $P_1 - M_1$ in straight lines for the required dart.

10. For front bell bottoms block cut along the points:

    $12 - 4_2 - 5_2 - 15 - 7_1 - 1 - 15_1 - 14 - 4 - 13 - M - 12$, where:

    $12 - 4_2 - 5_2 - 15 - 7_1$ is outside leg length/outside leg seams.

    $14 - 15_1 - 1$ is inside leg length/inside leg seams.

    13 – 4 – 14 is front fork.

    $7_1 - 1$ is hem line for bell bottoms.

    Cut two pieces of front block.

Add seam allowance of 1.5 cm (or as required) and hem allowance of 3 cm (or as required) and mark corresponding balance points and grain line on each draft and pattern piece.

Belt:

1. A – B = round waist = 68 cm
2. A – C = 4 cm (with intake)

   Complete the rectangle A – B – C – D.

3. For Overlap: B – E = D – F = 2.5 cm [horizontally outwards]

   Join E – F in a straight line or in a smooth outward curve for overlap.

   (Use interfacing equal to 1/2 of belt width to give firmness to the belt.)

Add seam allowance of 1.5 cm (or as required) and mark corresponding balance points and grain line on each draft and pattern piece.

Bell Bottoms:

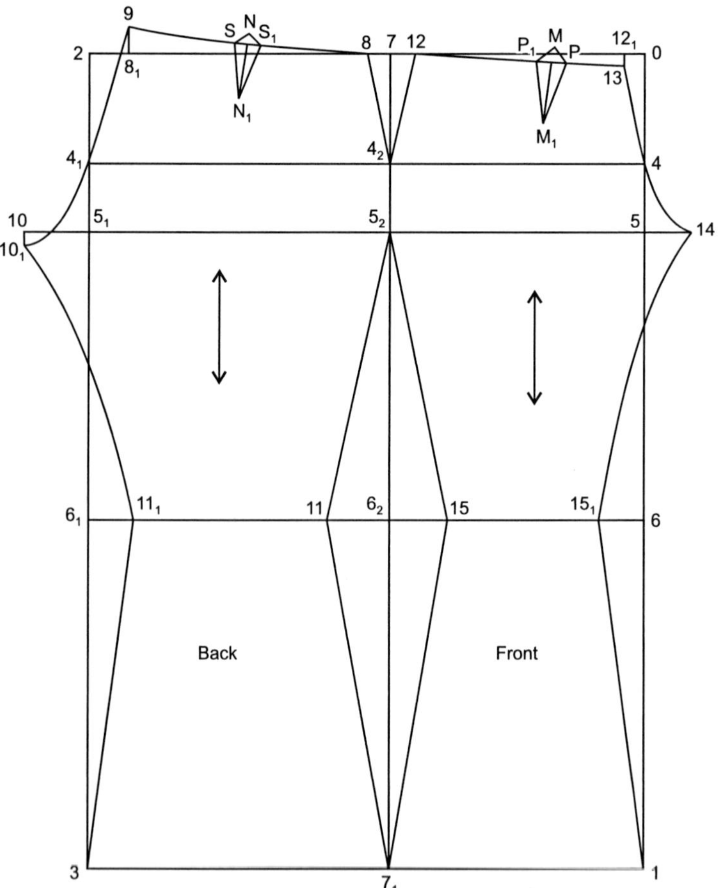

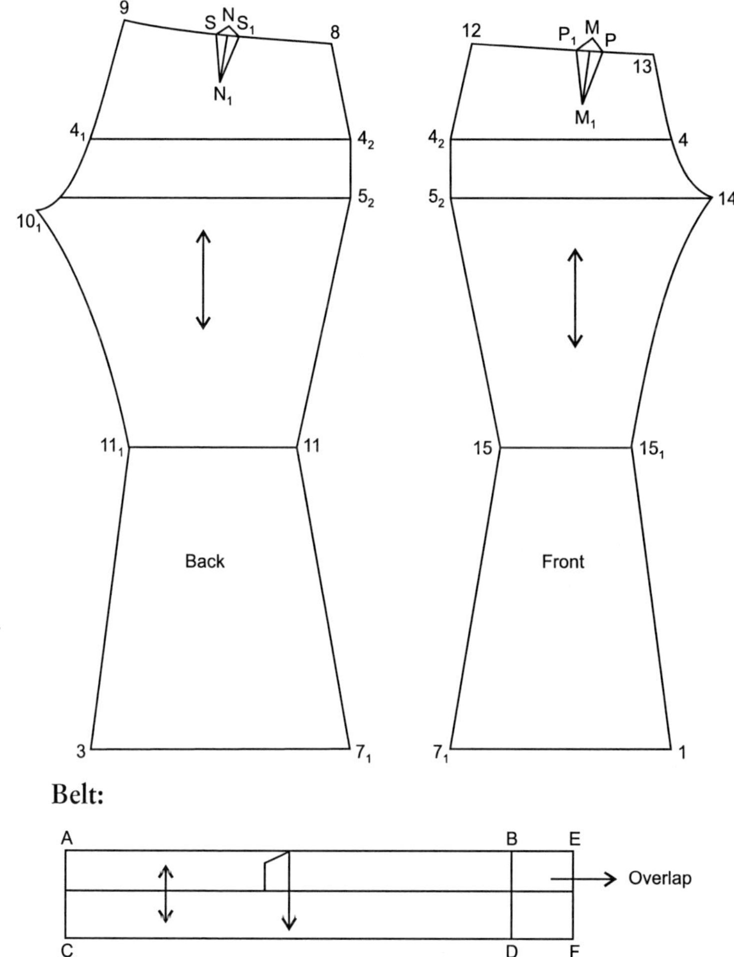

FLARED TROUSERS

Lower garment worn by women and girls length from waist to ankle (full length), with separate legs joined at crotch, and with or without waistline darts. Flared at hem from waist to give A-line appearance. Generally teamed with short shirt, etc.

Suitable Fabric: Cotton, denim, any medium to heavy weight fabric.

Age Group: Any

Size symbol – 10
Scale – cm
Drafting scale – 1/4th cm or 1/6th cm
Fabric required – 2.25 m × 57 cm (length × width)

Measurements:

Required length = 104 cm
Round waist = 72 cm
Round hips = 94 cm
Body rise = 25 cm
Hip level = 20 cm
Belt width = 3 cm

Construction:

1. 0 – 1 = required length + 1 cm – belt width [vertically downwards]
   = 102 cm
2. 0 – 2 = ½ round hips + 4 cm (ease) + 12 cm (flare) [horizontally]
   = 63 cm

   Complete the rectangle 0 – 1 – 2 – 3.
3. Hip Level:

   0 – 4 = hip level – belt width [vertically downwards on line 0 – 1]
   = 17 cm
4. Hip Line:

   Draw a horizontal line from point 4 to line 2 – 3 and mark as 4_1.
5. Body Rise:

   0 – 5 = body rise – belt width [vertically downwards on line 0 – 1]
   = 22 cm

6. Crotch Line:

   Draw a horizontal line from point 5 to line 2 – 3 and mark as 5_1.

7. To divide front and back flared trousers block:

   (i) 2 – 6 = ½ (0 – 2) + 1 cm [horizontally on line 2 – 0]
   = ½ × 63 cm + 1 cm
   = 32.5 cm

   (ii) Draw a vertical line downwards from point 6 to line 3 – 1 through lines 4 – 4_1 and 5 – 5_1 and mark as:

   4_2 on line 4 – 4_1

   5_2 on line 5 – 5_1, and

   6_1 on line 3 – 1.

   Line 6 – 6_1 divides front and back flared trousers block.

Back:

8. 4_1 – 7 = 1/4th round hips + 2 cm (ease) + 1 cm [horizontally on line 4_1 – 4_2]
   = 26.5 cm

9. 2 – 7_1 = 4_1 – 7 [horizontally on line 6 – 2]
   = 26.5 cm

   Join 7 – 7_1 in a straight line.

   Extend line 7 – 7_1 downwards to line 3 – 1 and mark as 7_2.

10. 7_1 – 8 = 2 cm [horizontally on line 7_1 – 2]

11. Join 8 – 7 in a smooth curve for side seams at hip level.

12. Waistline:

    8 – 9 – 1/4th round waist + 3 cm (dart width) [horizontally on line 8 – 2]
    = 20 cm

13. To Shape Waistline:

    $9 - 9_1 = 2.5$ cm [vertically upwards]

    Join $9_1 - 8$ in a smooth curve for waistline.

14. Crotch:

    $5_1 - 10 =$ 1/10th round hips (extend outwards) [horizontally]

    $= 9.4$ cm

    Join $9_1 - 4_1 - 10$ in a smooth curve for back crotch.

15. Inside Leg Seam:

    $3 - 10_1 = 5_1 - 10$ [horizontally]

    $= 9.4$ cm

    Join $10 - 10_1$ in a straight line.

16. For Flare:

    (a) Inside leg seam: Pivot line $10_1 - 10$ at point 10 by 6 cm (or as required) outwards and mark as 11.

    Join 11 – 3 in a smooth curve for hem line.

    (b) Outside leg seam: Pivot line $7_2 - 7$ at point 7 to meet the line $6 - 6_1$ and mark as 12.

    Join $12 - 7_2$ in a smooth curve for shaping hem line.

17. For Dart:

    (i) Dart position: $9 - N = 8 - N$ [on line $9_1 - 8$] $= 10.5$ cm

    i.e. point N is the mid-point of line $9_1 - 8$.

    (ii) Dart length: $N - N_1 =$ 1/12th round hips – 1 cm [perpendicular downwards to line $9_1 - 8$] $= 6.8$ cm

    (iii) Dart width: $N - S = N - S_1 = 1.5$ cm (on either side of point N) [on line $9_1 - 8$]

    Join $S - N_1$ and $S_1 - N_1$ in straight lines for the required dart.

18. For flared trousers back block cut along the points: $8 - 7 - 12 - 7_2 - 3 - 11 - 10 - 4_1 - 9_1 - N - 8$, where:

    $8 - 7 - 12$ is outside leg length/outside leg seam.

    $10 - 11$ is inside leg length/inside leg seam.

    $9_1 - 4_1 - 10$ is back crotch depth.

    $11 - 10_1 - 7_2 - 12$ is hem line.

Front:

1. $4 - 13$ = 1/4th round hips + 2 cm (ease) – 1 cm [horizontally on line $4 - 4_2$]

   = 24.5 cm

2. $0 - 13_1 = 4 - 13$ [horizontally on line $0 - 6$]

   = 24.5 cm

   Join $13 - 13_1$ in a straight line.

   Extend line $13_1 - 13$ downwards to line $1 - 3$ and mark as 13_2.

3. $13_1 - 14$ = 2 cm [horizontally on line $13_1 - 0$]

   Join $14 - 13$ in a smooth curve for side seams at hip level.

4. Waistline:

   $14 - 15$ = 1/4th round waist + 4 cm (dart width) – 1 cm [horizontally on line $14 - 0$]

   = 21 cm

5. Crotch:

   $5 - 16$ = 1/12th round hips (extend outwards) [horizontally]

   = 7.8 cm

   Join $15 - 4 - 16$ in a smooth curve for front crotch.

6. Inside Leg Seam:

   $1 - 16_1 = 5 - 16$ [horizontally]

   = 7.8 cm

   Join $16 - 16_1$ in a straight line.

7. For Flare:
   (a) Inside leg seam: Pivot line 16_1 – 16 at point 16 by 6 cm (or as required) outwards and mark as 17.

   Join 17 – 1 in a smooth curve for shaping hem line.

   (b) Outside leg seam: Pivot line 13_2 – 13 at point 13 to meet point 12.

   Join 12 – 13_2 in a smooth curve for shaping hem line.

8. For Darts:
   (a) First dart:
   (i) Dart position: 15 – M = 1/12th round hips – 2 cm [on line 15 – 14]
   = 5.8 cm
   (ii) Dart length: M – M_1 = 1/12th round hips – 1 cm [perpendicular downwards to line 15 – 14]
   = 6.8 cm
   (iii) Dart width: M – P = M – P_1 = 1 cm (on either side of point M) [on line 15 – 14]

   Join P – M_1 and P_1 – M_1 in straight lines for the required dart.

   (b) Second dart:
   (i) Dart position: M – T = 1/12th round hips – 1 cm [on line 15 – 14]
   = 6.8 cm
   (ii) Dart length: T – T_1 = 1/12th round hips – 1 cm [perpendicular downwards to line 15 – 14]
   = 6.8 cm
   (iii) Dart width: T – Q = T – Q_1 = 1 cm (on either side of point T) [on line 15 – 14]

   Join Q – T_1 and Q_1 – T_1 in straight lines for the required dart.

9. For flared trousers front block cut along the points:

   14 – 13 – 12 – 13_2 – 16_1 – 17 – 16 – 4 – 15 – M – T – 14, where:

   14 – 13 – 12 is outside leg length/outside leg seam.

   16 – 17 is inside leg length/inside leg seam.

   15 – 4 – 16 is front crotch depth.

   17 – 16_1 – 13_2 – 12 is hem line.

Add seam allowance of 1.5 cm (or as required) and hem allowance of 3 cm (or as required) and mark corresponding balance points and grain line on each draft and pattern piece.

Belt:

1. A – B = round waist [horizontally]

   = 72 cm

2. A – C = 4 cm (with intake) [vertically downwards]

   Complete the rectangle A – B – C – D.

3. For Overlap:

   B – E = D – F = 2.5 cm [horizontally outwards]

   Join E – F in a straight line or in a smooth outward curve for overlap.

   (Use interfacing equal to 1/2 of belt width to give firmness to the belt.)

Add seam allowance of 1.5 cm (or as required) and put up corresponding balance points and grain line on each draft and pattern piece.

Flared Trousers:

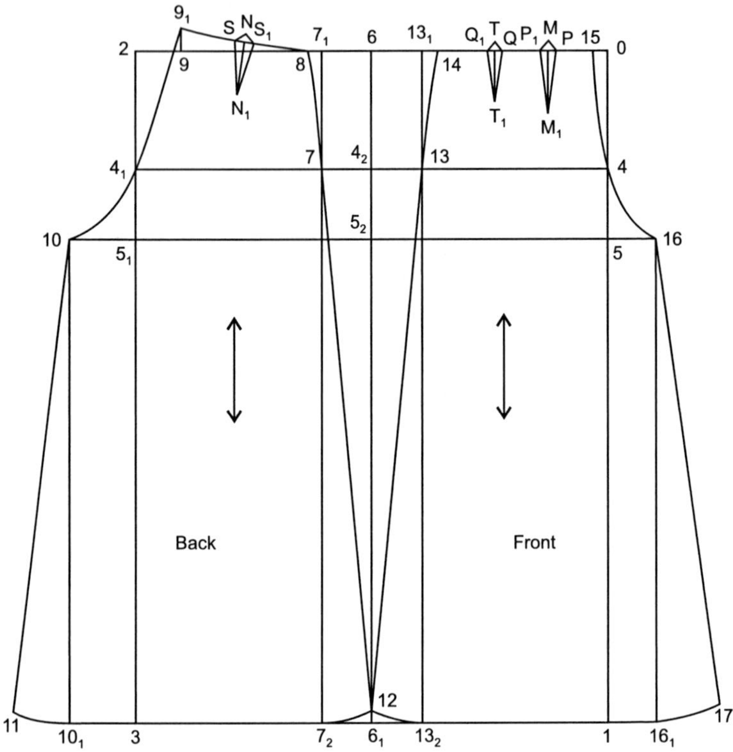

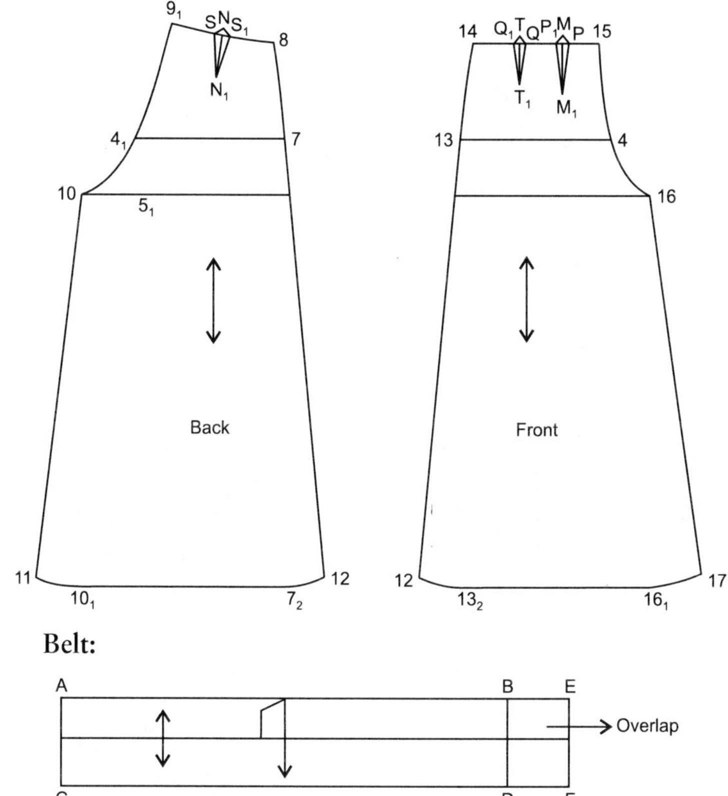

Belt:

BELL BOTTOMS & FLARED TROUSERS

Bell bottoms

Flared trousers

21 CAPRICE AND PEDAL PUSHERS

CAPRICE

Mid calf length lower garment worn by girls and women.

Suitable Fabric: Light to medium weight fabrics.

Age Group: Any

Size symbol – 10

Scale – cm

Drafting scale – 1/4th cm or 1/6th cm

Fabric required – 1.6 m × 90 cm (length × width)

Measurements:

Required length = 76 cm

Round waist = 72 cm (low waist)

Round hips = 94 cm

Round knee = 38 cm

Round bottom/calf muscles = 36 cm

Hip level = 17.3 cm

Body rise = 25 cm

Knee length = 55 cm

Belt width = 2 cm

Construction:

1. 0 – 1 = required length + 1 cm – belt width [vertically downwards]
   = 75 cm

2. $0 - 2$ = ½ round hips + 4 cm (ease) [horizontally]
   = 51 cm

   Complete the rectangle $0 - 1 - 2 - 3$,

   where:

   $2 - 3 = 0 - 1$ [vertically] and

   $1 - 3 = 0 - 2$ [horizontally]

3. $0 - 4$ = hip level – belt width [vertically downwards on line $0 - 1$]
   = 15.3 cm

   Draw a horizontal line from point 4 to line $2 - 3$ and mark as 4_1.

4. $0 - 5$ = body rise – belt width [vertically downwards on line $0 - 1$]
   = 23 cm

   Draw a horizontal line from point 5 to line $2 - 3$ and mark as 5_1.

5. $0 - 6$ = knee length – belt width [vertically downwards on line $0 - 1$]
   = 53 cm

   Draw a horizontal line from point 6 to line $2 - 3$ and mark as 6_1.

Back:

6. $2 - 7$ = ½ $(0 - 2)$ + 1 cm [horizontally on line $2 - 0$]
   = 26.5 cm

   Draw a vertical line downwards from point 7 to line $3 - 1$ through lines $4 - 4_1$, $5 - 5_1$ and $6 - 6_1$ and mark as:

   4_2 on line $4 - 4_1$,

   5_2 on line $5 - 5_1$,

   6_2 on line $6 - 6_1$, and

   7_1 on line $3 - 1$.

7. $7 - 8 = 1.5$ cm [horizontally on line $7 - 2$]

   Join $8 - 4_2$ in a smooth curve for shaping side seams at hip level.

8. For Waist:

   $8 - 8_1$ = 1/4th round waist + 3 cm (dart width) + 1 cm [horizontally on line $8 - 2$]

   = 22 cm

9. Waistline:

   $8_1 - 9 = 2.5$ cm [vertically upwards]

   Join $9 - 8$ in a smooth inward curve for waistline.

10. For Crotch:

    $5_1 - 10$ = 1/10th round hips [horizontally outwards]

    = 9.4 cm

    Join $9 - 4_1 - 10$ in a smooth curve for back crotch.

11. Round Knee:

    $6_2 - 11$ = ½ round knee + 2 cm (ease) + 1 cm [horizontally on line $6_2 - 6_1$]

    = 22 cm

12. Round Bottom/Round Calf Muscles:

    $7_1 - 12$ = ½ round bottom + 2 cm (ease) + 1 cm [horizontally on line $7_1 - 3$]

    = 21 cm

    Join $10 - 11 - 12$ in a smooth curve for inside leg seam.

13. For Dart:

    (i) Dart position: $9 - N = 8 - N$ [on line $9 - 8$] = 11 cm i.e. point N is the mid-point of line $9 - 8$.

    (ii) Dart length. $N - N_1$ - 1/12th round hips – 1 cm [perpendicular downwards to line $9 - 8$] = 6.8 cm

    (iii) Dart width: $N - S = N - S_1 = 1.5$ cm (on either side of point N) [on line $9 - 8$]

Join S – N_1 and S_1 – N_1 in straight lines for the required dart.

14. For back caprice block cut along the points:

    8 – 4_2 – 5_2 – 6_2 – 7_1 – 12 – 11 – 10 – 4_1 – 9 – N – 8,

    where:

    8 – 4_2 – 5_2 – 6_2 – 7_1 is outside leg seam/outside leg length.

    10 – 11 – 12 is inside leg seam/inside leg length.

    9 – 4_1 – 10 is back crotch.

    Cut two pieces of the above block to complete the caprice.

Front:

1. 7 – 13 = 1.5 cm [horizontally on line 7 – 0]
2. 13 – 14 = 1/4th round waist + 2 cm (dart width) – 1 cm [horizontally on line 13 – 0]

   = 19 cm
3. For Crotch:

   5 – 15 = 1/12th round hips [horizontally outwards]

   = 7.8 cm

   Join 14 – 4 – 15 in a smooth curve for front crotch depth.
4. Round Knee:

   6_2 – 16 = ½ round knee + 2 cm (ease) – 1 cm [horizontally on line 6_2 – 6]

   = 20 cm
5. Round Bottom/Calf Muscles:

   7_1 – 17 = ½ round bottom + 2 cm (ease) – 1 cm [horizontally on line 7_1 – 1]

   = 19 cm

   Join 15 – 16 – 17 in a smooth curve for inside leg seam.

6. For Dart:
   (i) Dart position: 14 – M = 1/12th round hips [horizontally on line 14 – 13]
   = 7.8 cm
   (ii) Dart length: M – M_1 = 1/12th round hips – 1 cm [vertically downwards]
   = 6.8 cm
   (iii) Dart width: M – P = M – P_1 = 1 cm (on either side of point M) [horizontally on line 14 – 13]

   Join P – M_1 and P_1 – M_1 in straight lines for the required dart.
7. For front caprice block cut along the points:

   13 – 4_2 – 5_2 – 6_2 – 7_1 – 17 – 16 – 15 – 4 – 14 – M – 13, where:

   13 – 4_2 – 5_2 – 6_2 – 7_1 is outside leg seam/outside leg length.

   15 – 16 – 17 is inside leg seam/inside leg length.

   14 – 4 – 15 is front crotch/fork.

   Cut two pieces of the above block to complete the caprice.

Add seam allowance of 1.5 cm (or as required) and hem allowance of 3 cm (or as required) and mark corresponding balance points and grain line on each draft and pattern piece.

Belt:

1. A – B = round waist [horizontally]
   = 72 cm
2. A – C = 4 cm (with intake) [vertically downwards]

   Complete the rectangle A – B – C – D.
3. For Overlap:

   B – E = D – F = 2.5 cm [horizontally outwards]

   Join E – F in a straight line or in a smooth outward curve for overlap.

(Use interfacing equal to ½ of belt width to give firmness to the belt.)

Add seam allowance of 1.5 cm (or as required) and put up corresponding balance points and grain line on each draft and pattern piece.

Caprice:

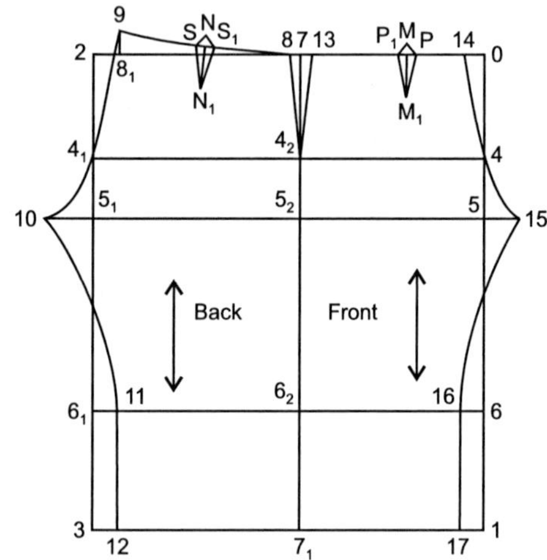

Belt:

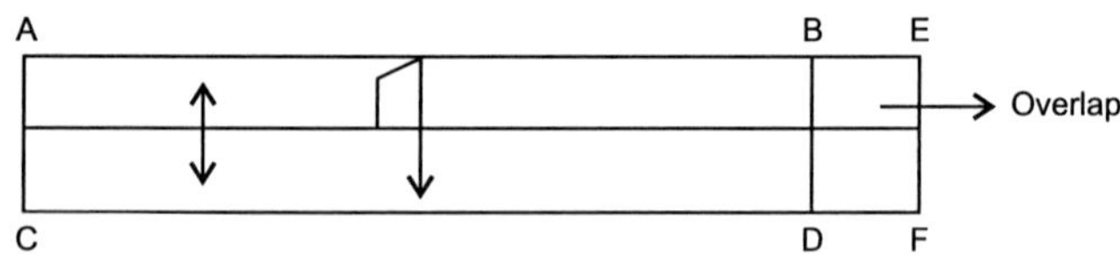

PEDAL PUSHERS

Mid calf length lower garment worn by girls and women, gathered or pleated at mid calf length into a band.

Suitable Fabric: Cotton, medium to heavy weight fabrics.

Age Group: Any

Size symbol – 10

Scale – cm

Drafting scale – 1/4th cm or 1/6th cm

Fabric required – 1.6 m × 90 cm (length × width)

Measurements:

Required length = 76 cm

Round waist = 72 cm (low waist)

Round hips = 94 cm

Round knee = 38 cm

Round bottom/calf muscles = 36 cm

Hip level = 17.3 cm

Body rise = 25 cm

Knee length = 55 cm

Belt width = 2 cm

Construction:

1. 0 – 1 = required length + 1 cm – belt width [vertically downwards]
   = 75 cm
2. 0 – 2 = ½ round hips + 4 cm [horizontally]
   = 51 cm

   Complete the rectangle 0 – 1 – 2 – 3, where:

   2 – 3 = 0 – 1 [vertically] and,

   1 – 3 = 0 – 2 [horizontally]
3. 0 – 4 = hip level – belt width [vertically downwards on line 0 – 1]
   = 15.3 cm

   Draw a horizontal line from point 4 to line 2 – 3 and mark as 4_1.
4. 0 – 5 = body rise – belt width [vertically downwards on line as 0 – 1]
   = 23 cm

   Draw a horizontal line from point 5 to line 2 – 3 and mark as 5_1.
5. 0 – 6 = knee length – belt width [vertically downwards on line 0 – 1]
   = 53 cm

Draw a horizontal line from point 6 to line 2 – 3 and mark as 6_1.

Back:

6. 2 – 7 = ½ (0 – 2) + 1 cm [horizontally on line 2 – 0]
 = 26.5 cm

 Draw a vertical line downwards from point 7 to line 3 – 1 through lines 4 – 4_1, 5 – 5_1 and 6 – 6_1 and mark as:

 4_2 on line 4 – 4_1,

 5_2 on line 5 – 5_1,

 6_2 on line 6 – 6_1, and

 7_1 on line 3 – 1.

7. 7 – 8 = 1.5 cm [horizontally on line 7 – 2]

 Join 8 – 4_2 in a smooth curve for shaping side seams at hip level.

8. For Waist:

 8 – 8_1 = 1/4th round waist + 3 cm (dart width) + 1 cm [horizontally on line 8 – 2]
 = 22 cm

9. Waistline:

 8_1 – 9 = 2.5 cm [vertically upwards]

 Join 9 – 8 in a smooth curve for waistline.

10. For Crotch:

 (i) 5_1 – 10 = 1/10th round hips [horizontally outwards]
 = 9.4 cm

 (ii) 10 – 10_1 = 1 cm [vertically downwards]

 Join 9 – 4_1 – 10_1 in a smooth curve for crotch depth.

11. Round Knee:

 6_2 – 11 = ½ round knee + 3 cm (ease) + 1 cm [horizontally on line 6_2 – 6_1]
 = 23 cm

12. Round Bottom/Calf Muscles:

    $7_1 - 12 = 6_2 - 11$ [horizontally]

    = 23 cm

13. Join $10_1 - 11$ in a smooth curve and 11 – 12 in a straight line for inside leg seam/inside leg length.
14. For Dart:
    (i) Dart position: 9 – N = 8 – N [on line 9 – 8] = 11 cm i.e. point N is the mid-point of line 9 – 8.
    (ii) Dart length: N – N_1 = 1/12th round hips – 1 cm [perpendicular downwards to line 9 – 8] = 7.8 cm
    (iii) Dart width: N – S = N – S_1 = 1.5 cm (on either side of point N) [on line 9 – 8]

    Join S – N_1 and S_1 – N_1 in straight lines for the required dart.
15. For back pedal pushers block cut along the points:

    $8 - 4_2 - 5_2 - 7_1 - 12 - 11 - 10_1 - 4_1 - 9 - N - 8$,

    where:

    $8 - 4_2 - 5_2 - 7_1$ is outside leg seam/outside leg length.

    $10_1 - 11 - 12$ is inside leg seam/inside leg length.

    $9 - 4_1 - 10_1$ is back crotch depth.

    $7_1 - 12$ is the hem of the pedal pushers

Front:

1. 7 – 13 = 1.5 cm [horizontally on line 7 – 0]
2. 13 – 14 = 1/4th round waist + 4 cm (pleats intake) – 1 cm [horizontally on line 13 – 0]

   = 20 cm
3. For Crotch:

   5 – 15 = 1/12th round hips [horizontally out wards]

   = 7.8 cm

   Join 14 – 4 – 15 in a smooth curve for crotch depth.

4. Round Knee:

   $6_2 - 16$ = ½ round knee + 3 cm (ease) – 1 cm [horizontally on line $6_2 - 6$]

   = 21 cm

5. Round Bottom:

   $7_1 - 17 = 6_2 - 16$ [horizontally on line $7_1 - 1$]

   = 21 cm

6. Join 15 – 16 in a smooth curve and join 16 – 17 in a straight line for inside leg seam/inside leg length.

7. For Pleats: Two pleats. Mark the pleat position and pleat intake.

   (a) First pleat:

   (i) Pleat position: 14 – M = 1/12th round hips [horizontally on line 14 – 13]

   = 7.8 cm

   (ii) Pleat intake: $M - M_1$ = 2 cm (towards point 14) [horizontally on line M – 14]

   (b) Second pleat:

   (i) Pleat position: M – P = 5 cm (towards point 13) [horizontally on line M – 13]

   (ii) Pleat intake: $P - P_1$ = 2 cm (towards point M) [horizontally on line P – 14]

8. For front pedal pushers block cut along the points:

   $13 - 4_2 - 5_2 - 7_1 - 17 - 16 - 15 - 4 - 14 - M - P - 13$, where:

   $13 - 4_2 - 5_2 - 7_1$ is outside leg seam/outside leg length.

   15 – 16 – 17 is inside leg seam/inside leg length.

   14 – 4 – 15 is the front crotch/fork.

   $7_1 - 17$ is hem of the front pedal pushers.

9. 12 – 17 is the hem of the pedal pushers which can be finished by gathering or pleating to a band or simply by inserting a draw string.

Add seam allowance of 1.5 cm (or as required) and hem allowance of 3 cm (or as required) and mark corresponding balance points and grain line on each draft and pattern piece.

Band:

1. 18 – 19 = 4 cm [vertically downwards]
2. 18 – 20 = ½ round bottom (calf muscles) + 1 cm (ease)
   = 19 cm

   Complete the rectangle 18 – 19 – 20 – 21.
3. For Overlap: Extend on one side of the band for overlap

   20 – 22 = 2 cm [horizontally outwards]

   21 – 23 = 2 – 4 [horizontally outwards]
   = 2 cm

   Join 23 – 24 in a straight line or in a smooth outward curve.

   Overlapping section can be finished with a Velcro or button as required.
4. 18 – 19 is on fold.

   20 – 21 – 22 – 23 is extra on only one side of the band.

   Cut two pieces of the above block for both the legs.

Add seam allowance of 1.5 cm (or as required) and mark corresponding balance points and grain line on each draft and pattern piece.

Belt:

1. A – B = round waist [horizontally]
   = 72 cm
2. A – C = 4 cm (with intake) [vertically downwards]

   Complete the rectangle A – B – C – D.
3. For Overlap:

   B – E = D – F = 2.5 cm [horizontally outwards]

   Join E – F in a straight line or in a smooth outward curve for overlap.

   (Use interfacing equal to ½ of belt width to give firmness to the belt.)

Add seam allowance of 1.5 cm (or as required) and put up corresponding balance points and grain line on each draft and pattern piece.

Pedal Pushers:

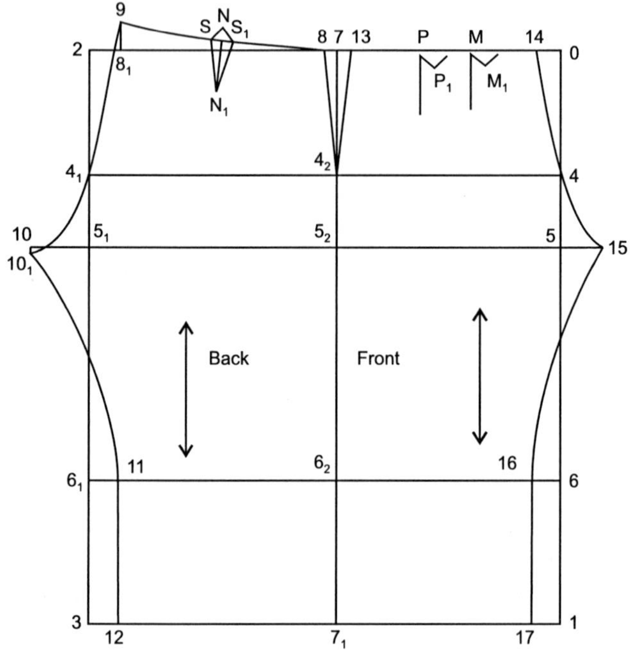

Band:

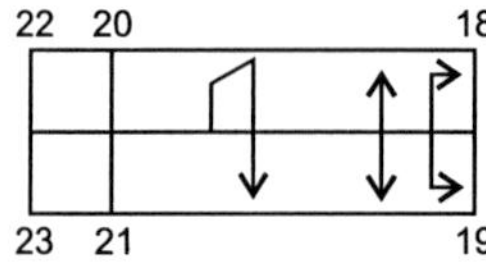

Belt:

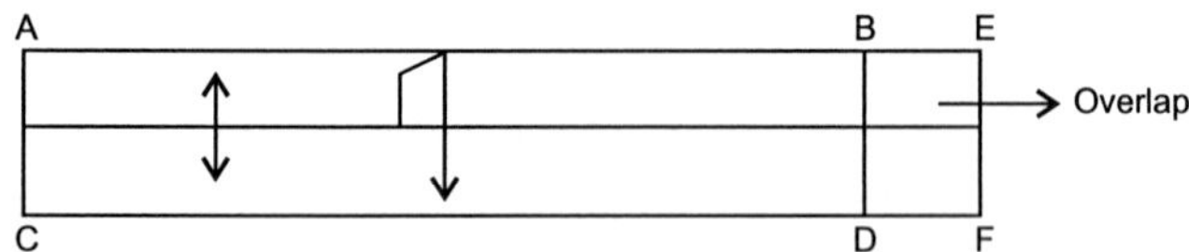

CAPRICE & PEDAL PUSHERS

Caprice

Pedal pushers

22 CULOTTES AND KNICKERS

CULOTTES

A women's knee to mid-calf length lower garment comparable to trousers but cut with full legs to resemble a skirt.

Suitable Fabric: Light to medium weight fabric.

Age Group: Any

Size symbol – 10

Scale – cm

Drafting scale – 1/4th cm or 1/6th cm

Fabric required – 1.5 m × 1 m (length × width)

Measurements:

Required length = 62 cm

Round waist = 68 cm

Round hips = 94 cm

Hip level = 20.3 cm

Body rise = 28 cm

Number of pleats = 16

Pleat intake = 6 cm

Belt width = 2 cm

Construction:

1. 0 – 1 = required length + 1 cm – belt width [vertically downwards]
   = 61 cm

2. 0 – 2 = 2 (1/4th round waist + 1/4th number of pleats × pleat intake) [horizontally]
   = 2 (17 cm + 24 cm)
   = 82 cm

   Complete the rectangle 0 – 1 – 2 – 3,

   where:

   2 – 3 = 0 – 1 [vertically] and

   1 – 3 = 0 – 2 [horizontally]

3. 0 – 4 = hip level – belt width [vertically downwards on line 0 – 1]
   = 18.3 cm

   Draw a horizontal line from point 4 to line 2 – 3 and mark as 4_1.

4. 0 – 5 = body rise + 3 cm – belt width [vertically downwards on line 0 – 1]
   = 29 cm

   Draw a horizontal line from point 5 to line 2 – 3 and mark as 5_1.

5. 2 – 6 = ½ (0 – 2) [horizontally]
   = 41 cm

   Draw a line vertically downwards from point 6 to line 1 – 3 through lines 4 – 4_1 and 5 – 5_1 and mark as:

   4_2 on line 4 – 4_1,

   5_2 on line 5 – 5_1, and

   6_1 on line 3 – 1.

Back:

6. For Waistline:

   2 – 7 = 2.5 cm [vertically upwards]

   Join 7 – 6 in a smooth curve for waistline.

7. For Crotch:

   5_1 – 8 = 1/10th round hips (extend outwards) [horizontally]
   = 9.4 cm

8 – 9 = 1 cm [vertically downwards]

Join 7 – 4_1 – 9 in a smooth curve for back crotch.

8. Join 9 – 3 in a straight line for inside leg seam.
9. For Pleats: Divide 7 – 6 into five equal parts and mark as A, B, C, D, i.e. 7 – A = A – B = B – C = C – D = D – 6 = 8.2 cm
   (i) First pleat: A – A_1 = A – A_2 = 3 cm (on either side of point A) [on line 7 – 6]

   A_1 – A_2 is the required pleat intake.

   (ii) Second pleat: B – B_1 = B – B_2 = 3 cm (on either side of point B) [on line 7 – 6]

   B_1 – B_2 is the required pleat intake.

   (iii) Third pleat: C – C_1 = C – C_2 = 3 cm (on either side of point C) [on line 7 – 6]

   C_1 – C_2 is the required pleat intake.

   (iv) Fourth pleat: D – D_1 = D – D_2 = 3 cm (on either side of point D) [on line 7 – 6]

   D_1 – D_2 is the required pleat intake.
10. Back culottes block is along the points:

    6 – 6_1 – 3 – 9 – 4_1 – 7 – A_1 – B_1 – C_1 – D_1 – 6.

Front:

1. For Crotch: 5 – 10 = 1/12th round hips (extend outwards) [horizontally]

   = 7.8 cm

   Join 0 – 4 – 10 in a smooth curve for front crotch.
2. Join 10 – 1 in a straight line for inside leg seam.
3. For Pleats: Divide 6 – 0 into five equal parts and mark as E, F, G, H, i.e. 6 – E = E – F = F – G = G – H = H – 0 = 8.2 cm
   (i) First pleat: E – E_1 = E – E_2 = 3 cm (on either side of point E) [on line 6 – 0]

   E_1 – E_2 is the required pleat intake.

   (ii) Second pleat: F – F_1 = F – F_2 = 3 cm (on either side of point F) [on line 6 – 0]

   F_1 – F_2 is the required pleat intake.

(iii) Third pleat: $G - G_1 = G - G_2 = 3$ cm (on either side of point G) [on line 6 – 0]

$G_1 - G_2$ is the required pleat intake.

(iv) Fourth pleat: $H - H_1 = H - H_2 = 3$ cm (on either side of point H) [on line 6 – 0]

$H_1 - H_2$ is the required pleat intake.

4. Front culottes block is along the points:

   $6 - 6_1 - 1 - 10 - 4 - 0 - H_1 - G_1 - F_1 - E_1 - 6$.

5. For culottes block cut along the points:

   $0 - 4 - 10 - 1 - 3 - 9 - 4_1 - 7 - A_1 - B_1 - C_1 - D_1 - 6 - E_1 - F_1 - G_1 - H_1 - O$, where:

   0 – 4 – 10 is front crotch.

   10 – 1 is inside leg seam.

   1 – 3 is hem line of the culottes.

   $7 - 4_1 - 9$ is back crotch.

   9 – 3 is inside leg seam.

Add seam allowance of 1.5 cm (or as required) and hem allowance of 3 cm (or as required) and mark corresponding balance points and grain line on each draft and pattern piece.

Belt:

1. A – B = round waist [horizontally]

   = 68 cm

2. A – C = 4 cm (with intake) [vertically downwards]

   Complete the rectangle A – B – C – D.

3. For Overlap:

   B – E = D – F = 2.5 cm [horizontally outwards]

   Join E – F in a straight line or in a smooth outward curve for overlap.

   (Use interfacing equal to ½ of belt width to give firmness to the belt.)

Add seam allowance of 1.5 cm (or as required) and put up corresponding balance points and grain line on each draft and pattern piece.

Culottes:

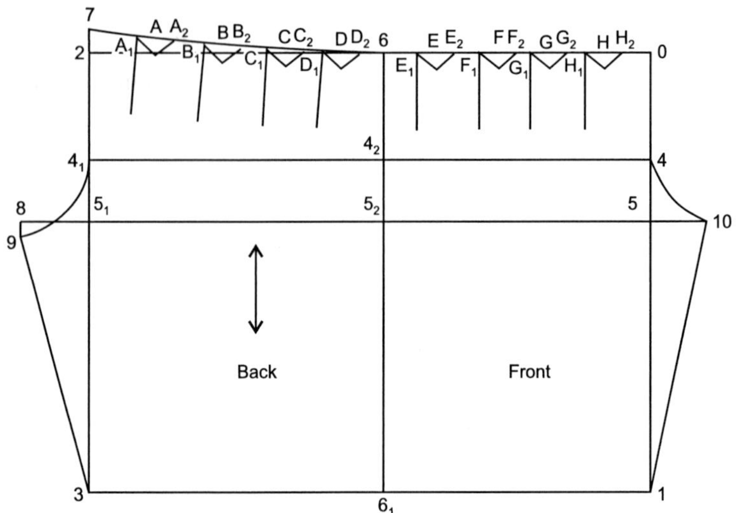

Belt:

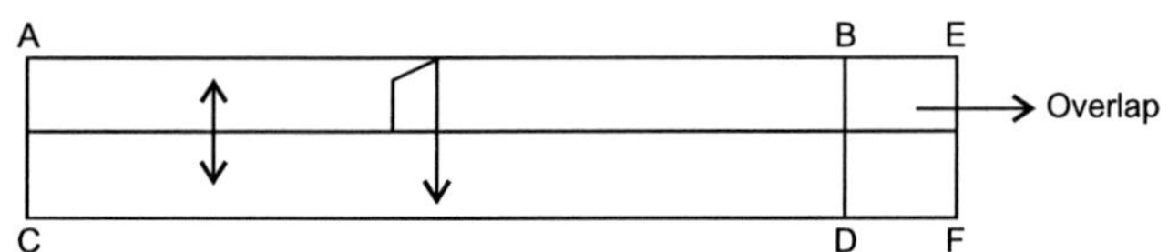

KNICKERS

Two legged outer garment that reaches knee from waist.

Suitable Fabric: Light to heavy fabric.

Age Group: Any

Size symbol – 10

Scale – cm

Drafting scale – 1/4th cm

Fabric required – 1.10 m × 1 m (length × width)

Measurements:

Required length (waist to knee) = 50 cm

Round waist = 75 cm

Round hips = 90 cm

Body rise = 25 cm

Hip level = 15 cm

Round knee = 42.5 cm

Belt width = 2.5 cm

Construction:

1. 0 – 1 = required length + 1.5 cm – belt width [vertically downwards]
   = 49 cm
2. 0 – 2 = ½ round hips + 5 cm (ease) [horizontally]
   = 50 cm

   Complete the rectangle 0 – 1 – 2 – 3.
3. 0 – 4 = hip level – belt width [vertically downwards]
   = 13 cm

   Draw a horizontal line from point 4 to line 2 – 3 and mark as 5.
4. 0 – 6 = body rise – belt width [vertically downwards]
   = 23 cm

   Draw a horizontal line from point 6 to line 2 – 3 and mark as 7.
5. 2 – 8 = ½ (2 to 0) – 1 cm [horizontally for dividing front and back block]
   = 24 cm

   Draw a vertical line downwards from point 8 to line 1 – 3 through line 4 – 5 and line 6 – 7 and mark as:

   9 on line 4 - 5.

   10 on line 6 – 7.

   11 on line 1 – 3.

   Line 8 – 9 is dividing front and back block.

Front:

6. 8 – 12 = 1.5 cm [horizontally inwards on line 8 – 2]

   Join 9 – 12 in a smooth outward curve.

   12 – 9 – 10 – 11 is outside leg length/side seam.

7. For Waistline:

   12 –13 = 1/4th round waist + 2.5 cm (dart width) – 1 cm [horizontally]

   = 20.25 cm

   Draw a vertical line downwards from point 13 to line 7 – 6 through line 5 – 4 and mark as 14 on line 5 – 4 and 15 on line 7 – 6.

8. For Shaping Front Waistline:

   13 – 16 = 1.5 cm [vertically downwards on line 13 – 15]

   Join 16 – 12 in a smooth inward curve for front waistline.

9. For Crotch Depth:

   7 – 17 = 1/12th round hips [extend horizontally outwards from point 7]

   = 7.5 cm

   Join 17 – 14 – 16 in a smooth inward curve for front crotch depth.

10. For Round Knee:

    11 – 18 = ½ round knee + 2.5 cm (ease) – 1 cm [horizontally on line 11 – 3]

    = 22.75 cm

    Join 18 – 17 in a smooth inward curve for inside leg length/inside leg seam.

11. For Dart:

    (i) Dart position: 13 – N = 1/12th round hips [on line 16 – 12]

    = 7.5 cm

    (ii) Dart length: N – O = 1/12th round hips [vertically downwards]

    = 7.5 cm

    (iii) Dart width: N – R = N – R_1 = 1.25 cm on (either side of point N)

    Join R – O and R_1 – O in straight lines for the required dart.

12. For knickers front block cut through the points:
    12 – 9 – 10 – 11 – 18 – 17 – 14 – 16 – N – 12.
    Cut two pieces of the above block to complete the knickers.

Back:

1. 8 – 19 = 1.5 cm [horizontally inwards on line 8 – 0]
   Join 9 – 19 in a smooth outward curve.
   19 – 9 – 10 – 11 is the outside leg length/side seam.
2. For Waistline:
   19 – 20 = 1/4th round waist + 2.5 cm (dart) + 1 cm [horizontally on line 8 – 0]
   = 22.25 cm
3. 20 – 21 = 1.5 cm [vertically upwards]
   Join 19 – 21 in a smooth inward curve to shape the waistline.
4. For Crotch Depth:
   (i) Draw a vertical line downwards from point 20 to line 6 – 7 through line 4 – 5 and mark as:
   22 on line 4 – 5 and
   23 on line 6 – 7.
   (ii) 6 – 24 = 1/10th round hips [extend horizontally outwards from point 6]
   = 9 cm
   (iii) 24 – 25 = 1.5 cm [vertically downwards]
   Join 25 – 22 – 21 in a smooth inward curve for crotch depth.
5. Inside Leg Length:
   11 – 26 = ½ round knee + 2.5 cm (ease) + 1 cm [horizontally on line 11 – 1]
   = 24.75 cm
   Join 26 – 25 in a smooth inward curve for inside leg length/inside leg seam.

6. For Darts:
   (i) Dart position: Divide 19 – 21 into two equal parts and mark as M.
   (ii) Dart length: M – P = 1/12th round hips – 0.5 cm = 7 cm

   Draw M – P perpendicular to line 19 – 21.
   (iii) Dart width: M – S = M – S_1 = 1.25 cm (on either side of point M)

   Join S – P and S_1 – P in straight lines for the required dart.
7. For knickers back block cut through:

   19 – 9 – 10 – 11 – 26 – 25 – 22 – 21 – M – 19.

   Cut two pieces of the above block to complete the knickers.

Add seam allowance of 1.5 cm (or as required) and hem allowance of 3 cm (or as required) and put up corresponding balance points and grain line on each pattern piece.

Belt:

1. A – B = round waist [horizontally]

   = 75 cm
2. A – C = 4 cm (with intake) [vertically downwards]

   Complete the rectangle A – B – C – D.
3. For Overlap: B – E = D – F = 2.5 cm [horizontally outwards]

   Join E – F in a straight line or in a smooth outward curve for overlap.

   (Use interfacing equal to ½ of belt width to give firmness to the belt.)

Add seam allowance of 1.5 cm (or as required) and mark corresponding balance points and grain line on each draft and pattern piece.

Knickers:

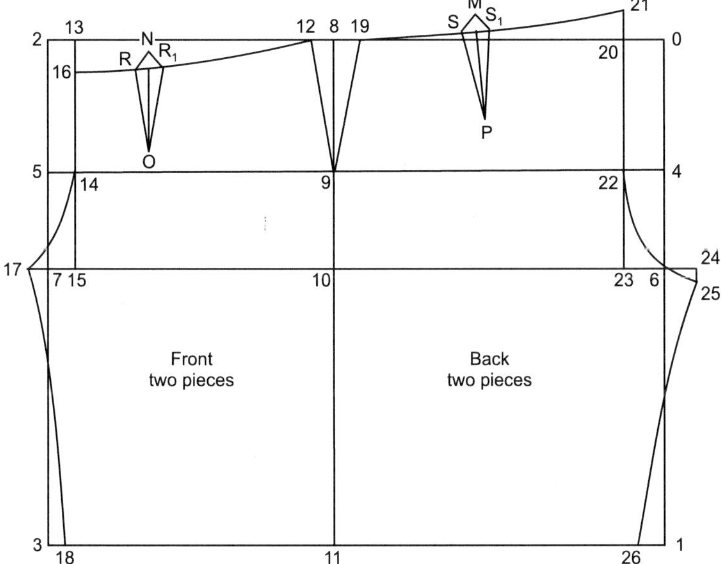

Belt:

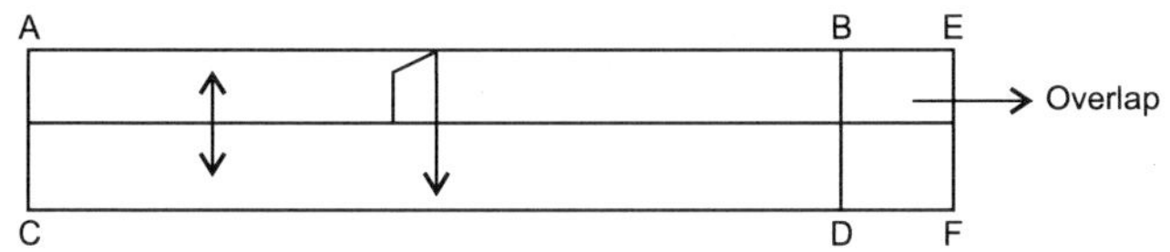

KNICKERS & CULOTTES

Knickers Culottes

23 PETTICOAT FOR SAREE

PETTICOAT FOR SAREE

Petticoat: A loose light weight inner garment in the form of a skirt generally worn by women and girls, on which a saree or skirt is draped.

4-gored Skirt/Petticoat

4-gored skirt is a 4-vertical paneled conical shaped lower inner garment generally worn by women and girls, on which a saree is draped. A draw string is used in its belt which allows fitting at waist and flare at hem.

Suitable Fabric: Light weight fabric.

Age Group: 13 yrs. and above (this construction method is suitable for the given age group).

Size symbol – 10

Scale – cm

Drafting scale – 1/4th cm or 1/6th cm

Required fabric – 2.1m × 90 cm (length × width)

Measurements:

Required length (waist to ankle) = 104 cm

Round waist = 68 cm

Round hips = 94 cm

Hip level = 21 cm

Belt width = 2 cm

Construction:

1. 0 – 1 = required length + 1 cm – belt width [vertically downwards]

   = 103 cm

2. Hip Level:

   0 – 2 = hip level – belt width [vertically downwards on line 0 – 1]

   = 19 cm

3. Hip Line:

   2 – 3 = 1/4th round hips + 4 cm (ease or as required) [horizontally]

   = 27.5 cm

4. Waistline:

   0 – 4 = 1/4th round waist + 3 cm (dart) + 2 cm (ease) [horizontally]

   = 22 cm

5. To Shape Waistline:

   4 – 5 = 2.5 cm [vertically upwards]

   Join 5 – 0 in a smooth curve for waistline.

6. Side Seams:

   Join 5 – 3 in a straight line and extend downwards and mark as 6, where:

   5 – 6 = 0 – 1 [downwards]

   = 103 cm

   Join 6 – 1 in a smooth curve for hem line.

7. Dart:

   (i) Dart position: 0 – N = 1/12th round hips [on line 0 – 5]

   = 7.8 cm

   (ii) Dart length: N – N_1 = 1/10th round hips [perpendicular to line 0 – 5]

   = 9.4 cm

(iii) Dart width: $N - S = N - S_1 = 1.5$ cm (on either side of point N) [on line 0 – 5]

Join $S - N_1$ and $S_1 - N_1$ in straight lines for the required dart.

8. 4-gored skirt block is along the points:

   0 – 1 – 6 – 3 – 5 – N – 0.

   Cut four pieces of the obtained pattern to complete the 4-gored skirt/petticoat.

   5 – 3 – 6 is side seam.

   0 – 1 is the central seam for front and back.

Add seam allowance of 1.5 cm (or as required) and hem allowance of 3 cm (or as required) and mark corresponding balance points and grain line on each draft and pattern piece.

Belt:

1. A – B = belt width [vertically downwards]

   = 4 cm (with intake)

2. A – C = 4 × (waistline – dart width) [horizontally]

   = 4 × (22 – 3)

   = 76 cm

   Complete the rectangle A – B – C – D.

Add seam allowance of 1.5 cm (or as required) and put up corresponding balance points and grain line on each draft and pattern piece.

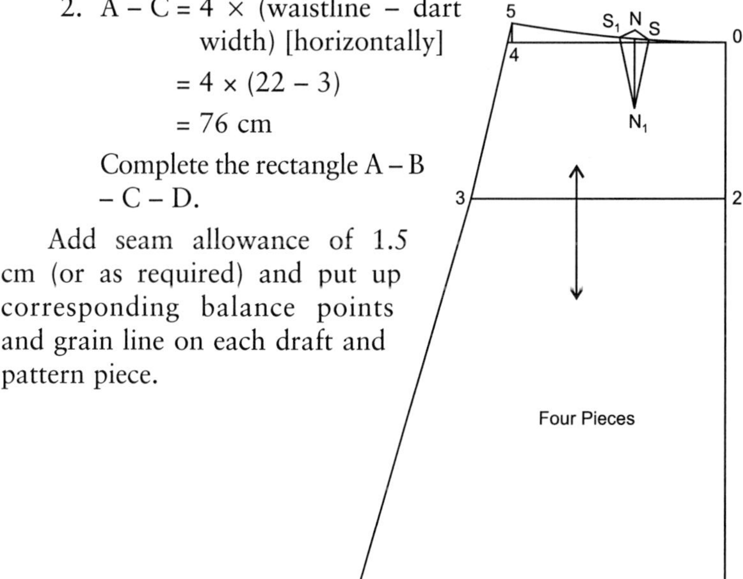

Belt:

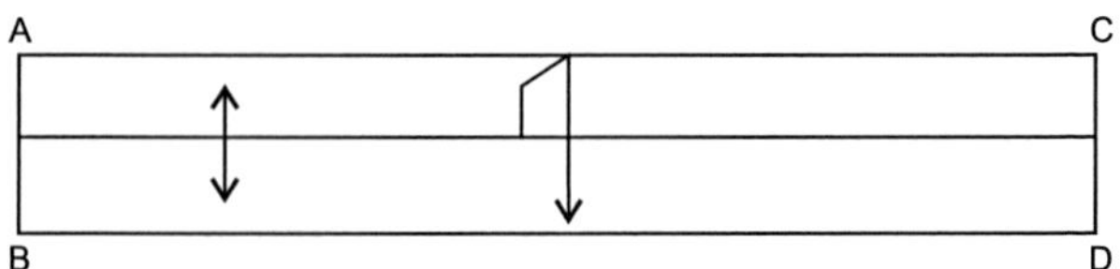

6-gored Skirt/Petticoat

6-gored skirt is a 6-vertical paneled conical shaped lower inner garment generally worn by women and girls, on which is a saree is draped. A draw string is used in its belt which allows fitting at waist and flare at hem. A 6-gored skirt has more flare at hem than 4-gored skirt.

Suitable Fabric: Light weight fabric.

Age Group: 13 yrs. and above. (this construction method is suitable for the given age group)

Size symbol – 10

Scale – cm

Drafting scale – 1/4th cm or 1/6th cm

Required fabric – 2.1 m × 90 cm (length × width)

Measurements:

Required length (waist to ankle) = 104 cm

Round waist = 68 cm

Round hips = 94 cm

Hip level = 21 cm

Belt width = 2 cm

Construction:

1. 0 – 1 = required length + 1 cm – belt width [vertically downwards]
   = 103 cm
2. Hip Level:
   0 – 2 = hip level – belt width [vertically downwards on line 0 – 1]
   = 19 cm

3. Hip Line:

   2 – 3 = 1/4th round hips + 4 cm (ease or as required) [horizontally]

   = 27.5 cm

4. Waistline:

   0 – 4 = 1/4th round waist + 3 cm (dart) + 1 cm (ease) [horizontally]

   = 21 cm

5. To Shape Waistline:

   4 – 5 = 2.5 cm [vertically upwards]

   Join 5 – 0 in a smooth curve for waistline.

6. Join 5 – 3 in a straight line and extend downwards and mark as 6, where:

   5 – 6 = 0 – 1

   = 103 cm

7. Hem Line:

   Join 6 – 1 in a smooth curve for hem line.

8. Central Gore:

   (i) 0 – 7 = 1/3rd (0 – 5) [on line 0 – 5]

   = 8 cm

   (ii) 2 – 8 = 1/3rd (2 – 3) [on line 2 – 3]

   = 9.17 cm

   Join 7 – 8 in a straight line and extend downwards to meet the line 1 – 6 and mark as 9.

   (iii) 7 – N = 1.5 cm [on line 7 – 0]

   Join N – 8 in a straight line.

   (iv) Central Gore (central panel) is along the points:

   0 – 1 – 9 – 8 – N – 0.

   Cut two pieces of central panel: one front and one back.

   0 – 1 is on fold.

   N – 8 – 9 is central side seam.

9. Side Panels:
   (i) $7 - N_1 = 1.5$ cm [on line 7 – 5]
   Join $N_1 - 8$ in a straight line.
   (ii) Side panel is along the points:
   $N_1 - 8 - 9 - 6 - 3 - 5 - N_1$.

   Cut four pieces of side panels to complete the 6-gored skirt/petticoat.

   5 – 3 – 6 is side seam.

Add seam allowance of 1.5 cm (or as required) and hem allowance of 3 cm (or as required) and mark corresponding balance points and grain line on each draft and pattern piece.

Belt:

1. A – B = 4 × (waistline – dart width) [horizontally]
   = 76 cm
2. A – C = 4 cm (with intake) [vertically downwards]
   Complete the rectangle A – B – C – D.

Add seam allowance of 1.5 cm (or as required) and put up corresponding balance points and grain line on each draft and pattern piece.

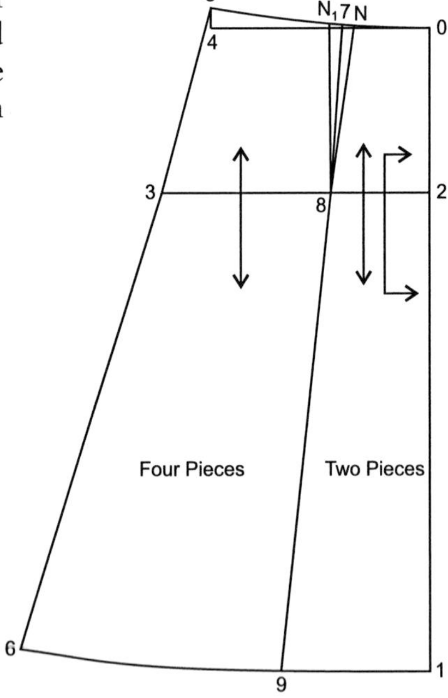

Belt:

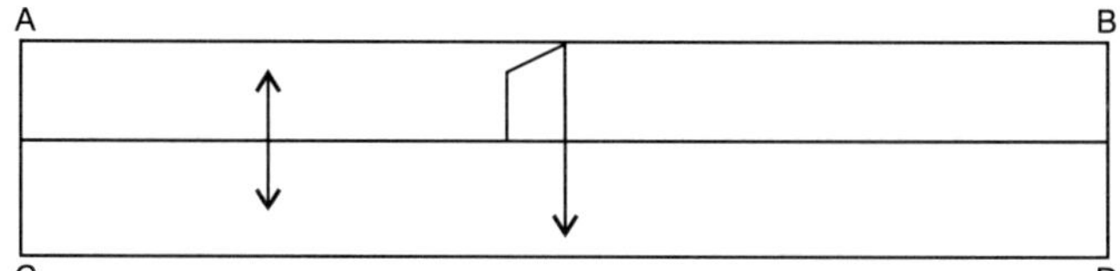

PETTICOAT

4-gored petticoat

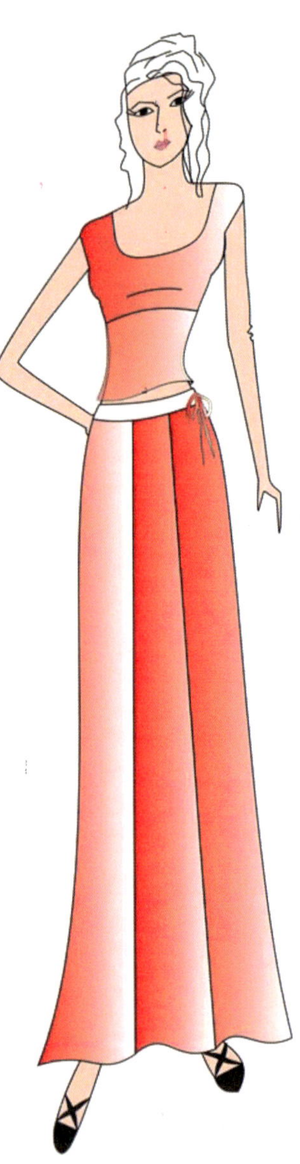

6-gored petticoat

24 CONSTRUCTION OF SAREE BLOUSES

PLAIN SAREE BLOUSE

Saree Blouse: A saree blouse is a fitting upper garment that ends right below the busts with short or long sleeves and is teamed up with a saree or ghagra-odhani, etc.

Note: Dart intake is based on cup size.

Suitable Fabric: Any light weight fabric.

Size Symbol: Any (B-cup size). This construction is suitable for the given cup size. For any other cup size the dart width should be changed accordingly.

Size symbol – 10

Scale – cm

Drafting scale – 1/4th cm

Fabric required – 1 m × 90 cm (length × width)

Measurements:

Required length = 32 cm

Round bust = 88 cm

Round waist (empire waist) = 72 cm

Across shoulder = 35 cm

Highest bust level = 25 cm

Sleeve:

Sleeve length = 23 cm

Round sleeve = 24 cm

Construction:

Back:

1. 0 – 1 = full length + 1 cm [vertically downwards]
   = 33 cm
2. Armhole Depth:
   0 – 2 = 1/4th round bust – 4 cm [vertically downwards on line 0 – 1]
   = 18 cm
3. Bust Line:
   2 – 3 = 1/4th round bust + 2 cm (ease) [horizontal]
   = 24 cm
4. Waistline:
   1 – 4 = 1/4th round waist + 3 cm (dart width) [horizontal]
   = 21 cm

   Join 4 – 3 in a straight line for side seam.
5. Shoulder:
   0 – 5 = ½ across shoulder + 1 cm [horizontal]
   = 18.5 cm

   Draw a vertical line downwards from point 5 to line 2 – 3 and mark as 6.
6. Neckline:
   0 – 7 = 1 /12th round bust (or as required) [horizontal]
   = 7.3 cm

   0 – 8 = 1.5 cm (or as required for depth) [vertically downwards]

   Join 7 – 8 in a smooth curve for neckline.
7. Shoulder Line:
   5 – 9 = 2 cm [vertically downwards]

   Join 7 – 9 in a straight line for shoulder.
8. Armhole:
   9 – 10 = 10 – 6 [vertically]

   i.e. 10 is the mid-point of 9 – 6.

   Join 9 – 10 – 3 in a smooth curve for armhole.

9. For Darts:

   (a) Waistline dart:

   (i) Dart position: $1 - N$ = 1/12th round bust
   = 7.3 cm

   (ii) Dart length: $N - N_1$ = 1/12th round bust [vertically upwards]
   = 7.3 cm

   (iii) Dart width: $N - S = N - S_1$ = 1.5 cm (on either side of point N) [horizontally]

   Join $S - N_1$ and $S_1 - N_1$ in straight lines for the required waistline dart.

10. For back plain saree blouse block cut along the points:

    8 – 1 – N – 4 – 3 – 10 – 9 – 7 – 8, where:

    3 – 4 is side seam.

    8 – 1 is on fold.

Front:

1. $0_f - 1_f$ = required length + 1 cm + 2 cm (dart width) [vertically downwards]
   = 35 cm

2. Armhole Depth:

   $0_f - 2_f$ = 1/4th round bust – 2.5 cm [vertically downwards on line $0_f - 1_f$]
   = 19.5 cm

3. Bust Line:

   $2_f - 3_f$ = 1/4th round bust + 1 cm (dart width) + 2 cm (ease) [horizontally]
   = 25 cm

4. Waistline:

   $1_f - 4_f$ = 1/4th round waist + 3 cm (dart width) [horizontally]
   = 21 cm

   Join $4_f - 3_f$ in a straight line for side seam.

5. Shoulder:

   $0_f - 5_f$ = ½ across shoulder + 1 cm [horizontally]
   = 18.5 cm

   Draw a vertical line downwards from point 5_f to line $2_f - 3_f$ and mark as 6_f.

6. Neckline:

   $0_f - 7_f$ = 0 – 7 (of back block) [horizontally]
   = 7.3 cm

   $0_f - 8_f$ = 1/12th round neck + 3 cm (or as required for depth) [vertically downwards]
   = 10.3 cm

   Join $7_f - 8_f$ in a smooth curve for scoop neck or in a straight line for deep V-neck.

7. Shoulder Line:

   $5_f - 9_f$ = 2 cm (shoulder drop according to shoulder type) [vertically downwards]

   Join $7_f - 9_f$ in straight line for shoulder.

8. Armhole:

   $6_f - 10_f$ = 3.5 cm [vertically upwards on line $6_f - 9_f$]

   Join $9_f - 10_f - 3_f$ in a smooth curve for armhole.

9. For Darts:

   0_f – A = highest bust level [vertically downwards on line $0_f - 1_f$]
   = 25 cm

   A – B = 1/12th round bust [horizontally]
   = 7.3 cm

   (a) Waistline dart:

   (i) Dart position: 1_f – M = 1/12th round bust [horizontally on line $1_f - 4_f$]
   = 7.3 cm

   (ii) Dart length: B – M_1 = 1.5 cm [vertically downwards on line B – M]

$M - M_1$ is the required dart length for the waistline dart.

(iii) Dart width: $M - P = M - P_1 = 1.5$ cm (on either side of point M) [horizontally]

Join $P - M_1$ and $P_1 - M_1$ in straight lines for the required waist line dart.

(b) Side seam dart:

(i) Dart position: $3_f - T$ = 1/6th round bust – 1.5 cm [downwards on line $3_f - 4_f$]
= 13 cm

(ii) Dart length: $B - T_1 = 2$ cm [on line B – T]

$T - T_1$ is the required dart length for the side seam dart.

(iii) Dart width: $T - Q = T - Q_1 = 1.25$ cm (on either side of point T) [on line $4_f - 3_f$]

Join $Q - T_1$ and $Q_1 - T_1$ in straight lines for the required side seam dart.

(c) Armhole dart:

(i) Dart position: Point 10_f is the position for armhole dart.

(ii) Dart length: $B - J = 2$ cm [on line $B - 10_f$]

$10_f - J$ is the required dart length for the armhole dart.

(iii) Dart width: $10_f - R = 10_f - R_1 = 1$ cm (on either side of point 10_f) [on line $3_f - 9_f$]

Join $R - J$ and $R_1 - J$ in straight lines for the required armhole dart.

(d) Center front dart:

(i) Dart position: Point A is the position for center front dart.

(ii) Dart length: $B - A_1 = 2$ cm [horizontal on line B – A]

$A - A_1$ is the required dart length for center front dart.

(iii) Dart width: $A - K = A - K_1 = 1$ cm [vertically on line $0_f - 1_f$]

Join $K - A_1$ and $K_1 - A_1$ in straight lines for the required center front dart.

10. For front saree blouse cut along the points:

$8_f - A - 1_f - M - 4_f - T - 3_f - 10_f - 9_f - 7_f - 8_f$, where:

$3_f - T - 4_f$ is side seams.

$8_f - A - 1_f$ is center front and should be finished with a placket.

Cut two pieces of the front saree blouse block to complete the saree blouse.

Add seam allowance 1.5 cm (or as required) and mark corresponding balance points and grain line on each draft and pattern piece.

Sleeve

Sleeve length = 23 cm

Round bust = 88 cm

Round sleeve = 24 cm

Sleeve:

1. Sleeve Length:

$0 - 1$ = sleeve length + 1 cm [vertically downwards]

= 24 cm

2. Crown Height:

$0 - 2$ = 1/12th round bust + 2 cm [vertically downwards on line $0 - 1$]

= 9.3 cm

3. Crown Width:

$2 - 3$ = 1/4th round bust – 5 cm [horizontally]

= 17 cm

4. Top Arm:

   1 – 4 = ½ round sleeve [horizontally]

   = 12 cm

5. To Shape Sleeve Crown:

   0 – 5 = 2 cm [horizontally]

   Join 3 – 5 in a straight line.

6. Divide 3 – 5 into four equal parts and mark as 6, 7, 8.

   (i) $6 - 6_1$ = 0.6 cm [perpendicular downwards to the line 3 – 5]

   (ii) $7 - 7_1$ = 1.25 cm [perpendicular upwards to the line 3 – 5]

   (iii) $8 - 8_1$ = 0.6 cm [perpendicular upwards to the line 3 – 5]

7. For Back Sleeve Crown:

   Join $5 - 7_1 - 6 - 3$ in a smooth 'S' shape.

8. For Front Sleeve Crown:

   Join $5 - 8_1 - 7 - 6_1 - 3$ in a smooth 'S' shape.

Add seam allowance of 1.5 cm (or as required) and hem allowance of 3 cm (or as required) and put up corresponding balance points and grain line on each pattern piece.

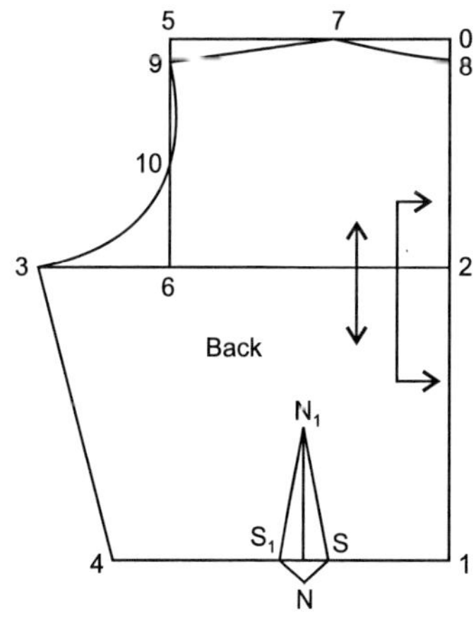

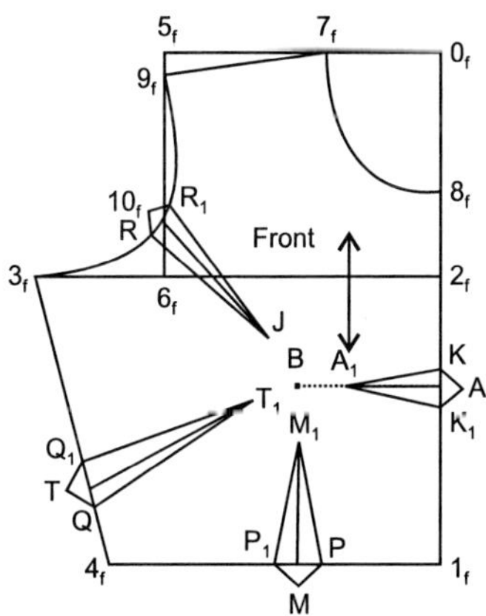

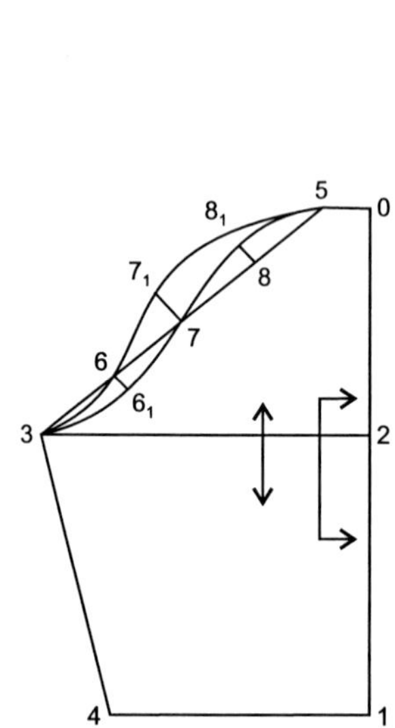

SLEEVELESS SAREE BLOUSE

Saree Blouse: A sleeveless saree blouse is a fitting upper garment that ends right below the busts and is teamed up with a saree or ghagra-odhani, etc.

Suitable Fabric: Any light weight fabric.

Size Symbol: Any (B-cup size). This construction is suitable for the given size symbol. For any other cup size the dart width should be changed accordingly.

Size symbol – 10

Scale – cm

Drafting scale – 1/4th cm

Fabric required – 80 cm × 90 cm (length × width)

Measurements:

Required length = 32 cm

Round bust = 88 cm

Round waist (empire waist) = 72 cm

Across shoulder = 35 cm

Highest bust level = 25 cm

Construction:

Back:

1. 0 – 1 = required length + 1 cm [vertically downwards]
   = 33 cm
2. Armhole Depth:
   0 – 2 = 1/4th round bust – 4 cm [vertically downwards on line 0 – 1]
   = 18 cm
3. Bust Line:
   2 – 3 = 1/4th round bust + 2 cm (ease) [horizontally]
   = 24 cm
4. Waistline:
   1 – 4 = 1/4th round waist + 3 cm (dart width) [horizontally]
   = 21 cm

   Join 3 – 4 in a straight line for side seam.
5. Shoulder:
   0 – 5 = ½ across shoulder [horizontally]
   = 17.5 cm

   Draw a vertical line downwards from point 5 to line 2 – 3 and mark as 6.
6. Neckline:
   0 – 7 = 1/12th round bust + 2 cm (or as required) [horizontally on line 0 – 5]
   = 9.3 cm

   0 – 8 = 1.5 cm (or as required for depth) [vertically downwards]

   Join 7 – 8 in a smooth curve for neck line.
7. Shoulder Line:
   5 – 9 = 1.5 cm (shoulder drop according to shoulder type) [vertically downwards]

   Join 9 – 7 in a straight line for shoulder.

8. Armhole:

   9 – 10 = 6 – 10 [vertically]

   i.e. point 10 is the mid-point of line 9 – 6

   = 8.25 cm

   Join 9 – 10 – 3 in a smooth curve for back armhole.

9. For Dart: waistline dart.

   (i) Dart position: 1 – N = 1/12th round bust [horizontally]

   = 7.3 cm

   (ii) Dart length: $N - N_1$ = 1/12th round bust – 1 cm [vertically upwards]

   = 6.3 cm

   (iii) Dart width: $N - S = N - S_1$ = 1.5 cm (on either side of point N) [horizontally]

   Join $S - N_1$ and $S_1 - N_1$ in straight lines for the required waistline dart.

10. Back sleeveless saree blouse cut along the points:

    8 – 1 – N – 4 – 3 – 10 – 9 – 7 – 8,

    where:

    8 – 1 is on fold.

    3 – 4 is side seams.

Front:

1. $0_f - 1_f$ = required length + 1 cm + 3 cm (dart width) [vertically downwards]

   = 36 cm

2. Armhole Depth:

   $0_f - 2_f$ = 1/4th round bust – 2.5 cm [vertically downwards on line $0_f - 1_f$]

   = 19.5 cm

3. Bust Line:

   $2_f - 3_f$ = 1/4th round bust + 1 cm (dart width) + 2 cm (ease) [horizontally]

   = 25 cm

4. Waistline:

   $1_f - 4_f$ = 1/4th round waist + 3 cm (dart width) [horizontally]

   = 21 cm

   Join $3_f - 4_f$ in a straight line for side seams.

5. Shoulder:

   $0_f - 5_f$ = ½ across shoulder [horizontally]

   = 17.5 cm

   Draw a vertical line downwards from point 5_f to line $2_f - 3_f$ and mark as 6_f.

6. Neckline:

   $0_f - 7_f$ = 0 – 7 (of back saree blouse) [horizontally]

   = 9.3 cm

   $0_f - 8_f$ = 1/12th round bust + 4 cm (or as required for depth) [vertically downwards]

   = 11.3 cm

   Join $7_f - 8_f$ in a smooth curve for deep and wide scoop neckline for front.

7. Shoulder Line:

   $5_f - 9_f$ = 1.5 cm (shoulder drop according to shoulder type) [vertically downwards]

   Join $9_f - 7_f$ in a straight line for shoulder.

8. Armhole:

   $6_f - 10_f$ = 3.5 cm [vertically upwards on line $6_f - 9_f$]

   Join $9_f - 10_f - 3_f$ in a smooth curve for front armhole.

9. For Darts:

   0_f – A = highest bust level [vertically downwards]

   = 25 cm

   A – B = 1/12th round bust [horizontally]

   = 7.3 cm

(a) Waistline dart:

(i) Dart position: $1_f - M$ = 1/12th round bust [horizontally]
= 7.3 cm

(ii) Dart length: $B - M_1$ = 2 cm [vertically downwards on line B – M]

$M - M_1$ is the required dart length for the waistline dart.

(iii) Dart width: $M - P = M - P_1$ = 1.5 cm (on either side of point M) [horizontally]

Join $P - M_1$ and $P_1 - M_1$ in straight lines for the required waistline dart.

(b) Side seam dart:

(i) Dart position: $3_f - T$ = 1/6th round bust – 1.5 cm [downwards on line $3_f - 4_f$]
= 13 cm

(ii) Dart length: $B - T_1$ = 2 cm [on line B – T]

$T - T_1$ is the required length for side seam dart.

(iii) Dart width: $T - Q = T - Q_1$ = 1.25 cm (either side of point T) [on line $4_f - 3_f$]

Join $Q - T_1$ and $Q_1 - T_1$ in straight lines for the required side seam dart.

(c) Armhole dart:

(i) Dart position: Point 10_f is the position for armhole dart.

(ii) Dart length: $B - J$ = 2 cm [on line $B - 10_f$]

$10_f - J$ is the required length for armhole dart.

(iii) Dart width: $10_f - R = 10_f - R_1$ = 1 cm (on either side of point 10_f) [on line $3_f - 9_f$]

Join $R - J$ and $R_1 - J$ in straight lines for the required armhole dart.

(d) Center front dart:

(i) Dart position: Point A is the position for center front dart.

(ii) Dart length: $B - A_1 = 1.5$ cm [horizontally on line $B - A_1$]

$A - A_1$ is the required dart length for the center front dart.

(iii) Dart width: $A - K = A - K_1 = 1.5$ cm (on either side of point A) [vertically on line $0_f - 1_f$]

Join $K - A_1$ and $K_1 - A_1$ in straight lines for the required center front dart.

10. For front sleeveless saree blouse cut along the points:

$8_f - A - 1_f - M - 4_f - T - 3_f - 10_f - 9_f - 7_f - 8_f$, where:

$3_f - T - 4_f$ is side seams.

$8_f - A - 1_f$ is center front.

Cut two pieces of front sleeveless saree blouse to complete the saree blouse.

Add seam allowance of 1.5 cm and put up corresponding balance points and grain line on each pattern piece.

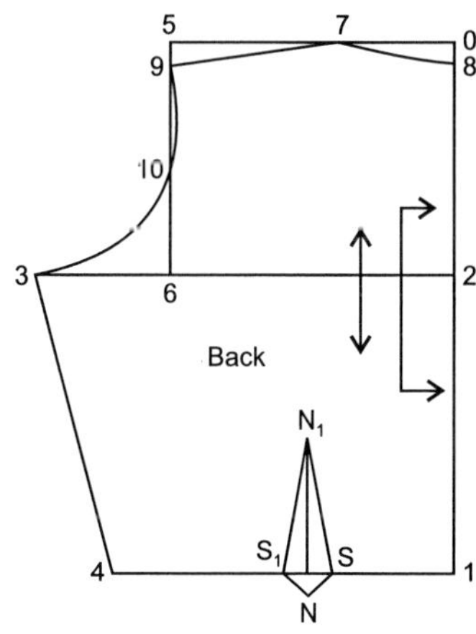

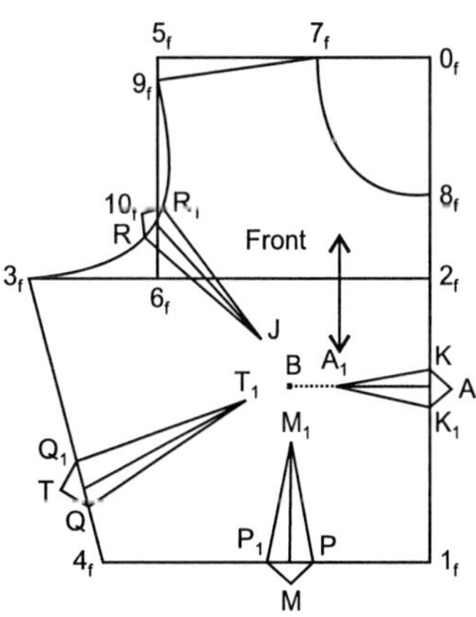

PLEATED SLEEVELESS SAREE BLOUSE

A pleated sleeveless saree blouse is a fitting upper garment that ends right below the busts and is teamed up with a saree or ghagra-odhani, etc. In this blouse pleats substitute the darts.

Suitable Fabric: Any light weight fabric.

Size Symbol: Any (B-cup size). This construction is suitable for the given size symbol. In this blouse darts are replaced by pleats.

Size symbol – 10

Scale – cm

Drafting scale – 1/4th cm

Fabric required – 80 cm × 90 cm (length × width)

Measurements:

Required length = 36 cm

Round bust = 88 cm

Round waist (empire waist) = 72 cm

Highest bust level = 25 cm
Across shoulder = 35 cm

Construction:

Back:

1. 0 – 1 = required length + 1 cm [vertically downwards]
   = 33 cm
2. Armhole Depth:
   0 – 2 = 1/4th round bust – 4 cm [vertically downwards on line 0 – 1]
   = 18 cm
3. Bust Line:
   2 – 3 = 1/4th round bust + 2 cm (ease) [horizontally]
   = 24 cm
4. Waistline:
   1 – 4 = 1/4th round waist + 3 cm (dart width) [horizontally]
   = 21 cm

   Join 3 – 4 in a straight line for side seams.
5. Shoulder:
   0 – 5 = ½ across shoulder [horizontally]
   = 17.5 cm

   Draw a vertical line downwards from point 5 to line 2 – 3 and mark as 6.
6. Neckline:
   0 – 7 = 1/12th round bust + 2 cm (or as required) [horizontally on line 0 – 5]
   = 9.3 cm

   0 – 8 = 8 cm (or as required for depth) [vertically downwards on line 0 – 1]

   Join 7 – 8 in a smooth curve for back neckline.
7. Shoulder Line:
   5 – 9 = 1.5 cm (shoulder drop) [vertically downwards on line 5 – 6]

   Join 9 – 7 in a straight line for the shoulder.

8. Armhole:

   9 – 10 = 6 – 10 [vertically]

   i.e. point 10 is the mid-point of line 9 – 6

   = 8.25 cm

   Join 9 – 10 – 3 in a smooth curve for armhole.

9. For Dart: waistline dart.

   (i) Dart position: 1 – N = 1/12th round bust [horizontally]

   = 7.3 cm

   (ii) Dart length: N – N_1 = 1/12th round bust – 1 cm [vertically upwards]

   = 6.3 cm

   (iii) Dart width: S – N = S_1 – N = 1.5 cm (on either side of point N) [horizontally on line 1 – 4]

   Join S – N_1 and S_1 – N_1 in straight lines for the required waistline dart.

10. For back blouse block cut along the points:

    8 – 1 – N – 4 – 3 – 10 – 9 – 7 – 8,

    where:

    8 – 1 is on fold.

    3 – 4 is side seams.

    7 – 8 is neck line.

Font:

1. 0_f – 1_f = required length + 1 cm + 3 cm (pleats intake) [vertically downwards]

   = 36 cm

2. Armhole Depth:

   0_f – 2_f = 1/4th round bust – 2.5 cm [vertically downwards on line 0_f – 1_f]

   = 19.5 cm

3. Bust Line:

   2_f – 3_f = 1/4th round bust + 2 cm (ease) [horizontally]

   = 24 cm

4. Waistline:

   $1_f - 4_f$ = 1/4th round waist + 3 cm (pleats intake) [horizontally]

   = 21 cm

   Join $3_f - 4_f$ in a straight line for side seams.

5. Shoulder:

   $0_f - 5_f$ = ½ across shoulder [horizontally]

   = 17.5 cm

   Draw a vertical line downwards from point 5_f to line $2_f - 3_f$ and mark as 6_f.

6. Neckline:

   $0_f - 7_f$ = 0 – 7 (of back block) [horizontally]

   = 9.3 cm

   $0_f - 8_f$ = 1/12th round bust + 4 cm (or as required for depth) [vertically downwards]

   = 11.3 cm

   Join $7_f - 8_f$ in a smooth curve for deep and wide scoop neck for front.

7. Shoulder Line:

   $5_f - 9_f$ = 1.5 cm (shoulder drop according to shoulder type) [vertically downwards]

   Join $9_f - 7_f$ in a straight line for shoulder.

8. Armhole:

   $6_f - 10_f$ = 3.5 cm [vertically upwards on line $6_f - 9_f$]

   Join $9_f - 10_f - 3_f$ in a smooth curve for armhole.

9. For Pleats: Mark the pleat position and pleat intake for every pleat.

   (a) Waistline pleats: (three pleats)

   First pleat:

   (i) Pleat position: 1_f – M = 1/12th round bust – 1.5 cm [horizontally on line $1_f - 4_f$]

   = 5.8 cm

(ii) Pleat intake: $M - M_1$ = 1 cm [horizontally on line $M - 4_f$]

Second pleat:

(i) Pleat position: $M_1 - P$ = 0.6 cm [horizontally on line $M_1 - 4_f$]

(ii) Pleat intake: $P - P_1$ = 1 cm [horizontally on line $P - 4_f$]

Third pleat:

(i) Pleat position: $P_1 - R$ = 0.6 cm [horizontally on line $P_1 - 4_f$]

(ii) Pleat intake: $R - R_1$ = 1 cm [horizontally on line $R - 4_f$]

(b) Armhole pleats: (two pleats)

First pleat:

(i) Pleat position: $10_f - T$ = 0.6 cm [on line $10_f - 3_f$]

(ii) Pleat intake: $T - T_1$ = 1 cm [on line $T - 3_f$]

Second pleat:

(i) Pleat position: $10_f - G$ = 1.6 cm [on line $T_1 - 9_f$]

(ii) Pleat intake: $G - G_1$ = 1 cm [on line $G - 3_f$]

(c) Center front pleats:

First pleat:

(i) Pleat position: $0_f - A$ = highest bust level – 1.25 cm [vertically downwards]
= 23.75 cm

(ii) Pleat intake: $A - A_1$ = 1 cm [vertically downwards on line $A - 1_f$]

Second pleat:

(i) Pleat position: $A_1 - D$ = 0.6 cm [vertically downwards on line $A_1 - 1_f$]

(ii) Pleat intake: $D - D_1$ = 1 cm [vertically downwards on line $D - 1_f$]

10. $4_f - 11_f$ = 3 cm [upwards on line $4_f - 3_f$]

Join 11_f – R_1 in a smooth curve to shape the waistline.

11. For front pleated sleeveless blouse cut along the points:

    8_f – A – D – 1_f – M – P – R – 11_f – 3_f – T – 10_f – G – 9_f – 7_f – 8_f, where:

    3_f – 11_f is side seams.

    8_f – A – B – 1_f is center front and should be finished with placket and dress hooks or as required.

    Cut two pieces of front blouse block to complete the pleated sleeveless saree blouse.

Add seam allowance 1.5 cm (or as required) and put up corresponding balance points and grain line on each pattern piece.

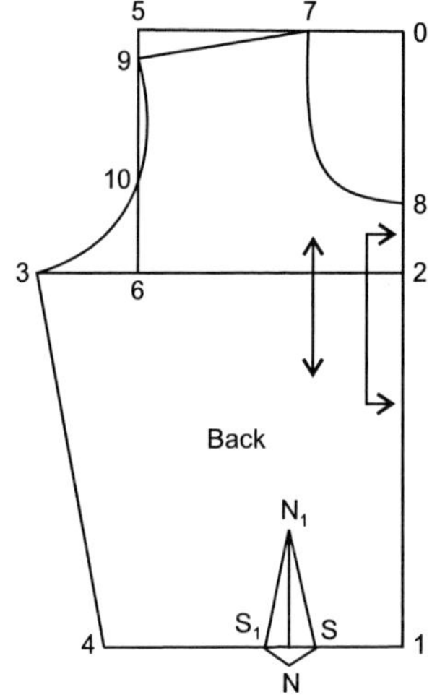

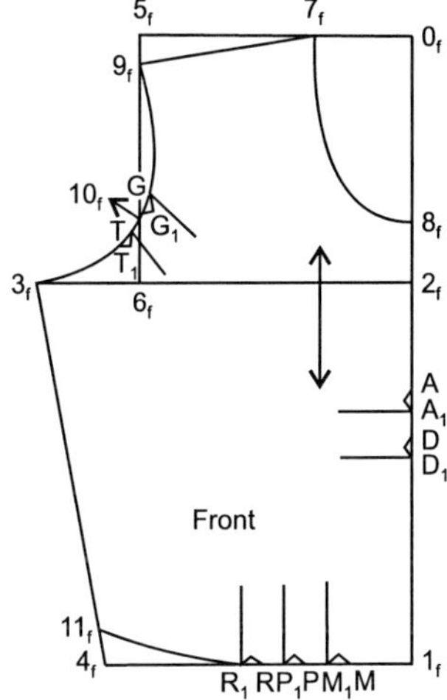

25 KATORI CHOLI

KATORI CHOLI 1

A small blouse that ends right below the busts and has a very good fitting and front section of blouse is cut in two sections and then stitched. Generally teamed with saree or ghagra, etc.

Suitable Fabric: Any light weight fabric.

Size Symbol: Any (B-cup size). This construction is suitable for the given size symbol. For any other cup size the dart width should be changed accordingly.

Size symbol – 10

Scale – cm

Drafting scale – 1/4th cm

Fabric required – 1 m × 90 cm (length × width)

Measurements:

Required length = 32 cm

Round bust = 88 cm

Round waist = 72 cm

Highest bust level = 25 cm

Across shoulder = 35 cm

Base band width = 2 cm

Sleeve:

Sleeve length = 22 cm

Round sleeve = 24 cm

Construction:

Back:

1. 0 – 1 = required length + 1 cm [vertically downwards]
   = 33 cm
2. Armhole Depth:
   0 – 2 = 1/4th round bust – 4 cm [vertically downwards]
   = 18 cm
3. Bust Line:
   2 – 3 = 1/4th round bust + 2 cm (ease) [horizontally]
   = 24 cm
4. Waistline:
   1 – 4 = 1/4th round waist + 3 cm (dart width) [horizontally]
   = 21 cm

   Join 3 – 4 in a straight line for side seams.
5. Shoulder:
   0 – 5 = ½ across shoulder + 1 cm [horizontally]
   = 18.5 cm

   Draw a vertical line downwards from point 5 to line 2 – 3 and mark as 6.
6. Neckline:
   0 – 7 = 1/12th round bust + 2 cm [horizontally on line 0 – 5]
   = 9.3 cm

   0 – 8 = 1.5 cm (or as required for depth) [vertically downwards]

   Join 7 – 8 in a smooth curve for neckline.
7. Shoulder Line:
   5 – 9 = 1.5 cm (shoulder drop according to shoulder type) [vertically downwards]

   Join 9 – 7 in a straight line for shoulder.

8. Armhole:
   $9 - 10 = 6 - 10$ [vertically]
   $= 8.25$ cm
   i.e. point 10 is the mid-point of line $9 - 6$.
   Join $9 - 10 - 3$ in a smooth curve for armhole.
9. For Dart: waistline dart.
   (i) Dart position: $1 - N =$ 1/12th round bust [horizontally on line $1 - 4$]
   $= 7.3$ cm
   (ii) Dart length: $N - N_1 =$ 1/12th round bust $- 1$ cm [vertically upwards]
   $= 6.3$ cm
   (iii) Dart width: $N - S = N - S_1 = 1.5$ cm (on either side of point N) [horizontally on line $1 - 4$]
   Join $S - N_1$ and $S_1 - N_1$ in straight lines for the required waistline dart.
10. For back blouse cut along the points:
   $8 - 1 - N - 4 - 3 - 10 - 9 - 7 - 8$,
   where:
   $8 - 1$ is on fold.
   $3 - 4$ is side seams.
   $7 - 8$ is neckline.
   $9 - 10 - 3$ is armhole.

Front:

1. $0_f - 1_f =$ required length + 2 cm (dart width) + 1 cm – base band width [vertically downwards]
   $= 33$ cm
2. Shoulder:
   $0_f - 2_f =$ ½ across shoulder + 1 cm [horizontally]
   $= 18.5$ cm
3. Waistline Section:
   $1_f - 3_f = 0_f - 2_f$ [horizontally]
   $= 18.5$ cm
   Join $2_f - 3_f$ in a straight line.

4. Armhole Depth:

   $0_f - 4_f$ = 1/4th round bust – 4 cm [vertically downwards]
   = 18 cm

5. Bust Line:

   $4_f - 5_f$ = 1/4th round bust + 2 cm (ease) [horizontally]
   = 24 cm

   Mark the point as 6_f on line $4_f - 5_f$. Where lines $2_f - 3_f$ and $4_f - 5_f$ intersect.

6. Waistline:

   $1_f - 7_f$ = 1/4th round waist + 3 cm (dart width) [horizontally]
   = 21 cm

   Extend line $1_f - 3_f$ by 2.5 cm for point 7_f.

7. Neckline: Sweet heart neck.

   $0_f - 8_f$ = 1/12th round bust + 2 cm [horizontally on line $0_f - 2_f$]
   = 9.3 cm

   $0_f - 9_f$ = 1/6th round bust (or as required) [vertically downwards on line $0_f - 1_f$]
   = 14.6 cm

   $0_f - 10_f = 9_f - 10_f$ [vertically]
   = 7.3 cm

   $10_f - 11_f$ = 1/12th round bust + 3 cm [horizontally]
   = 10.3 cm

   Join $8_f - 11_f$ in a smooth outward curve and $11_f - 9_f$ in a smooth outward curve.

   $8_f - 11_f - 9_f$ is the required sweet heart shape.

8. Shoulder Line:

   $2_f - 12_f$ = 1.5 cm (shoulder drop) [vertically downwards on line $2_f - 3_f$]

   Join $12_f - 8_f$ in a straight line for shoulder.

9. Armhole:

   $6_f - 13_f$ = 2.5 cm [vertically upwards on line $6_f - 2_f$]

   Join $12_f - 13_f - 5_f$ in a smooth curve for armhole.

10. For Katori:

    (i) $0_f - D$ = highest bust level [vertically downwards]
    = 25 cm

    Draw a horizontal line from point D to line $2_f - 3_f$ and mark as E.

    (ii) $D - B$ = 1/12th round bust [horizontally on line D – E]
    = 7.3 cm

11. For Section A:

    (a) Waistline dart:

    (i) Dart position: $1_f - M$ = 1/12th round bust [horizontally on line $1_f - 7_f$]
    = 7.3 cm

    (ii) Dart length: $B - M_1$ = 2 cm [vertically downwards on line B – M]

    $M - M_1$ is the required dart length.

    (iii) Dart width: $M - P = M - P_1$ = 1.5 cm (on either side of point M) [horizontally on line $1_f - 7_f$]

    Join $P - M_1$ and $P_1 - M_1$ in straight lines for the required waistline dart.

    (b) For shaping on line $3_f - 2_f$:

    E – T = 1 cm [vertically downwards on line E 3_f]

    $B - E_1$ = 1.5 cm [horizontally on line B – E]

    Join $T - E_1$ in a straight line.

    (c) For shaping on line $9_f - 1_f$:

    D – R = 1 cm [vertically downwards on line $D - 1_f$]

    $B - D_1$ = 1.5 cm [horizontally on line B – D]

    Join $D_1 - R$ in a straight line.

(d) For shaping on line $1_f - 9_f$:

$1_f - 14_f$ = 1.5 cm [vertically upwards on line $1_f - 9_f$]

Join 14_f – P in a smooth curve.

(e) Section A is along the points:

R – 14_f – P – M – 3_f – T – E_1 – B – D_1 – R.

12. For Section B:

(a) For shaping on line $3_f - 2_f$:

E – T_1 = 1 cm [vertically upwards on line E – 2_f]

Join $E_1 - T_1$ in a straight line.

(b) For shaping on line $9_f - 1_f$:

D – R_1 = 1 cm [vertically upwards on line D – 9_f]

Join $D_1 - R_1$ in a straight line.

(c) Join $T_1 - 11_f$ in a smooth curve for katori (cup) shape.

(d) Section B is along the points:

9_f – R_1 – D_1 – B – E_1 – T_1 – 11_f – 9_f.

13. For Section C:

(a) $3_f - 15_f$ = 2 cm [vertically upwards on line $3_f - 2_f$]

Draw a horizontal line from point 15_f to line $7_f - 5_f$ and mark as 16_f.

Cut out the section: $3_f - 15_f - 16_f - 7_f - 3_f$, to level section C with sections A and B.

(b) Section C is along the points:

8_f – 11_f – T_1 – E – T – 15_f – 16_f – 5_f – 13_f – 12_f – 8_f.

14. For katori choli 1 cut along the points:

For Section A: R – 14_f – P – M – 3_f – T – E_1 – B – D_1 – R.

For Section B: 9_f – R_1 – D_1 – B – E_1 – T_1 – 11_f – 9_f.

For Section C: 8_f – 11_f – T_1 – E – T – 15_f – 16_f – 5_f – 13_f – 12_f – 8_f.

Cut two pieces of the above block one piece for right and one piece for left side of the katori choli 1.

Add seam allowance 1.5 cm (or as required) and put up corresponding balance points and grain line on each pattern piece.

Base Band:

1. 0 – 1 = 2 cm [vertically downwards]
2. 0 – 2 = 1/4th round waist [horizontally]
   = 18 cm

   Complete the rectangle 0 – 1 – 2 – 3.
3. 0 – 4 = 1.5 cm [vertically upwards]
4. 0 – 5 = 1_f – P (of katori choli 1) [horizontally on line 0 – 2]
   = 5.8 cm

   Join 4 – 5 in a smooth curve to shape base band.
5. For base band block cut along the points:

   4 – 1 – 3 – 2 – 5 – 4.

   Cut two pieces of the above base band block, one piece for right and one piece for left side of the katori choli 1.

Add seam allowance 1.5 cm (or as required) and put up corresponding balance points and grain line on each pattern piece.

Sleeve:

Sleeve length = 22 cm

Round bust = 88 cm

Round sleeve = 24 cm

1. 0 – 1 = required sleeve length + 1 cm [vertically downwards]
   = 23 cm
2. Sleeve Crown:

   0 – 2 = 1/12th round bust + 2 cm [vertically downwards on line 0 – 1]
   = 9.3 cm

3. Crown Width:

   2 – 3 = 1/4th round bust – 5 cm [horizontally]

   = 17 cm

4. Top Arm:

   1 – 4 = ½ round sleeve [horizontally]

   = 12 cm

5. 0 – 5 = 2 cm [horizontally]

   Join 3 – 5 in a straight line.

6. Divide 3 – 5 into four equal parts and mark as 6, 7, 8.

   (i) $6 - 6_1$ = 0.6 cm [perpendicular downwards to the line 3 – 5]

   (ii) $7 - 7_1$ = 1.25 cm [perpendicular upwards to the line 3 – 5]

   (iii) $8 - 8_1$ = 0.6 cm [perpendicular upwards to the line 3 – 5]

7. For Back Sleeve Crown:

   Join $5 - 7_1 - 6 - 3$ in a smooth 'S' shape.

8. For Front Sleeve Crown:

   Join $5 - 8_1 - 7 - 6_1 - 3$ in a smooth 'S' shape.

Add seam allowance of 1.5 cm (or as required) and hem allowance of 3 cm (or as required) and put up corresponding balance points and grain line on each pattern piece.

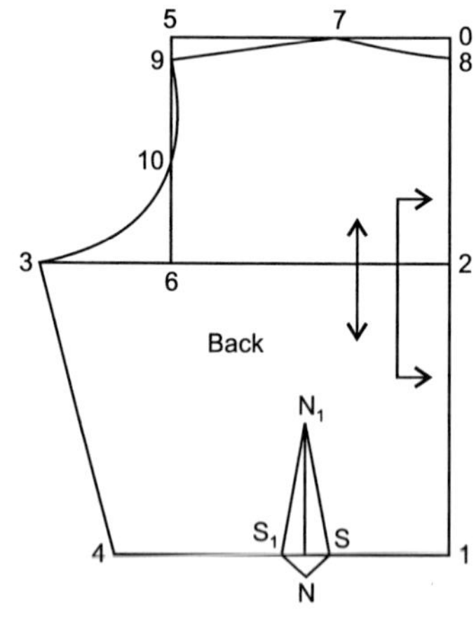

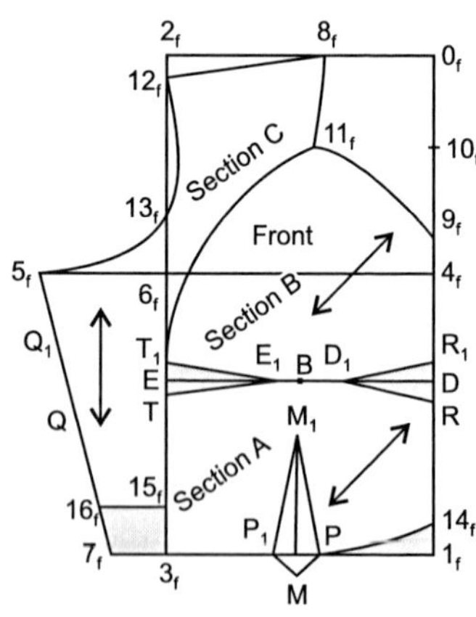

Base Band:

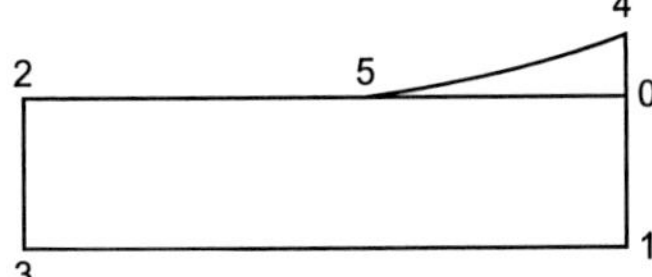

Sleeve:

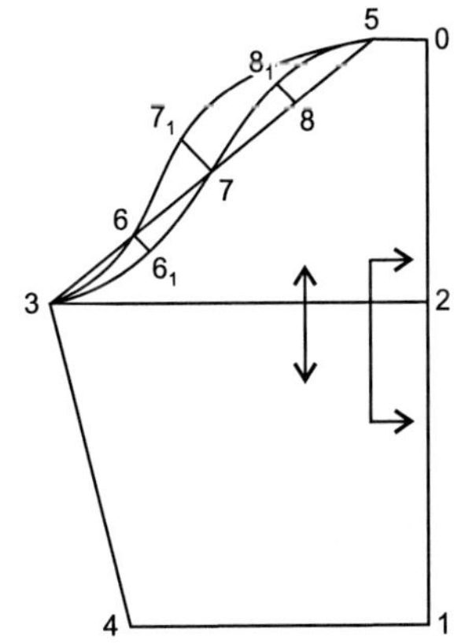

KATORI CHOLI 2

A small blouse that ends right below the busts and has a very good fitting and front section of blouse is cut in three sections and then stitched. Generally teamed with saree or ghagra, etc.

Suitable Fabric: Any light weight fabric.

Size Symbol: Any (B-cup size). This construction is suitable for the given size symbol. For any other cup size the dart width/ seams should be changed accordingly.

Size symbol – 10

Scale – cm

Drafting scale – 1/4th cm

Fabric required – 1 m × 90 cm (length × width)

Measurements:

Required length = 32 cm

Round bust = 88 cm

Round waist = 72 cm

Highest bust level = 25 cm

Across shoulder = 35 cm

Base band width = 2 cm

Sleeve:

Sleeve length = 22 cm

Round sleeve = 24 cm

Construction:

Back:

1. 0 – 1 = required length + 1 cm [vertically downwards]
   = 33 cm
2. Armhole Depth:
   0 – 2 = 1/4th round bust – 4 cm [vertically downwards]
   = 18 cm
3. Bust Line:
   2 – 3 = 1/4th round bust + 2 cm [horizontally]
   = 24 cm

4. Waistline:

   1 – 4 = 1/4th round waist + 3 cm (dart width) [horizontally]

   = 21 cm

   Join 3 – 4 in a straight line for side seams.

5. Shoulder:

   0 – 5 = ½ across shoulder + 1 cm [horizontally]

   = 18.5 cm

   Draw a vertical line downwards from point 5 to line 2 – 3 and mark as 6.

6. Neckline:

   0 – 7 = 1/12th round bust + 2 cm [horizontally on line 0 – 5]

   = 9.3 cm

   0 – 8 = 1.5 cm (or as required for depth) [vertically downwards]

   Join 7 – 8 in a smooth curve for neckline.

7. Shoulder Line:

   5 – 9 = 1.5 cm (shoulder drop according to shoulder type) [vertically downwards]

   Join 9 – 7 in a straight line for shoulder.

8. Armhole:

   9 – 10 = 6 – 10 [vertically]

   = 8.25 cm

   i.e. point 10 is the mid-point of line 9 – 6.

   Join 9 – 10 – 3 in a smooth curve for armhole.

9. For Dart: waistline dart.

   (i) Dart position: 1 – N = 1/12th round bust [horizontally on line 1 – 4]

   = 7.3 cm

   (ii) Dart length: N – N_1 = 1/12th round bust – 1 cm [vertically upwards]

   = 6.3 cm

(iii) Dart width: $N - S = N - S_1$ = 1.5 cm (on either side of point N) [horizontally on line 1 – 4]

Join $S - N_1$ and $S_1 - N_1$ in straight lines for the required waistline dart.

10. For back blouse cut along the points:

8 – 1 – N – 4 – 3 – 10 – 9 – 7 – 8,

where:

8 – 1 is on fold.

3 – 4 is side seams.

7 – 8 is neckline.

9 – 10 – 3 is armhole.

Front:

1. $0_f - 1_f$ = required length + 2 cm (dart width) + 1 cm – base band width [vertically downwards]

   = 33 cm

2. Shoulder:

   $0_f - 2_f$ = ½ across shoulder + 1 cm [horizontally]

   = 18.5 cm

3. Waistline Section:

   $1_f - 3_f = 0_f - 2_f$ [horizontally]

   = 18.5 cm

   Join $2_f - 3_f$ in a straight line.

4. Armhole Depth:

   $0_f - 4_f$ = 1/4th round bust – 4 cm [vertically downwards]

   = 18 cm

5. Bust Line:

   $4_f - 5_f$ = 1/4th round bust + 2 cm [horizontally]

   = 24 cm

   Mark the point as 6_f on line $4_f - 5_f$. Where lines $2_f - 3_f$ and $4_f - 5_f$ intersect.

6. Waistline:

   $1_f - 7_f$ = 1/4th round waist + 3 cm (dart width) [horizontally]
   = 21 cm

   Extend line $1_f - 3_f$ by 2.5 cm for point 7_f.

7. Neckline: Sweet heart neck.

   $0_f - 8_f$ = 1/12th round bust + 2 cm [horizontally on line $0_f - 2_f$]
   = 9.3 cm

   $0_f - 9_f$ = 1/6th round bust (or as required) [vertically downwards on line $0_f - 1_f$]
   = 14.6 cm

   $0_f - 10_f = 9_f - 10_f$ [vertically]
   = 7.3 cm

   $10_f - 11_f$ = 1/12th round bust + 3 cm [horizontally]
   = 10.3 cm

   Join $8_f - 11_f$ in a smooth outward curve and $11_f - 9_f$ in a smooth outward curve.

   $8_f - 11_f - 9_f$ is the required sweet heart shape.

8. Shoulder Line:

   $2_f - 12_f$ = 1.5 cm (shoulder drop) [vertically downwards on line $2_f - 3_f$]

   Join $12_f - 8_f$ in a straight line for shoulder.

9. Armhole:

   $6_f - 13_f$ = 2.5 cm [vertically upwards on line $6_f - 2_f$]

   Join $12_f - 13_f - 5_f$ in a smooth curve for armhole.

10. For Katori:

    (i) 0_f – D = highest bust level [vertically downwards]
    = 25 cm

    Draw a horizontal line from point D to line $2_f - 3_f$ and mark as E.

    (ii) D – B = 1/12th round bust [horizontally on line D – E]
    = 7.3 cm

11. For Section A:
    (a) For shaping on line $3_f - 2_f$:
        E – T = 1 cm [vertically downwards on line $E - 3_f$]
        $B - E_1$ = 1.5 cm [horizontally on line B – E]
        Join $T - E_1$ in a straight line.
    (b) For shaping section A at side:
    (i) $3_f - M$ = 3 cm [horizontally on line $3_f - 1_f$]
        Join M – T in a straight line.
    (ii) M – P = 0.5 cm [upwards on line M – T]
        $M - P_1$ = 1/12th round bust – 2 cm [horizontally on line $3_f - 1_f$]
        = 5.3 cm
        Join $P - P_1$ in smooth curve.
    (c) For shaping on line $9_f - 1_f$ (center front):
        D – R = 1 cm [vertically downwards on line $D - 1_f$]
        $B - D_1$ = 1.5 cm [horizontally on line B – D]
        Join $D_1 - R$ in a straight line.
    (d) For shaping on line $1_f - 9_f$:
        $1_f - 14_f$ = 1.5 cm [vertically upwards on line $1_f - 9_f$]
        $1_f - P_2$ = 1/12th round bust – 2 cm [horizontally on line $1_f - 3_f$]
        = 5.3 cm
        Join $14_f - P_2$ in a smooth curve.
    (e) Section A is along the points:
        $R - 14_f - P_2 - P_1 - P - T - E_1 - B - D_1 - R$.
12. For Section B:
    (a) For shaping on line $3_f - 2_f$:
        $E - T_1$ = 1 cm [vertically upwards on line $E - 2_f$]
        Join $E_1 - T_1$ in a straight line.

(b) For shaping on line $9_f - 1_f$:

$D - R_1 = 1$ cm [vertically upwards on line $D - 9_f$]

Join $D_1 - R_1$ in a straight line.

(c) Join $T_1 - 11_f$ in a smooth curve for katori (cup) shape.

(d) Section B is along the points:

$9_f - R_1 - D_1 - B - E_1 - T_1 - 11_f - 9_f$.

13. For Section C:

(a) $3_f - 15_f = 2$ cm [vertically upwards on line $3_f - 2_f$]

Draw a horizontal line from point 15_f to line $7_f - 5_f$ and mark as 16_f.

Cut out the section: $3_f - 15_f - 16_f - 7_f - 3_f$, to level section C with sections A and B.

(b) Section C is along the points:

$8_f - T_1 - E - T - 15_f - 16_f - 5_f - 13_f - 12_f - 8_f$.

14. For katori choli 2 cut along the points:

For Section A: $R - 14_f - P_2 - P_1 - P - T - E_1 - B - D_1 - R$.

For Section B: $9_f - R_1 - D_1 - B - E_1 - T_1 - 11_f - 9_f$.

For Section C: $8_f - T_1 - E - T - 15_f - 16_f - 5_f - 13_f - 12_f - 8_f$.

Cut two pieces of the above blocks, one piece for right and one piece for left side of the katori choli 2.

Add seam allowance 1.5 cm (or as required) and put up corresponding balance points and grain line on each pattern piece.

Base Band:

1. $0 - 1 = 2$ cm [vertically downwards]
2. $0 - 2 = 1/4$th round waist [horizontally]

   $= 18$ cm

   Complete the rectangle $0 - 1 - 2 - 3$.
3. $0 - 4 = 1.5$ cm [vertically upwards]

4. 0 – 5 = 1_f – P (of katori choli 2) [horizontally on line 0 – 2]
   = 5.8 cm

   Join 4 – 5 in a smooth curve to shape base band.
5. For base band block cut along the points:

   4 – 1 – 3 – 2 – 5 – 4.

   Cut two pieces of the above base band block, one piece for right and one piece for left side of the katori choli 2.

Add seam allowance 1.5 cm (or as required) and put up corresponding balance points and grain line on each pattern piece.

Sleeve:

Sleeve length = 22 cm

Round bust = 88 cm

Round sleeve = 24 cm

1. 0 – 1 = required sleeve length + 1 cm [vertically downwards]
   = 23 cm
2. Sleeve Crown:

   0 – 2 = 1/12th round bust + 2 cm [horizontally]
   = 9.3 cm
3. Crown Width:

   2 – 3 = 1/4th round bust – 5 cm [horizontally]
   = 17 cm
4. Top Arm:

   1 – 4 = ½ round sleeve [horizontally]
   = 12 cm
5. To Shape Sleeve Crown

   0 – 5 = 2 cm [horizontally]

   Join 3 – 5 in a straight line.
6. Divide 3 – 5 into four equal parts and mark as 6, 7, 8.

(i) $6 - 6_1 = 0.6$ cm [perpendicular downwards to the line 3 – 5]

(ii) $7 - 7_1 = 1.25$ cm [perpendicular upwards to the line 3 – 5]

(iii) $8 - 8_1 = 0.6$ cm [perpendicular upwards to the line 3 – 5]

7. For Back Sleeve Crown:

   Join $5 - 7_1 - 6 - 3$ in a smooth 'S' shape.

8. For Front Sleeve Crown:

   Join $5 - 8_1 - 7 - 6_1 - 3$ in a smooth 'S' shape.

Add seam allowance of 1.5 cm (or as required) and hem allowance of 3 cm (or as required) and put up corresponding balance points and grain line on each pattern piece.

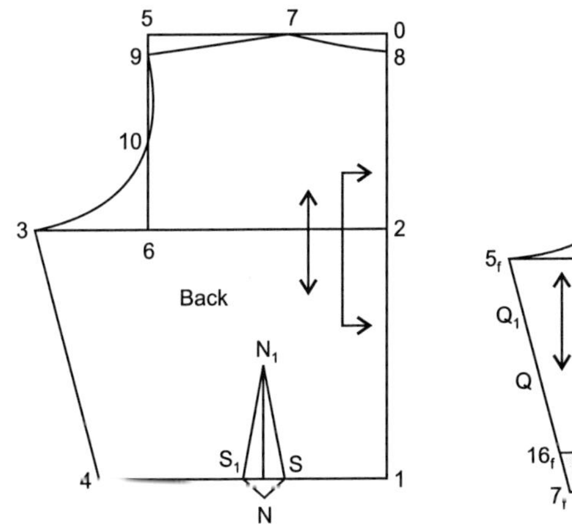

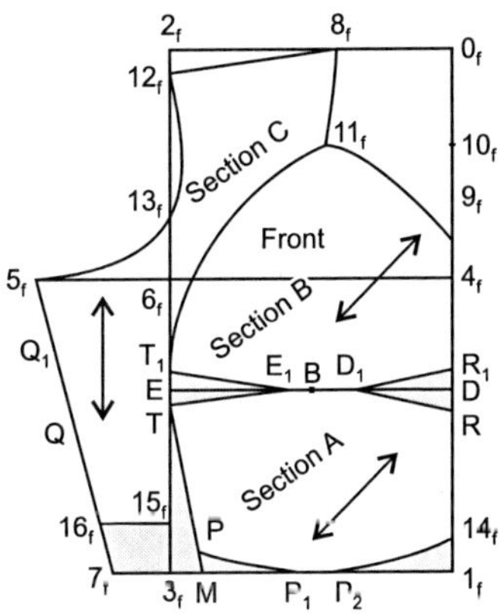

Base Band:

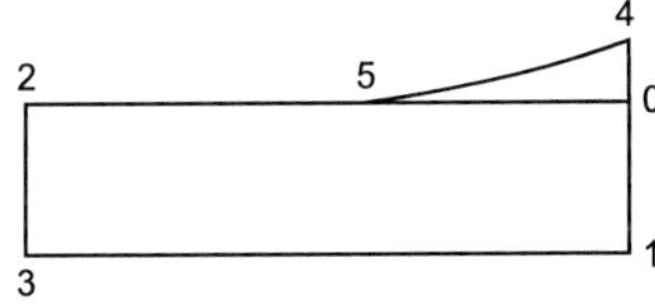

Sleeve:

26 RAGLAN SLEEVE SAREE BLOUSE

RAGLAN SLEEVE BLOUSE

Suitable Fabric: Cotton, any light weight fabric.

Size Symbol: Any (B-cup size). This construction is suitable for the given cup-size. For any other cup size the dart width should be changed accordingly.

Size symbol – 10

Scale – cm

Drafting scale – 1/4th cm

Fabric required – 1 m × 90 cm (length × width)

Measurements:

Required length = 32 cm

Round bust = 88 cm

Round waist (empire waist) = 72 cm

Across shoulder = 35 cm

Highest bust level = 25 cm

Sleeve:

Sleeve length = 20 cm

Round sleeve = 24 cm

Construction:

Back:

1. 0 – 1 = full length + 1 cm [vertically downwards]
   = 33 cm

2. Armhole Depth:

   0 – 2 = 1/4th round bust – 4 cm [vertically downwards on line 0 – 1]

   = 18 cm

3. Bust Line:

   2 – 3 = 1/4th round bust + 2 cm (ease) [horizontally]

   = 24 cm

4. Waistline:

   1 – 4 = 1/4th round waist + 3 cm (dart width) [horizontally]

   = 21 cm

   Join 4 – 3 in a straight line for side seam.

5. Shoulder:

   0 – 5 = ½ across shoulder + 1 cm [horizontally]

   = 18.5 cm

   Draw a vertical line downwards from point 5 to line 2 – 3 and mark as 6.

6. Neckline:

   0 – 7 = 1 /12th round bust (or as required) [horizontally on line 0 – 5]

   = 7.3 cm

   0 – 8 = 1.5 cm (or as required for depth) [vertically downwards on line 0 – 1]

   = 7.3 cm

   Join 7 – 8 in a smooth curve for neckline.

7. Shoulder Line:

   5 – 9 = 1 cm [vertically downwards]

   Join 7 – 9 in a straight line for shoulder.

8. Armhole:

   9 – 10 = 10 – 6 [vertically]

   = 8.5 cm

   i.e. point 10 is the mid-point of line 9 – 6.

   Join 9 – 10 – 3 in a smooth curve for armhole.

9. For Darts:
   (a) Waistline dart:
   (i) Dart position: 1 – N = 1/12th round bust
   = 7.3 cm
   (ii) Dart length: N – N_1 = 1/12th round bust [vertically upwards]
   = 7.3 cm
   (iii) Dart width: N – S = N – S_1 = 1.5 cm (on either side of point N) [horizontally]
   Join S – N_1 and S_1 – N_1 in straight lines for the required waistline dart.
10. For shaping the back blouse block for Raglan sleeves:
   (i) 7 – 11 = 2 cm [downwards on line 7 – 8 of neckline]
   (ii) Join 10 – 11 in a smooth upward curve as shown in the diagram.
11. Mark the shoulder section and blouse and cut along the points:
   (i) For shoulder section (back) cut along the points:
   7 – 11 – 10 – 9 – 7,
   where:
   9 – 7 is shoulder line.
   9 – 10 is armhole section.
   7 – 11 is neckline section.
   (ii) For raglan sleeve blouse (back) cut along the points:
   11 – 8 – 1 – N – 4 – 3 – 10 – 11,
   where:
   8 – 1 is on fold.
   3 – 4 is side seams.
   10 – 3 is the remaining armhole.
   11 – 8 is the remaining neckline.

Front:

1. $0_f - 1_f$ = required length + 2 cm (dart width) + 1 cm [vertically downwards]
   = 35 cm
2. Armhole Depth:
   $0_f - 2_f$ = 1/4th round bust – 4 cm [vertically downwards on line $0_f - 1_f$]
   = 18 cm
3. Bust Line:
   $2_f - 3_f$ = 1/4th round bust + 2 cm (ease) [horizontally]
   = 24 cm
4. Waistline:
   $1_f - 4_f$ = 1/4th round waist + 3 cm (dart width) [horizontally]
   = 21 cm

   Join $4_f - 3_f$ in a straight line for side seam.
5. Shoulder:
   $0_f - 5_f$ = ½ across shoulder + 1 cm [horizontally]
   = 18.5 cm

   Draw a vertical line downwards from point 5_f to line $2_f - 3_f$ and mark as 6_f.
6. Neckline:
   $0_f - 7_f$ = 1/12th round bust [horizontally on line $0_f - 5_f$]
   = 7.3 cm

   $0_f - 8_f$ = 1/12th round neck + 3 cm (or as required for depth) [vertically downwards on line $0_f - 1_f$]
   = 10.3 cm

   Join $7_f - 8_f$ in a smooth curve for scoop neck.
7. Shoulder Line:
   $5_f - 9_f$ = 1 cm (shoulder drop) [vertically downwards on line $5_f - 6_f$]

   Join $7_f - 9_f$ in straight line for shoulder.

8. Armhole:

$6_f - 10_f = 9_f - 10_f$ [vertically]

$= 8.5$ cm

$10_f - 11_f = 1.5$ cm [horizontally inwards]

Join $9_f - 11_f - 3_f$ in a smooth curve for armhole.

9. For Darts:

$0_f - A$ = highest bust level [vertically downwards]

$= 25$ cm

$A - B = 1/12$th round bust [horizontally]

$= 7.3$ cm

(a) Waistline dart:

(i) Dart position: $1_f - M = 1/12$th round bust [horizontally]

$= 7.3$ cm

(ii) Dart length: $B - M_1 = 2$ cm [vertically downwards on line $B - M$]

$M - M_1$ is the required dart length for the waistline dart.

(iii) Dart width: $M - P = M - P_1 = 1.5$ cm (on either side of point M) [horizontally]

Join $P - M_1$ and $P_1 - M_1$ in straight lines for the required waistline dart.

(b) Side seam dart: straight side seam dart.

(i) Dart position: Extend line $A - B$ horizontally to meet the line $3_f - 4_f$ and mark as T.

Point T is the required dart position for side seam dart.

(ii) Dart length: $B - T_1 = 2$ cm [on line $B - T$]

$T - T_1$ is the required dart length for the straight side seam dart.

(iii) Dart width: $T - Q = T - Q_1 = 1.25$ cm (on either side of point T) [on line $4_f - 3_f$]

Join $Q - T_1$ and $Q_1 - T_1$ in straight lines for the required side seam dart.

(c) Center front dart: straight center front dart.

(i) Dart position: Point A is the position for straight center front dart.

(ii) Dart length: $B - A_1 = 2$ cm [horizontally on line $B - A$]

$A - A_1$ is the required dart length for the straight center front dart.

(iii) Dart width: $A - K = A - K_1 = 1$ cm (on either side of point A) [vertically on line $0_f - 1_f$]

Join $K - A_1$ and $K_1 - A_1$ in straight lines for the required center front dart.

10. For shaping the front blouse block for Raglan sleeves:

(i) $7_f - 12_f = 2$ cm [downwards on line $7_f - 8_f$ of neckline]

(ii) Join $11_f - 12_f$ in a smooth upward curve as shown in the diagram.

11. Mark the shoulder section and blouse and cut along the points:

(i) For shoulder section (front) cut along the points:

$7_f - 12_f - 11_f - 9_f - 7_f$,

where:

$9_f - 7_f$ is shoulder line.

$9_f - 11_f$ is armhole.

$7_f - 12_f$ is neckline.

(ii) For raglan sleeve blouse (front) cut along the points:

$12_f - 8_f - A - 1_f - M - 4_f - T - 3_f - 11_f - 12_f$,

where:

$3_f - T - 4_f$ is side seams.

$11_f - 3_f$ is the remaining armhole.

$12_f - 8_f$ is the remaining neckline.

$8_f - A - 1_f$ is the center front and should be finished with placket.

Cut two pieces of the front Raglan sleeve saree blouse block to complete the saree blouse.

Add seam allowance 1.5 cm (or as required) and mark corresponding balance points and grain line on each pattern piece.

Sleeve:

Sleeve length = 20 cm

Round bust = 88 cm

Round sleeve = 24 cm

Shoulder line = 11 cm (7 – 9 of blouse block)

Sleeve:

1. 0 – 1 = required sleeve length + shoulder of blouse [vertically downwards]
   = 33 cm
2. Sleeve Crown:
   0 – 2 = shoulder line +1/12th round bust – 1.5 cm [vertically downwards on line 0 – 1]
   = 16.8 cm
3. Crown Width:
   $2 - 3 = 2 - 3_1$ = 1/4th round bust – 5 cm (on either side of point 2) [horizontally]
   = 17 cm
4. Top Arm:
   $1 - 4 = 1 - 4_1$ = ½ round sleeve + 0.5 cm (ease) (on either side of point 1) [horizontally]
   = 12.5 cm

   Join 3 – 4 in a straight line and $3_1 - 4_1$ in a straight line for side seams.
5. $0 - 5 = 0 - 5_1$ = 2 cm (on either side of point 0) [horizontally]

Join 3 – 5 in a straight line and join 3_1 – 5_1 in a straight line.

Join 5 – 5_1 in a smooth inward curve for neckline.

6. For Shaping Back Sleeve Crown:

   Divide 3 – 5 into four equal parts and mark as R, S and T, respectively.

   (i) R – R_1 = 2.5 cm [perpendicular downwards to the line 3 – 5]

   (ii) S – S_1 = 3.5 cm [perpendicular downwards to the line 3 – 5]

   (iii) T – T_1 = 2.5 cm [perpendicular downwards to the line 3 – 5]

   Join 3 – R_1 – S_1 – T_1 – 5 in a smooth inward curve for back sleeve crown.

7. For Shaping Front Sleeve Crown:

   Divide 3_1 – 5_1 into four equal parts and mark as L, M and N respectively.

   (i) L – L_1 = 2.5 cm [perpendicular downwards to the line 3_1 – 5_1]

   (ii) M – M_1 = 4 cm [perpendicular downwards to the line 3_1 – 5_1]

   (iii) N – N_1 = 2.5 cm [perpendicular downwards to the line 3_1 – 5_1]

   Join 3_1 – L_1 – M_1 – N_1 – 5_1 in a smooth inward curve for front sleeve crown.

8. For the required raglan sleeve block cut along the points:

   5_1 – N_1 – M_1 – L_1 – 3_1 – 4_1 – 4 – 3 – R_1 – S_1 – T_1 – 5 – 5_1, where;

   5 – T_1 – S_1 – R_1 – 3 is the back sleeve crown.

   5_1 – N_1 – M_1 – L_1 – 3_1 is the front sleeve crown.

   4 – 4_1 is round sleeve.

   5 – 5_1 is neckline.

   3 – 4 and 3_1 – 4_1 are side seams.

Add seam allowance of 1.5 cm (or as required) and hem allowance of 3 cm (or as required) and put up corresponding balance points and grain line on each pattern piece.

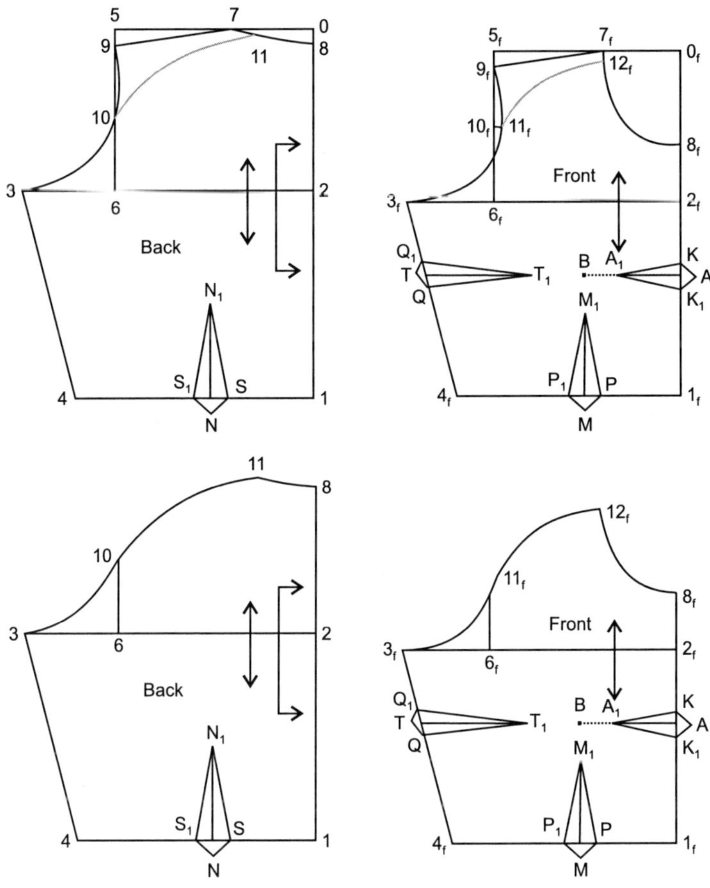

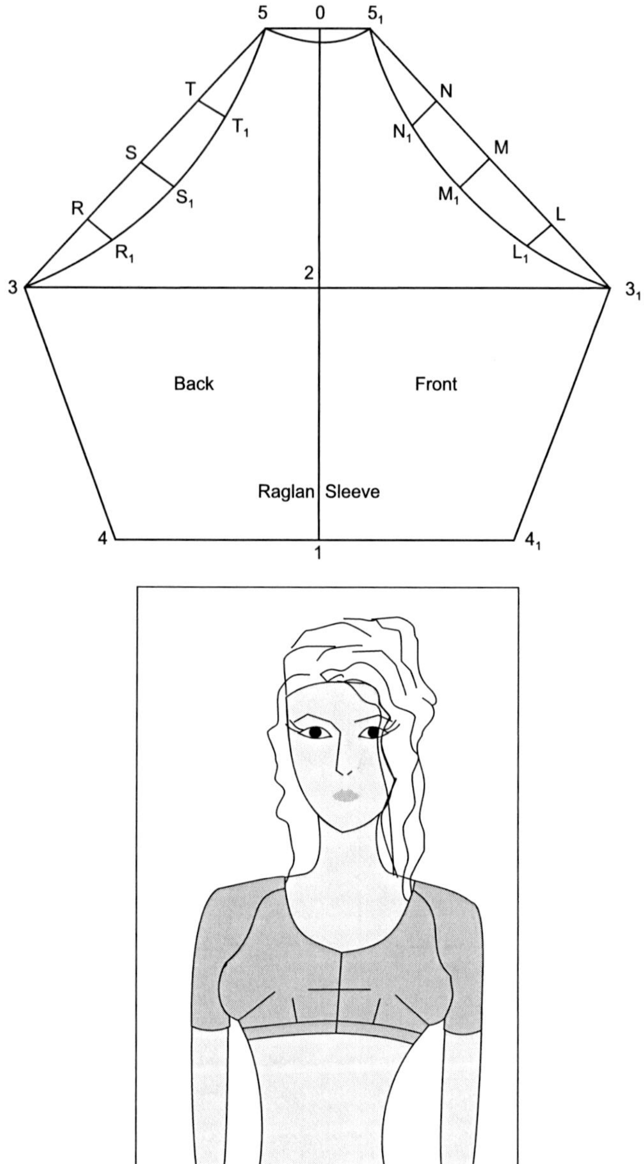
5
0
5₁
T
T₁
S
S₁
R
R₁
N
N₁
M
M₁
L
L₁
3
2
3₁
Back
Front
Raglan Sleeve
4
1
4₁

27 HALTER NECK SAREE BLOUSE

HALTER NECK SAREE BLOUSE

A small blouse that ends right below the busts and generally teamed up with saree or ghagra, etc.

Suitable Fabric: Any light weight fabric.

Size Symbol: Any (A-cup size). This construction is suitable for the given cup size. For any other cup size the dart width should be changed accordingly.

Size symbol – 10

Scale – cm

Drafting scale – 1/4th cm

Fabric required – 60 cm × 90 cm (length × width)

Measurements:

Required length = 32 cm

Round bust = 88 cm

Round waist (empire waist) = 72 cm

Across shoulder = 35 cm

Highest bust level = 25 cm

Construction:

Front:

1. $0_f - 1_f$ = required length + 2 cm (dart width) + 1 cm [vertically downwards]

   = 35 cm

2. Armhole Depth:

   $0_f - 2_f$ = 1/4th round bust – 3 cm [vertically downwards on line $0_f - 1_f$]

   = 19 cm

3. Bust Line:

   $2_f - 3_f$ = 1/4th round bust + 1 cm (ease) [horizontally]

   = 23 cm

4. Waistline:

   $1_f - 4_f$ = 1/4th round waist (empire waist) + 2 cm (dart width) [horizontally]

   = 20 cm

   Join $4_f - 3_f$ in a straight line for side seams.

5. Shoulder:

   $0_f - 5_f$ = ½ across shoulder [horizontally]

   = 17.5 cm

   Draw a vertical line downwards from point 5_f to line $2_f - 3_f$ and mark as 6_f.

6. Neckline:

   $0_f - 7_f$ = 1/12th round bust [horizontally on line $0_f - 5_f$]

   = 7.33 cm

   $0_f - 8_f$ = 1/4th round bust – 4 cm (or as required) [vertically downwards]

   = 18 cm

   Join $7_f - 8_f$ in a smooth curve for scoop neck or straight line for v-neck.

7. Shoulder Line:

   $5_f - 9_f$ = 2 cm (shoulder drop) [vertically downwards on line $5_f - 6_f$]

   Join $9_f - 7_f$ in a straight line for shoulder line.

8. Required Shoulder Line:

   $7_f - 10_f$ = 4 cm (or as required for shoulder strap) [on line $7_f - 9_f$]

$7_f - 10_f$ is the required shoulder width for halter neck saree blouse.

9. Armhole:

   $6_f - 11_f$ = 2.5 cm [vertically upwards on line $6_f - 9_f$]

   Join $10_f - 11_f - 3_f$ in a smooth curve for armhole.

10. Darts:

    0_f – A = highest bust level [vertically downwards on line $0_f - 1_f$]
    = 25 cm

    A – B = 1/12th round bust [horizontally]
    = 7.33 cm

    (a) Waistline dart:

    (i) Dart position: 1_f – M = 1/12th round bust [horizontally on line $1_f - 4_f$]
    = 7.33 cm

    (ii) Dart length: B – M_1 = 1.5 cm [vertically downwards on line B – M]

    M – M_1 is the required dart length for waistline dart.

    (iii) Dart width: M – P = M – P_1 = 1 cm (on either side of point M) [on line $1_f - 4_f$]

    Join P – M_1 and P_1 – M_1 in straight lines for the required waistline dart.

    (b) Side seam dart:

    (i) Dart position: 4_f – T = 1/12th round bust – 2 cm [upwards on line $4_f - 3_f$]
    = 5.33 cm

    (ii) Dart length: B – T_1 = 2 cm [on line B – T]

    T – T_1 is the required dart length for side seam dart.

    (iii) Dart width: T – R = T – R_1 = 1 cm (on either side of point T) [on line $4_f - 3_f$]

Join R – T_1 and R_1 – T_1 in straight lines for the required side seam dart.

11. Neck Strap:

    0_f – 12 = 1.5 cm [vertically upwards]

    Join 12 – 7_f in smooth curve for back neckline.

12. 12 – 13 = 4 cm (or as required) [vertically upwards]

    Join 13 – 10_f in a smooth curve.

13. 13 – 14 = 2 cm (deduct the shoulder drop) [on line 13 – 10_f]

    Join 12 – 14 in a straight line.

14. Front halter neck saree blouse is along the points:

    12 – 7_f – 8_f – 1_f – M – 4_f – T – 3_f – 11_f – 10_f – 14 – 12,

    where:

    8_f – 1_f is on fold.

    12 – 7_f – 8_f is the neckline for front and back together.

    10_f – 11_f – 3_f is the armhole.

    1_f – M – 4_f is the hem line which can be finished with a facing or as required.

Back:

1. 0 – 1 = 2_f – 1_f (of front blouse block) [vertically downwards]

   = 16 cm

2. Bust Line:

   0 – 2 = 1/4th round bust + 1 cm (ease) [horizontally]

   = 23 cm

3. Waistline:

   1 – 3 = 1/4th round waist + 2 cm (dart width) [horizontally]

   = 20 cm

   Join 3 – 2 in a straight line for side seams.

4. For Strap:

   1 – 4 = 7 cm (or as required for back strap) [vertically upwards on line 1 – 0]

   Join 2 – 4 in a smooth curve for back neckline.

5. Darts:

   Waistline dart

   (i) Dart position: 1 – N = 1/12th round bust [horizontally on line 1 – 3]
   = 7.3 cm

   (ii) Dart length: N – N_1 = 1/12th round bust – 1 cm [vertically upwards]
   = 6.33 cm

   [*Note:* Point N_1 should be at least 2 cm below the line 2 – 4]

   (iii) Dart width: N – S = N – S_1 = 1 cm (on either side of point N) [horizontally on line 1 – 3]

   Join S – N_1 and S_1 – N_1 in straight lines for the required waistline dart.

6. Back halter neck saree blouse is along the points:

   4 – 1 – N – 3 – 2 – 4,

   where:

   2 – 3 is side seams.

   4 – 1 is for back opening and should be finished with dress hooks or as required.

   1 – 3 is hem line which should be finished as front block.

Add seam allowance 1.5 cm and put up corresponding balance points and grain line on each pattern piece.

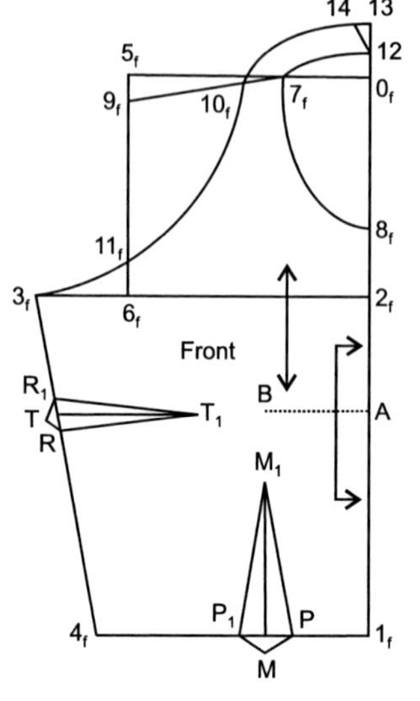
14
13
5_f
12
9_f
10_f
7_f
0_f
8_f
11_f
3_f
6_f
2_f
Front
R_1
T
R
T_1
B
A
M_1
P_1
P
4_f
1_f
M

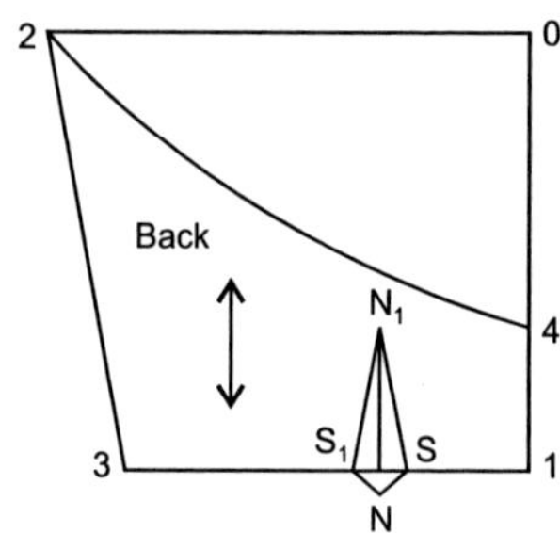
2
0
Back
N_1
4
S_1
S
3
1
N

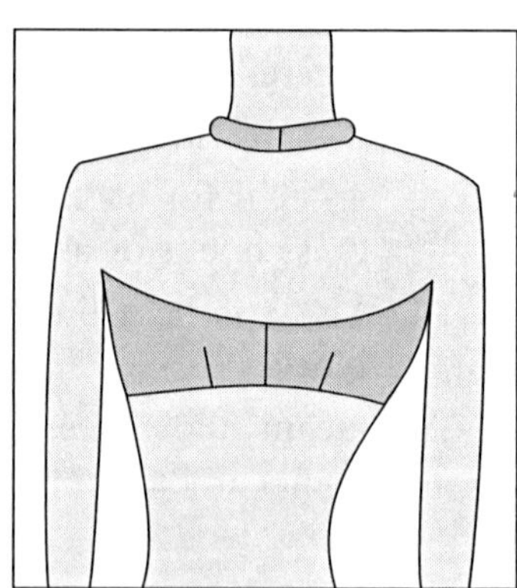

28 MAGYAR SLEEVE SAREE BLOUSE

Saree Blouse: A small blouse that ends right below the busts and generally teamed up with saree or ghagra, etc.

Suitable Fabric: Any light weight fabric.

Size Symbol: Any (B-cup size). This construction is suitable for the given cup size. For any other cup size the dart width should be changed accordingly.

Size symbol – 10

Scale – cm

Drafting scale – 1/4th cm

Fabric required – 80 cm × 90 cm (length × width)

Measurements:

Required length = 32 cm

Round bust = 88 cm

Round waist (empire waist) = 72 cm

Across shoulder = 35 cm

Highest bust level = 25 cm

Construction:

Back:

1. 0 – 1 = required length + 1 cm [vertically downwards]
   = 33 cm
2. Armhole Depth:
   0 – 2 = 1/4th round bust – 4 cm [vertically downwards on line 0 – 1]
   = 18 cm

3. Bust Line:

   2 – 3 = 1/4th round bust + 2 cm (ease) [horizontally]

   = 24 cm

4. Waistline:

   1 – 4 = 1/4th round waist + 3 cm (dart width) [horizontally]

   = 21 cm

   Join 3 – 4 in a straight line for side seam.

5. Shoulder:

   0 – 5 = ½ across shoulder + 1 cm [horizontally]

   = 18.5 cm

   Draw a vertical line downwards from point 4 to line 2 – 3 and mark as 6.

6. Neckline:

   0 – 7 = 1/12th round bust (or as required) [horizontally]

   = 7.3 cm

   0 – 8 = 2 cm (or as required for depth) [vertically downwards]

   Join 7 – 8 in a smooth curve for neckline.

7. Shoulder Line:

   5 – 9 = 1.5 cm [vertically downwards]

   Join 9 – 7 in a straight line for shoulder.

8. Magyar Sleeve:

   9 – 10 = 8 cm [extend line 7 – 9 by 8 cm for point 10]

   Join 3 – 10 in a straight line for Magyar sleeves.

9. Darts:

   (a) Waistline dart:

   (i) Dart position: 1 – N = 1/12th round bust [horizontally]

   = 7.3 cm

   (ii) Dart length: $N - N_1$ = 1/12th round bust [vertically upwards]

   = 7.3 cm

(iii) Dart width: $N - S = N - S_1 = 1.5$ cm (on either side of point N) [on line 1 – 4]

Join $S - N_1$ and $S_1 - N_1$ in straight lines for the required waistline dart.

10. For back Magyar sleeve blouse block cut along the points:

8 – 1 – N – 4 – 3 – 10 – 7 – 8,

3 – 4 is side seam.

10 – 3 is sleeve line for Magyar sleeve blouse.

Front:

1. $0_f - 1_f$ = required length + 1 cm + 2 cm (dart width) [vertically downwards]

= 35 cm

2. Armhole Depth:

$0_f - 2_f$ = 1/4th round bust – 4 cm [vertically downwards on line $0_f - 1_f$]

= 18 cm

3. Bust Line:

$2_f - 3_f$ = 1/4th round bust + 2 cm (ease) [horizontally]

= 24 cm

4. Waistline:

$1_f - 4_f$ = 1/4th round waist + 3 cm (dart width) [horizontally]

= 21 cm

Join $3_f - 4_f$ in a straight line for side seam.

5. Shoulder:

$0_f - 5_f$ = 0 – 5 (of back blouse block) [horizontally]

= 18.5 cm

Draw a vertical line downwards from point 5_f to line $2_f - 3_f$ and mark as 6_f.

6. Neckline:

$0_f - 7_f$ = 0 – 7 (of back blouse block) [horizontally]

= 7.3 cm

$0_f - 8_f$ = 1/12th round bust + 4 cm (or as required for depth) [vertically downwards]

= 11.3 cm

Join $7_f - 8_f$ in a smooth curve for scoop neck.

7. Shoulder Line:

$5_f - 9_f$ = 5 – 9 (of back blouse block) [vertically downwards]

= 1.5 cm

8. Magyar Sleeve:

$9_f - 10_f$ = 9 – 10 (of back blouse block)

= 8 cm [extend $7_f - 9_f$ by 8 cm for point 10_f]

Join $10_f - 3_f$ in a straight line for Magyar sleeve.

9. For Darts:

0_f – A = highest bust level [vertically downwards on line $0_f - 1_f$]

= 25 cm

A – B = 1/12th round bust [horizontally]

= 7.3 cm

(a) Waistline dart:

(i) Dart position: 1_f – M = 1/12th round bust [horizontally on line $1_f - 4_f$]

= 7.3 cm

(ii) Dart length: B – M_1 = 2 cm [vertically downwards on line B – M]

M – M_1 is the required dart length for waistline dart.

(iii) Dart width: M – P = M – P_1 = 1.5 cm (on either side of point M) [horizontally]

Join P – M_1 and P_1 – M_1 in straight lines for the required waistline dart.

(b) Side seam dart:

(i) Dart position: $3_f - T$ = 1/6th round bust [downwards on line $3_f - 4_f$]
= 14.6 cm

(ii) Dart length: $B - T_1$ = 2 cm [on line B – T]

$T - T_1$ is the required dart length for the side seam dart.

(iii) Dart width: $T - Q = T - Q_1$ = 1.25 cm (on either side of point T) [on line $4_f - 3_f$]

Join $Q - T_1$ and $Q_1 - T_1$ in straight lines for the required side seam dart.

(c) Center front dart:

(i) Dart position: Point A is the position for center front dart.

(ii) Dart length: $B - A_1$ = 1.5 cm [horizontally on line B – A]

$A - A_1$ is the required dart length for the center front dart.

(iii) Dart width: $A - K = A - K_1$ = 1 cm (on either side of point A) [vertically on line $0_f - 1_f$]

Join $K - A_1$ and $K_1 - A_1$ in straight lines for the required center front dart.

10. For front Magyar sleeve blouse cut along the points:

$8_f - A - 1_f - M - 4_f - T - 3_f - 10_f - 7_f - 8_f$,

$3_f - T - 4_f$ is side seam.

$10_f - 3_f$ is sleeve line for Magyar sleeve blouse.

$8_f - A - 1_f$ is center front and should be finished with placket.

Cut two pieces of the front blouse block to complete the Magyar sleeve blouse.

Add seam allowance 1.5 cm (or as required) and put up corresponding balance points and grain line on each pattern piece.

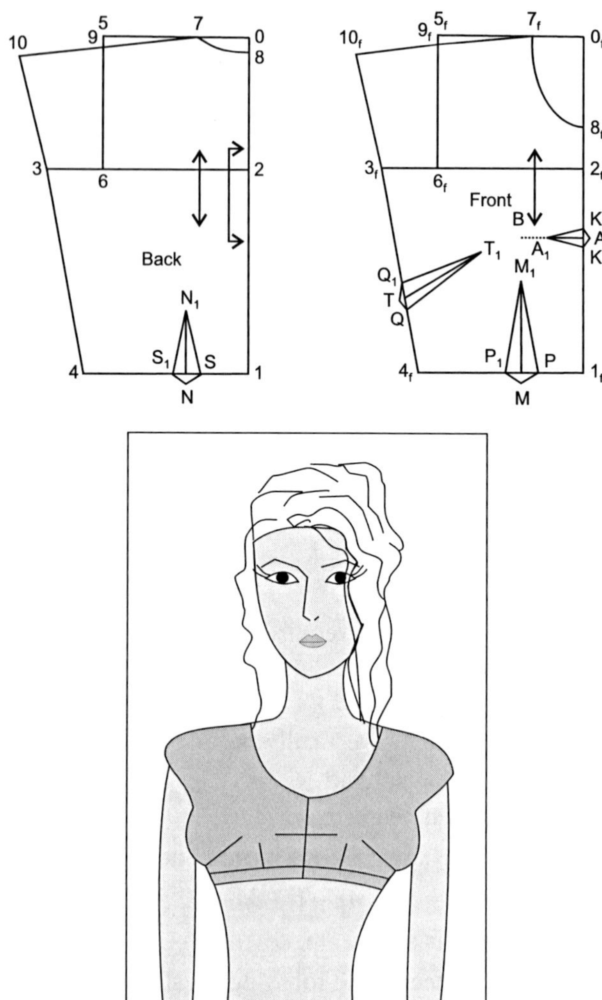
10
9
5
7
0
8
3
6
2
Back
N1
S1
S
4
1
N
10f
9f
5f
7f
0f
8f
3f
6f
2f
Front
B
K
A
A1
K1
T1
M1
Q1
T
Q
P1
P
4f
1f
M

29 KURTAS

Kurta: A kurta is a knee to calf length upper garment worn generally by women which is teamed with a salwaar, chudidaar or trousers.

STRAIGHT FIT/PUNJABI KURTA

Straight fit/Punjabi kurta is a comfortably fitting knee length upper garment worn generally by women in India that falls straight from hip level to the hem line with side slits. It is generally teamed with a salwar or chudidar.

Suitable Fabric: Light weight to medium weight fabric.

Size Symbol: Any (B-cup size). This construction is suitable for the given cup size. For any other cup size the dart width should be changed accordingly.

Size symbol – 10

Scale – cm

Drafting scale – 1/4th cm or 1/6th cm

Fabric required – 2 m × 90 cm (length × width)

Measurements:

Required length = 98 cm

Round bust = 88 cm

Round waist = 68 cm

Round hips = 94 cm

Highest bust level = 25 cm

Neck to waist/waist length = 42 cm

Hip level = 17 cm

Across shoulder = 35 cm

Construction:

Back:

1. 0 – 1 = required length + 1 cm [vertically downwards]
   = 99 cm
2. Armhole Depth:
   0 – 2 = 1/4th round bust – 4 cm [vertically downwards]
   = 18 cm
3. Bust Line:
   2 – 3 = 1/4th round bust + 2 cm (ease) [horizontally]
   = 24 cm
4. Waist Length:
   0 – 4 = waist length [vertically downwards]
   = 42 cm
5. Waistline:
   4 – 5 = 1/4th round waist + 3 cm (dart) + 1 cm (ease) [horizontally]
   = 21 cm
   Join 5 – 3 in a straight line.
6. Hip Level:
   4 – 6 = hip level [vertically downwards on line 4 – 1]
   = 17 cm
7. Hip Line:
   6 – 7 = 1/4th round hips + 2 cm (ease) [horizontally]
   = 25.5 cm
   Join 7 – 5 in a straight line.
8. Hem Line:
   1 – 8 = 6 – 7 [horizontally]
   = 25.5 cm
   Join 7 – 8 in a straight line for side slits.

9. Shoulder:

   0 – 9 = ½ across shoulder + 1 cm [horizontally]

   = 18.5 cm

   Draw a vertical line downwards from point 9 to line 2 – 3 and mark as 10.

10. Neckline:

    0 – 11 = 1/12th round bust + 1 cm (or as required) [horizontally]

    = 8.3 cm

    0 – 12 = 2 cm (or as required for depth) [vertically downwards]

    Join 11 – 12 in a smooth curve for back neck.

11. Shoulder Line:

    9 – 13 = 2 cm (shoulder drop according to shoulder type) [vertically downwards]

    Join 13 – 11 in a straight line for shoulder.

12. Armhole:

    13 – 14 = 10 – 14 [vertically downwards]

    i.e. point 14 is the mid-point of line 13 – 10.

    = 8 cm

    Join 13 – 14 – 3 in a smooth curve for armhole.

13. Darts:

    (i) Dart position: 4 – N = 1/12th round bust (on line 4 – 5) [horizontally]

    = 7.3 cm

    (ii) Dart length: Double headed dart.

    Upward dart length:

    $N - N_1$ = 1/8th round bust 8 [vertically upwards]

    = 11 cm

    Downward dart length:

    $N - N_2$ = 1/10th round hips [vertically downwards]

    = 9.4 cm

    $N_1 - N_2$ is the required length for double-headed dart.

(iii) Dart width: $N - S = N - S_1 = 1.5$ cm (on either side of point N) [horizontally]

Join $S - N_1$ and $S - N_2$ in straight lines and join $S_1 - N_1$ and $S_1 - N_2$ in straight lines to complete the required double headed dart.

14. Back Punjabi kurta/straight fit kurta is along the points:

    11 – 12 – 1 – 8 – 7 – 5 – 3 – 14 – 13 – 11, where:

    12 – 1 is on fold.

    3 – 5 – 7 is side seams.

    7 – 8 is side slits.

Give a back opening to kurta as Punjabi kurta is much fitting. The opening should be finished with a fly or as desired.

Front:

1. $0_f - 1_f$ = required length + 2.5 cm [vertically downwards]
   = 100 cm
2. Armhole Depth:

   $0_f - 2_f$ = 1/4th round bust – 2.5 cm [vertically downwards on line $0_f - 1_f$]
   = 19.5 cm
3. Bust Line:

   $2_f - 3_f$ = 1/4th round bust + 1 cm (dart) + 2 cm (ease) [horizontally]
   = 25 cm
4. Waist Length:

   $0_f - 4_f$ = waist length + 1.5 cm [vertically downwards on line $0_f - 1_f$]
   = 43.5 cm
5. Waistline:

   $4_f - 5_f$ = 1/4th round waist + 3 cm (dart) + 1 cm (ease) [horizontally]
   = 21 cm

   Join $3_f - 5_f$ in a straight line.

6. Hip Level:

   $4_f - 6_f$ = hip level [vertically downwards on line $4_f - 1_f$]
   = 17 cm

7. Hip Line:

   $6_f - 7_f$ = 1/4th round hips + 2 cm (ease) [horizontally]
   = 25.5 cm

   Join $5_f - 7_f$ in a straight line.

8. Hem Line:

   $1_f - 8_f$ = $6_f - 7_f$ [horizontally]
   = 25.5 cm

   Join $7_f - 8_f$ in a straight line for side slits.

9. Shoulder:

   $0_f - 9_f$ = ½ across shoulder + 1 cm [horizontally]
   = 18.5 cm

   Draw a vertical line downwards from point 9_f to line $2_f - 3_f$ and mark as 10_f.

10. Neckline:

    $0_f - 11_f$ = 1/12th round bust + 1 cm [horizontally on line $0_f - 9_f$]
    = 7.3 cm

    $0_f - 12_f$ = 1/12th round bust + 4 cm (or as required for depth) [vertically downwards on line $0_f - 1_f$]
    = 11.3 cm

    Join $11_f - 12_f$ in a smooth curve for scoop neck.

11. Shoulder Line:

    $9_f - 13_f$ = 2 cm (shoulder drop) [vertically downwards on line $9_f - 10_f$]

    Join $13_f - 11_f$ in a straight line for shoulder.

12. Armhole:

    $10_f - 14_f$ = 3 cm [vertically upwards]

    Join $13_f - 14_f - 3_f$ in a smooth curve for armhole.

13. Darts:

$0_f - A$ = highest bust level [vertically downwards on line $0_f - 1_f$]

= 25 cm

$A - B$ = 1/12th round bust [horizontally]

= 7.3 cm

(a) Waistline dart:

(i) Dart position: $4_f - M$ = 1/12th round bust [horizontally]

= 7.3 cm

(ii) Dart length: double-headed dart.

$B - M_1$ = 1.5 cm [vertically downwards on line $M - B$]

$M - M_1$ is the required length of upward dart.

$M - M_2$ = 1/8th round hips [vertically downwards]

= 11.75 cm

$M_1 - M_2$ is the required dart length for double-headed dart.

(iii) Dart width: $M - P = M - P_1$ = 1.5 cm (on either side of point M) [horizontally]

Join $P - M_1$ and $P - M_2$ in straight lines and join $P_1 - M_1$ and $P_1 - M_2$ in straight lines for the required double-headed dart.

(b) Armhole dart:

(i) Dart position: Point 14_f is the dart position.

(ii) Dart length: $B - T$ = 2 cm [on line $B - 14_f$]

i.e. $T - 14_f$ is the required dart length.

(iii) Dart width: $14_f - R = 14_f - R_1$ = 1 cm (on either side of point 14_f) [on line $3_f - 13_f$]

Join $R - T$ and $R_1 - T$ in straight lines for the required armhole dart.

14. Front kurta block is along the points:

$11_f - 12_f - 1_f - 8_f - 7_f - 5_f - 3_f - 14_f - 13_f - 11_f$,

where:

$12_f - 1_f$ is on fold.

$3_f - 5_f - 7_f$ is side seam.

$7_f - 8_f$ is side slits.

Add seam allowance of 1.5 cm (or as required) and hem allowance of 3 cm (or as required) and mark corresponding balance points and grain line on each pattern piece.

Sleeve:

Sleeve length = 22 cm

Round bust = 88 cm

Round sleeve = 24 cm

1. 0 – 1 = required sleeve length + 1 cm [vertically downwards]

   = 23 cm

2. Sleeve Crown:

   0 – 2 = 1/12th round bust + 2 cm [horizontally]

   = 9.3 cm

3. Crown Width:

   2 – 3 = 1/4th round bust – 5 cm [horizontally]

   = 17 cm

4. Top Arm:

   1 – 4 = ½ round sleeve [horizontally]

   = 12 cm

   Join 4 – 3 in a straight line for side seam.

5. To Shape Sleeve Crown:

   0 – 5 = 2 cm [horizontally]

   Join 3 – 5 in a straight line.

6. Divide 3 – 5 into four equal parts and mark as 6, 7, 8.

   (i) $6 - 6_1$ = 0.6 cm [perpendicular downwards to the line 3 – 5]

   (ii) $7 - 7_1$ = 1.25 cm [perpendicular upwards to the line 3 – 5]

   (iii) $8 - 8_1$ = 0.6 cm [perpendicular upwards to the line 3 – 5]

7. For Back Sleeve Crown:

   Join 5 – 7_1 – 6 – 3 in a smooth 'S' shape.

8. For Front Sleeve Crown:

   Join 5 – 8_1 – 7 – 6_1 – 3 in a smooth 'S' shape.

Add seam allowance of 1.5 cm (or as required) and hem allowance of 3 cm (or as required) and put up corresponding balance points and grain line on each pattern piece.

Straight Fit Kurta:

Back Kurta Pattern:

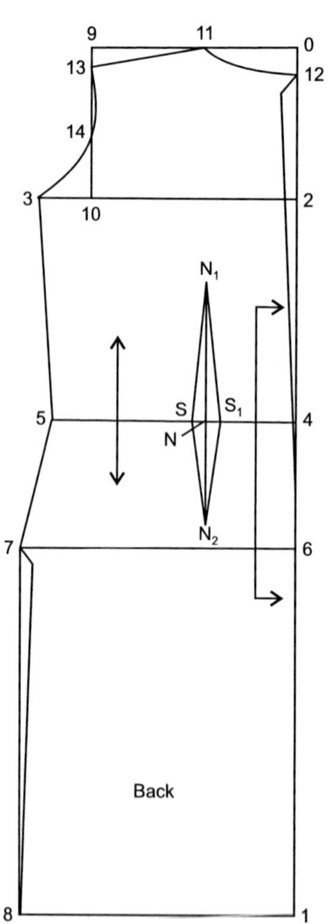

Front Kurta Pattern:

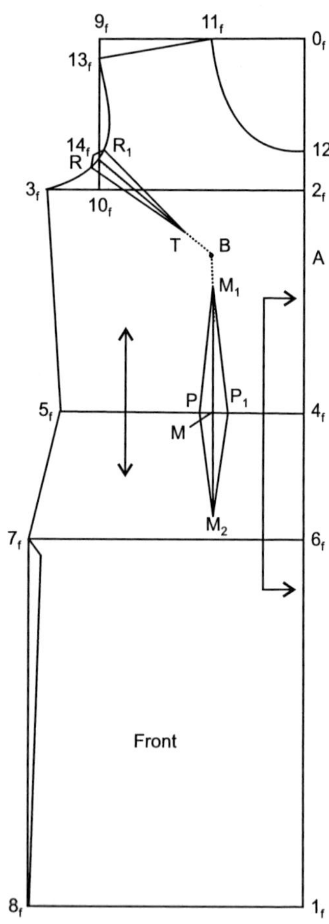

Sleeve:

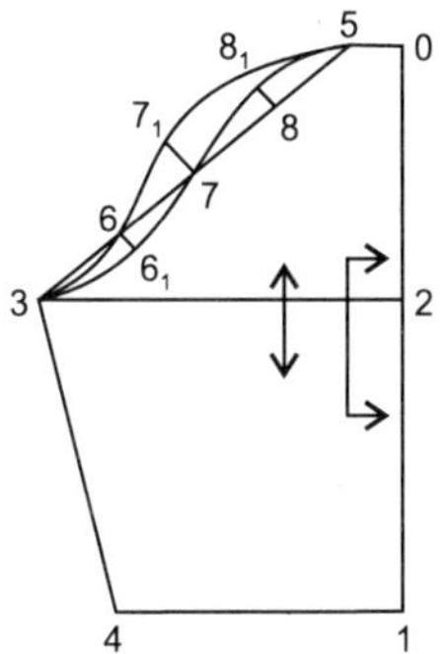

A-LINE KURTA

A-line kurta is a loose fit knee length to calf length upper garment worn generally by women. It has a conical shape and is flared at hem. It is generally teamed with a salwar or chudidar.

Suitable Fabric: Any light weight smooth fabric.

Size Symbol: Any (B-cup size). This construction is suitable for the given cup size. For any other cup size the dart width should be changed accordingly.

Size symbol – 10

Scale – cm

Drafting scale – 1/4th cm or 1/6th cm

Fabric required – 2 m × 1 m (length × width)

Measurements:

Required length = 98 cm

Round bust = 88 cm

Round hips = 94 cm

Highest bust level = 25 cm

Neck to waist/waist length = 42 cm

Hip level = 17 cm

Across shoulder = 35 cm

STRAIGHT FIT KURTA/PUNJABI KURTA & VARIATION

Straight fit kurta with salwar

Straight fit kurta with kurta placket and chudidar

Construction:

Back:

1. 0 – 1 = required length + 1 cm [vertically downwards]

   = 99 cm

2. Armhole Depth:

   0 – 2 = 1/4th round bust – 4 cm [vertically downwards]

   = 18 cm

3. Bust Line:

   2 – 3 = 1/4th round bust + 2.5 cm (ease) (or as required) [horizontally]

   = 24.5 cm

4. Waist Length:

   0 – 4 = waist length [vertically downwards]

   = 42 cm

5. Hip Level:

   4 – 5 = hip level [vertically downwards]

   = 17 cm

6. Hip Line:

   5 – 6 = 1/4th round hips + 4 cm (or as required for shape) [horizontally]

   = 27.5 cm

7. Side Seams:

   Join 3 – 6 in a straight line and extend downwards and mark as 7, so as; 3 – 7 = 2 – 1

   = 81 cm

   Join 7 – 1 in a smooth curve for hem line.

8. Draw a horizontal line from point 4 to line 3 – 7 and mark as 8.

9. Shoulder:

   0 – 9 = ½ across shoulder + 1 cm [horizontally]

   = 18.5 cm

Draw a vertical line downwards from point 9 to line 2 – 3 and mark as 10.

10. Neckline:

    0 – 11 = 1/12th round bust [horizontally]

    = 7.3 cm

    0 – 12 = 2 cm [vertically downwards]

    Join 11 – 12 in a smooth curve for neckline.

11. Shoulder Line:

    9 – 13 = 2 cm (shoulder drop according to the shoulder type) [vertically downwards]

    Join 13 – 11 in a straight line for shoulder.

12. Armhole:

    13 – 14 = 14 – 10

    = 8 cm

    i.e. point 14 is the mid-point of line 13 – 10.

    Join 13 – 14 – 3 in a smooth curve for armhole.

13. Dart:

    Waistline dart: double-headed dart.

    (i) Dart position: 4 – N = 1/12th round bust [horizontally]

    = 7.3 cm

    (ii) Dart length: double-headed dart.

    Upward dart length:

    $N - N_1$ = 1/8th round bust [vertically upwards]

    = 11 cm

    Downward dart length:

    $N - N_2$ = 1/10th round hips [vertically downwards]

    = 9.4 cm

    $N_1 - N_2$ is the required dart length for double-headed dart.

    (iii) Dart width: $N - S = N - S_1$ = 1.5 cm (on either side of point N) [horizontally]

Join $S - N_1$ and $S - N_2$ in straight lines and join $S_1 - N_1$ and $S_1 - N_2$ in straight lines for the required double-headed dart.

14. Back A-line kurta is along the points:

    12 – 1 – 7 – 6 – 8 – 3 – 14 – 13 – 11 – 12,

    where:

    12 – 1 is on fold.

    3 – 8 – 6 – 7 is side seams without side slits.

    With side slits:

    3 – 8 – 6 is side seams.

    6 – 7 is side slits.

Front:

1. $0_f - 1_f$ = required length + 2.5 cm [vertically downwards]

   = 100.5 cm

2. Armhole Depth:

   $0_f - 2_f$ = 1/4th round bust – 2.5 cm [vertically downwards on line $0_f - 1_f$]

   = 19.5 cm

3. Bust Line:

   $2_f - 3_f$ = 1/4th round bust + 2.5 cm (ease) (or as required) [horizontally]

   = 24.5 cm

4. Waist Length:

   $0_f - 4_f$ = waist length + 1.5 cm [vertically downwards on line $0_f - 1_f$]

   = 43.5 cm

5. Hip Level:

   $4_f - 5_f$ = hip level [vertically downwards on line $4_f - 1_f$]

   = 17 cm

6. Hip Line:

   $5_f - 6_f$ = 1/4th round hips + 4 cm (equal to back block) [horizontally]

   = 27.5 cm

7. Side Seams:

   Join $3_f - 6_f$ in a straight line and extend downwards and mark as point 7_f, so as; $3_f - 7_f = 2_f - 1_f$

   = 81 cm

   Join $7_f - 1_f$ in a smooth curve for hem line.

8. Draw a horizontal line from point 4_f to line $3_f - 7_f$ and mark as 8_f.

9. Shoulder:

   $0_f - 9_f$ = ½ across shoulder + 1 cm [horizontally]

   = 18.5 cm

   Draw a vertical line downwards from point 9_f to line $2_f - 3_f$ and mark as 10_f.

10. Neckline:

    $0_f - 11_f$ = 0 – 11 of back block [horizontally]

    = 7.3 cm

    $0_f - 12_f$ = 1/12th round bust + 2 cm (or as required for depth) [vertically downwards]

    = 9.3 cm (but care should be taken not to make the neckline much deep as A-line kurta is a loose garment)

    Join $11_f - 12_f$ in a smooth curve for neckline.

11. Shoulder Line:

    $9_f - 13_f$ = 2 cm (as of back) [vertically downwards]

    Join $13_f - 11_f$ in a straight line for shoulder.

12. Armhole:

    $10_f - 14_f$ = 2.5 cm [vertically upwards]

    Join $13_f - 14_f - 3_f$ in a smooth curve for armhole.

13. Darts:

    0_f – A = highest bust level [vertically downwards]

    = 25 cm

    A – B = 1/12th round bust [horizontally]

    = 7.3 cm

(a) Waistline dart: double-headed dart.

(i) Dart position: $4_f - M$ = 1/12th round bust [horizontally]
= 7.3 cm

(ii) Dart length: double-headed dart.

Upward dart: $B - M_1$ = 2 cm [vertically downwards on line $B - M$]

$M - M_1$ is the upward dart.

Downward dart: $M - M_2$ = 1/8th round hips [vertically downwards]
= 11.75 cm

$M_1 - M_2$ is the required length for double headed dart.

(iii) Dart width: $M - P = M - P_1$ = 1.5 cm [horizontally on either side of point M]

Join $P - M_1$ and $P - M_2$ in straight lines and join $P_1 - M_1$ and $P_1 - M_2$ in straight lines for the required waistline dart.

(b) Armhole dart:

(i) Dart position: Point 14_f is the position for armhole dart.

(ii) Dart length: $B - T$ = 2 cm [on line $B - 14_f$]

$T - 14_f$ is the required dart length for the armhole dart.

(iii) Dart width: $14_f - R = 14_f - R_1$ = 1 cm (on either side of point 14_f)

Join $R - T$ and $R_1 - T$ in straight lines for the required armhole dart.

14. Front A-line kurta is along the points:

$12_f - 1_f - 7_f - 6_f - 8_f - 3_f - 14_f - 13_f - 11_f - 12_f$,

where:

$12_f - 1_f$ is on fold.

$3_f - 7_f$ is side seams without slits.

With side slits:

$3_f - 8_f - 6_f$ is side seams with side slits.

$6_f - 7_f$ is side slits.

Add seam allowance of 1.5 cm (or as required) and hem allowance of 3 cm (or as required) and mark corresponding balance points and grain line on each pattern piece.

Sleeve:

Sleeve length = 18 cm

Round bust = 88 cm

Round sleeve = 24 cm

1. 0 – 1 = required sleeve length + 1 cm [vertically downwards]
   = 19 cm
2. Sleeve crown:
   0 – 2 = 1/12th round bust + 2 cm [horizontally]
   = 9.3 cm
3. Crown width
   2 – 3 = 1/ 4th round bust – 5 cm [horizontally]
   = 17 cm
4. Top arm
   1 – 4 = ½ round sleeve [horizontally]
   = 12 cm
5. To shape sleeve crown
   0 – 5 = 2 cm [horizontally]
   Join 3 – 5 in a straight line.
6. Divide 3 – 5 into 4 equal parts and mark as 6, 7, 8.
   (i) $6 - 6_1$ = 0.6 cm [perpendicular downwards to the line 3 – 5]
   (ii) $7 - 7_1$ = 1.25 cm [perpendicular upwards to the line 3 – 5]
   (iii) $8 - 8_1$ = 0.6 cm [perpendicular upwards to the line 3 – 5]

7. For back sleeve crown:

   Join 5 – 7_1 – 6 – 3 in a smooth 'S' shape.

8. For front sleeve crown:

   Join 5 – 8_1 – 7 – 6_1 – 3 in a smooth 'S' shape.

Add seam allowance of 1.5 cm (or as required) and hem allowance of 3 cm (or as required) and put up corresponding balance points and grain line on each pattern piece.

A-line Kurta:

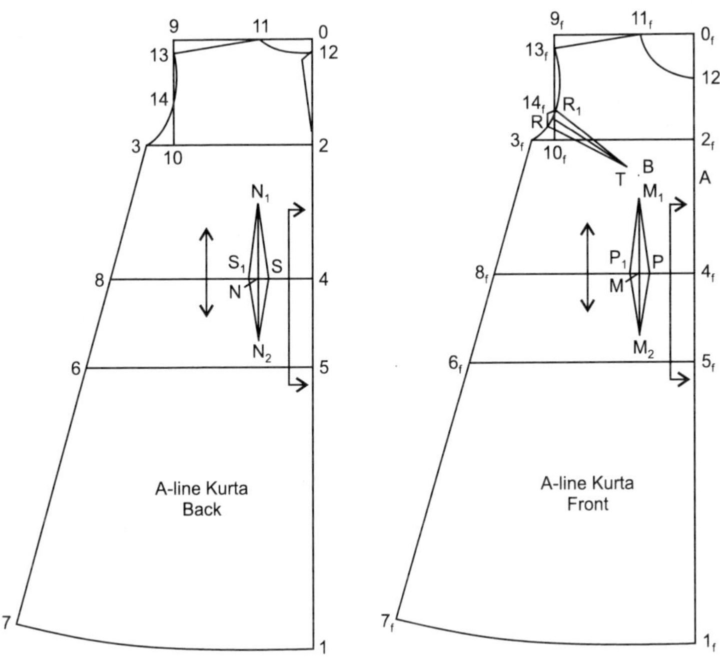

Sleeve:

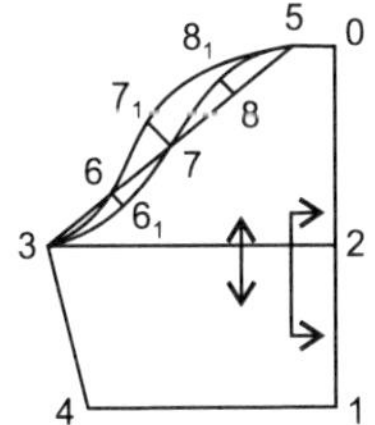

A-LINE KURTA & VARIATION

A-line kurta with salwar

A-line kurta with chudidar

30 KALIDAAR KURTA

KALIDAAR KURTA 1

Kalidaar kurta is a knee length to calf length upper garment worn generally by women in India. It is comparable to A-line kurta that is cut in longitudinal panels and stitched with princess seams. It is generally teamed with a salwar or chudidar.

Suitable Fabric: Light weight fabric.

Size Symbol: Any (B-cup size). This construction is suitable for the given cup size. For any other cup size the dart width should be changed accordingly.

Size symbol – 10

Scale – cm

Drafting scale – 1/4th cm or 1/6th cm

Fabric required – 2.5 m × 1 m (length × width)

Measurements:

Required length = 110 cm

Round bust = 88 cm

Round waist = 68 cm

Round hips = 94 cm

Waist length = 42 cm

Hip level = 17 cm

Highest bust level = 25 cm

Across shoulder = 35 cm

Construction:

Back:

1. 0 – 1 = required length + 1 cm [vertically downwards]
   = 111 cm
2. Armhole Depth:
   0 – 2 = 1/4th round bust – 3 cm [vertically downwards on line 0 – 1]
   = 19 cm
3. Bust Line:
   2 – 3 = 1/4th round bust + 2.5 cm (ease or as required) [horizontally]
   = 24.5 cm
4. Waist Length:
   0 – 4 = waist length [vertically downwards]
   = 42 cm
5. Waistline:
   4 – 5 = 1/4th round waist + 3 cm (dart width) + 2 cm (ease) [horizontally]
   = 22 cm

   Join 3 – 5 in a straight line.
6. Hip Level:
   4 – 6 = hip level [vertically downwards on line 4 – 6]
   = 17 cm
7. Hip Line:
   6 – 7 = 1/4th round hips + 3 cm (ease for shape) [horizontally]
   = 26.5 cm

   Join 5 – 7 in a straight line and extend downwards and mark as 8 where:

   5 – 8 = 4 – 1
8. Hem Line:
   Join 1 – 8 in a smooth curve for hem line.

9. Shoulder:

   0 – 9 = ½ across shoulder + 2 cm (dart width) [horizontally]

   = 19.5 cm

   Draw a vertical line downwards from point 9 to line 2 – 3 and mark as 10.

10. Neckline:

    0 – 11 = 1/12th round bust (or as required) [horizontally]

    = 7.3 cm

    0 – 12 = 1.5 cm [vertically downwards for neckline depth]

    Join 11 – 12 in a smooth curve for back neckline.

11. Shoulder Line:

    9 – 13 = 2.5 cm [vertically downwards on line 9 – 10]

    Join 13 – 11 in a straight line for shoulder.

12. Armhole:

    13 – 14 = 14 – 10 [on line 13 – 10]

    i.e. point 14 is the mid-point of line 13 – 10.

    Join 13 – 14 – 3 in a smooth curve for armhole.

13. For Darts:

    (a) For shoulder dart: Draw a horizontal line from point 14 to line 0 – 1 and mark as 14_1.

    (i) Dart position: 11 – 15 = 13 – 15 [on line 11 – 13] i.e. point 15 is the mid-point of line 11 – 13.

    (ii) Dart length: Draw a line from point 15 perpendicular to line 11 – 13 to line 14 – 14_1 and mark as Q. 15 – Q is the required dart length.

    (iii) Dart width: 15 – R = 15 – R_1 = 1 cm (on either side of point 15) [on line 11 – 13]

    Join R – Q and R_1 – Q in straight lines for the required shoulder dart.

    (b) Waistline dart:

    (i) Dart position: 4 – N = 1/12th round bust [horizontally on line 4 – 5]

    = 7.3 cm

(ii) Dart length: double-headed dart.

Upward dart length:

$N - N_1$ = 1/8th round bust [vertically upwards]
= 11 cm

Downward dart length:

$N - N_2$ = 1/10th round hips [vertically downwards]
= 9.4 cm

$N_1 - N_2$ is the required dart length for double-headed dart.

(iii) Dart width: $N - S = N - S_1$ = 1.5 cm (on either side of point N) [horizontally]

Join $S - N_1$ and $S - N_2$ in straight lines and join $S_1 - N_1$ and $S_1 - N_2$ in straight lines for the required double-headed dart.

14. 1 – L = 1/3rd hem line [on line 1 – 8]
= 13.3 cm

Join $L - N_2$ in a straight line.

15. For Kali/Panels:

3 – B = 1/12th round bust [horizontally]
= 7.3 cm

Join Q – B in a straight line and join N_1 – B in a straight line and smooth out the line Q – B – N_1 at point B.

(i) For central kali/central panel cut along the points: 12 – 1 – L – N_2 – S – N_1 – B – Q – R – 11 – 12, where:

12 – 1 is on fold.

(ii) For side kali/side panel cut along the points: R_1 – Q – B – N_1 – S_1 – N_2 – L – 8 – 5 – 3 – 14 – 3 – R_1, where:

3 – 5 – 7 – 8 is side seams (without side slits)

With side slits:

3 – 5 – 7 is side seams.

7 – 8 is side slits.

Cut two pieces of side kali/panel to complete back section of kalidaar kurta.

Front:

1. $0_f - 1_f$ = required length + 2 cm [vertically downwards]
   = 112 cm
2. Armhole Depth:
   $0_f - 2_f$ = 1/4th round bust – 2 cm [vertically downwards on line $0_f - 1_f$]
   = 20 cm
3. Bust Line:
   $2_f - 3_f$ = 1/4th round bust + 1 cm (dart width) + 2.5 cm (ease) [horizontally]
   = 25.5 cm
4. Waist Length:
   $0_f - 4_f$ = waist length + 1 cm [vertically downwards on line $4_f - 1_f$]
   = 43 cm
5. Waistline:
   $4_f - 5_f$ = 1/4th round waist + 3 cm (dart width) + 2 cm (ease) [horizontally]
   = 22 cm

   Join $5_f - 3_f$ in a straight line.
6. Hip Level:
   $4_f - 6_f$ = hip level [vertically downwards]
   = 17 cm
7. Hip Line:
   $6_f - 7_f$ = 1/4th round hips + 3 cm (ease) [horizontally]
   = 26.5 cm

   Join $5_f - 7_f$ in a straight line and extend downwards and mark as 8_f, where: $5_f - 8_f = 4_f - 1_f$.
8. Hem Line:
   Join $8_f - 1_f$ in a smooth curve for hem line.

9. Shoulder:

   $0_f - 9_f$ = ½ across shoulder + 3 cm (dart width) [horizontally]

   = 20.5 cm

   Draw a vertical line downwards from point 9_f to line $2_f - 3_f$ and mark as 10_f.

10. Neckline:

    $0_f - 11_f$ = 0 – 1 (of back kurta block) [horizontally]

    = 7.3 cm

    $0_f - 12_f$ = 1/12th round bust (or as required for depth) [vertically downwards]

    = 7.3 cm (but care should be taken not to make the neckline much deep as kalidaar kurta is a loose garment)

    Join $11_f - 12_f$ in a smooth curve for round neck.

11. Shoulder Line:

    $9_f - 13_f$ = 3.5 cm [vertically downwards on line $9_f - 10_f$]

    Join $13_f - 11_f$ in a straight line for shoulder.

12. Armhole:

    $13_f - 14_f = 14_f - 10_f$

    i.e. point 14_f is the mid-point of line $13_f - 10_f$.

    Join $13_f - 14_f - 3_f$ in a smooth curve for armhole.

13. For Darts:

    0_f – A = highest bust level [vertically downwards]

    = 25 cm

    A – D = 1/12th round bust [horizontally]

    = 7.3 cm

    (a) Shoulder dart:

    (i) Dart position: $11_f - 15_f = 15_f - 13_f$ [on line $11_f - 13_f$] i.e. point 15_f is the mid-point of line $11_f - 13_f$.

    (ii) Dart length: D – T – 3 cm (upwards on line D – 15_f)

15_f – T is the required dart length for shoulder dart.

(iii) Dart width: 11_f – T_1 = 11 – R (of back block) 13_f – T_2 = 13 – R_1 (of back block) T_1 – T_2 is the required dart width.

Join T_1 – T and T_2 – T in straight lines for the required shoulder dart.

(b) Waistline dart:

(i) Dart position: 4_f – M = 1/12th round bust [horizontally]
= 7.3 cm

(ii) Dart length: double-headed dart.

Upward dart length: D – M_1 = 2 cm [vertically downwards on line D – M] M – M_1 is the required upward dart length.

Downward dart length:

M – M_2 = 1/10th round hips [vertically downwards]
= 9.4 cm

M_1 – M_2 is the required dart length for double-headed dart.

(iii) Dart width: M – P = M – P_1 = 1.5 cm (on either side of point M) [horizontally]

Join P – M_1 and P – M_2 in straight lines and join P_1 – M_1 and P_1 – M_2 in straight lines for the required waistline double-headed dart.

14. 1_f – J = 1/3rd hem line [on line 1_f – 8_f]
= 13.3 cm

Join M_2 – J in a straight line.

15. For Kali/Panels:

Join T – D and join D – M_1 in straight lines and smooth out line T – D – M_1 at point D.

(i) For central kali/central panel cut along the points: 12_f – 1_f – J – M_2 – P – M_1 – D – T – T_1 – 11_f – 12_f, where:

12_f – 1_f is on fold.

(ii) For side kali/longitudinal panel cut along the points: $T_2 - T - D - M_1 - P_1 - M_2 - J - 8_f - 5_f - 3_f - 14_f - 13_f - T_2$,

where:

$3_f - 5_f - 7_f - 8_f$ is side seams (without side slits)

With side slits:

$3_f - 5_f - 7_f$ is side seams.

$7_f - 8_f$ is side slits.

Cut two pieces of side kali/panel to complete front section of kalidaar kurta.

Add seam allowance of 1.5 cm (or as required) and hem allowance of 3 cm (or as required) and mark corresponding balance points and grain line on each pattern piece.

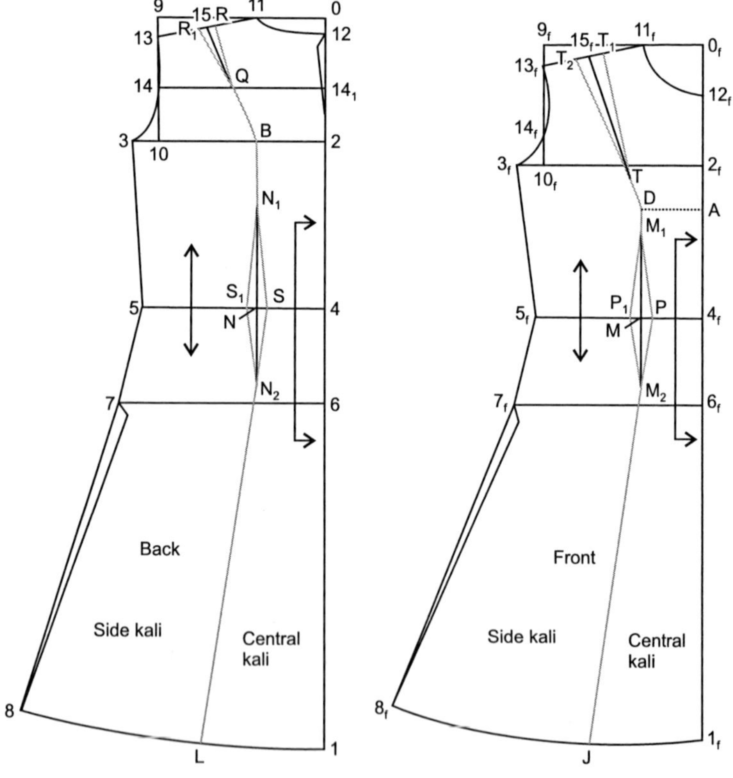

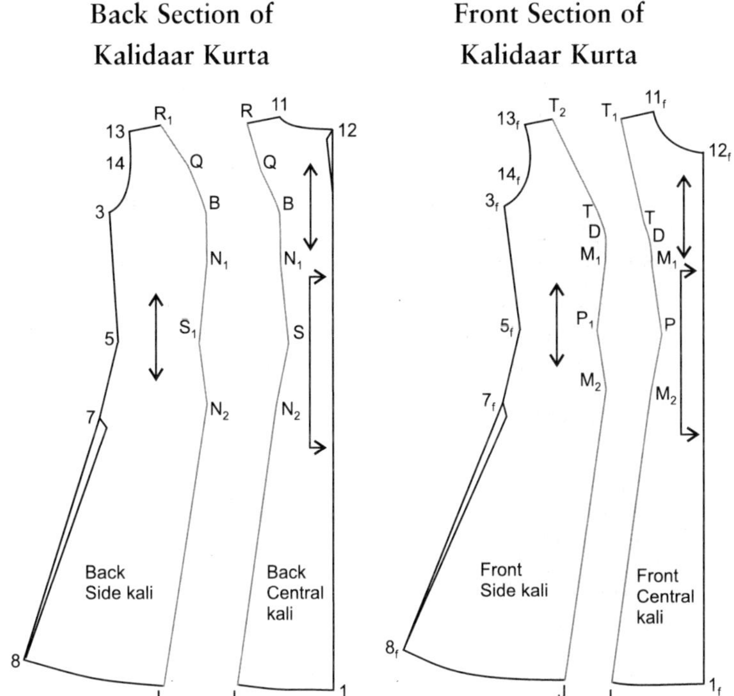

KALIDAAR KURTA 2

Flared kalidaar kurta is a knee length to calf length upper garment worn generally by women. It is comparable to A-line kurta that is cut in longitudinal panels and stitched with princess seams and is more flared at hem. It is generally teamed with a salwar or chudidar.

Suitable Fabric: Cotton, satin, any smooth light weight fabric.

Size Symbol: Any (B-cup size). This construction is suitable for the given cup size. For any other cup size the dart width should be changed accordingly.

Size symbol – 10

Scale – cm

Drafting scale – 1/4th cm or 1/6th cm

Fabric required – 3 m × 1 m (length × width)

KALIDAR KURTA & VARIATION

Kalidar kurta with salwar

Kalidar kurta with chudidar

Measurements:

Required length = 110 cm

Round bust = 88 cm

Round waist = 68 cm

Round hips = 94 cm

Waist length = 42 cm

Hip level = 17 cm

Highest bust level = 25 cm

Across shoulder = 35 cm

Construction:

1. Trace back and front block of kalidaar kurta on a new paper for pattern.

Back:

2. Back Central Kali/Longitudinal Panel:

   12 – 1 – L – N_2 – S – N_1 – B – Q – R – 11 – 12.

   (i) For flare: Pivot line L – N_2 at point N_2 till points L – N_2 – S are on same line and mark as L_C.

   (ii) For flared central kali/longitudinal panel cut along: 12 – 1 – L_C – S – N_1 – B – Q – R – 11 – 12.

   (iii) 12 – 1 is on fold.

3. Back Side Kali/Longitudinal Panel:

   R_1 – Q B – N_1 – S_1 – N_2 – L – 8 – 5 – 3 – 14 – 3 – R_1.

   (i) For flare: Pivot line L – N_2 at point N_2 till point L – N_2 – S_1 are on the same line and mark as L_S.

   (ii) For flared side kali/longitudinal panel cut along:

   R_1 – Q – B – N_1 – S_1 – L_S – 8 – 5 – 3 – 14 – 13 – R_1.

   (iii) Cut two pieces of the side kali/longitudinal panel to complete the back section of flared kalidaar kurta.

Front:

1. Front Central Kali/Longitudinal tPanel:

   $12_f - 1_f - J - M_2 - P - M_1 - D - T - T_1 - 11_f - 12_f$.

   (i) For flare: Pivot line $J - M_2$ at point M_2 till points $J - M_2 - P$ are on same line and mark as J_C.

   (ii) For flared central kali/longitudinal panel cut along:

   $12_f - 1_f - J_C - P - M_1 - D - T - T_1 - 11_f - 12_f$.

   (iii) $12_f - 1_f$ is on fold.

2. Front Side Kali/Longitudinal Panel:

   $T_2 - T - D - M_1 - P_1 - M_2 - J - 8_f - 5_f - 3_f - 14_f - 13_f - T_2$.

   (i) For flare: Pivot line $J - M_2$ at point M_2 till points $J - M_2 - S_1$ are on same line and mark as J_S.

   (ii) For flared side kali/longitudinal panel cut along:

   $T_2 - T - D - M_1 - P_1 - J_S - 8_f - 5_f - 3_f - 14_f - 13_f - T_2$.

   (iii) Cut two pieces of the side kali/longitudinal panel to complete the front section of flared kalidaar kurta.

Add seam allowance of 1.5 cm (or as required) and hem allowance of 3 cm (or as required) and mark corresponding balance points and grain line on each pattern piece.

Kalidaar Kurta: Back:

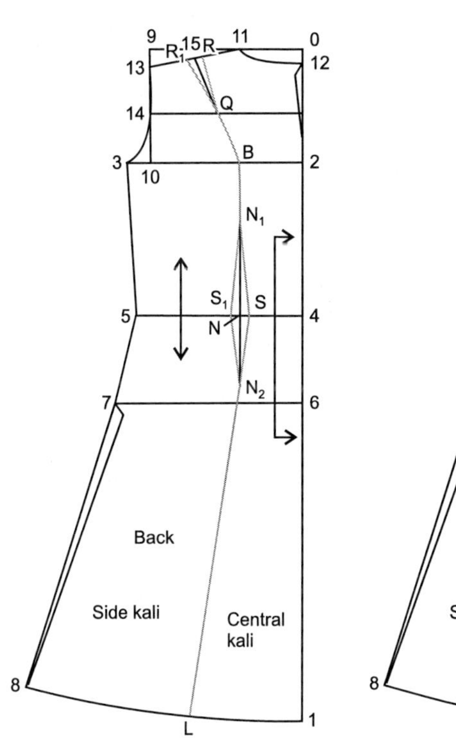

Kalidaar Kurta: (cut and separated)

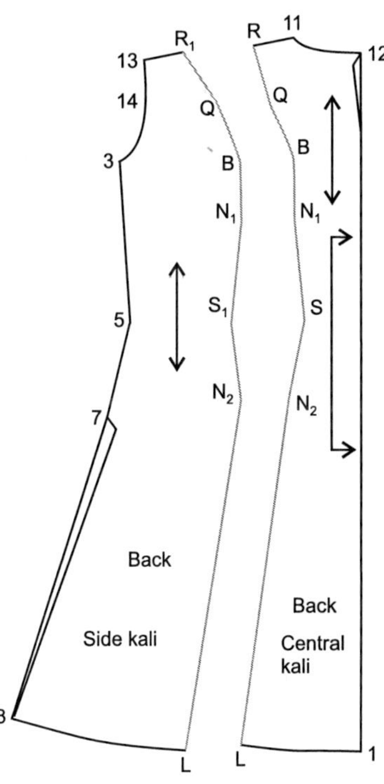

Kalidaar Kurta Flared:

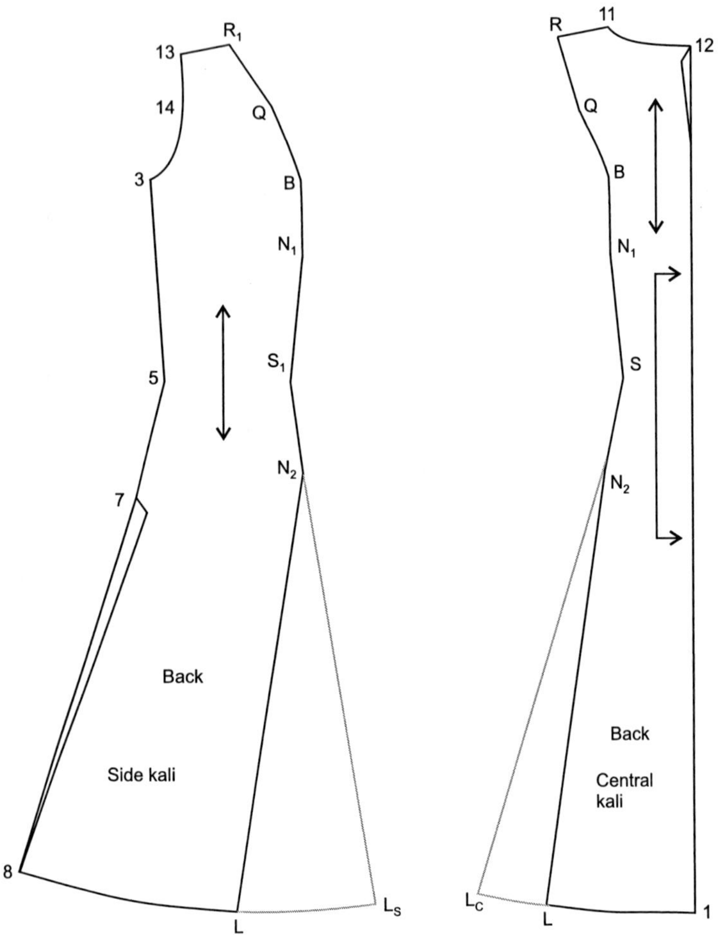

Kalidaar Kurta: Front:

Front

Side kali

Central kali

Kalidaar Kurta: (cut and separated)

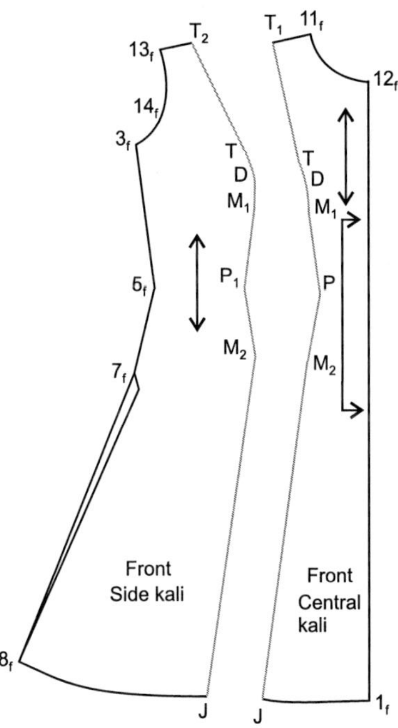

Kalidaar Kurta Flared:

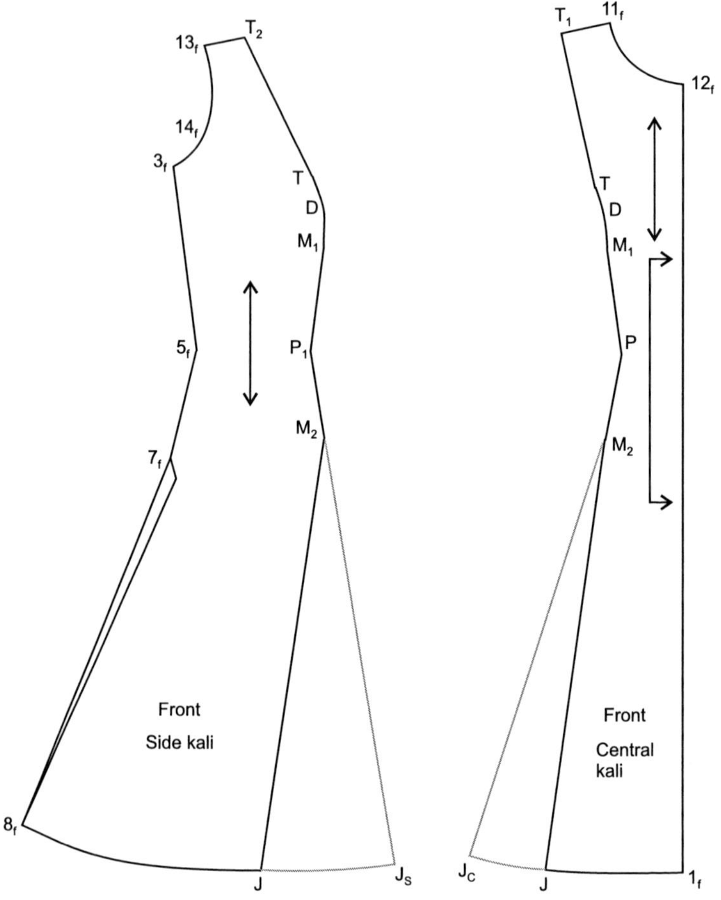

FLARED KALIDAR KURTA & VARIATION

Flared kalidar kurta with salwar

Flared kalidar kurta with chudidar

31 ANGARAKHA KURTA/ WRAPAROUND KURTA

STRAIGHT FIT ANGARAKHA KURTA

A straight fit wraparound kurta is a comfortably fitting knee length upper garment worn by women, generally teamed with salwar, chudidaar or trousers.

Suitable Fabric: Cotton, satin or any light weight fabric.

Size Symbol: Any (A-cup size). This construction is suitable for the given cup size. For any other cup size the dart width should be changed accordingly.

Size symbol – 10

Scale – cm

Drafting scale – 1/4th cm or 1/6th cm

Fabric required – 2.31 m × 75 cm (length × width)

Measurements:

Required length = 110 cm

Round bust = 88 cm

Round waist = 68 cm

Round hips = 94 cm

Waist length = 42 cm

Hip level = 20 cm

Highest bust level = 25 cm

Across shoulder = 35 cm

Construction:

Back:

1. 0 – 1 = required length + 1.5 cm [vertically downwards]
   = 111.5 cm
2. Armhole Depth:
   0 – 2 = 1/4th round bust – 4 cm [vertically downwards on line 0 – 1]
   = 18 cm
3. Bust Line:
   2 – 3 = 1/4th round bust + 2 cm (ease) [horizontally]
   = 24 cm
4. Waist Length:
   0 – 4 = waist length [vertically downwards on line 0 – 1]
   = 42 cm
5. Waistline:
   4 – 5 = 1/4th round waist + 2 cm (dart width) + 1 cm (ease) [horizontally]
   = 20 cm
   Join 5 – 3 in a straight line.
6. Hip Level:
   4 – 6 = hip level [vertically downwards on line 4 – 1]
   = 20 cm
7. Hip Line:
   6 – 7 = 1/4th round hips + 2 cm (ease) [horizontally]
   = 25.5 cm
   Join 7 – 5 in a straight line.
8. Hem Line:
   1 – 8 = 6 – 7 [horizontally]
   = 25.5 cm
   Join 8 – 7 in a straight line for side slits.

9. Shoulder:

   0 – 9 = ½ across shoulder [horizontally]

   = 17.5 cm

   Draw a vertical line downwards from point 9 to line 2 – 3 and mark as 10.

10. Neckline:

    0 – 11 = 1/12th round bust [horizontally on line 0 – 9]

    = 7.3 cm

    0 – 12 = 1.5 cm [vertically downwards on line 0 – 1]

    Join 11 – 12 in a smooth curve for neckline.

11. Shoulder Line:

    9 – 13 = 2 cm (shoulder drop) [vertically downwards on line 9 – 10]

    Join 13 – 11 in a straight line for shoulder line.

12. Armhole:

    13 – 14 = 14 – 10 [vertically on line 13 – 10]

    = 8 cm

    i.e. point 14 is the mid-point of line 13 – 10.

    Join 13 – 14 – 3 in a smooth curve for armhole.

13. Dart: Waistline dart (double-headed dart)

    (i) Dart position: 4 – N = 1/12th round bust [horizontally on line 4 – 5]

    = 7.3 cm

    (ii) Dart length: Upward dart length:

    $N - N_1$ = 1/8th round bust [vertically upwards]

    = 11 cm

    Downward dart length:

    $N - N_2$ = 1/10th round hips [vertically downwards]

    = 9.4 cm

    $N_1 - N_2$ is the required dart length for double-headed waistline dart.

(iii) Dart width: $N - S = N - S_1 = 1$ cm (on either side of point N) [horizontally on line 4 – 5]

Join $S - N_1$ and $S - N_2$ in straight lines and join $S_1 - N_1$ and $S_1 - N_2$ in straight lines for the required double-headed dart.

14. Back straight fit angarakha kurta block is along the points:

12 – 1 – 8 – 7 – 5 – 3 – 14 – 13 – 11 – 12,

where:

0 – 1 is on fold.

11 – 12 is neckline.

13 – 11 is shoulder line.

13 – 14 – 3 is armhole.

3 – 5 – 7 is side seams.

7 – 8 is side slits.

Front:

1. $0_f - 1_f$ = required length + 3 cm [vertically downwards]
   = 113 cm
2. Armhole Depth:
   $0_f - 2_f$ = 1/4th round bust – 4 cm [vertically downwards on line $0_f - 1_f$]
   = 18 cm
3. Bust Line:
   $2_f - 3_f$ = 1/4th round bust + 2 cm (ease) [horizontally]
   = 24 cm
4. Waist Length:
   $0_f - 4_f$ = waist length + 1.5 cm (dart width) [vertically downwards on line $0_f - 1_f$]
   = 43.5 cm
5. Waitline:
   $4_f - 5_f$ = 1/4th round waist + 2 cm (dart width) + 1 cm (ease) [horizontally]
   = 20 cm

   Join $5_f - 3_f$ in a straight line.

6. Hip Level:

   $4_f - 6_f$ = hip level [vertically downwards on line $4_f - 1_f$]
   = 20 cm

7. Hip Line:

   $6_f - 7_f$ = 1/4th round hips + 2 cm (ease) [horizontally]
   = 25.5 cm

   Join $7_f - 5_f$ in a straight line.

8. Hem Line:

   $1_f - 8_f = 6_f - 7_f$ [horizontally]
   = 25.5 cm

   Join $8_f - 7_f$ in a straight line for side slits.

9. Shoulder:

   $0_f - 9_f$ = ½ across shoulder [horizontally]
   = 17.5 cm

   Draw a vertical line downwards from point 9_f to line $2_f - 3_f$ and mark as 10_f.

10. Overlap (bust line):

    $2_f - 11_f$ = 1/12th round bust + 1 cm (extend outwards) [horizontally]
    = 8.3 cm

    Overlap (hem line):

    $1_f - 12_f = 2_f - 11_f$ (extend outwards) [horizontally]
    = 8.3 cm

    Join $12_f - 11_f$ in a straight line for overlap angarakha style.

11. Neckline:

    $0_f - 13_f$ = 1/12th round bust [horizontally on line $0_f - 9_f$]
    = 7.3 cm

    Join $13_f - 11_f$ in a smooth curve for neckline.

12. Shoulder Line:

    $9_f - 14_f$ = 2 cm [vertically downwards on line $9_f - 10_f$]

    Join $14_f - 13_f$ in a straight line for shoulder line.

13. Armhole:

    $10_f - 15_f$ = 2.5 cm [vertically upwards on line $10_f - 14_f$]

    Join $14_f - 15_f - 3_f$ in a smooth curve for armhole.

14. Darts:

    0_f – A = highest bust level [vertically downwards on line $0_f - 1_f$]
    = 25 cm

    A – B = 1/12th round bust [horizontally]
    = 7.3 cm

    (a) Waistline dart: double-headed dart

    (i) Dart position: 4_f – M = 1/12th round bust [horizontally on line $4_f - 5_f$]
    = 7.3 cm

    (ii) Dart length: Upward dart length: B – M_1 = 2 cm [vertically downwards on line B – M]

    Join M – M_1 in straight line.

    M – M_1 is the upward dart length.

    Downward dart length:

    M – M_2 = 1/10th round hips [vertically downwards]
    = 9.4 cm

    M_1 – M_2 is the required dart length for double-headed dart.

    (iii) Dart width: M – P = M – P_1 = 1 cm (on either side of point M) [horizontally on line $4_f - 5_f$]

    Join P – M_1 and P – M_2 in straight lines and join P_1 – M_1 and P_1 – M_2 in straight lines for the required double headed waistline dart.

(b) Side seam dart:

(i) Dart position: $3_f - T$ = 1/8th round bust [downwards on line $3_f - 5_f$]
= 11 cm

(ii) Dart length: $B - T_1$ = 4 cm [on line $B - T$]
Join $T_1 - T$ in a straight line for the side seam dart.

(iii) Dart width: $T - R = T - R_1$ = 0.8 cm (on either side of point T) [on line $3_f - 5_f$]
Join $R - T_1$ and $R_1 - T_1$ in straight lines for the required side seam dart.

15. Front straight fit angarakha kurta block is along the points:

$11_f - 12_f - 8_f - 7_f - 5_f - T - 3_f - 15_f - 14_f - 13_f - 11_f$, where:

$11_f - 12_f$ is front open for overlap.

$13_f - 11_f$ is neckline.

$14_f - 13_f$ is shoulder line.

$14_f - 15_f - 3_f$ is armhole.

$3_f - 5_f - 7_f$ is side seams.

$7_f - 8_f$ is side slits.

$8_f - 12_f$ is hem line.

Cut two pieces of front block each for right and left side.

Add seam allowance of 1.5 cm (or as required) and hem allowance of 3 cm (or as required) and mark corresponding balance points and grain line on each pattern piece.

Straight Fit Angarakha Kurta:

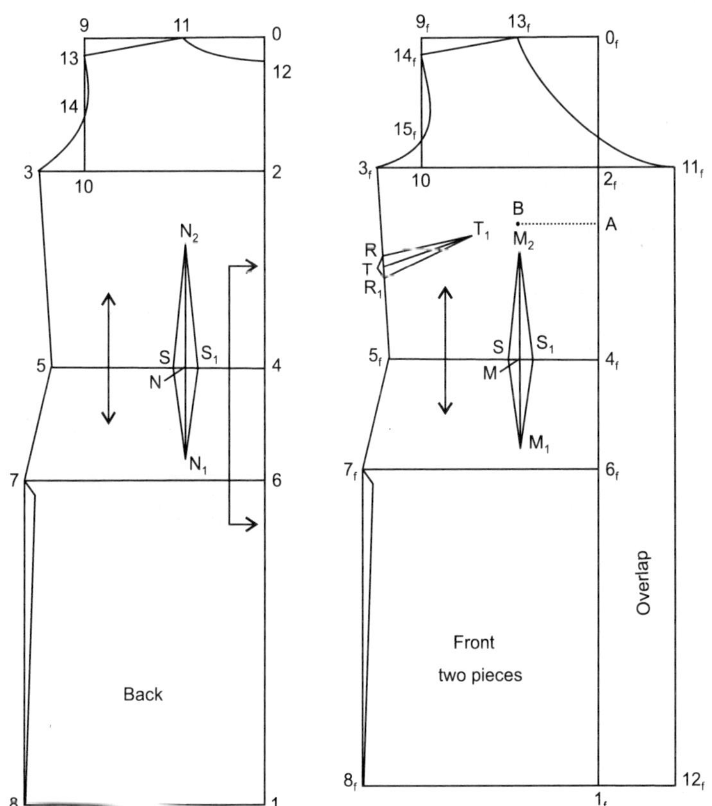

FLARED ANGARAKHA KURTA

A slightly fitting and flared at hem kurta is a knee to calf length upper garment worm by girls and women, generally teamed with salwar, chudidaar or trousers.

Suitable Fabric: Cotton, satin or any light weight fabric.

Size Symbol: Any (B-cup size). This construction is suitable for the given cup size. For any other cup size the dart width should be changed accordingly.

Size symbol – 10

Scale – cm

STRAIGHT FIT ANGARAKHA KURTA & VARIATION

Straight fit angarakha kurta with salwar

Straight fit angarakha kurta with chudidar

Drafting scale – 1/4th cm or 1/6th cm

Fabric required – 2.31 m × 90 cm (length × width)

Measurements:

Required length = 110 cm

Round bust = 88 cm

Round waist = 68 cm

Round hips = 94 cm

Waist length = 42 cm

Hip level = 20 cm

Highest bust level = 25 cm

Across shoulder = 35 cm

Construction:

Back:

1. 0 – 1 = required length + 1.5 cm [vertically downwards]
   = 111.5 cm
2. Armhole Depth:
   0 – 2 = 1/8th round bust + 7 cm [vertically downwards on line 0 – 1]
   = 18 cm
3. Bust Line:
   2 – 3 = 1/4th round bust + 2 cm (ease or as required) [horizontally]
   = 24 cm
4. Waist Length:
   0 – 4 = waist length [vertically downwards on line 0 – 1]
   = 42 cm
5. Waistline:
   4 – 5 = 1/4th round waist + 3 cm (dart width) + 1 cm (ease) [horizontally]
   = 21 cm

   Join 3 – 5 in a straight line.

6. Hip Level:

   4 – 6 = hip level [vertically downwards on line 4 – 1]
   = 20 cm

7. Hip Line:

   6 – 7 = 1/4th round hips + 3 cm (ease and shape) [horizontally]
   = 26.5 cm

   Join 7 – 5 in a straight line.

8. Hem Line:

   1 – 8 = 1/4th round hips + 8 cm (for flare) [horizontally]
   = 31.5 cm

9. Side Seams:

   Join 8 – 7 in a straight line for side seams.

10. To Shape Hem Line:

    8 – 9 = 1.5 cm [upwards on line 8 – 7]

    Join 9 – 1 in a smooth curve for hem line.

11. Shoulder:

    0 – 10 = ½ across shoulder + 1 cm [horizontally]
    = 18.5 cm

    Draw a vertical line downwards from point 10 to line 2 – 3 and mark as 11.

12. Neckline:

    0 – 12 = 1/12th round bust [horizontally on line 0 – 10]
    = 7.3 cm

    12 – 13 = 1.5 cm [vertically upwards]

    Join 13 – 0 in a smooth curve for neckline.

13. Shoulder Line:

    10 – 14 = 0.5 cm [vertically downwards on line 10 – 11]

    Join 14 – 13 in a straight line for shoulder line.

14. Armhole:

    14 – 15 = 15 – 11 [vertically downwards on line 14 – 11]
    = 8.75 cm

    i.e. point 15 is the mid-point of line 14 – 11.

    Join 14 – 15 – 3 in a smooth curve for armhole.

15. Dart: Waistline dart (double-headed dart)

    (i) Dart position: 4 – N = 1/12th round bust [horizontally on line 4 – 5]
    = 7.3 cm

    (ii) Dart length: Upward dart length:

    $N - N_1$ = 1/8th round bust [vertically upwards]
    = 11 cm

    Downward dart length:

    $N - N_2$ = 1/10th round hips [vertically downwards]
    = 9.4 cm

    $N_1 - N_2$ is the required dart length for double-headed dart.

    (iii) Dart width: $N - S = N - S_1$ = 1.5 cm (on either side of point N) [horizontally on line 4 – 5]

    Join $S - N_1$ and $S - N_2$ in straight lines and join $S_1 - N_1$ and $S_1 - N_2$ in straight lines for the required double-headed dart.

15. Back flared angarakha kurta block is along the points:

    0 – 1 – 9 – 7 – 5 – 3 – 15 – 14 – 13 – 0,

    where:

    0 – 1 is on fold.

    13 – 0 is neckline.

    13 – 14 is shoulder line.

    14 – 15 – 3 is armhole.

    3 – 5 – 7 – 9 is side seams.

    1 – 9 is hem line.

Front:

1. $0_f - 1_f$ = required length + 3 cm [vertically downwards]
   = 113 cm
2. Armhole Depth:
   $0_f - 2_f$ = 1/8th round bust + 7 cm [vertically downwards on line $0_f - 1_f$]
   = 18 cm
3. Bust Line:
   $2_f - 3_f$ = 1/4th round bust + 2 cm (ease) [horizontally]
   = 24 cm
4. Waist Length:
   $0_f - 4_f$ = waist length + 1.5 cm (dart width) [vertically downwards on line $0_f - 1_f$]
   = 43.5 cm
5. Waitline:
   $4_f - 5_f$ = 1/4th round waist + 3 cm (dart width) + 1 cm (ease) [horizontally]
   = 21 cm

   Join $5_f - 3_f$ in a straight line.
6. Hip Level:
   $4_f - 6_f$ = hip level [vertically downwards on line $4_f - 1_f$]
   = 20 cm
7. Hip Line:
   $6_f - 7_f$ = 1/4th round hips + 3 cm (ease and shape) [horizontally]
   = 26.5 cm

   Join $7_f - 5_f$ in a straight line.
8. Hem Line:
   $1_f - 8_f$ = 1/4th round hips + 8 cm (as of back block) [horizontally]
   = 31.5 cm

9. Side Seams:

   Join $8_f - 7_f$ in a straight line for side seam.

10. To Shape Hemline:

    $8_f - 9_f$ = 1.5 cm [upwards on line $8_f - 7_f$]

    Join $9_f - 1_f$ in a smooth curve for hem line.

11. Shoulder:

    $0_f - 10_f$ = ½ across shoulder + 1 cm [horizontally]
    = 18.5 cm

    Draw a vertical line downwards from point 10_f to line $2_f - 3_f$ and mark as 11_f.

12. Overlap (bust line):

    $2_f - 12_f$ = 1/12th round bust + 1 cm (extend outwards) [horizontally]
    = 8.3 cm

    Overlap (hem line):

    $1_f - 13_f = 2_f - 12_f$ (extend outwards) [horizontally]
    = 8.3 cm

    Join $12_f - 13_f$ in a straight line for overlap angarakha style.

13. Neckline:

    $0_f - 14_f$ = 1/12th round bust [horizontally on line $0_f - 10_f$]
    = 7.3 cm

    $0_f - 15_f$ = 1/12th round bust [vertically downwards on line $0_f - 1_f$]
    = 7.3 cm

    Join $14_f - 15_f$ in a smooth curve and extend horizontally (straight line) outwards and mark as 16_f for neckline, where:

    $15_f - 16_f = 2_f - 12_f$ [horizontally]
    = 8.3 cm

14. Shoulder Line:

$10_f - 17_f$ = 2 cm [vertically downwards on line $10_f - 11_f$]

Join $17_f - 14_f$ in a straight line for shoulder line.

15. Armhole:

$11_f - 18_f$ = 2.5 cm [vertically upwards on line $11_f - 17_f$]

Join $17_f - 18_f - 3_f$ in a smooth curve for armhole.

16. Darts:

0_f – A = highest bust level [vertically downwards on line $0_f - 1_f$]
= 25 cm

A – B = 1/12th round bust [horizontally]
= 7.3 cm

(a) Waistline dart: double-headed dart

(i) Dart position: 4_f – M = 1/12th round bust [horizontally on line $4_f - 5_f$]
= 7.3 cm

(ii) Dart length: Upward dart length: B – M_1 = 2 cm [vertically downwards on line B – M]

Join M_1 – M in a straight line for upward dart length.

Downward dart length:

M – M_2 = 1/10th round hips [vertically downwards]
= 9.4 cm

$M_1 - M_2$ is the required dart length for double-headed dart.

(iii) Dart width: M – P = M – P_1 = 1.5 cm (on either side of point M) [horizontally on line $4_f - 5_f$]

Join P – M_1 and P – M_2 in straight lines and join $P_1 - M_1$ and $P_1 - M_2$ in straight lines for the required double-headed waistline dart.

(b) Side seam dart:

(i) Dart position: $5_f - T$ = 1/8th round bust + 2 cm [upwards on line $5_f - 3_f$]
= 13 cm

(ii) Dart length: $B - T_1$ = 3 cm [downwards on line B – T]

Join $T - T_1$ in a straight line.

$T - T_1$ is the required dart length for side seam dart.

(iii) Dart width: $T - R = T - R_1$ = 0.8 cm (on either side of point T) [on line $5_f - 3_f$]

Join $R - T_1$ and $R_1 - T_1$ in straight lines for the required side seam dart.

17. Front flared angarakha kurta block is along the points:

$16_f - 13_f - 1_f - 9_f - 7_f - 5_f - T - 3_f - 18_f - 17_f - 14_f - 15_f - 16_f$, where:

$16_f - 13_f$ is front open for overlap.

$14_f - 15_f - 16_f$ is neckline.

$14_f - 17_f$ is shoulder line.

$17_f - 18_f - 3_f$ is armhole.

$3_f - T - 5_f - 7_f - 9_f$ is side seams.

$9_f - 1_f - 13_f$ is hem line.

Cut two pieces of front block each for right and left side.

Add seam allowance of 1.5 cm (or as required) and hem allowance of 3 cm (or as required) and mark corresponding balance points and grain line on each pattern piece.

Flared Angarakha Kurta:

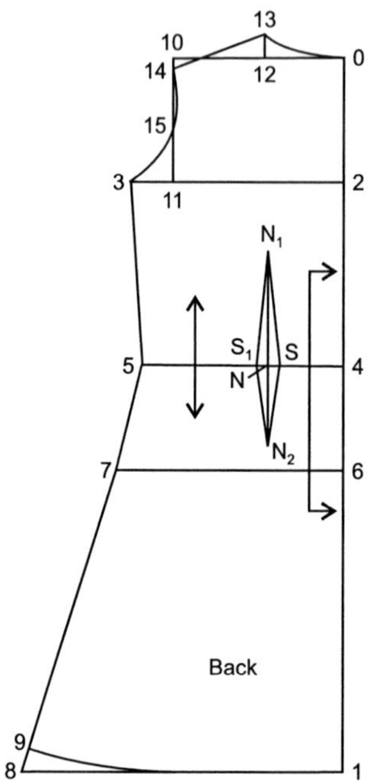

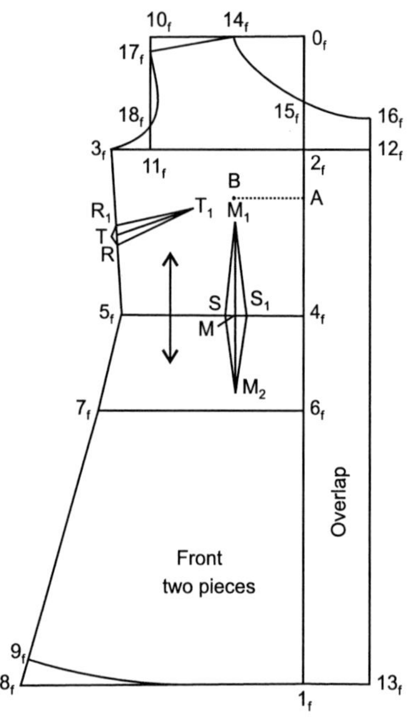

FLARED ANGARAKHA KURTA & VARIATION

Flared angarakha kurta
with salwar

Flared angarakha kurta
with chudidar

32 PANELED KURTA (HORIZONTAL PANELS STITCHED TO SAREE BLOUSE)

PANELED KURTA

Horizontal panels are stitched to a small blouse at the level of empire waist. These type of kurtas should be teamed with a churidaar to enhance the look.

Suitable Fabric: Light weight smooth fabric, e.g. chiffon, linen, etc.

Size Symbol: Any (B-cup size). This construction is suitable for the given cup size. For any other cup size the dart width should be changed accordingly.

Size symbol – 10

Scale – cm

Drafting scale – 1/4th cm or 1/6th cm

Fabric required – 2.5 m × 1 m (length × width)

Measurements:

Required length = 110 cm

Round bust = 88 cm

Round waist (empire waist) = 72 cm

Blouse length = 34 cm

Highest bust level = 25 cm

Across shoulder = 35 cm

Sleeve length = 14 cm

Top arm = 26 cm

Construction:

Back:

1. 0 – 1 = blouse length + 1 cm [vertically downwards]
   = 35 cm
2. Armhole Depth:
   0 – 2 = 1/4th round bust – 4 cm [vertically downwards on line 0 – 1]
   = 18 cm
3. Bust Line:
   2 – 3 = 1/4th round bust + 2 cm (ease) [horizontally]
   = 24 cm
4. Empire Waistline
   1 – 4 = 1/4th round empire waist + 2 cm (dart width) [horizontally]
   = 20 cm
   Join 4 – 3 in a straight line for side seams.
5. Shoulder:
   0 – 5 = ½ across shoulder + 1 cm [horizontally]
   = 18.5 cm
   Draw a vertical line downwards from point 5 to line 2 – 3 and mark as 6.
6. Neckline:
   0 – 7 = 1/12th round bust (or as required) [horizontally on line 0 – 5]
   = 7.3 cm
   0 – 8 = 1.5 cm [vertically downwards on line 0 – 1]
   Join 7 – 8 in a smooth curve for neckline.
7. Shoulder Line:
   5 – 9 = 2 cm (shoulder drop) [vertically downwards on line 5 – 6]
   Join 9 – 7 in a straight line for shoulder line.

8. Armhole:

   9 – 10 = 10 – 6 [vertically on line 9 – 6]

   = 8 cm

   i.e. point 10 is the mid-point of line 9 – 6.

   Join 9 – 10 – 3 in a smooth curve for armhole.

9. Dart: Waistline dart

   (i) Dart position: 1 – N = 1/12th round bust [horizontally on line 1 – 4]

   = 7.3 cm

   (ii) Dart length: N – N_1 = 1/12th round bust [vertically upwards]

   = 7.3 cm

   (iii) Dart width: N – S = N – S_1 = 1 cm (on either side of point N) [horizontally on line 1 – 4]

   Join S – N_1 and S_1 – N_1 in straight lines for the required dart.

10. Back blouse block is along the points:

    8 – 1 – N – 4 – 3 – 10 – 9 – 7 – 8,

    where:

    8 – 1 is on fold.

    7 – 9 is shoulder line.

    9 – 10 – 3 is armhole.

    3 – 4 is side seams.

    1 – N – 4 is empire waistline.

Front:

1. $0_f - 1_f$ = required length + 2.5 cm [vertically downwards]

   = 36.5 cm

2. Armhole Depth:

   $0_f - 2_f$ = 1/4th round bust – 4 cm [vertically downwards on line $0_f - 1_f$]

   = 18 cm

3. Bust Line:

   $2_f - 3_f$ = 1/4th round bust + 2 cm (ease) [horizontally]
   = 24 cm

4. Empire Waistline:

   $1_f - 4_f$ = 1/4th round waist + 3 cm (dart width) [horizontally]
   = 21 cm

5. Shoulder:

   $0_f - 5_f$ = ½ across shoulder + 1 cm [horizontally]
   = 18.5 cm

   Draw a vertical line downwards from point 5_f to line $2_f - 3_f$ and mark as 6_f.

6. Neckline:

   $0_f - 7_f$ = 1/12th round bust [horizontally on line $0_f - 5_f$]
   = 7.3 cm

   $0_f - 8_f$ = 1/12th round bust + 1 cm (or as required for depth) [vertically downwards on line $0_f - 1_f$]
   = 7.3 cm

   Join $7_f - 8_f$ in a smooth curve for neckline.

7. Shoulder Line:

   $5_f - 9_f$ = 2 cm (shoulder drop) [vertically downwards on line $5_f - 6_f$]

   Join $9_f - 7_f$ in a straight line for shoulder line.

8. Armhole:

   (i) $5_f - 10_f = 6_f - 10_f$ [vertically on line $9_f - 6_f$]
   = 8 cm

   i.e. point 10_f is the mid-point of line $9_f - 6_f$.

   (ii) $10_f - 11_f$ = 1.5 cm [horizontally inwards]

   Join $9_f - 11_f - 3_f$ in a smooth curve for armhole.

9. Darts:

   0_f – A = highest bust level [vertically downwards on line $0_f - 1_f$]
   = 25 cm

A – B = 1/12th round bust [horizontally]

= 7.3 cm

(a) Waistline dart:

(i) Dart position: 1_f – M = 1/12th round bust [horizontally on line $1_f – 4_f$]

= 7.3 cm

(ii) Dart length: B – M_1 = 2 cm [vertically downwards on line B – M]

Join M – M_1 in a straight line.

M – M_1 is the required dart length.

(iii) Dart width: M – P = M – P_1 = 1.5 cm (on either side of point M) [horizontally on line $1_f – 4_f$]

Join P – M_1 and P_1 – M_1 in straight lines for the required waistline dart.

(b) Side seam dart:

(i) Dart position: 4_f – T = 1/12th round bust – 2 cm [upwards on line $4_f – 3_f$]

= 5.3 cm

(ii) Dart length: B – T_1 = 4 cm [on line B – T]

Join T – T_1 in a straight line.

T – T_1 is the required dart length.

(iii) Dart width: T – R = T – R_1 = 0.8 cm (on either side of point T) [on line $4_f – 3_f$]

Join R – T_1 and R_1 – T_1 in straight lines for the required side seam dart.

10. Front blouse block is along the points:

$8_f – 1_f$ – M – 4_f – T – $3_f – 11_f – 9_f – 7_f – 8_f$,

where:

$8_f – 1_f$ is center front and should be finished with plackets and dress hooks or as desired.

$7_f – 8_f$ is neckline.

$7_f – 9_f$ is shoulder line.

$9_f - 11_f - 3_f$ is armhole.

$3_f - T - 4_f$ is side seams.

$1_f - M - 4_f$ is empire waistline.

Sleeve:

1. 0 – 1 = sleeve length + 1 cm [vertically downwards]
   = 15 cm
2. Sleeve Crown:
   0 – 2 = 1/4th round bust – 4 cm [vertically downwards]
   = 18 cm
3. Crown Width:
   2 – 3 = 1/4th round bust + 10 cm (gathers) [horizontally]
   = 32 cm
   Join 3 – 0 in a straight line.
4. Top Arm:
   1 – 4 = ½ top arm + 10 cm (gathers) [horizontally]
   = 23 cm
   Join 4 – 3 in a straight line for side seams.
5. To Shape Sleeve Crown:
   (i) Divide 3 – 0 into four equal parts and mark as 5, 6 and 7, respectively.
   (ii) $5 - 5_1$ = 1 cm [perpendicular to line 3 – 0 downwards]
   (iii) $6 - 6_1$ – 2.5 cm [perpendicular to line 3 – 0 upwards]
   (iv) $7 - 7_1$ = 1 cm [perpendicular to line 3 – 0 upwards]
      (a) For back sleeve crown join points: $0 - 6_1 - 5 - 3$ in a 'S' shape as shown in the diagram.
      (b) For front sleeve crown join points: $0 - 7_1 - 6 - 5_1 - 3$ in a 'S' shape as shown in the diagram.

6. Sleeve block is along the points:
   back sleeve block: $0 - 1 - 4 - 3 - 5 - 6_1 - 0$.
   front sleeve block: $0 - 1 - 4 - 3 - 5_1 - 6 - 7_1 - 0$.
   where:
   0 – 1 is on fold.
   3 – 4 is side seams.
   1 – 4 is round arm which should be gathered to a band or elasticized as required.

Skirt for Kurta:

1. Skirt Length:
   11 – 12 = required length – bodice length [vertically downwards]
   = 76 cm
2. First Horizontal Panel:
   (a) 11 – 13 = 1/4th round bust + 10 cm (gathers or as required) [horizontally]
   = 32 cm
   (b) 11 – 14 = 1/3rd skirt length – 2 cm (or as required) [vertically downwards on line 11 – 12]
   = 23.3 cm
   (c) 14 – 15 = 11 – 13 [horizontally]
   = 32 cm
   Join 15 – 13 in a straight line for side seams.
3. Second Horizontal Panel:
   (a) 15 – 16 = 15 cm (or as required) [extend outwards horizontally]
   (b) 14 – 17 = 1/3rd skirt length – 1 cm [vertically downwards on line 11 – 12]
   = 24.3 cm
   (c) 17 – 18 = 14 – 16 [horizontally]
   = 38.3 cm
   Join 18 – 16 in a straight line for side seams.

4. Third Horizontal Panel:
   (a) 18 – 19 = 20 cm (or as required) [extend outwards horizontally]
   (b) 17 – 12 is the length of third panel.
   (c) 12 – 20 = 17 – 19 [horizontally]
       = 58.3 cm

   Join 20 – 19 in a straight line for side seams.
5. Skirt block for horizontal paneled kurta is along the points:

   For first panel cut along the points:

   11 – 14 – 15 – 13 – 11,

   where:

   11 – 14 is on fold.

   11 – 13 is waistline and should be gathered to 1 – 4 and $1_f - 4_f$ of blouse block. This seam can be finished with a fancy linear lace or as required.

   For second panel cut along the points;

   14 – 17 – 18 – 16 – 14,

   where:

   14 – 17 is on fold.

   16 – 14 should be gathered to 14 – 15 of first panel. This seam can be finished with a fancy linear lace or as required.

   For third panel cut along the points:

   17 – 12 – 20 – 19 – 17,

   where:

   17 – 12 is on fold.

   17 – 19 should be gathered to 17 – 18 of second panel. This seam can be finished with a fancy linear lace or as required.

   12 – 20 is hem line.

Add seam allowance of 1.5 cm (or as required) and hem allowance of 3 cm (or as required) and mark corresponding balance points and grain line on each pattern piece.

Paneled Kurta:

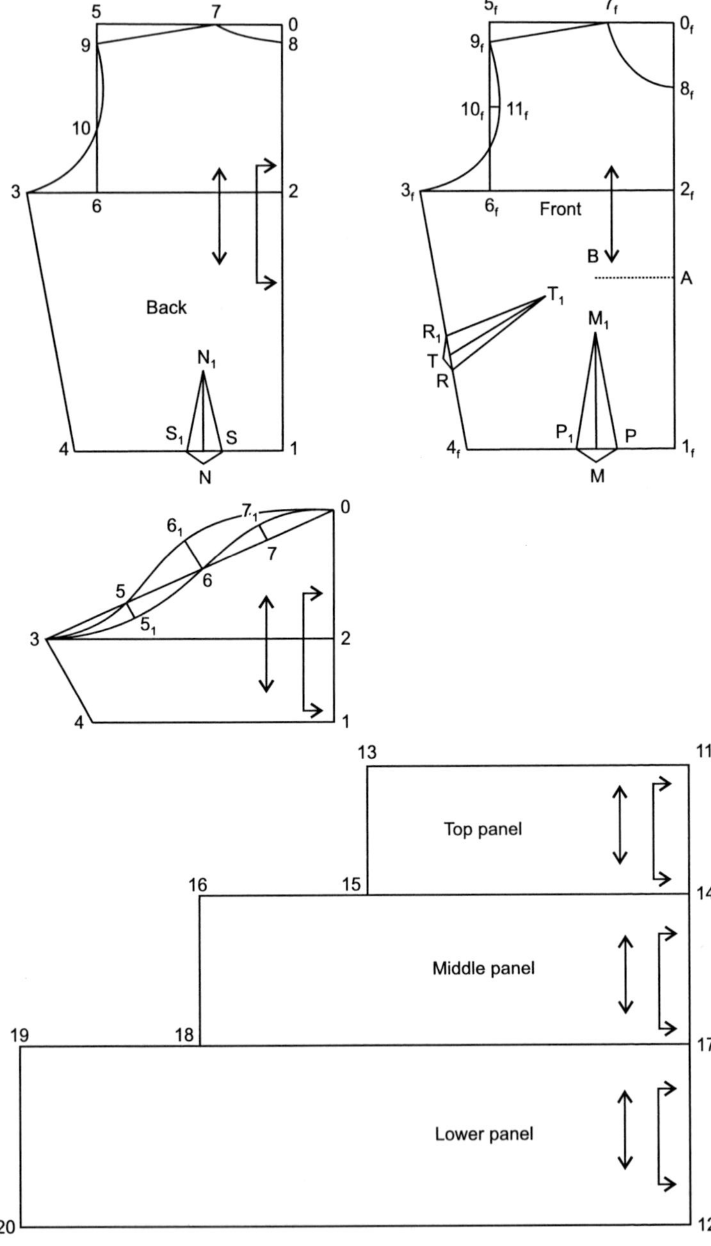

PANELED KURTA & VARIATION

Paneled kurta with chudidaar

Paneled kurta with salwar

33 SHOULDERLESS KURTA

SHOULDERLESS KURTA

A skirt like upper garment without shoulder and sleeves worn at chest level. A designer garment generally worn by women and teamed with salwar, chudidaar or trousers.

Suitable Fabric: Cotton, satin, any smooth light weight fabric.

Size Symbol: Any (B-cup size). This construction is suitable for the given cup size. For any other cup size the dart width should be changed accordingly.

Size symbol – 10

Scale – cm

Drafting scale – 1/4th cm or 1/6th cm

Fabric required – 1.80 m × 1 m (length × width)

Measurements:

Required length = 80 cm

Round chest = 78 cm

Round bust = 88 cm

Round waist = 68 cm

Round hips = 94 cm

Waist length = 42 cm

Hip level = 17 cm

Highest bust level = 25 cm

Across shoulder = 35 cm

Construction:

Back:

1. 0 – 1 = required length + 1 cm [vertically downwards]
   = 81 cm
2. Chest Line:
   0 – 2 = 1/4th round chest + 3 cm (dart width) [horizontally]
   = 22.5 cm
3. Distance between Chest Line and Bust Line:
   0 – 3 = 3 cm [vertically downwards]
4. Bust Line:
   3 – 4 = 1/4th round bust + 1 cm (dart width) + 0.5 cm (ease) [horizontally]
   = 23.5 cm

   Join 2 – 4 in a straight line.
5. Waist Length:
   3 – 5 = waist length – armhole depth [vertically downwards]
   = 42 cm – (1/4th round bust – 4 cm)
   = 24 cm
6. Waistline:
   5 – 6 = 1/4th round waist + 3 cm (dart width) + 0.5 cm (ease) [horizontally]
   = 20.5 cm

   Join 4 – 6 in a straight line.
7. Hip Level:
   5 – 7 = hip level [vertically downwards]
   = 17 cm
8. Hip Line:
   7 – 8 = 1/4th round hips + 2 cm (ease) [horizontally]
   = 25.5 cm

   Join 8 – 6 in straight line.

9. Hem Line:

   1 – 9 = 7 – 8 [horizontally]

   = 25.5 cm

   Join 9 – 8 in a straight line for side slits.

10. For Darts:

   (a) Waistline dart: double-headed dart:

   (i) Dart position: 5 – N = 1/12th round bust [horizontally]

   = 7.3 cm

   (ii) Dart length: Double-headed dart. Upward dart length: N – N_1 = 1/8th round bust [vertically upwards]

   = 11 cm

   Downward dart length:

   N – N_2 = 1/10th round hips [vertically downwards]

   = 9.4 cm

   N_1 – N_2 is the required length for double headed dart.

   (iii) Dart width: N – S = N – S_1 = 1.5 cm (on either side of point N) [horizontally]

   Join S – N_1 and S – N_2 in straight lines and join S_1 – N_1 and S_1 – N_2 in straight lines for the required double-headed dart.

   (b) Chest line dart:

   (i) Dart position: 0 – L = 1/12th round bust + 2 cm [horizontally]

   = 9.3 cm

   (ii) Dart length: L – N_1 is the required dart length [downwards]

   (iii) Dart width: L – Q = L – Q_1 = 1.5 cm (on either side of point L) [horizontally]

   Join Q – N_1 and Q_1 – N_1 in straight lines for the required chest line dart.

11. For Back Opening:

    0 – C = (0 – 5) + 4 cm [vertically downwards]

    = 28 cm

    As shoulder less kurta is fitting so a opening longer than 0 – 5 has to be given to slip in, which should be finished with a fly (zip) or as required.

12. For back shoulderless kurta cut along the points:

    0 – 1 – 9 – 8 – 6 – 4 – 2 – L – 0,

    where:

    0 – 1 is on fold.

    2 – 4 – 6 – 8 is side seams.

    8 – 9 is side slits.

    0 – C is for back opening.

Front:

1. $0_f - 1_f$ = required length + 2.5 cm [vertically downwards]

   = 82.5 cm

2. Chest Line:

   $0_f - 2_f$ = 1/4th round chest + 3 cm (dart width) [horizontally]

   = 22.5 cm

3. Distance between Chest Line and Bust Line:

   $0_f - 3_f$ = 3 cm [vertically downwards]

4. Bust Line:

   $3_f - 4_f$ = 1/4th round bust + 1 cm (dart width) + 0.5 cm (ease) [horizontally]

   = 23.5 cm

   Join $2_f - 4_f$ in a straight line.

5. Waist Length:

   $3_f - 5_f$ = waist length – armhole depth + dart width [vertically downwards]

   = 42 cm – (1/4th round bust – 4 cm) + 1 cm

   = 25 cm

6. Waistline:

   $5_f - 6_f$ = 1/4th round waist + 3 cm (dart width) + 0.5 cm (ease) [horizontally]

   = 20.5 cm

   Join $4_f - 6_f$ in a straight line.

7. Hip Level:

   $5_f - 7_f$ = hip level [vertically downwards]

   = 17 cm

8. Hip Line:

   $7_f - 8_f$ = 1/4th round hips + 2 cm (ease) [horizontally]

   = 25.5 cm

   Join $6_f - 8_f$ in a straight line.

9. Hem Line:

   $1_f - 9_f$ = $7_f - 8_f$ [horizontally]

   = 25.5 cm

   Join $8_f - 9_f$ in a straight line for side slits.

10. For Darts:

    3_f – A = highest bust level – scye depth [vertically downwards]

    = 25 cm – (1/4th round bust – 4 cm)

    = 7 cm

    A – B = 1/12th round bust [horizontally]

    = 7.3 cm

    (a) Waistline dart: double-headed dart.

    (i) Dart position: 5_f – M = 1/12th round bust [horizontally]

    = 7.3 cm

    (ii) Dart length: double-headed dart. Upward dart: B – M_1 = 1.5 cm [vertically downwards]

    M – M_1 is the required upward dart length.

    Downward dart: M – M_2 = 1/10th round hips [vertically downwards]

    = 9.4 cm

$M_1 - M_2$ is the required dart length for the double-headed dart.

(iii) Dart width: $M - P = M - P_1 = 1.5$ cm (on either side of point M) [horizontally]

Join $P - M_1$ and $P - M_2$ in straight lines and join $P_1 - M_1$ and $P_1 - M_2$ in straight lines for the required double headed dart.

(b) Chest line dart:

(i) Dart position: $0_f - G$ = 1/12th round bust + 2 cm [horizontally]

= 9.3 cm

(ii) Dart length: $B - G_1$ = 2 cm [upwards on line $B - G$]

$G - G_1$ is the required dart length.

(iii) Dart width: $G - J = G - J_1 = 1.5$ cm (on either side of point G) [horizontally]

Join $J - G_1$ and $J_1 - G_1$ in straight lines for the required chest line dart.

(c) Side seam dart:

(i) Dart position: $6_f - T$ = 1/8th round bust [upwards on line $6_f - 4_f$]

= 11 cm

(ii) Dart length: $B - T_1$ = 2 cm [on line $B - T$]

$T - T_1$ is the required dart length.

(iii) Dart width: $T - R = T - R_1 = 1$ cm (on either side of point T) [on line $6_f - 4_f$]

Join $R - T_1$ and $R_1 - T_1$ in straight lines for the required side seam dart.

11. For front shoulderless kurta cut along the points:

$0_f - 1_f - 9_f - 8_f - 6_f - T - 4_f - 2_f - G - 0_f$,

where:

$0_f - 1_f$ is on fold.

$2_f - 4_f - 6_f - 8_f$ is side seams.

$8_f - 9_f$ is side slits.

Add seam allowance of 1.5 cm (or as required) and hem allowance of 3 cm (or as required) and mark corresponding balance points and grain line on each pattern piece.

Shoulderless Kurta (back)

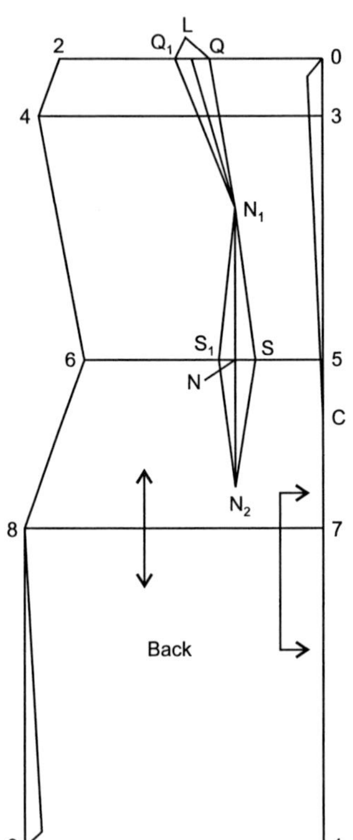

Shoulderless Kurta (front)

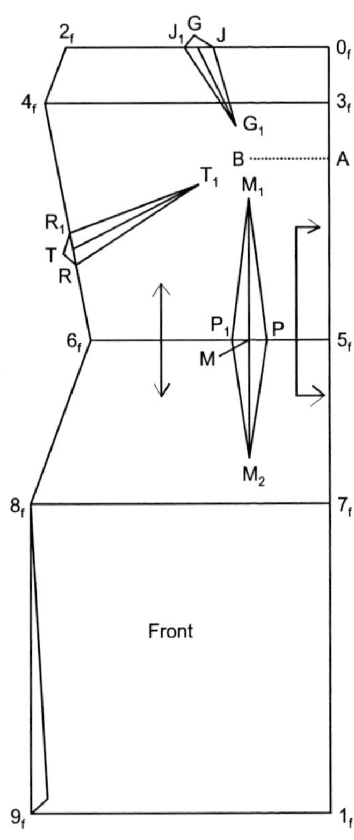

SHOULDERLESS KURTA & VARIATION

Shoulderless kurta with salwar

Shoulderless kurta shaped with chudidar

34 SALWAR

PLAIN SALWAR

A simple trouser like lower garment generally worn by men and women in India and few Asian countries which is teamed with kurta.

Suitable Fabric: Cotton, any light weight fabric.

Size Symbol: Any

Size symbol – 10

Scale – cm

Drafting scale – 1/4th cm

Fabric required – 2.25 m × 90 cm (length × width)

Measurements:

Required length = 104 cm

Round hip = 94 cm

Hip level = 20.3 cm

Round ankle = 24 cm

Round bottom = round ankle + 12 cm (ease or as required)
= 36 cm

Construction:

Central Panel:

1. 0 – 1 = full length +1 cm [vertically downwards]
   = 105 cm

2. 1 – 2 = ½ round bottom – 2.5 cm [horizontally]
   = 15.5 cm

   Complete the rectangle 0 – 1 – 2 – 3,

   where:

   3 – 2 = 0 – 1 [vertically], and

   0 – 3 = 1 – 2 [horizontally].

Side Panel:

3. Crotch Level:

   3 – 4 = 1/3rd round hips + 5 cm [vertically downwards on line 3 – 2]
   = 36.3 cm
4. 4 – 5 = 1/3rd round hips + 5 cm (or as required) [horizontally]
   = 36.3 cm
5. 3 – 6 = 4 – 5 [horizontally]
   = 36.3 cm

   Join 5 – 6 in a straight line for crotch level.
6. For Crotch:
   (i) 6 – 7 = hip level + 2 cm [vertically downwards on line 6 – 5]
   = 22.3 cm

   (ii) 5 – 8 = 1/10th round hips (extend outwards) [horizontally]
   = 9.4 cm

   (iii) 6 – 9 = 2.5 cm [horizontally on line 6 – 3]

   Join 9 – 7 – 8 in a smooth curve for crotch depth.
7. Inside Leg Seam:
   (i) 8 – 10 = 1/12th round hips – 2 cm [horizontally on line 8 – 4]
   = 5.8 cm

   (ii) 10 – 11 = 1/12th round hips – 2 cm [vertically downwards]
   = 5.8 cm

(iii) 2 – 12 = 2.5 cm (value deducted from ½ round bottom) [horizontally]

Join 7 – 11 – 12 in a smooth curve for inside leg seam.

8. For salwar cut along the points:

Central Panel:

0 – 1 – 2 – 3 – 0,

where:

0 – 1 is on fold.

3 – 2 is central side seam.

Side Panel:

3 – 2 – 12 – 11 – 8 – 7 – 9 – 3,

where:

7 – 11 – 12 is inside leg seam.

9 – 7 – 8 is crotch depth.

3 – 2 is side central seam that is to be stitched to 3 – 2 of central panel.

9. To cut salwar in one piece cut along the points:

0 – 1 – 12 – 11 – 8 – 7 – 9 – 0,

where:

0 – 1 is on fold.

7 – 11 – 12 is inside leg seam.

9 – 8 – 7 is crotch depth.

Cut two pieces of the above block one piece for each side, i.e. right and left leg.

Add seam allowance of 1.5 cm (or as required) and hem allowance of 3 cm (or as required) and mark corresponding balance points and grain line on each pattern piece.

Plain Salwar:

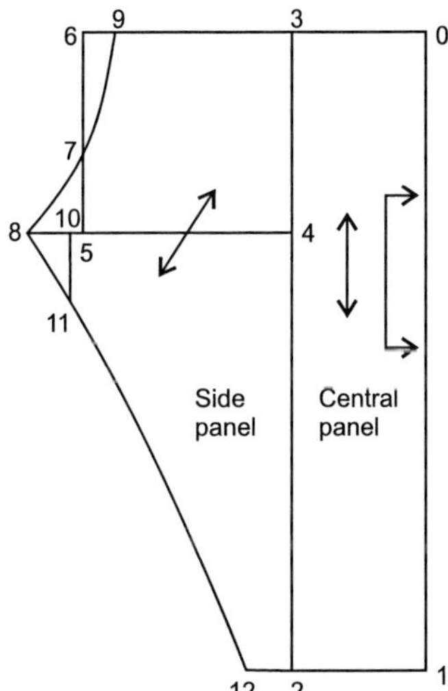

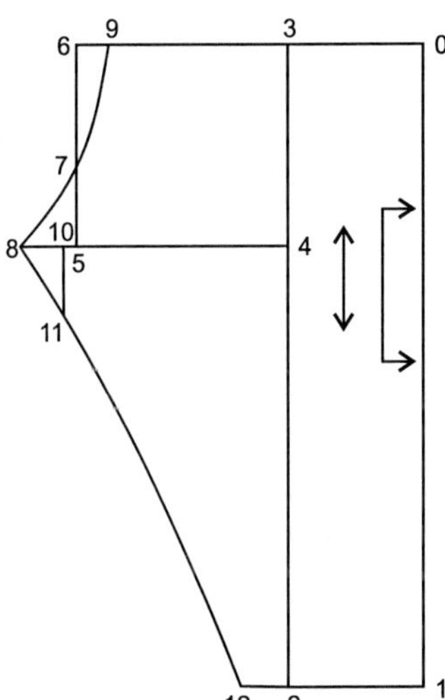

SALWAR WITH YOKE

Salwar with Belt: This is a lower garment worn generally by women in India where salwar is cut in two sections, i.e. yoke and salwar. This type of construction is used to decrease the volume around the hips but still maintaining the structure and ease.

Suitable Fabric: Cotton, any light weight fabric.

Size Symbol: Any

Size symbol – 10

Scale – cm

Drafting scale – 1/4th cm

Fabric required – 2.25 m × 1 m (length × width)

Measurements:

Required length = 104 cm

Round hip = 94 cm

Round ankle = 24 cm

Round bottom = 24 cm + 12 cm

= 36 cm

Yoke length = 1/8th round hips + 5 cm [vertically]
= 16.75 cm

Construction:

Salwar:

Central Panel:

1. 0 – 1 = required length + 1 cm – yoke length [vertically downwards]
   = 93.25 cm
2. 0 – 2 = ½ round bottom – 4 cm [horizontally]
   = 14 cm

   Complete the rectangle 0 – 1 – 2 – 3.
3. 0 – 1 is on fold.

Side Panels:

4. Crotch Level:

   2 – 4 = 1/3rd round hips + 5 cm – yoke length [vertically downwards]
   = 19.58 cm
5. 4 – 5 = 1/3rd round hips + 5 cm (or as required) [horizontally]
   = 36.3 cm
6. 2 – 6 = 4 – 5 [horizontally]

   Join 5 – 6 in a straight line.
7. 5 – 7 = 1/10th round hips (extend outwards) [horizontally]
   = 9.4 cm
8. 7 – 8 = 1/12th round hips [horizontally on line 7 – 5]
   = 7.8 cm
9. 8 – 9 = 1/12th round hips [vertically downwards]
   = 7.8 cm
10. 3 – 10 = 4 cm (value deducted from ½ round bottom) [horizontally]

    Join 7 – 9 – 10 in a smooth curve for inside leg seam.

Back:

11. 6 – 11 = 2.5 cm [vertically upwards]

    Join 6 – 2 in a smooth curve for waistline.

12. Join 11 – 7 in a smooth curve for back crotch.

13. Back side panel is along the points:

    2 – 3 – 10 – 9 – 7 – 11 – 2.

Front:

1. 6 – 12 = 2 cm [horizontally in wards on line 6 – 2]

   Join 7 – 12 in a smooth curve for front crotch.

2. Front side panel is along the points:

   2 – 3 – 10 – 9 – 7 – 12 – 2.

For making pattern: Take a paper of:

(i) Length = 89.5 cm, and

Width = twice of (0 – 2) + (4 – 7), i.e.

= 59.7 cm

(ii) Fold the paper along the points 0 – 1.

(iii) Follow the construction method and first shape back block and then open the paper and shape the front block, for salwar without separating central and side panels.

(iv) For seperate panels: Cut through line 2 – 3 to separate central and side panels.

Cut two pieces of the above block one piece for each side, i.e. right and left leg.

Yoke:

1. A – B = yoke length + 1 cm [vertically downwards]

   = 17.75 cm

2. A – C = ½ round hips + 4 cm (or as required) [horizontally]

   = 51 cm

   Complete the rectangle A – B – C – D for belt.

3. A – B is on fold.

4. Finish the salwar by gathering salwar to yoke on front.

Add seam allowance of 1.5 cm (or as required) and hem allowance of 3 cm (or as required) and mark corresponding balance points and grain line on each pattern piece.

Salwar with Belt:

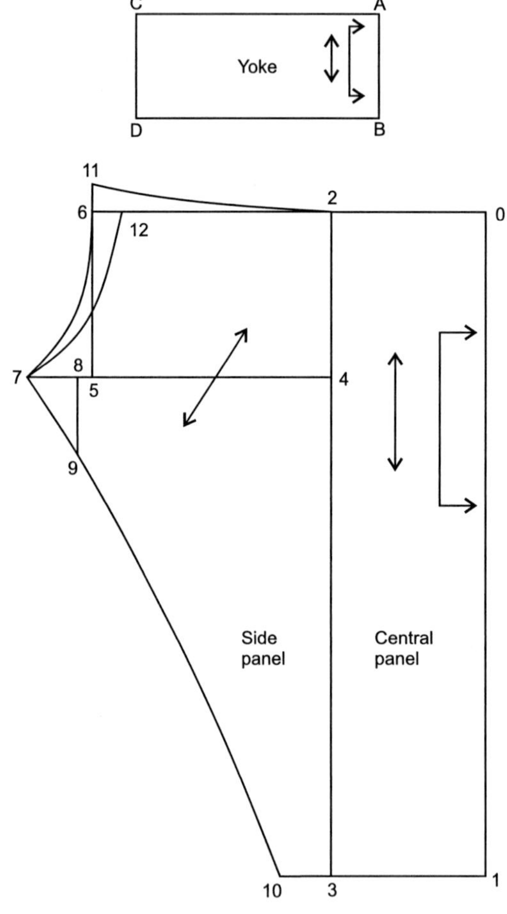

SALWARS-1

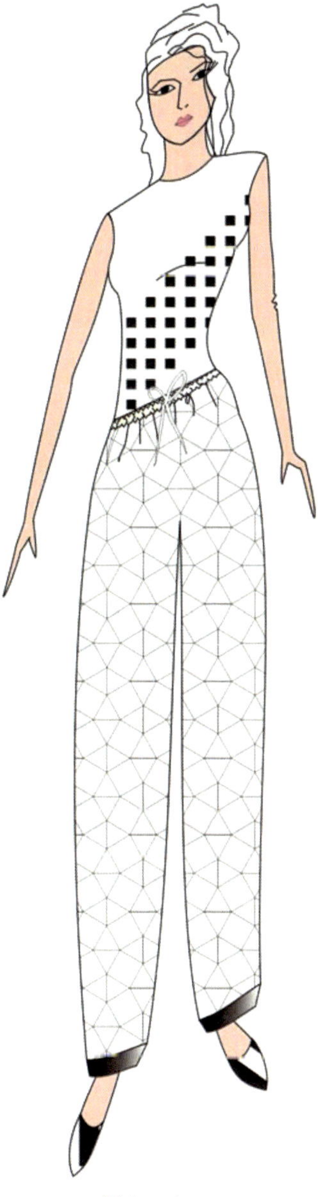

Plain salwar

Salwar with belt

SIDDHA PAJAMA

This is a ankle lower garment generally worn by women in India where inside leg length is cut straight and is generally teamed with Punjabi kurta.

Suitable Fabric: Cotton, satin, silk, any smooth light weight fabric.

Size symbol: Any

Size symbol – 10

Scale – cm

Drafting scale – 1/4th cm or 1/6th cm

Required fabric – 2.25 m × 1 m (length × width)

Measurements:

Required length = 104 cm

Round waist = 68 cm

Round hips = 94 cm

Round ankle = 24 cm

Yoke length = 18 cm

Construction:

1. 0 – 1 = required length + 1 cm – yoke length [vertically downwards]

   = 87 cm
2. 0 – 2 = 1/3rd round hips + 5 cm – yoke length [vertically downwards on line 0 – 1]

   = 18.3 cm
3. 2 – 3 = 1/3rd round hips + 10 cm (or as required) [horizontally]

   = 41.3 cm
4. 0 – 4 = 2 – 3 [horizontally]

   Join 3 – 4 in a straight line
5. 3 – 5 = 1/12th round hips [extend outwards horizontally]

   = 7.8 cm

6. 1 – 6 = ½ round ankle + 6 cm (ease or as required) [horizontally]
   = 18 cm

   Join 5 – 6 in a straight line for inside leg seam.

Back:

7. 4 – 7 = 2.5 cm [vertically upwards]

   Join 5 – 7 in a smooth curve for back crotch depth.

8. Join 7 – 0 in a smooth curve for shaping the back waistline.

Front:

1. 4 – 8 = 2.5 cm [horizontally inwards on line 4 – 0]

   Join 5 – 8 in a smooth curve for front crotch depth.

2. 0 – 1 is on fold.

For making pattern: Take a paper of:

(i) Length = 89.5 cm, and
    Width = twice of (0 – 2) + (4 – 7)
    = 59.7 cm

(ii) Fold the paper along the points 0 – 1.

(iii) Follow the construction method and first shape back block and then open the paper and shape the front block.

    Cut two pieces of the above block one piece for each side, i.e. right and left leg.

Yoke:

1. A – B = yoke length + 1 cm [vertically downwards]
   = 17.75 cm

2. A – C = ½ round hips + 4 cm (or as required) [horizontally]
   = 51 cm

   Complete the rectangle A – B – C – D for yoke.

3. A – B is on fold.

4. Finish the salwar by gathering/pleating salwar to yoke on front.

Add seam allowance of 1.5 cm (or as required) and hem allowance of 3 cm (or as required) and mark corresponding balance points and grain line on each pattern piece.

Siddha Pajama:

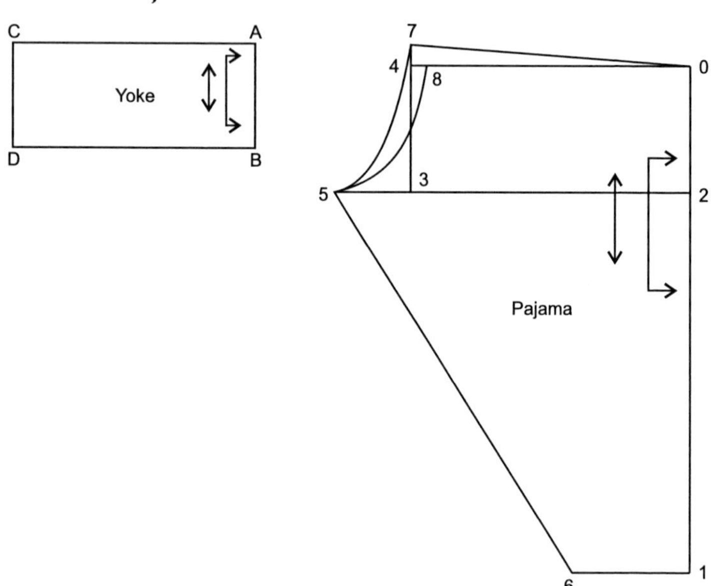

PATHANI SALWAR

This is a ankle length lower garment generally worn by women where inside leg length is cut straight and the salwar has more gathers and ease than plain salwar and is generally teamed with Punjabi kurta.

Suitable Fabric: Cotton, satin, silk, any smooth light weight fabric.

Size symbol: Any

Size symbol – 10

Scale – cm

Drafting scale – 1/4th cm or 1/6th cm

Required fabric – 2.25 m × 1 m (length × width)

Measurements:

Required length = 104 cm

Round waist = 68 cm

Round hips = 94 cm

Round ankle = 24 cm

Yoke length = 1/6th round hips + 4 cm

= 19.6 cm

Construction:

1. 0 – 1 = required length + 1 cm – yoke length [vertically downwards]

   = 85.4 cm
2. 1 – 2 = ½ round ankle + 7 cm (ease) [horizontally]

   = 19 cm

   Complete the rectangle 0 – 1 – 2 – 3.
3. For Crotch Depth: 3 – 4 = 1/3rd round hips + 5 cm – yoke length [vertically downwards on line 3 – 2]

   = 20.7 cm
4. 4 – 5 = ½ round hips [horizontally]

   = 47 cm
5. 3 – 6 = 4 – 5 [horizontally]

   = 47 cm

   Join 5 – 6 in a straight line.
6. 2 – 7 = 3 cm [horizontally]

   Join 5 – 7 in a straight line for inside leg seam.
7. 6 – 8 = 1/12th round hips [horizontally inwards on line 6 – 3]

   = 7.3 cm

Back:

8. For Shaping Back Crotch:

   8 – 9 = 2.5 cm [vertically upwards]

   Join 9 – 5 in a straight line for back crotch.

9. For Waistline: Join 9 – 3 in a smooth curve for waistline.

Front:

1. For Shaping Front Crotch:

   Join 5 – 8 in a straight line for front crotch.

2. For salwar block pattern take a paper 2 × (0 – 6) (horizontally)

   = 66 cm fold it along the line 0 – 1 and follow the construction method. For salwar in one piece cut along the points:

   0 – 1 – 7 – 5 – 9 – 3 – 0.

   Open the pattern paper and cut for front salwar along the points:

   0 – 8 – 5.

3. For Separate Central and Side Panels:

   (i) For central panel (two pieces) cut along the points:

   0 – 1 – 2 – 3 – 0.

   0 – 1 is on fold.

   (ii) For side panels (two pieces) cut along the points:

   Back: 3 – 2 – 7 – 5 – 9 – 3,

   where:

   5 – 9 is back crotch.

   5 – 7 is inside leg seam.

   3 – 2 is central side seam.

   Front: 3 – 2 – 7 – 5 – 8 – 3,

   where:

   5 – 8 is front crotch.

   5 – 7 is inside leg seam.

   3 – 2 is side central seam.

   Cut two pieces of the above block one piece for each leg, i.e. 2 pieces of each block for right and left.

Add seam allowance of 1.5 cm (or as required) and hem allowance of 3 cm (or as required) and mark corresponding balance points and grain line on each pattern piece.

Yoke:

1. A – B = yoke length + 1 cm [vertically downwards]
   = 17.75 cm
2. A – C = ½ round hips + 4 cm (or as required) [horizontally]
   = 51 cm

   Complete the rectangle A – B – C – D for yoke.
3. A – B is on fold.
4. Finish the salwar by gathering salwar to yoke on front.

Add seam allowance of 1.5 cm (or as required) and 5 cm (or as required) for nefa fold and mark corresponding balance points and grain line on each pattern piece.

Nefa fold is made in salwar's and pajama's so that a draw string can be inserted into it and tied into a knot as comfortable.

Pathani Salwar:

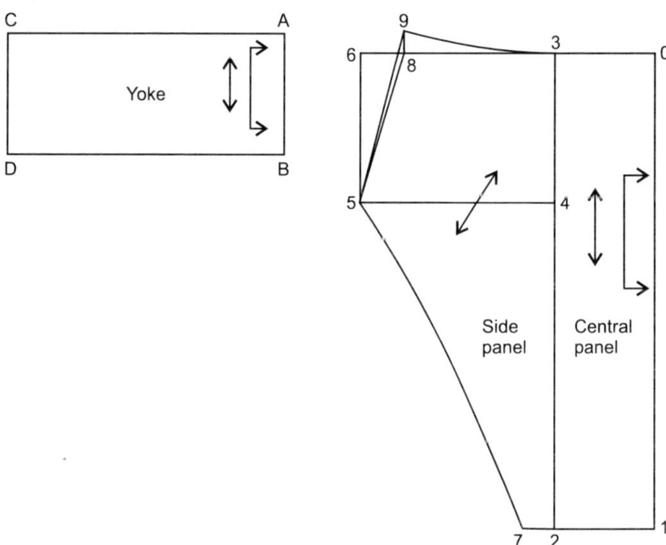

SALWARS-2

Sidha pajama

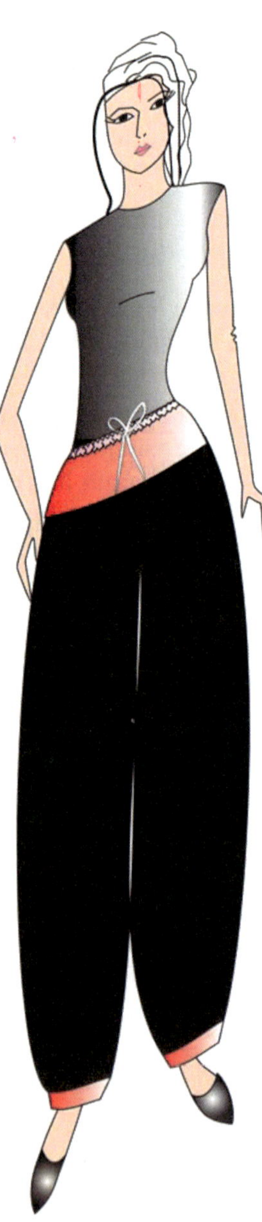

Pathani salwar

35 CHUDIDAAR

CHUDIDAAR

This is a ankle length bias cut lower garment generally worn by women which has extra fabric incorporated from calf to ankle length to give bangles like appearance and is generally teamed with kurta.

Suitable Fabric: Cotton, satin, any smooth light weight fabric.

Size Symbol: Any

Size symbol – 10

Scale – cm

Drafting scale – 1/4th cm or 1/6th cm

Required fabric – 2 m × 90 cm (length × width)

Measurements:

Required length = 104 cm

Round hips = 94 cm

Round calf muscles = 36 cm

Round ankle = 24 cm

Hip level = 20.3 cm

Mid-calf length (waist to mid-calf length) = 64 cm

Construction:

1. 0 – 1 = required length + 1 cm [vertically downwards]
   = 105 cm

2. 1 – 2 = 1/4th required length (or as required for churis) [vertically downwards]
   = 21 cm
3. Crotch Level: 0 – 3 = 1/3rd round hips + 5 cm [vertically downwards]
   = 36.3 cm
4. 3 – 4 = 1/3rd round hips + 5 cm [horizontally]
   = 36.3 cm
5. 0 – 5 = 3 – 4 [horizontally]
   = 36.3 cm

   Join 4 – 5 in a straight line.
6. 0 – 6 = hip level + 3 cm [vertically downwards on line 0 – 1]
   = 23.3 cm

   Draw a horizontal line from point 6 to line 4 – 5 and mark as 7.
7. 4 – 8 = 1/10th round hips (extend outwards) [horizontally]
   = 9.4 cm
8. 5 – 9 = 2 cm [horizontally on line 5 – 0]

   Join 9 – 7 – 8 in a smooth curve for crotch depth.
9. 0 – 10 = mid-calf length [vertically downwards on line 0 – 2]
   = 64 cm
10. Round Calf Muscles: 10 – 11 = ½ round calf muscles + 1 cm (ease) [horizontally]
    = 19 cm
11. Round Ankle: 2 – 12 = ½ round ankle + 1 cm (ease) [horizontally]
    = 13 cm
12. 8 – 13 = 1/12th round hips – 2.5 cm [horizontally on line 8 – 3]
    = 5.3 cm

13. 13 – 14 = 1/12th round hips – 2.5 cm [vertically downwards]

= 5.3 cm

Join 8 – 14 – 11 – 12 in a smooth curve for the required inside leg seam.

14. For chudidaar block cut along the points:

0 – 2 – 12 – 11 – 14 – 8 – 7 – 9 – 0,

where:

0 – 1 is on fold.

10 – 2 is churis.

8 – 14 – 11 – 12 is inside leg seam.

9 – 7 – 8 is crotch depth.

0 – 9 is waistline which should be given nefa allowance of 5 cm (or as required) upwards and be finished with a dori or an elastic inserted into the nefa fold or as required.

Cut two pieces of the above block one piece for each side i.e. right and left leg.

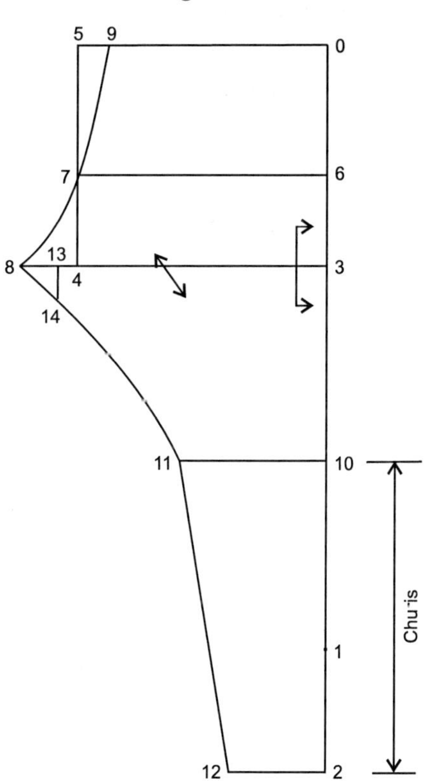

Add seam allowance of 1.5 cm (or as required) and hem allowance of 1.5 cm (or as required) and mark corresponding balance points and grain line on each pattern piece.

Chudidaar:

PUFFED CHUDIDAAR

This is a ankle length lower garment generally worn by women which is gathered at hip level and at knee length to give a skirt like look and also has extra fabric incorporated from knee to ankle length to give bangles like appearance and is generally teamed with a short kurti, tunic or waist length top.

Suitable Fabric: Georgette, chiffon, or any soft and sheer fabric.

Size Symbol: Any

Size symbol – 10

Scale – cm

Drafting scale – 1/4th cm or 1/6th cm

Required fabric – 2.5 m × 1 m (length × width)

Measurements:

Required length = 104 cm

Round hips = 94 cm

Knee length = 58 cm

Round knee = 36 cm

Round ankle = 24 cm

Hip level = 20.3 cm

Body rise = 28 cm

Yoke length = 1/8th round hips [vertically downwards]
= 11.75 cm

This chudidaar is cut into three sections:

(i) Yoke section,

(ii) Middle chudidaar section, and

(iii) Chudis section respectively.

Construction:

Yoke Section:

1. A – B = yoke length + 1 cm [vertically downwards]
   = 12.75 cm

2. A – C = 1/4th round hips + 3 cm (ease) [horizontally]
   = 26.5 cm

   Complete the rectangle A – B – C – D.

Back:

3. C – E = 2.5 cm [vertically upwards]

   Join E – A in a smooth curve to shape back yoke.

4. For yoke block cut along the points:

   A – B – D – E – A,

   where:

   A – B is on fold.

   A – B – D – C – A is front yoke.

   A – E – D – B – A is back yoke.

5. For Making Pattern: Take a paper of:
   (i) Length = (C – D) + 2.5 cm [vertically downwards]
   = 15.25 cm

   Width = twice of A – C [horizontally]
   = 53 cm
   (ii) Fold the paper along the points A – B.
   (iii) Follow the construction method and first shape back yoke block and then open the paper and shape the front yoke block.

Middle Chudidaar Section:

1. 0 – 1 = knee length + 4 cm – yoke length [vertically downwards]
   = 50.25 cm
2. 0 – 2 = 1/4th round hips + 25 cm (or as required for gathers) [horizontally]
   = 48.5 cm
3. 0 – 3 = hip level – yoke length [vertically downwards on line 0 – 1]
   = 16.25 cm
4. 3 – 4 = 0 – 2 [horizontally]
   = 48.5 cm

5. 0 – 5 = body rise + 2 cm (ease) – yoke length [vertically downwards on line 0 – 1] = 18.25 cm
6. 5 – 6 = 3 – 4 = 0 – 2 [horizontally]

   = 48.5 cm

   Join 2 – 4 – 6 in a straight line for crotch level.
7. For Crotch: 6 – 7 = 1/10th round hips (extend outwards) [horizontally]

   = 9.4 cm

   Join 7 – 4 – 2 in a smooth curve for crotch depth.
8. 1 – 8 = ½ round knee + 20 cm (for gathers) [horizontally]

   = 38 cm

   Join 8 – 7 in a smooth curve for inside leg seam.
9. For middle chudidaar section cut along the points:

   0 – 1 – 8 – 7 – 4 – 2 – 0,

   where:

   0 – 1 is on fold.

   7 – 8 is the required inside leg seam.

   2 – 4 – 7 is the crotch depth.
10. Gather 0 – 2 of middle chudidaar section to B – D of yoke section.

Chudi Section:

1. 9 – 10 = required length – knee length + 20 cm (for churis) [vertically downwards]

   = 66 cm
2. 9 – 11 = ½ round knee [horizontally]

   = 18 cm
3. 10 – 12 = ½ round ankle + 1 cm (ease) [horizontally]

   = 13 cm

   Join 11 – 12 in a straight line for inside leg seam of chudi section.

4. For chudi section cut along the points:

   9 – 10 – 12 – 11 – 9,

   where:

   9 – 10 is on fold.

   11 – 12 is inside leg seam.

5. Gather 1 – 8 of middle chudidaar section to 9 – 11 of chudi section.

Add seam allowance of 1.5 cm (or as required) and hem allowance of 1.5 cm (or as required) and mark corresponding balance points and grain line on each pattern piece.

Puffed Chudidaar:

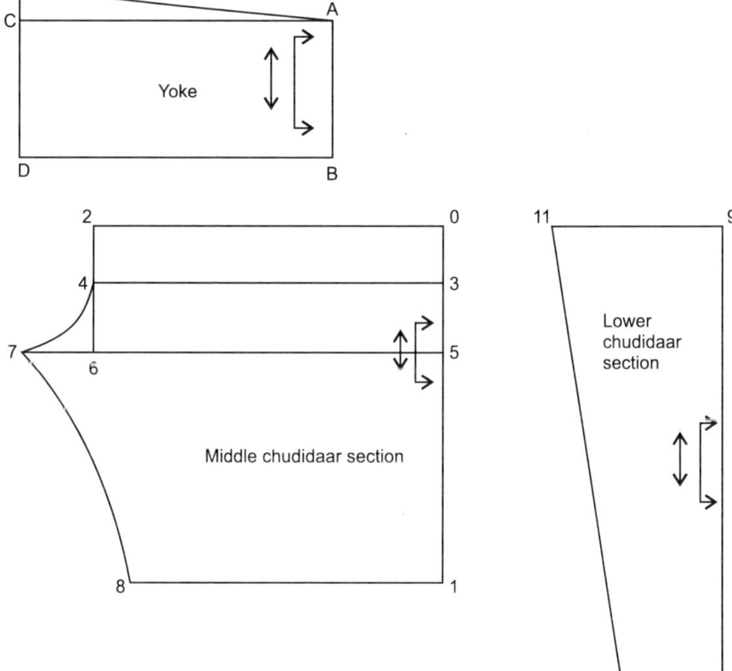

PLAIN CHUDIDAR & PUFFED CHUDIDAR

Plain chudidar

Puffed chudidar

QUESTIONS FOR PRACTICE

Chapter – 1: Introduction to Fabrics

Q.1. What do you understand by fabric – garment relationship? Explain.

Q.2. What do you understand by fabric qualities? Describe and give examples for the following:

(i) Shrinkable fabrics

(ii) Preshrunk fabrics

(iii) Stretch fabrics

(iv) Light weight fabrics, medium weight fabrics and heavy weight fabrics

(v) Chemically treated fabrics

Chapter – 2: Understanding Different Aspects of Body

Q.1. What is the importance of face shapes for a designer? Explain different face shapes and support with illustrations.

Q.2. What is the importance of neck types for a designer? Explain different neck types and support with illustrations.

Q.3. What is the importance of figure types for a designer? Explain figure types and support with illustrations.

Chapter – 3: Adult Bodice Block and Sleeve Block

Q.1. Draft a basic adult bodice block and give complete construction methods for the given measurements:

Required length = 42 cm

Round bust = 88 cm

Round waist = 68 cm

Across front = 28 cm

Across back = 35 cm

Highest bust level = 25 cm

Across shoulder = 35 cm

Also make the pattern and construct the garment.

Q.2. Draft a sleeve block for the above bodice block and give complete construction methods for with the given measurements:

Round bust = 88 cm

Sleeve length = 20 cm

Top arm/round sleeve = 29 cm

Also make the pattern and construct the sleeve to the bodice block.

Chapter – 4: Dart Manipulation Theory

Q.1. Describe draft manipulation theory and explain with illustrations the various darts.

Chapter – 5: Skirts

Q.1. Draft basic skirt block for adults and give complete construction methods for size symbols – 8, 10, 12. Mention suitable fabrics.

Q.2. Draft fish cut skirt block and give complete construction methods for size symbols – 8, 10, 12. Mention suitable fabrics.

Q.3. Draft pencil skirt block and give complete construction methods for size symbols – 8, 10, 12. Mention suitable fabrics.

Q.4. Draft A-line skirt block and give complete construction methods for size symbols – 8, 10, 12. Mention suitable fabrics.

Chapter – 6: Mini Skirt

Q.1. Draft straight fit mini skirt and give complete construction methods for size symbols – 8, 10, 12. Mention suitable fabrics.

Q.2. Draft mini skirt with inverted box pleats and give complete construction methods for size symbols – 8, 10, 12. Mention suitable fabrics.

Q.3. Draft A-line mini skirt and give complete construction methods for size symbols – 8, 10, 12. Mention suitable fabrics.

Chapter – 7: Gored Skirt

Q.1. Draft 4-gored skirt and give complete construction methods for size symbols – 8, 10, 12. Mention suitable fabrics.

Q.2. Draft 6-gored skirt and give complete construction methods for size symbols – 8, 10, 12. Mention suitable fabrics.

Q.3. Draft 12-gored skirt and give complete construction methods for size symbols – 8, 10, 12. Mention suitable fabrics.

Chapter – 8: Wraparound Skirt

Q.1. Draft straight fit wraparound skirt and give complete construction methods for size symbols – 8, 10, 12. Mention suitable fabrics.

Q.2. Draft half circular wraparound skirt and give complete construction methods for size symbols – 8, 10, 12. Mention suitable fabrics.

Chapter – 9: Paneled Skirt

Q.1. Draft paneled skirt and give complete construction methods for size symbols – 8, 10, 12. Mention suitable fabrics.

Q.2. Draft pixie skirt-1 and give complete construction methods for size symbols – 8, 10, 12. Mention suitable fabrics.

Q.3. Draft pixie skirt with a yoke and give complete construction methods for size symbols – 8, 10, 12. Mention suitable fabrics.

Chapter – 10: Women's Vest

Q.1. Draft women vest and give complete construction methods for size symbols – 8, 10, 12. Mention suitable fabrics.

Chapter – 11: Shirts: Plain Shirt with Full Sleeves

Q.1. Draft women plain shirt with blouse collar and give complete construction methods for size symbols – 8, 10 and 12. Mention suitable fabrics.

Q.2. Draft a full sleeve for the above shirt size and give complete construction methods.

Chapter – 12: Corset

Q.1. Draft Edwardian corset and give complete construction methods for size symbols – 8, 10 and 12. Cup size – A, B and C. Mention suitable fabrics.

Q.2. Draft corset bodice and give complete construction methods for size symbols – 8, 10 and 12. Cup size – A, B and C. Mention suitable fabrics.

Chapter – 13: Tunics (Sleeveless)

Q.1. Draft a straight fit tunic and give complete construction methods for size symbols – 8, 10 and 12. Cup size – A, B and C. Mention suitable fabrics.

Q.2. Draft a sleeve block for the above straight fit tunic and give complete construction methods. Mention suitable fabrics.

Q.3. Draft A-line tunic (first garment) and give complete construction methods for size symbols – 8, 10 and 12. Cup size – A, B and C. Mention suitable fabrics. Draft a sleeve block for the A-line tunic and give complete construction methods. Mention suitable fabrics.

Q.4. Draft A-line tunic (second garment) and give complete construction methods for size symbols – 8, 10 and 12. Cup size – A, B and C. Mention suitable fabrics.

Chapter – 14: Frocks

Q.1. Draft a mini frock with different necklines and give complete construction methods for size symbols – 8, 10 and 12. Mention suitable fabrics.

Q.2. Draft a middy with different necklines and give complete construction methods for size symbols – 8, 10 and 12. Mention suitable fabrics.

Q.3. Draft a puffed and gathered frock with different necklines and give complete construction methods for size symbols – 8, 10 and 12. Mention suitable fabrics.

Chapter – 15: Evening Gown

Q.1. Draft a evening gown with different necklines and give complete construction methods for size symbols – 8, 10 and 12. Mention suitable fabrics.

Chapter – 16: Nigh-tie

Q.1. Draft a nigh-tie and give complete construction methods for size symbols – 8, 10 and 12. Mention suitable fabrics.

Chapter – 17: Over Coat

Q.1. Draft a over coat and give complete construction methods for size symbols – 8, 10 and 12. Mention suitable fabrics.

Chapter – 18: Trousers

Basic Trousers

Q.1. Draft the basic trousers block and give complete construction methods for size symbols – 8, 10 and 12. Mention suitable fabrics.

Q.2. Draft a flat fronts (trousers) and give complete construction methods for size symbols – 8, 10 and 12. Mention suitable fabrics.

Chapter – 19: Pants

Q.1. Draft harem pants and give complete construction methods for size symbols – 8, 10 and 12. Mention suitable fabrics.

Chapter – 20: Bell Bottoms

Q.1. Draft bell bottoms and give complete construction methods for size symbols – 8, 10 and 12. Mention suitable fabrics.

Q.2. Draft flared pants and give complete construction methods for size symbols – 8, 10 and 12. Mention suitable fabrics.

Chapter – 21: Caprice and Pedal Pushers

Q.1. Draft a caprice and give complete construction methods for size symbols – 8, 10 and 12. Mention suitable fabrics.

Q.2. Draft a pedal pushers and give complete construction methods for size symbols – 8, 10 and 12. Mention suitable fabrics.

Chapter – 22: Culottes and Knickers

Q.1. Draft a culottes and give complete construction methods for size symbols – 8, 10 and 12. Mention suitable fabrics.

Q.2. Draft knickers and give complete construction methods for size symbols – 8, 10 and 12. Mention suitable fabrics.

Chapter – 23: Petticoat for Saree

Q.1. Draft a 4-gored petticoat and give complete construction methods for size symbols – 8, 10 and 12. Mention suitable fabrics.

Q.2. Draft a 6-gored petticoat and give complete construction methods for size symbols – 8, 10 and 12. Mention suitable fabrics.

Chapter – 24: Construction of Saree Blouse

Q.1. Draft a plain saree blouse and give complete construction methods for size symbols – 8, 10 and 12. Cup sizes – A, B and C. Mention suitable fabrics.

Q.2. Draft a sleeveless saree blouse and give complete construction methods for size symbols – 8, 10 and 12. Cup sizes – A, B and C. Mention suitable fabrics.

Q.3. Draft a sleeveless pleated saree blouse and give complete construction methods for size symbols – 8, 10 and 12. Cup sizes – A, B and C. Mention suitable fabrics.

Chapter – 25: Katori Choli

Q.1. Draft katori choli 1 and give complete construction methods for size symbols – 8, 10 and 12. Cup sizes – A, B and C. Mention suitable fabrics.

Q.2. Draft katori choli 2 and give complete construction methods for size symbols – 8, 10 and 12. Cup sizes – A, B and C. Mention suitable fabrics.

Chapter – 26: Raglan Sleeve Saree Blouse

Q.1. Draft a raglan sleeve saree blouse and give complete construction methods for size symbols – 8, 10 and 12. Cup sizes – A, B and C. Mention suitable fabrics.

Chapter – 27: Halter Neck Saree Blouse

Q.1. Draft a Halter neck saree blouse and give complete construction methods for size symbols – 8, 10 and 12. Cup sizes – A, B and C. Mention suitable fabrics.

Chapter – 28: Magyar Sleeve Saree Blouse

Q.1. Draft a magyar sleeve saree blouse and give complete construction methods for size symbols – 8, 10 and 12. Cup sizes – A, B and C. Mention suitable fabrics.

Chapter – 29: Kurtas

Q.1. Draft a Punjabi kurta/straight fit kurta and give complete construction methods for size symbols – 8, 10 and 12. Mention suitable fabrics.

Q.2. Draft a A-line kurta and give complete construction methods for size symbols – 8, 10 and 12. Mention suitable fabrics.

Chapter – 30: Kalidaar Kurta

Q.1. Draft kalidaar kurta 1 and give complete construction methods for size symbols – 8, 10 and 12. Mention suitable fabrics.

Q.2. Draft kalidaar kurta 2 and give complete construction methods for size symbols – 8, 10 and 12. Mention suitable fabrics.

Chapter – 31: Angarakha Kurta/Wraparound Kurta

Q.1. Draft a straight fit kurta (Angarakha kurta/wraparound kurta) and give complete construction methods for size symbols – 8, 10 and 12. Mention suitable fabrics.

Q.2. Draft a flared angarakha kurta/wrap around kurta and give complete construction methods for size symbols – 8, 10 and 12. Mention suitable fabrics.

Chapter – 32: Paneled Kurta (Horizontal Panels Stitched to Saree Blouse)

Q.1. Draft a paneled kurta and give complete construction methods for size symbols – 8, 10 and 12. Mention suitable fabrics.

Chapter – 33: Shoulderless Kurta

Q.1. Draft a shoulderless kurta and give complete construction methods for size symbols – 8, 10 and 12. Mention suitable fabrics.

Chapter – 34: Salwar

Q.1. Draft a plain salwar and give complete construction methods for size symbols – 8, 10 and 12. Mention suitable fabrics.

Q.2. Draft salwar with belt and give complete construction methods for size symbols – 8, 10 and 12. Mention suitable fabrics.

Q.3. Draft a sidha pajama and give complete construction methods for size symbols – 8, 10 and 12. Mention suitable fabrics.

Q.4. Draft a Pathaani salwar and give complete construction methods for size symbols – 8, 10 and 12. Mention suitable fabrics.

Chapter – 35: Chudidaar

Q.1. Draft a plain chudidaar and give complete construction methods for size symbols – 8, 10 and 12. Mention suitable fabrics.

Q.2. Draft a puffed chudidaar and give complete construction methods for size symbols – 8, 10 and 12. Mention suitable fabrics.

GLOSSARY OF FABRICS

This glossary gives the distinct qualities of each fabric which makes it easier to distinguish each fabric from the other.

Albatross: Plain weave, soft, fleecy surface.

Alpaca: Plain weave. Soft and light weight.

Alpaca crepe: Plain weave. Soft.

Armure: Jacquard weave. Has a raised, pebbled or embossed surface.

Art linen: Plain weave, crisp fabric. Light to heavy weight.

Astrakhan: Woven or knitted. Rough fabric.

Backed cloth: Twill weave or satin weave. Medium to heave weight fabric, warm.

Backing or back cloth: Gray goods.

Bagheera velvet: Pile fabric. Fine, uncut pile velvet, rough surface.

Balloon cloth: Lustrous fabric.

Banbury plush: Pile fabric. Soft uncut long loops.

Barathea: Rib weave or basket weave. Fine fabric with luster.

Barege: Plain weave. Light weight sheer fabric.

Bark crepe: Crepe. Rough surface.

Baronet satin: Satin weave. Lustrous, soft.

Bathrobe blanketing: Double faced fabric, napped. Soft, thick and warm.

Beach cloth: Plain weave. Heavy weight fabric, rough surface.

Beaver: Pile fabric. Napped surface, soft.

Bengaline: Rib weave. Heavy weight fabric.

Bird's eye: Dobby weave. Small indentations suggesting eye of a bird.

Billiard cloth: Twill weave. Compact weave, smooth surface.

Bisso linen: Fine, sheer linen. Crispy feel.

Bolivia: Soft, plush like surface.

Book cloth: Plain weave. Coarse, either pyroxylin coated or embossed.

Bouche: Plain weave. Woolen surface.

Boucle: Woven or knitted. Small loops at interval, kinky appearance.

Bourette: Nub yarns. Hairy surface.

Bourrelet: Double knit. Raised loops. Corded or ripple effect.

Box cloth: Heavy weight fabric. Coarse.

Brilliantine: Plain weave or twill weave. Fine, smooth and wiry fabric.

Broadcloth: Plain weave or rib weave. Fine and smooth fabric.

Brocade: Satin weave or jacquard weave. Raised designs on satin ground.

Brocatelle: Jacquard weave. Lustrous surface.

Bunting: Plain weave. Soft or woolen surface.

Burlap: Plain weave. Heavy weight coarse fabric.

Butcher linen: Plain weave. Stiff fabric.

Butcher rayon: Plain weave. Coarse fabric.

Calico: Coarse fabric with small prints.

Cambric: Plain weave. Light weight soft fabric.

Camel hair: Plain or twill weave. Soft nap fabric.

Candle wick: Plain weave with tufted yarns. Soft with fuzzy designs. Caterpillar like appearance.

Canton crepe: Crepe weave. Pebbled surface.

Canton flannel: Twill weave. Soft nap, brushed surface.

Canvas: Plain weave. Generally gray goods, rough and heavy weight fabric.

Casement: Variation of plain weave.

Casha: Twill weave. Very fine woolen fabric.

Cashmere: Twill weave, napped fabric. Extremely soft fabric.

Cavalry twill: Twill weave (right hand twill). Pronounced narrow and wide wale's. Strong and rugged fabric.

Challis: Plain weave. Light weight soft fabric. Either dyed or printed with a delicate floral pattern, paisleys, or geometric patterns and pale designs.

Chambray: Plain weave. Woven tiny checks or mottled designs. Soft, brushed surface.

Chamois cloth: Plain weave with nap. Slightly stiff, smooth and thick fabric.

Charmesue: Satin weave. Semi-lustrous surface with dull back.

Charvet silk: Rib weave (diagonal ribs). Soft fabric with high luster.

Cheese cloth: Plain weave or gauze weave. Light weight thin fabric. Soft.

Chenille: Plain weave. Fluffy or fuzzy faced fabric.

Cheviot: Twill or plain weave. Rough, harsh and uneven woolen fabric.

Chevron: Broken twill or herringbone weave. Wide V's across width of the fabric.

Chiffon: Plain weave. Light weight sheer fabric. Transparent.

China silk: Plain weave. Extremely light weight and soft.

Chinchilla: Sateen weave or twill weave with extra floats. Small nubs on the fabric.

Chintz: Plain weave. Brightly printed floral or geometrical designs.

Chite: Plain weave. Printed linen.

Cisele velvet: Pile. Cut and uncut loops form patterned velvet design.

Cobourg: Twill weave. Medium to heavy weight fabric. Piece dyed or printed.

Cloque: Blistered appearance.

Corduroy: Rib weave. Ribbed fabric with soft luster.

Coutil: Twill weave with herringbone pattern. Can be soft to medium according to starching. Smooth finish.

Covert: Twill weave. Light weight fabric. Clear finish and hard texture. Made with two shades of same color.

Crash: Plain weave or twill weave. Rugged and substantial feel.

Crepe: Plain weave. Crinkled or pebbled surface.

Crepe-back satin: Satin weave face and crepe on back. Soft reversible fabric.

Crepe charmeuse: Smooth fabric with soft luster.

Crepe de chine: Plain weave. Soft, fairly sheer and considerable luster.

Crepe de laine: Plain or crepe weave. Light weight sheer fabric.

Crepe marocain: Plain weave or crepe weave. Heavy pronounced crepe fabric.

Crepe meteor: Similar to georgette on back and satin on face. Light weight fabric with soft feel finish.

Crepe (wool): Light weight worsted fabric with crinkled appearance.

Cretonne: Plain weave or twill weave. Medium to heavy weight cotton fabric. Bright and large printed patterns.

Crinoline: Plain weave. Smooth, stiff and excellent straight.

Damask: Figured or jacquard weave. Firm and compact fabric with lustrous jacquard pattern. Flatter and smoother than brocade.

Denim: Twill weave. Light to heavy weight fabric. Strong with smooth finish.

Dimity: Plain weave with crosswise or length wise spaced ribs. Crisp texture.

Doeskin: Satin weave or twill weave nap on one side. Slight short naps. Smooth and lustrous. Leather like appearance.

Dommett flannel: Plain or twill weave. Soft and fleecy appearance.

Dorian: Plain weave. Muslin with stripes.

Dotted swiss: Plain weave for base fabric with swivel, lappet or flocked dots. Semi-sheer and usually crisp fabric.

Drill: Twill weave (left hand twill weave). Medium weight coarse fabric.

Duchesse: Satin weave. Excellent luster and smooth texture.

Duck: Plain weave. Heavy weight cotton fabric.

Duvetyne: Satin weave. Soft hand, smooth, plush texture.

Egyptian cotton: Plain weave. Smooth finish with fine texture.

Elastique: Twill weave with double diagonal ribs. Fine ribs with smooth hand and surface.

Eolienne: Usually plain weave. Light weight fabrc. Very lustrous.

Eponge: Plain weave or novelty weaves. Light weight fabric. Soft and squishy.

Eskimo cloth: Satin weave or twill weave with thick nap. Heavy weight bulky fabric.

Etamine: Leno weave. Sheer and fuzzy fabric.

Express stripe: Twill weave with woven strips. Durable fabric.

Faconne velvet: Burnt out velvet giving pattern or design on sheer flat background.

Faille: Plain weave with flat ribs. Loose weave with slight luster.

Faille crepe: Plain weave with crepe filling. Light weight fabric.

Faille taffeta: Cross rib weave. Stiff and crisp fabric.

Farmer's satin: Twill weave. Smooth fabric with glossy surface.

Fearnaught: Twill weave or plain weave. Heavy weight fabric. Hirsute face.

Flannel: Twill weave with nap. Heavy weight fabric. Soft fabric.

Flannelette: Similar to flannel.

Flat crepe: Plain weave. Soft, fairly sheer, considerable luster with flat surface.

Fleece: Woven or knit fabric with airy space. Deep and soft nap.

Florentine: Twill weave. Light weight fabric. Lustrous.

Foulard: Twill weave. Light weight fabric. Very soft with small prints on a dark background.

Frenchback: Back with corded twill weave and face with a different weave. Clear finish and superior hand.

Frenchback serge: Twill weave (diagonal). Medium weight fabric. Clear finish with weave visible on face and back.

French serge: Twill weave. Superior quality fabric with condescending and spongy hand.

Frieze: Pile weave. Light weight or heavy weight fabric. Frizzy face and harsh board like hand.

Friezette: Rib weave. Light weight fabric. Rib effect created with alternate slack tension. Frizzy face and harsh.

Fustian: Cross weave. Soft.

Gabardine: Twill weave (steep - 45° or 63°). Clear finish, smooth, firm and lustrous can be dull.

Galatea: Twill weave (left hand) or plain weave. Rugged and lustrous.

Gamsa: Twill weave base with satin or crepe face. Soft hand with lustrous surface.

Gattar: Satin weave. Elegant luster and drape.

Gauze: Plain weave, leno weave or knitted. Light weight sheer fabric. Soft with open space.

Georgette: Plain weave or crepe weave. Crinkly, harsh and dull.

Gingham: Plain weave. Medium weight or light weight fabric. Usually in stripes or checks. Soft and dull luster.

Glissade: Satin weave. Polished fabric. Soft and lustrous.

Gloria: Plain weave, twill weave or satin weave. Light weight fabric. Smooth and lustrous.

Gossamer: Gauze weave. Very soft with open spaces.

Glove silk: Knitted (double knit). Soft and strong.

Granada: Twill weave (broken). Fine finish with granular surface.

Granite (momie cloth): Twill weave. Impression of crepe with crinkled surface.

Grenadine: Leno weave. Stiff fabric.

Gros de' londres: Plain weave with ribs. Light weight fabric. Lustrous finish.

Grosgrain: Plain weave with horizontal ribs. Large grains like appearance.

Habutai: Plain weave. Light weight fabric. Soft and lustrous.

Handkerchief linen: Plain weave corded. Light weight fabric. Soft.

Henrietta: Twill weave. Soft and lustrous.

Hickory cloth: Twill weave. Light weight fabric. Warp stripes.

Himalaya: Plain weave. Irregular slubs in fillings. Pebbled appearance.

Holland: Plain weave. Light weight fabric. Smooth finish. Can be glazed.

Homespun: Plain weave. Coarse, rugged and spongy. Appearance of tweed.

Honan: Plain weave. Uneven texture.

Hopsacking: Basket weave. Light weight to heavy weight fabric. Rough texture and bulky.

Huck a buck: Dobby weave or basket weave. Rough surface. Lustrous. Common design is small squares that stand out from the background.

India silk: Plain weave (hand loom). Light weight thin fabric. Soft.

Irish poplin: Plain weave with fine ribs. Lustrous.

Italian cloth: Twill weave. Lustrous.

Ixtle: Dobby weave or basket weave. Fine finish. Rough surface and lustrous.

Jaconet: Plain weave. Light weight fabric. Glazed surface with crisp finish.

Jaspe: Plain weave. Irregular lengthwise stripes of different shades of same color is its distinct quality.

Jeans: Twill weave or herring bone weave. Medium weight fabric. Smooth finish.

Jersey: Flat-bed knit or warp knit. Elastic and crease resistant.

Jute (Burlap): Plain weave. Heavy weight fabric. Rough, coarse and lustrous. Natural colors.

Kasha cloth: Twill weave with nap face. Soft filled sheeting. Tan or brown color.

Kashmir: All weaves, mostly plain or twill weave. Light weight fabric. Soft and silky finish. Delicate fabric.

Kersey: Obscure weave with nap. Medium weight fabric. Closely sheared surface with high luster.

Khaki: Twill weave. Tan or earthy color only. Soft and fine.

Lame: Any weave with metallic threads. Shine and glitter.

Lawn: Plain weave. Light weight sheer fabric. Soft and crispy.

Liama: Light weight fabric. Impressive luster.

Loden cloth: Felt fabric. Thick, soft and durable.

Long cloth: Plain weave. High count fabric, moderate luster and soft.

Luana: Plain weave. Crosswise ribs.

Luster fabric: Plain weave. High luster.

Lyons velvet: Pile fabric. Thick and stiff.

Mackinaw: Twill weave or double cloth. Heavy weight fabric. Heavily napped or felted fabric. Heavy and thick.

Madras: Plain weave or dobby or jacquard. Colors not fast. Usually stripes, checks or plaids are common.

Marble silk: Light weight fabric. Mottled appearance.

Marquisette: Gauze weave or leno weave. Light weight sheer fabric. Open space with dots or figures woven or clip spots.

Marvello/a: Pile fabric. Heavy weight fabric. High luster.

Matelasse: Double cloth. Blistered or quilted appearance.

Marceline: Plain weave. Light weight sheer fabric. Thin and lustrous.

Melton: Twill weave, satin weave or fancy weave. Double cloth. Fuller nap or felted fabric. Smooth and hard finish.

Merveilleux: Twill weave. Lustrous and smooth.

Messaline: Satin weave. Soft and lustrous.

Milanese: Knitted fabric. Soft, lustrous and light weight.

Mohair: Plain weave, twill weave or knitted. Bright and lustrous.

Moiré: Plain weave fabric with cross ribs. Water mark embossed fabric. Quite stiff.

Moleskin: Sateen weave. Heavy weight fabric. Thick soft nap on back.

Monk's cloth: Basket weave. Rough and heavy fabric.

Mousseline de soie: Plain weave. Light weight sheer fabric. Stiff or crisp finish.

Montagnac: Twill weave. Soft and lustrous luxurious fabric.

Moss crepe: Plain weave or dobby weave. Coarse and bulky fabric.

Muslin: Plain weave. Delicate fabric with open spaces.

Nacre velvet: Pile. Back of one color and pile of other color. Pearly changeable appearance.

Nainsook: Plain weave. Light weight fabric. Extremely soft fabric.

Ninnon: Plain weave with open mesh. Light weight sheer fabric. Fairly crisp and bulky.

Nun's veiling: Plain weave. Light weight fabric. Very soft and transparent.

Opaline: Lawn fabric with soft finish.

Organdy: Plain weave. Light weight sheer fabric. Crisp finish.

Organza: Plain weave. Light weight sheer fabric. Transparent, stiff and wiry.

Osnaburg: Plain weave. Medium weight to heavy weight fabric. Coarse, low grade fabric.

Ottoman: Plain weave with crosswise ribs. Heavy weight fabric. Stiff.

Outing flannel: Plain weave or twill weave. Light weight or medium weight fabric. Nap on face and back. Soft fabric.

Oxford: Basket weave. Medium weight or heavy weight fabric. Slight luster.

Paddock: Twill weave. Clear finish, smooth, firm and lustrous can be dull.

Pajama check: Plain weave. Light weight or medium weight fabric. Small or medium size corded checks.

Panama: Plain weave. Light weight fabric. Soft.

Panne satin: Satin weave. Light weight fabric. Extremely lustrous.

Panne velvet: Pile. Velvet with high luster.

Paper taffeta: Plain weave. Light weight fabric. Crisp pare like fabric.

Peau de soie: Satin weave. Soft, satin face with grainy appearance. Dull lusture.

Percale: Plain weave. Medium weight fabric. Soft, smooth and dull appearance.

Percaline: Plain weave. Light weight fabric. Soft fabric with bright finish.

Pigment taffeta: Pigmented taffeta. Dull appearance.

Pilot cloth: Twill weave. Heavy weight fabric. Napped and brushed. Dull appearance.

Pin check: Twill weave. Tiny white dots in rows vertically or horizontally. Shine with wear.

Pina cloth: Twill weave. Tiny white dots in rows vertically or horizontally. Shine with wear.

Pin head: Twill weave. Tiny white dots in rows vertically or horizontally. Shine with wear.

Pique: Fancy pique weave. Medium to heavy weight fabric. Bulky fabric.

Plisse: Plain weave. Crinkled fabric.

Plush: Pile. Higher pile. Soft.

Poiret: Twill weave (45° or 63°). Medium weight fabric. Soft.

Polo cloth: Plain weave, twill weave or basket weave or knitted. Heavy nap or pile. Medium to heavy weight fabric. Soft.

Pongee: Plain weave. Light to medium weight fabric. Nubs or irregular cross ribs.

Poplin: Crosswise rib. High luster.

Rabbit: Fur. Brownish or gray color (wild rabbits) and white or black (tamed rabbits).

Raccoon: Fur. Brown and black in color.

Radium: Plain weave. Soft and smooth fabric with high luster.

Rajah: Plain weave. Irregularities and slubs. Strong fabric.

Ratine: Plain weave. Rough, uneven and pebbled surface.

Rep: Plain weave with crosswise ribs. High luster. Frays.

Romaine: Plain weave. Light weight fabric. Uneven appearance. Lustrous.

Ruche: Lace or gauze weave. Light weight sheer fabric. Crimped.

Sailcloth: Plain weave. Heavy weight fabric. Strong.

Sateen: Sateen weave. Smooth fabric with high luster.

Satin: Twill weave. Lustrous surface with dull back.

Saxony: Fancy weave or knitted. Soft and smooth.

Scrim: Plain weave. Stiff finish.

Seersucker: Plain weave. Medium to heavy weight fabric. Alternate stripes crinkled. Dull surface.

Serge: Twill weave. Various weights. Smooth and hard finish. Lustrous.

Serpentine crepe: Plain weave. Light weight fabric. Crisp.

Shadowy organdy: Plain weave. Light weight sheer fabric. Crisp fabric with shadowy effect.

Shantung: Plain weave. Various weights. Irregular surface. Rough with slubs.

Sharkskin: Twill weave. Light weight fabric. Smooth fabric with luster.

Shatush: One of the finest and most expensive fabrics.

Shetland: Twill weave or knitted. Light weight fabric. Soft and smooth fabric with protruding fibers.

Shot taffeta: Plain weave. Iridescent fabric.

Soufflé: Novelty weave. Very soft, sponge like fabric.

Spun rayon: Plain weave. Soft and fuzzy face.

Suede cloth: Plain weave, twill weave or knitted. Close short nap. Soft and smooth.

Surah: Twill weave. Light weight fabric. Soft, flexible and lustrous.

Taffeta: Plain weave with fine cross ribs. Crisp and stiff fabric.

Terry cloth: Pile, jacquard or dobby with pile. Either looped on both side of the fabric or loops patterned to form designs.

Ticking: Twill weave, jacquard weave, dobby weave or satin weave. Strong, smooth and lustrous fabric.

Tissue taffeta: Plain weave. Light weight fabric. Transparent.

Tricolette (Mignonette): Knitted fabric. Soft hand and lustrous.

Tricot: Knitted. Vertical wales on face and crosswise ribs on back of the fabric.

Tricotine: Twill weave (63°). Medium weight fabric. Double twill on face of the fabric. Clear finish.

Tropical worsted: Plain weave. Light weight fabric. Clear finish with open spaces and stiffness.

Tulle: Gauze weave, leno weave or knotted. Stiff and delicate.

Tussah: Plain or twill weave. Uneven and coarse fabric with slubs and knots. Stiff fabric with dull luster.

Tweed: Plain weave, twill weave or novelty weave. Wide range of tweed fabrics—rough surface and sturdy fabrics, and; smooth and soft fabrics.

Velour: Thick or plush pile on plain weave or satin weave background. Light and shade appearance.

Velvet: Pile. Thick short pile. Lustrous.

Velveteen: Pile with plain weave or twill weave back. Short and compact pile. Lustrous.

Velveteen plush: Pile with plain weave or twill weave back. Longer pile than velveteen. Lustrous.

Venetian: Twill weave or sateen weave. Clear finish. Some fabrics have slight nap. Lustrous.

Vichy: Plain weave. Fabric weave comprises of light horizontal bands and strong vertical bands of same color.

Viscose: Plain weave or satin weave. Supple and soft. Silky to dull luster.

Viyella: Twill weave. Light weight fabric. Soft, fine and warm.

Voile: Plain weave. Light weight sheer fabric. Soft and firm with crisp hand. Hard finish.

Waffle cloth: Honey comb weave. Soft.

Whipcord: Twill weave (steep 63°). Back napped. Shines with use. Bulky.

Wool broadcloth: Twill weave or plain weave. Closely cut and polished nap. Lustrous.

Wool flannel: Plain weave or twill weave. Soft with a napped surface with dull finish. Higher nap and bulkier hand than worsted flannel.

Wool jersey: Knitted on circular, flat-bed or warp knitting methods. Lengthwise ribs on face and crosswise ribs on back. Elastic and appears like woven fabric.

Worsted flannel: Twill weave. Harder than wool flannel. Slight nap on one side.

Zibeline: Satin weave. Long nap. Very lustrous, sleek, smooth finish and soft hand.